World History

DeMYSTiFieD®

DeMYSTiFieD® Series

The Demystified Series publishes over 125 titles in all areas of academic study. For a complete list of titles, please visit www.mhprofessional.com.

World History
DeMYSTiFieD®

Stephanie Muntone

New York Chicago San Francisco Lisbon London Madrid Mexico City
Milan New Delhi San Juan Seoul Singapore Sydney Toronto

ISBN   978-0-07-175452-1
MHID   0-07-175452-0

e-ISBN   978-0-07-175453-8
e-MHID   0-07-175453-9

Library of Congress Control Number   2011922823

Interior illustrations by Paradigm Data Services, Ltd.

McGraw-Hill books are available at special quantity discounts to use as premiums and
sales promotions or for use in corporate training programs. To contact a representative,
please e-mail us at bulksales@mcgraw-hill.com.

This book is printed on acid-free paper.

Contents

How to Use This Book

The important questions a historian asks are "What happened?" and "Why did it happen?" This book should help you to answer those questions on the topic of World History—that is, from the first human civilizations up to the end of the Cold War in 1991.

History students are often confused by a wealth of information being thrown at them at once—names, dates, monarchs, and battles following one another in a bewildering array. The easiest way to sort out the confusion is to think about how events connect with one another. History is a long story of causes and effects. For example, the spread of Christianity led indirectly to the fall of the Roman Empire. Provisions of the peace treaty signed at the end of World War I created conditions that led to World War II. And so on. It's much easier to remember events when you understand how they relate to one another.

This book tells you the political, social, and cultural history of the world in a narrative format, emphasizing the key ideas so you will understand why they are important—why Christianity had such a powerful effect on the world, what caused a major wave of migration or immigration, or why Japan closed its ports to the West for more than two centuries. Each chapter deals with an important era or event in history, such as the Roman Empire or medieval China. Chapter topics often overlap in time, but the order of topics is basically chronological. The book is divided into three major sections:

- Part 1 begins with the earliest human civilizations in the Fertile Crescent and ends with the mighty empires of Asia and the Mediterranean.

- Part 2 covers the world from roughly AD 500–1750, including the settlement of Europe, the colonization of the Americas, and the rise of the Turks to world power.

- Part 3 narrates the course of world history in the modern era, including major political and cultural revolutions, the expansion of empires, and the eventful twentieth century to 1991.

Each chapter ends with a 10-question quiz. Each section ends with a 50-question section exam, and there is a 100-question final exam at the end of the book. The questions are all multiple-choice, similar to the sorts of questions used on standardized tests. Many of the questions ask you about causes and effects: Why did this event happen? What happened as a result of that decision?

You might try taking the chapter quiz first, before reading the chapter. This will tell you which sections of each chapter you already know well, and which sections you need to study further. Read and study the chapter, then take the quiz again. Keep working on each chapter until you can answer at least 9 of the 10 questions correctly.

Take the section exam after you finish reading the section, and take the final exam once you have mastered the entire book. Check your work against the Answer Key; if you answer at least 92 of the 100 questions correctly, you can consider that you have mastered the subject satisfactorily. Go back and study any areas of the book that cover questions you did not answer correctly.

If you are using this book as a course companion, follow along at the same pace your professor is taking. Use the book for extra tutorial and practice in addition to what is covered in class. If you are using the book as a substitute for taking the course, or to prepare yourself for an exam, then allow yourself time to get the most out of it. Allow three months, one month for each section of the book, to complete your study. Read the narrative, take the quizzes, and make a list of questions on aspects of world history that aren't clear to you. Use the sources recommended in the Bibliography or similar titles from the library or bookstore to find the answers. When you're done with the course, you can use this book, with its comprehensive index, as a permanent reference.

Introduction

A Note on Dates

The calendar that we use to measure history and time has a dividing line between two eras. This book distinguishes them with the abbreviations BC and AD. BC stands for "before Christ" and refers to all dates before the year 1. AD stands for the Latin phrase *anno domini*, which means "in the year of the Lord" and refers to all dates from the year 1 to the present. Some contemporary textbooks and secondary sources use the abbreviations BCE ("before the Christian Era") and CE ("Christian Era") instead of BC and AD.

Beginning history students are sometimes confused by BC dates because they seem to go backward. Think of the calendar as if it were a number line, with the negative (BC) numbers decreasing from left to right as they approach 0. The year 500 BC is followed by 499, then 498, and so on down to the year 1 BC, which is immediately followed by the year 1 AD. From there on, the numbers increase from left to right. There is, of course, no "year 0."

It is very important to remember that all dates before the early modern era are *approximate*. They refer to times so far in the past that historians cannot be certain of exact dates. All BC dates and all early AD dates may be approximate within a year or two, or they may be approximate within a few centuries. They represent the best consensus of historians, according to the most reliable evidence we have.

A Note on Spelling

Many languages are not written in the same alphabet we use to write English; therefore, you may find different spellings of Asian, Arabic, Russian, and other foreign words in different historical sources. For example, the full name of Chairman Mao of China is sometimes written Mao Tse-tung and sometimes Mao Zedong.

Understanding the Themes of World History

History, like a great work of literature, has themes—major motifs and concerns that arise again and again over the course of time. Understanding these themes helps you make sense of history. Themes show connections—causes and effects that can help you understand not only what happened, but why it happened. Themes show you the important factors that shape the course of history of a nation, a region, and a continent.

Geography

The history of any civilization or nation is inseparable from its geography: its position in relation to other nations, its climate, its topography, its natural resources, its major rivers, its seacoast or lack thereof, and similar factors. Here are some examples of how geography affects history:

- There is little rainfall in the Central Asian steppes, hence this region has no large sources of fresh water. The steppes are grasslands with very few trees, perfect for herd animals that graze for a while in one place, then move on to fresh pastures. Because this was their environment, the peoples of the steppes developed a nomadic culture. They followed their herds instead of establishing settled civilizations.

- Japan is an island nation, geographically detached from the Asian mainland. The broad stretch of sea between Japan and Korea/China served as a defense against invasion until the twentieth century; around 1600, it enabled the Japanese to close off the country to the entry of any foreigner—something no mainland nation could possibly do.

- France was the largest nation-state in central Europe until German unification in 1871, which made it the dominant European power until the downfall of Napoleon in 1815. A contiguous land mass like France is much easier to defend than an empire made of small states scattered over the map.

- The ancient Assyrian Empire, located on the Tigris River some distance from the Persian Gulf, had no natural features to define its borders or protect it from invasion. This was the direct cause of its aggressive foreign policy. An empire that is vulnerable to attack on all sides is equally in a strategic position to attack others.

War and the Force of Arms

Almost all nations of the world have one thing in common: the desire for territorial expansion. They all want to acquire more natural resources, to expand their power bases, to control major trade routes, and to secure their borders from attack. From the beginning, territorial expansion generally meant invading and taking over land that already belonged to another group—in other words, war.

Another powerful motivation for war is domination or suppression of what the attacker perceives as a hostile or unfriendly culture. For example, European wars from the Crusades to 1700 were often caused by deep differences over religious faith.

There is one basic historical axiom about the force of arms: the nation with bigger, stronger, or more guns always wins the fight. Although a small army has very occasionally defeated a larger one, it has always been because of greatly superior strategy. For example, the nineteenth-century gunboats of the European nations forced both China and Japan to sign trade agreements highly favorable to the West; the Chinese and Japanese had never developed such guns.

The same force of arms is responsible for all of history's successful dictatorships. Only the loyalty of the army has allowed military dictators to rise to power and keep it—for the simple reason that guns (or swords, in ancient times) are a powerful deterrent to any attack on the dictator. Armies have always been loyal to dictators because under dictators, they occupy a privileged position in society and government. The people fear and obey them—not out of patriotism or personal loyalty to the dictator, but because the army has the guns.

Empire

This book tells the story of a number of vast empires, all of which sooner or later fell. It is an axiom of history that an empire can only expand to a certain size before it has outgrown the emperor's ability to control it. The larger an empire, the less control the central government can have over its outlying areas. Those empires that had the most efficient bureaucracies and the best-organized armies and transportation systems lasted the longest.

Tolerance of diversity is also a crucial factor in the longevity of an empire. Because an empire, by definition, includes several small states, it is rarely homogenous. The population of most empires is religiously, ethnically, culturally, and linguistically mixed. When the diverse cultures within an empire begin to clamor for self-determination, the empire almost always falls. If an empire is tolerant, treating its different populations equally in terms of privileges, rights, and the potential for social and economic advancement, it will last much longer.

Rank or Class

Through most of world history, social class was the decisive factor in a person's life. One was born into a certain social position and had very few choices as to one's own future. Artisans married other artisans; shopkeepers passed down their businesses to their children; aristocrats arranged marriages with other aristocrats; and princes and princesses married other royal persons in arrangements based on diplomacy.

Change came about gradually. The rise of literacy meant that a person could get an education, and an educated person could find ways to rise in class. In prosperous nations, the merchant families often became so wealthy that they were very desirable marriage partners for the nobility—an exchange of cash for prestige. Over time, it became possible to rise in society according to talent, luck, and ambition.

Part One

Early Civilization: Empires of Asia and the Mediterranean

chapter 1

Early Civilizations

The word *civilization* means something beyond "human life" or even "human society." Certain basic elements are necessary to support human life: a source of fresh water, the ability to procure food, and a habitable climate. A civilization is the next step toward social organization. All civilizations have certain common factors.

First and perhaps most important, civilization requires a surplus of food. That means that the people have learned not just to hunt food and gather it but also to plant and grow it. The surplus of food naturally leads to a rise in population and the existence of wealth and disposable income. Society grows more complicated: it organizes itself into classes and begins to build cities. It also becomes literate; all early civilizations had classes of people who could read and write. Advanced human civilizations are also noted for their scientific and artistic achievements. In the field of science, the first sophisticated societies invented the wheel, established the 365-day calendar, and plotted the stars, while their artists created paintings, statues, and jewelry at whose charm and beauty we continue to marvel to this day. The Great Pyramids of Egypt, which still stand after four thousand years, are universally agreed to be one of the great architectural achievements of history.

The first human civilizations all appeared in the same region, which is known as the Fertile Crescent. This area includes present-day Egypt, Pakistan, and Iraq.

The presence of rivers, fertile soil, and hot climates combined in this region to make the beginning of human civilization possible.

CHAPTER OBJECTIVES

- Define the term *civilization*.
- Identify the earliest human civilizations and locate them on a map.
- Identify the major achievements of each early civilization.

Chapter 1 Time Line

(all dates are BC)

3500	Sumerian culture and the development of the first urban centers
3200–2334	Sumerian city-states in Mesopotamia
3200–3100	Menes unifies Upper and Lower Egypt
	Date of oldest written records yet discovered (Mesopotamian clay tablets)
2686–2181	Old Kingdom in Egypt
2600	Indus Valley civilization
2334–2191	Akkadian dynasty in Mesopotamia
2000–1900	First appearance of the *Epic of Gilgamesh*
1894–1595	Babylonian dynasty in Mesopotamia
1700s	Hyskos invade and conquer Lower Egypt

The First Human Civilizations

Information about the first human civilizations is changing all the time. Archaeologists add to our knowledge with each new excavation, but many areas, such as the Indus Valley, have not yet been thoroughly explored for their evidence. Archaeologists and historians are still struggling to interpret ancient written records and other artifacts. In addition, techniques such as carbon dating con-

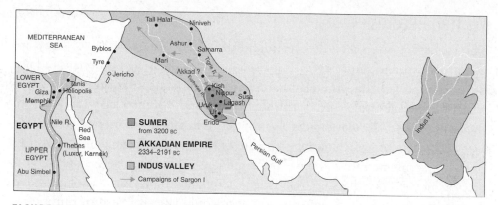

FIGURE 1.1 Civilizations of the Fertile Crescent

stantly improve our ability to understand the materials we find and to place them in their proper context.

All dates in the early chapters of this book are BC. They are also approximate; early civilizations belong to such a remote past that present-day historians cannot be exact about dates. Thus, we tend to speak of events occurring within a range of dates that represent the best of our current knowledge.

Human beings began to organize themselves into civilizations around 3500 to 3000 BC, or 5500 to 5000 years before the present day. The period from about 3000 to 1000 BC is called the Bronze Age, named for the hard, durable metal created by mixing copper with tin. Before about 3000 BC, people made weapons and tools from copper alone. When people first got the idea of creating a copper-tin alloy, they quickly discovered that it produced stronger, more effective, and longer-lasting tools and weapons. All successful civilizations from this era worked in bronze (see Figure 1.1).

Mesopotamia: The Sumerian Culture

The earliest human civilization was at the confluence of the Tigris and Euphrates rivers in present-day Iraq. This area was probably settled at least a thousand years earlier, but it did not become a civilization until about 3500 to 3200 BC. Shifting riverbeds left deposits of silt that made the soil unusually fertile. This, in turn, attracted settlers and eventually led to large urban centers.

The culture that developed in Mesopotamia was remarkably sophisticated. This civilization gave the world its first written language, its first organized religion, the basics of modern mathematics, the wheel, and the first literary epic.

Written Records

The earliest written records ever found date from about 3100 BC. They are inventory lists and similar records incised in clay tablets; the Sumerians did not have paper. Over time, the clay hardened; in that state, it is practically indestructible, and archaeologists continue to find and decipher clay tablets from the remote past. The clay tablets also contained fragments of literary works. *The Descent of Inanna*, which narrates the life of the goddess Inanna, is the world's oldest surviving narrative poem. The Sumerians prided themselves on their literary achievements; the Sumerian language remained the language of educated people in this region for centuries, as Latin would later in Western Europe.

Religion

By 2250 BC, the Sumerians had refined their religious beliefs into a system. They were polytheistic, meaning that they believed in many gods. Each god or goddess oversaw an aspect of nature or human relations such as air, water, or war. The creation of a sophisticated theology led to the development of a class of priests. As in many later civilizations, priests were better educated and more literate than most other people. This gave them standing and authority within the community.

The Sumerians built impressive shrines and temples in honor of their gods. Ziggurats—stepped pyramids, in which each level has a smaller perimeter than the one below it—were simple in design but massive in size. Their large scale shows the central importance of religion to the Sumerian culture.

Mathematics and Science

Sumerian achievements in science and math were equally impressive. They developed the wheel for use in making pottery and then realized its enormous potential for transportation. Sumerians also understood the concept of the decimal point and the seven-day week.

Politics and Government

In its early days, the Sumerian civilization was a loose collection of city-states that often warred with one another, jockeying for control. The most important urban centers were Ur, Uruk, Akkad, and Mari. These cities were religious centers as well as seats of government.

In about 2334 BC, Sargon I, king of Akkad, conquered all of Mesopotamia. It remained united under his rule and that of his successors for about the next two hundred years. This period in Sumerian history is called the Akkadian era. It was characterized by a divergence between church and state and the evolution of a professional class of soldiers. The size of the Akkadian Empire led inevitably to the development of a large bureaucracy; no empire could be run efficiently without an army of civil servants. The Akkadian era ended about 2191 BC, when the Sumerians retook power and Ur became the center of the Mesopotamian civilization. As time went on, Akkadian and Sumerian culture would diverge more and more.

Archaeologists have unearthed many luxury objects at Sumerian sites, including musical instruments, game boards, and jewelry. These artifacts allow us to draw numerous conclusions about the Sumerians. First, there must have been a wealthy class in the society: people can order and purchase jewelry and musical instruments only when they have disposable income. Second, the objects' fine quality shows that the Sumerians were skilled artisans and jewelers. Third, the presence of many metal items proves that the Sumerians traded with other civilizations, since there are no natural sources of metal in this area. Historians believe that the Sumerians traded their surplus crops to the Indus Valley civilizations in exchange for metals.

The Babylonian Empire

The Babylonian Empire came into being after the fall of Ur, perhaps as early as 2000 BC. It lasted until the 1500s BC, when the Kassites destroyed it. (See Chapter 2).

Like other early civilizations, Babylon boasted vast public buildings, including the palace at Mari. The builders of this 350-room palace dug 30 feet deep to lay pipes for drainage of waste. The grand scale of the building and the care lavished on its construction demonstrate how important the ruler had become in society.

Literature

Many written records of the Babylonian civilization have survived, including the version of *Gilgamesh* that has come down to us. Gilgamesh was king of Uruk in about 2800 BC. The people told, retold, and collected legends about Gilgamesh; these stories date back to the earliest Sumerian civilization. The Babylonians wrote down the epic in the form we know it today. *Gilgamesh* is the oldest example of a classic literary genre, the epic—a book-length narrative poem about an epic hero.

The epic hero is a leader of his people and is thus a national symbol. He undergoes adventures that test his moral and physical strength. The epic is considered to be something between fiction and nonfiction: people of the ancient world knew or believed that the hero existed and that his adventures were true, although they accepted that the tales told by poets were exaggerated versions of what really happened.

Law

Hammurabi became the king of Babylon about the year 1792 BC. He is famous in history as the author of one of the earliest codes of laws, which was carved on a *stele* (a stone pillar) in a public area of Mari, where all citizens could see and read it. Hammurabi's Code is similar to other law codes of its time, of which fragments have been discovered. It sets forth the proper punishments for various offenses, dealing with crimes against persons and property. The most famous rule is "an eye for an eye"—in other words, retribution in kind. The existence of such codes of laws, and their public display, shows that in this era, people understood and valued the concept of abstract justice and the importance of punishing aggressors.

Mathematics

The Babylonian culture was highly advanced in mathematics and astronomy. Babylonian scholars could plot the fixed stars, accurately follow the course of the sun and some of the planets, and predict lunar eclipses. The Babylonians perfected the Sumerian system of measuring circles, spheres, and time using 60 as a base; we use this system to this day. Their mathematicians were the first to use multiplication and square-root tables and understand algebraic geometry. The Babylonians also invented the sundial, the first artificial means of measuring time.

Egypt: The Old and Middle Kingdoms

The single most important factor in the history of Egypt is the Nile River. The Nile is literally an oasis, providing the only relief in an otherwise vast desert. Without the river, Egypt would be unfit for human habitation. To this day, more than 99 percent of all Egyptians live along the banks of the Nile.

Since at least 5000 BC, the Nile has provided Egyptians with fish and seafood for eating and fresh water for drinking, bathing, and irrigation. In ancient times, the Nile overflowed its banks each year, depositing silt that created some of the world's richest and most fertile soil. This annual flood was a fact of Egyptian life until the building of the Aswan Dams in the twentieth century.

The earliest Egyptians were good at crafts of all kinds. They soon learned to make small boats, using sails to harness the wind and travel south along the Nile or flow north with the current. This made trade possible. Two distinct Egyptian kingdoms developed. Because the Nile flows from south to north, the southern river valley is called Upper Egypt and the northern river delta is called Lower Egypt.

Three factors combined to mark the beginning of Egyptian civilization: the unification of the two kingdoms, the establishment of a capital city at Memphis, and the appearance of writing.

Government

Menes, the king of Upper Egypt, united the entire Nile delta under one rule between 3200 and 3100 BC. With two relatively brief intermissions, Egypt remained united under central rule for many generations. Through the periods known as the Old Kingdom and the Middle Kingdom, Egypt was a remarkably stable and prosperous civilization.

The Old Kingdom of Egypt ended about 2180 to 2160 BC. A weakening of the central monarchy, aggressive claims of power by local officials, and a period of drought and famine are possible reasons for its end. Nearly two hundred years—known to history as the First Intermediate Period—went by before Mentuhotep II reunited Upper and Lower Egypt into one kingdom. About 1985, his successor Amenemhet I strengthened the unification and inaugurated an era of prosperity and efficient rule known as the Middle Kingdom.

Like the later Roman Empire (see Chapter 6), Egypt was a well-organized bureaucracy under a strong central monarch, with classes of officials, priests, and scribes. Surviving Egyptian records show that this was a society that loved rules, order, and method. Under the first pharaohs of the Middle Kingdom, Egypt attacked Libya, the gold-rich kingdom of Nubia, and the Semitic Bedouin tribes to the east, thus securing its borders on all three sides. This freed Egypt to turn its attention to improvements in agriculture, which led to greater prosperity for all, even for the lowest ranks of society.

Egypt differed from the Mesopotamian civilization in one very striking respect—there was no tension between the forces of church and state. In Egypt, church and state were the same thing. The king, or pharaoh, was descended from gods and was himself (or herself) considered a god. Egyptians believed that the pharaoh controlled the ebb and flow of the Nile and its annual flooding. The pharaoh was an absolute ruler, omniscient and all-powerful, and the only being in Egypt who was granted the blessing of life after death. This belief in the pharaoh's afterlife is the reason for the most famous of all ancient Egyptian achievements—the pyramids.

The Great Pyramids

A pyramid is a final resting place for the pharaoh. The impressive size and scale of the pyramids at Saqqara and Giza make three things clear. First, they demonstrate the pharaoh's power, authority, and central importance in Egyptian society. Second, they prove the Egyptians were able to organize and carry through a project on a grand scale. Some of the Great Pyramids took more than twenty years to build, and some of the stones were brought to the Nile River valley from five hundred miles away. Third, they provide evidence of an orderly society. The pyramids represent the combined efforts of thousands of laborers who had to fit every stone into place with no technology except levers, sleds, and their own strength. It is clear that only a stable and well-organized society could have carried through such massive projects over such a length of time.

There is clear archaeological evidence of Mesopotamian influence on the early Egyptians. The styles of art and architecture, the systems of writing, and the use of official seals all came from the Mesopotamians. This indicates a certain degree of trade and cultural exchange between the civilizations.

Surviving Egyptian art and architecture are remarkable both for their state of preservation and their beauty and style. Egyptian artists portrayed gods and goddesses, ordinary mortals, and animals in a variety of settings and activities—everything from battles and royal ceremonies to fishing, cooking, and farming. This extraordinary level of artistic achievement and the prominence given to its display are typical of highly advanced human civilizations.

Writing

The Egyptians were the first to use papyrus—a plant material similar to thick paper or parchment—as a writing surface. Papyrus is prone to curl, and thus the scroll format was adopted for texts of any length. The Egyptians developed a complex writing system of hieroglyphs—a small picture to represent each word. This system took a long time to learn and was used only by priests.

Scribes, of whom there were hundreds throughout the bureaucracy, wrote in a kind of shorthand called hieratic script.

Mathematics and Science

The Egyptians achieved little of note in the areas of mathematics and science; the pyramids are impressive feats of engineering, but they are not the result of sophisticated mathematical ability. The Egyptians did invent the embalming process by which corpses are preserved as mummies—the hot, dry climate of Egypt, of course, was a powerful aid in preservation. Egyptians also devised the first calendar that divided the year into twelve 30-day months, with an extra five-day week at the end to account for the full 365-day year.

Women

Egyptian women seem to have had more choices, more power, and greater opportunities than women in other ancient civilizations—more, in fact, than most women would have in any culture for many centuries to come. The records show that women served as pharaohs, priestesses, and scribes. Female pharaohs were considered just as divine and powerful as their male counterparts; the fact that both men and women were given the same title, *pharaoh*, shows that they were considered equals.

Egypt: The Second Intermediate Period

The prosperous and successful Middle Kingdom era ended for two reasons. The first caused the second—the historical accident of several weak and ineffectual pharaohs in a row led to the successful invasion and conquest of Egypt by a foreign people.

Historians know very little about the Hyskos before their arrival in Lower Egypt. They came from the eastern Mediterranean, probably from the area later called Palestine. Factional disputes over royal power caused confusion and disorder throughout Egypt in the 1700s BC; the Hyskos took advantage of this situation to invade and conquer Lower Egypt. They succeeded largely by virtue of military superiority, as their bronze armor, strong bows, and iron chariots were better and stronger than anything the Egyptians could offer. By 1650 BC, the Hyskos had achieved total control of Lower Egypt and were poised to take over Upper Egypt. In the face of this threat to their civilization, the Thebans united against the Hyskos. In 1570 BC, brothers Kamose and Ahmose led their people against the invaders, forcing them to retreat. Ahmose and his army chased the Hyskos out of Egypt altogether; Ahmose returned in triumph to Thebes as pharaoh of a reunited Egypt. This ushered in the long-lasting era known to history as the New Kingdom (see Chapter 2).

The Indus Valley

The earliest Indus Valley civilization lasted from about 2500 to 1500 BC and was located in the Indus River valley in present-day Pakistan. This civilization is sometimes called Harappan, after one of its most important cities.

There are written records from this early civilization, but archaeologists and historians have not yet been able to decipher the language. Therefore, we know much less about this civilization than about Sumer or Egypt, which flourished at the same time.

It is possible, however, to study other evidence and come to some conclusions about the Indus Valley. Since no elaborate or advanced weapons have been discovered in the area, it was probably a peaceful society. The lack of major temples among the public buildings suggests that religion was practiced privately rather than controlled or encouraged as a matter of state. The cities of Harappan and Mohenjo-dara appear to be results of the same urban plan; both have identical street patterns. The public buildings have impressive indoor plumbing leading to sewage systems.

Evidence is too scarce for historians to be sure what caused the decline of this earliest Indian civilization. Natural disaster, such as a series of earthquakes, is one possibility.

QUIZ

1. The word *civilization* refers to _____.
   A. any region densely populated with human beings
   B. groups of small villages that maintain economic and social relations
   C. a sophisticated, literate human society living in and around a city or cities
   D. a human society from the ancient past

2. _____ is an important historical figure because he is the author of one of the earliest law codes.
   A. Sargon
   B. Hammurabi
   C. Menes
   D. Gilgamesh

3. In _____, women enjoyed an unusual measure of equality and freedom of choice.
   A. Egypt
   B. Mesopotamia
   C. Babylon
   D. the Indus River valley

4. We know less about the Indus Valley civilization than about other early civilizations because _____.
   A. its people did not celebrate religion in an organized, public way
   B. scholars have not yet been able to decipher the surviving written records
   C. it was located along the Indus River in present-day Pakistan
   D. it was a loose collection of city-states rather than a central monarchy

5. Which is the most important factor in Egyptian history?
   A. the Nile River
   B. the Great Pyramids
   C. the hieroglyphic writing system
   D. the position of women

6. The world's oldest surviving literary epic comes from which civilization?
   A. Egypt
   B. the Indus Valley
   C. the Hittites
   D. Mesopotamia

7. Menes is an important historical figure because he _____.
   A. united Upper and Lower Egypt under one rule
   B. conquered the Sumerians and inaugurated the Akkadian era
   C. established 60 as the base for measuring circles, spheres, and time
   D. wrote one of the world's earliest codes of law

8. The discovery of _____ in Mesopotamian excavations proves that the Sumerians traded with the Indus Valley civilization.
   A. jewelry
   B. clay tablets
   C. metal objects
   D. papyrus

9. Which of these most clearly demonstrates the importance of the pharaoh in Egyptian society?
   A. the public display of the code of laws
   B. the size and scale of the Great Pyramids
   C. the annual flooding of the Nile
   D. the use of papyrus as a writing surface

10. The Indus Valley civilization was located in present-day _____.
    A. Egypt
    B. Iraq
    C. Turkey
    D. Pakistan

chapter **2**

The New Kingdom to the Fall of Babylon, 1550–550 BC

Civilizations changed much more slowly in ancient times than they do in our own time. For the majority of the people, the New Kingdom in Egypt was almost unchanged from the Old Kingdom or the Middle Kingdom.

The major change in the era between about 1500 and 500 BC was the rise and fall of empires. The Egyptian, Hittite, and Assyrian empires all expanded beyond a manageable size; all these empires either contracted in size or disappeared altogether.

The Bronze Age ended around 1200 BC and was succeeded by the Iron Age. Iron tools and weapons were substantially stronger than bronze ones; therefore, the first civilizations that learned to work with iron had a significant advantage over others. Iron affected not only a culture's military might but also its agricultural production. The use of iron therefore led to both strength and prosperity.

As early civilizations became empires, certain common patterns began to emerge. A successful empire always contained the same elements. The first necessity for an empire was a strong, charismatic ruler; without such a ruler, a civilization simply would not make the effort to expand. Second, all the early empires had efficient bureaucracies; an empire could not be administered without a literate class of scribes and other officials. Third, each successful empire had a powerful, well-organized standing army loyal to the monarch and the state. The army was needed both to conquer new areas and to prevent uprisings; troops were maintained throughout the empire during peacetime for this purpose. Fourth, the emperor delegated authority to local rulers, since he could not be everywhere at once. As long as all these factors functioned smoothly together, an empire was successful. When one or more of them failed, the empire would weaken and eventually fall.

CHAPTER OBJECTIVES

- Compare and contrast Egypt's New Kingdom with the Old and Middle Kingdoms.
- Describe the Hittite Empire and its culture.
- Describe the later Mesopotamian cultures and empires.

Chapter 2 Time Line

(all dates are BC)

●	1570–1065	New Kingdom in Egypt
●	1415–1154	Kassite Dynasty in Mesopotamia
●	1380–1190	Hittite Empire
●	1379–1362	Amenhotep IV rules Egypt as Akhenaton
●	1200	Iron Age begins
		Invasions of "Sea Peoples"
●	1150–612	Assyrian Empire
●	625–538	Second Babylonian Empire
●	612	Sack of Nineveh by Medes

Egypt: The New Kingdom

The New Kingdom era in Egypt began in 1570 BC and lasted for five hundred years. Throughout this era of Egyptian history, there was remarkably little change in the everyday lives of the people. Pharaohs succeeded one another, territorial borders shifted, and neighboring empires rose and fell, but through it all there was no particular scientific or technological progress. The ebb and flow of the Nile controlled the rhythms of life in Egypt as it always had.

During the fourteenth century BC, the various pharaohs expanded their sphere of influence northward, as well as once again establishing control over Libya and Nubia. Thutmose I led his troops as far as the Euphrates River; later in the century, Hatshepsut and her consort and successor Thutmose III extended the Egyptian Empire throughout Syria and ancient Palestine. The Egyptians followed the same pattern as most other successful empires in the ancient world. They allowed local authority figures in conquered areas to govern, but all had to pay tribute to the pharaoh and all were under his or her authority. The court at Thebes developed a literate civil service of bureaucrats to manage affairs such as taxes and the payment of tributes throughout the empire. The Egyptian military was garrisoned throughout the empire to quell any potential rebellions and to ensure that local rulers remained loyal.

Amenhotep IV inherited the pharaoh's throne in 1379. His tastes ran more to religion than to administrative tasks. One of his first acts as pharaoh was to reorganize Egyptian religious practices by outlawing worship of all the gods except Aton, the sun god. Amenhotep established a new city, Amarna, three hundred miles north of Thebes, and ordered a new temple built to the sun god. Amenhotep even changed his own name to Akhenaton, specifically to identify himself as Aton's representative on earth. His goal may have been to secure his own position of authority by weakening the powerful priestly class, but the actual result of his decision was to weaken the Egyptian Empire. With the pharaoh's attention on religious matters, Egypt's military might suffered and the Hittites took advantage of the situation to seize control over Syria (see "The Hittites in Asia Minor" later in this chapter).

In 1362 BC, Tutakhaton succeeded Akhenaton and promptly changed his name to Tutankhamen to mark the restoration of the old polytheistic religious practices. Tutankhamen's reign was very short and uneventful; he is famous for the historical accident of the survival, unlooted, of his tomb in the Valley of the Kings. The magnificent collection of artifacts in his tomb shows a surprising level of veneration for a relatively uninspiring ruler and also demonstrates the great cultural renaissance in the arts that occurred during the New Kingdom. Some historians believe Tutankhamen was given such a lavish burial out of gratitude for his restoration of the old religious ways; Egypt was a religiously conservative society and the changes made under Akhenaton had not been popular.

During the twelfth century BC, Egypt attempted to regain control of its New Kingdom empire. Ramses II led the Egyptians against the Hittites at Syria. The battle ended more or less in a stalemate, in which the two combatants agreed that they would exist side by side in peace and that Egypt would accept Hittite authority in Syria.

The Egyptian Empire continued to decline. By the 1100s BC, Egypt had withdrawn its influence throughout the region; it was once again centered on its original home on the banks of the Nile. The New Kingdom was followed by an era called the Late Period. Two things characterized this era: internal strife and external attack.

Internally, the Egyptian court was chaotic throughout the Late Period. It can best be described as a long round of court intrigue, factionalism, and political squabbles. From the outside, a succession of foreign powers invaded Egypt one after another, and each held sway over it for a shorter or longer period. From about 945 BC to about AD 330, the following powers successfully attacked Egypt in turn: Libyans, Nubians, Assyrians, Persians, Greeks, and Romans. Remarkably, Egypt was able to retain its culture throughout all these successive takeovers; at the same time, it absorbed many elements of the conquering cultures.

The Hittites in Asia Minor

Historians know little about the origin of the Hittites, who settled in present-day Turkey about 2000 BC. Their language belonged to the Indo-European linguistic family, and they appear to have come from the west, from the Balkan region of Europe. They were a herding, horse-breeding tribe.

Hittite culture was highly advanced in some ways. The Hittites used both cuneiform and hieroglyphic writing, and as their empire grew, they both preserved and shared elements of all the cultures in the region. They developed a law code of their own. Their military was the strongest and most sophisticated of the time; they were the first to create iron weapons and to use iron for their chariot wheels. Eventually, the Bronze Age gave way to the Iron Age, in which all the various cultures acquired the ability to work with iron, but this technology was exclusive to the Hittites for a long time. The use of iron contributed significantly to their agricultural production as well as to their military success.

The Hittites prospered economically for at least three reasons. First, as already noted, they were capable of working with iron before other peoples in the region, which gave them an advantage in making stronger tools and weapons. Second, they controlled many of the Mediterranean trade routes. Third, they had settled in an area that was rich in mineral resources.

Both the Hittites and the Kassites occupied Babylon at different times; these two peoples may have been related. Again, the origins of tribes of this early era of civilization are still obscure, and historians differ in their interpretation of the evidence.

As of about 1400 BC, the Kassite kingdom followed the course of the Tigris and Euphrates rivers, reaching as far northwest as the city of Mari on the Euphrates and Sippar on the Tigris. At that time, the Hittites controlled a large area of present-day Turkey north of Cyprus in the Mediterranean. They would soon expand their empire to every part of the Fertile Crescent except the Nile River valley in Egypt.

The zenith of the Hittite Empire was in the early thirteenth century BC under Suppiluliumas, who ruled from 1380 to 1346. Under Suppiluliumas, Hittite influence expanded throughout the Fertile Crescent; his rise to power coincided with a weak Egypt, and he led the Hittites into Syria.

The Hittite Empire faded around 1200 BC, due to attacks from the Assyrians and Phrygians. The Sea Peoples (see the following section) also invaded Hittite strongholds and helped bring the empire to the point of collapse.

The "Sea Peoples"

Historians have given the name *Sea Peoples* to a variety of belligerent tribes that roamed the eastern Mediterranean throughout the early twelfth century BC. The Sea Peoples were wholly or partly responsible for the destruction of the Hittite Empire; they attacked and destroyed various cities in the region, particularly along the Syrian coast. The invasion of the Sea Peoples also coincided with the fall of the Mycenaean civilization (see Chapter 5).

The Sea Peoples attacked Egypt twice but were defeated on both occasions. Some of them settled in Egypt, assimilating with the local population.

The Assyrian Empire

When the Kassites conquered Babylon (see Chapter 1), they adopted its culture. The Kassites ruled in the area for about four hundred years. The Assyrians took advantage of the invasions of the Sea Peoples to overthrow Kassite rule and create their own empire.

Geography played a major role in the history of the Assyrian kingdom, which was centered on the Tigris some distance upriver from the Persian Gulf. Because the kingdom had no natural features to serve as frontiers or fortifications, it was vulnerable to attack from all sides. Throughout history, nation-states in this position have generally built up their armies. A mighty standing army is, of course, a powerful offensive weapon; it is also a defensive weapon because its sheer size and strength frightens other nations out of any notion of attack. The Assyrian army was the best organized in history up to that time. Soldiers were grouped into divisions under professional commanders, and the army boasted specialized corps of engineers and cavalry. Additionally, the Assyrian army was strong because all its weapons were iron.

Assyrian officials rode into neighboring areas, making it clear that they expected gifts from local rulers. If gifts were not forthcoming, then the Assyrian army marched in, conquered the area, and extracted tributes. In this way, the Assyrians spread out over the Fertile Crescent, eventually taking control of Mesopotamia, Syria, and Palestine; the Assyrians even took over Egypt for a time. Troops were posted throughout the empire and were used to put down any attempt at rebellion. Assyrian troops were noted for their brutality; Assyrian stone reliefs and other records describe torture, enslavement, deportations, and massacres of conquered peoples as well as the sacking of numerous cities.

Tiglath-Pileser III ruled Assyria from 746 to 727 BC and was perhaps the most capable of the Assyrian kings. Tiglath-Pileser's empire was unified in several ways that were not common among other empires of his era. First, he established a system of Assyrian royal governors in outlying territories of the empire; this differed from the usual practice of ancient empires, in which local leaders were left to rule their own cultures within the imperial structure.

Second, Tiglath-Pileser maintained a standing army that was personally loyal to him as the head of the state. Third, he oversaw the creation of a post office and the construction of a system of roads, which helped the court maintain contact with the outlying cities and also facilitated troop movements. Fourth, the king made the Aramaic language the standard throughout the empire. The capital city of Nineveh was notable for its sizeable royal library, which contained tablets, scrolls, and manuscripts from cultures throughout the region. Sargon II, who ruled Assyria from 721 to 705 BC, was an enthusiastic collector of written records, both literary and informational. Most of our present-day knowledge of Mesopotamian literature, including what survives of the *Epic of Gilgamesh*, comes from the surviving works in Sargon's collection.

In the end, the Assyrian Empire fell for the same reason empires always fall—it was too large and unwieldy to sustain. In the sixth century, it fell to the Second Babylonian Empire. The city of Nineveh was sacked in 612 BC, marking the end of the Assyrian Empire.

The Second Babylonian Empire and the Median Empire

The Second Babylonian Empire was centered in Chaldea, at the juncture of present-day Kuwait and Iraq. Under Tiglath-Pileser, this area had been absorbed into the Assyrian Empire around 727 BC.

In 627 BC, the Chaldean king Nabopolassar led a revolt against the Assyrians and thus created the Second Babylonian Empire. Nabopolassar formed an alliance with the king of the Medes, an Iranian tribe. With the help of the Medes, Nabopolassar and his son Nebuchadnezzar took over Assyria, Syria, Palestine, and Judea. Meanwhile, Media expanded to cover a vast area stretching from the Black Sea and the Caucasus in the west to the Indian Ocean and the Indus River in the east.

The Babylonian and Median empires did not last; economic problems, religious conflicts, and outside threats all caused trouble. Around 550 BC, the Persians conquered Media; soon after, they took over Babylon (see Chapter 3).

QUIZ

1. Amenhotep IV instituted a major change in Egyptian society when he _____.
   A. extended the Egyptian Empire into Syria and Palestine
   B. outlawed worship of all Egyptian gods except Aton
   C. built new temples to the gods
   D. created a powerful class of priests

2. Around 1200 BC, which two empires agreed to a nonaggression pact that would allow them both to remain strong without fear of mutual attack?
   A. the Egyptians and the Hittites
   B. the Hittites and the Assyrians
   C. the Assyrians and the Babylonians
   D. the Babylonians and the Egyptians

3. At the height of their civilization, the Hittites were prosperous for all these reasons except _____.
   A. they worked with iron before other cultures had this technology
   B. they controlled major Mediterranean trade routes
   C. they made the proper sacrifices to the gods
   D. the area where they settled was rich in mineral resources

4. Assyrian emperor Sargon II is a notable figure in history for _____.
   A. the manner in which he organized the professional army
   B. collecting a vast library of early Mesopotamian literature and documents
   C. declaring that he was the supreme deity's representative on earth
   D. presiding over the fall of the once-mighty Assyrian Empire

5. One of the major factors in the fall of the Assyrian Empire was the rebellion of _____.
   A. the Chaldeans
   B. the Medes
   C. the Sea Peoples
   D. the Egyptians

6. _____ is the most likely cause for the buildup of the Assyrian army into the greatest one in the region.
    A. Geographic vulnerability
    B. Economic poverty
    C. Religious fervor
    D. A series of strong rulers

7. The Bronze Age gave way to the Iron Age around what date?
    A. 2000 BC
    B. 1500 BC
    C. 1200 BC
    D. 500 BC

8. The center of the Hittite Empire was the present-day nation of _____.
    A. Iraq
    B. Syria
    C. Greece
    D. Turkey

9. What was the result of the twelfth-century battle between the Hittites and Egyptians at Syria?
    A. The Hittites conquered the Egyptians.
    B. The Egyptians conquered the Hittites.
    C. The Egyptians and the Hittites agreed to rule side by side in peace.
    D. The Hittites and the Egyptians agreed to merge their empires into one.

10. The rise to power around 500 BC of _____ marked the end of the first era of Fertile Crescent civilizations.
    A. the Medes
    B. the Chaldeans
    C. the Persians
    D. the Sea Peoples

chapter 3

The Ancient Middle East: Israel, Phoenicia, and Persia, 1800–323 BC

The area we today call the Middle East was the center of western civilization in ancient times. By the end of the period discussed in this chapter, civilization can really begin to be called Western, as the peoples of Europe—first Greek and then Roman—took over supremacy from the peoples of the Fertile Crescent.

By the turn of the millennium in 1000 BC, two tiny civilizations that settled on the eastern shore of the Mediterranean Sea had developed systems that were of lasting influence on the Western world. The Phoenicians perfected an alphabet in which each character stood for a sound rather than a whole word, and the Israelites set the example of a belief in one unique god who had created human beings in his own image.

About five hundred years later, the Persian Empire absorbed both of these civilizations and many more besides. It became the greatest empire of the ancient world. Unwieldy, diverse, and internally quarrelsome, it lasted only two hundred years or so before it was conquered by the mighty Alexander the Great.

CHAPTER OBJECTIVES

- Identify the major kingdoms and empires of the ancient Middle East on a map.
- Identify the major contributions of the Hebrews and Phoenicians and explain their significance.
- Describe the rise and fall of the Persian Empire.

Chapter 3 Time Line

(all dates are BC)

- 1800   Hebrews move to Canaan
- 1280   Moses leads the Israelites from Egypt to Israel
- 1050   Phoenician alphabet
- 1020–922   Kingdom of Israel
- 550   Birth of Persian Empire under Cyrus the Great
- 492–479   Persian Wars
- 323   Fall of the Persian Empire

Ancient Israel

History

Probably about 1800 BC, a Semitic people later called the Hebrews migrated from the Mesopotamian city of Ur to Canaan, where they settled on a narrow slice of land between the Dead Sea and the Mediterranean. Very little is known about their origins. At least one group of them traveled to Egypt, possibly during the Hyskos conquest (see Chapter 1). During the thirteenth century BC, according to legend, Moses led the Hebrews out of Egypt and into the Sinai Desert. They settled in the land we know today as Israel.

There is no historical record of the ancient Hebrews before about 1200 BC other than the Hebrew Bible; there is no outside evidence to confirm or disprove the stories of Abraham or Moses. Most historians have cautiously accepted that the biblical narrative of the Hebrews' exodus from Egypt and settlement in Israel has a basis in fact.

Around 1200 BC, the Philistines, a neighboring tribe, occupied a tiny piece of the Mediterranean coastline on Israel's western border. This challenge to their supremacy formed the Israelites into a kingdom by about 1020. The Kingdom of Israel lasted for about a century under three strong and charismatic rulers: Saul, David, and Solomon. Under Saul, the Philistines defeated the Israelites; under David, the Israelites fought the Philistines again and won a victory. David established Israel's capital city in Jerusalem, where Solomon oversaw the building of the Temple.

On Solomon's death, Israel was divided roughly in half, with the northern half called Israel and the southern half called Judah. In 721, the Assyrians under Sargon II conquered Israel and deported many of the Israelites, who apparently resettled throughout the Assyrian Empire and blended in with the local populations. Nebuchadnezzar, king of the Chaldeans, invaded Judah and led the destruction of Jerusalem in 587, during the Second Babylonian Empire. The Israelites aided Cyrus of Persia in establishing the Persian Empire (see "The Persian Empire" later in this chapter). About 538 BC, they returned to Israel and built the Second Temple. Throughout this period of exile, the prophets continued to teach the precepts of the religion we now call Judaism, thus ensuring a continuum of Hebrew belief and culture.

Religion

The Hebrews or Israelites— the term *Jews* was not used until much later—are important because, over time, they developed the first coherent, lasting monotheistic religion. The Israelites believed in the god Yahweh, who created the world and peopled it with men and women in his own image. According to legend, Yahweh gave the Ten Commandments directly to Moses; they constituted a moral code of behavior that was equally binding on all people, from monarchs to slaves.

Both these concepts were revolutionary. The various ancient peoples of the region believed in many gods, not just one. While the idea of monotheism had been tried—under Akhenaton in Egypt, for example—it never took firm hold until the Israelites. Ancient peoples also believed in the absolute authority of their rulers. The gods could affect life on earth by whim or by force; equally, the emperors and kings could command obedience. The idea of a moral code that made the slave the equal of the master was new to the world.

The Israelites compiled their legends, religious beliefs, and early history in a series of books collectively known as the Hebrew Bible. In their present form, the books of the Bible were probably written around the seventh century BC, though the stories they tell date back much earlier.

After the rise of Christianity, the Hebrew Bible (known to Christians as the Old Testament) was combined with the later New Testament; together, they are called simply the Bible. The Bible can safely be called the most important literary work in the history of the Western world (see Chapter 6).

The Phoenicians

Unlike the Hebrews, who came to the area from Mesopotamia, the Phoenicians were the descendants of the original settlers of Canaan. The age of Phoenician supremacy began around 1200 BC in present-day Lebanon, just north of the Kingdom of Israel. The Phoenicians built the free city-states of Byblos, Sidon, and Tyre. They developed a thriving mercantile economy and began establishing trading posts and colonies throughout the Mediterranean region.

By the end of the ninth century, the Phoenician civilization included a long stretch of the North African coast, well west of Egypt; the North African city of Carthage was a major trading center for the Phoenicians. They also established footholds on the southernmost tip of Spain and on the islands of Sicily, Sardinia, and Cyprus. Although Phoenicia was absorbed into the Assyrian Empire in the eighth century, the Phoenicians maintained their trading supremacy in the Mediterranean.

Competition for trade appeared with the rise and geographical expansion of the Greek civilization. By around 750, the Greeks had established footholds throughout the Mediterranean, which was the beginning of the end for Phoenician supremacy. The Phoenicians were eventually absorbed into the Persian Empire.

The Phoenicians are historically notable for the Phoenician alphabet, which appeared about 1050 BC. This alphabet was revolutionary because each of its letters represented a sound; writing systems of the time were usually pictographic, using a character or hieroglyph to represent a word or an idea. The Persian Empire and the Greek civilization both adapted the Phoenician alphabet to their own uses. The Persians developed it into the Aramaic alphabet, which later gave rise to the Arabic and Hebrew alphabets. The Greeks modified it only slightly by making it represent vowel sounds more consistently. The

Greek alphabet later gave rise to the Latin alphabet, used throughout most of the West, and the Cyrillic alphabet, used in Russia and the Russian republics.

The Persian Empire

The first Persians came to the Fertile Crescent around 2000 BC from the north (present-day Russia). Many of them settled on the Iranian plateaus, where they bred cattle and horses; others roamed farther east, eventually finding their way to the Indus Valley and present-day India. In both areas, Persians merged with the local populations, imposing their own languages on them and thus disseminating the Indo-European language family.

The Assyrians controlled the Mesopotamian region until the seventh century, when the Assyrian Empire fell to the Second Babylonian and Median empires (see Chapter 2). The Medes were themselves of Persian origin; the Median Empire was the first great success of the Persian peoples on the Iranian plateau. In 559, Cyrus succeeded to the throne of the small kingdom of Persia, united the other Persian tribes against the Medes, and in 550 declared himself king of a united Persian empire. This success against the Medes was the result of Persian military superiority. Cyrus is known to history as "the Great"; the title pays tribute to both his military skills and his charitable and just policies toward conquered peoples. These took the shape of tolerance and encouragement of local customs, beliefs, and laws.

Cyrus hoped to secure the eastern borders of the new Persian Empire and expand his territory into the west. In 547, a Persian victory over the Lydians extended Cyrus's control over the Anatolian peninsula (present-day Turkey), including the Ionian city-states of the Greek civilization. The next step was to conquer the Second Babylonian Empire. Cyrus was killed in battle in 530; his son and heir Cambyses carried out his father's ambitions, extending the Persian Empire into Egypt, Libya, and the Sudan. He also oversaw a buildup of the Persian fleet.

Cambyses died in 522 BC with no direct heir. After a period of factional squabbling, Darius I assumed control of the empire. Under his rule, the Persians conquered Macedonia and expanded their control into the Indus Valley. This made the Persian Empire the largest in the ancient world; it included more than twenty-five different ethnic groups.

Darius, who became known as Darius the Great, followed the pattern of most of the successful ancient empires. As emperor, he ruled by divine right.

Local authority in the empire's twenty provinces was in the hands of royal governors, called satraps, who were personally loyal to the emperor (often through family ties). Each satrap was all-powerful in his own province, collecting the tributes due to the emperor and maintaining the laws. The Persian army, which was loyal only to the emperor, was deployed throughout the empire both to protect the borders from outside invasions and to guard against the possibility of internal rebellion.

Darius established Aramaic as the official language of the Persian Empire. Under his rule, the Persians built a highway system and established a postal service, both of which eased communication throughout the empire. A uniform system of weights and measures ensured fair trade between and among the provinces.

The Persian Empire was mighty and vast, but it contained the seeds of its own destruction. First, government by an absolute monarch depends largely on the personality and talent of that monarch. Many of Darius's successors were weak or incompetent. Second, the empire was physically too large for central control in an age of slow communication and travel. Third, the empire was too diverse for its own stability. Persians were a small minority within their own empire, which was also home to Phoenicians, Israelites, Medes, Assyrians, Egyptians, and so on. There was plenty of resentment and irritation present among these varied ethnic groups (see Figure 3.1).

By the time of Darius, the Greek civilization had grown so much and become so prosperous that it became a distinct threat to the supremacy of the Persian Empire (see Chapter 5). In 499 BC, the Greek city-states rose up in rebellion against Persia. The rebels proved unexpectedly stubborn, but Persian troops succeeded in stamping out all resistance by 493—except in Athens and Sparta, which refused to give in. The enraged Darius sent his ships out against Athens and Sparta in 492, but nature intervened on the side of the Greeks, and storms off Mount Athos destroyed most of the Persian ships.

Darius, however, had no intention of accepting Greek defiance. In 490, the Persians sacked Eretria. Soon after, the Athenian army faced the Persians at Marathon and defeated them. Darius's successor, Xerxes, rallied the Persians in a full-scale invasion of Greece, which proved to be a serious strategic error. The Greeks took an important step forward in their civilization by unifying all their armies against the Persians. Before this, each state had fought its own battles without the help of the others.

The Greek army was under Spartan command. Meanwhile, the Athenian leader Themistocles ordered a massive buildup of the Athenian navy, which

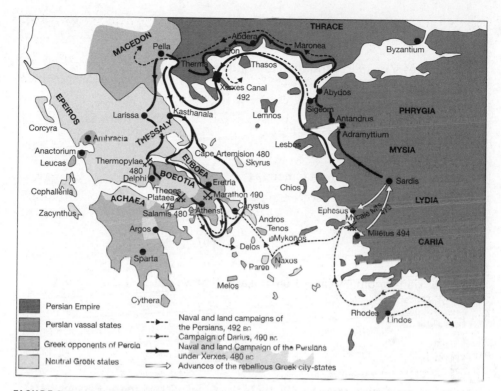

FIGURE 3.1   The Persian Wars

he believed would be crucial in the fight against the Persians. The Persians defeated the Greek troops under Leonidas at Thermopylae in 480; the Athenians took this as a sign that they would never be able to win a decisive victory against the Persians on land and retreated from their city. The Persians swept into Athens and burned it to the ground, but it was not long before the Athenians drove the Persian ships out of Greek waters. The war ended in 479 when the Spartans defeated the Persians on land at Plataea and Mount Mycale.

The Persian Empire, greatly weakened by the Greek victory, was finally vanquished in the fourth century under Alexander the Great (see Chapter 5). Alexander's Macedonian Empire did not long survive his death in 323; the former Persian Empire broke up into smaller kingdoms, which were eventually absorbed into the Roman Empire (see Chapter 6).

QUIZ

1. **The Hebrews' major contribution to world history was _____.**
   A. the alphabet
   B. monotheistic religion
   C. a barter economy
   D. the invention of writing

2. **The Phoenicians were most famous as _____.**
   A. warriors
   B. scholars
   C. traders
   D. scientists

3. **The Persians originally came from the area that we call _____ today.**
   A. Russia
   B. China
   C. Iran
   D. India

4. **What was the most important factor in the Greek victory in the Persian Wars?**
   A. The Greeks had established footholds throughout the Mediterranean.
   B. The Greek city-states were a civilization rather than an empire.
   C. The Persians were better sailors than the Greeks.
   D. The Greek city-states united their troops against the enemy.

5. **_____ conquered the Persian Empire and thus brought its supremacy to an end.**
   A. Cyrus the Great
   B. Alexander the Great
   C. King David
   D. Themistocles

6. **The ancient land of Canaan is located closest to present-day _____.**
   A. Lebanon
   B. Sicily
   C. Egypt
   D. Greece

7. All of these were inherent weaknesses in the Persian Empire except _____.
   A. ethnic diversity
   B. vast physical size
   C. linguistic unity
   D. autocratic government

8. All these writing systems are adaptations of the Phoenician alphabet except _____.
   A. Chinese
   B. Cyrillic
   C. Hebrew
   D. Arabic

9. Which aspect of the Greek civilization made it a threat to the Phoenicians?
   A. scientific discoveries
   B. religious beliefs
   C. military might
   D. geographical expansion

10. At its height, the Phoenician civilization maintained colonies or outposts in all of the following places except _____.
    A. Sicily
    B. Spain
    C. Egypt
    D. Carthage

Ancient China and India

Today, it is hard to imagine a world in which human societies, however far apart, are not aware of each other's existence. However, this was very much the case in ancient times. The civilizations of the Mediterranean and Near East were separated from China by distance and also by geographical barriers; therefore, these two regions developed along separate lines without ever making contact. Westerners did, however, invade India in large numbers, and there is some evidence that the ancient Chinese and Indian civilizations may have had limited contact with one another.

Today, India and China are two of the world's largest and most densely populated nations. They are generally referred to as "developing" nations—an irony, considering that their civilizations date substantially further back than Western ones.

There have been human settlements in China since at least the Neanderthal era of prehistory. China has existed as a culturally unified entity since at least 1000 BC; aspects of Chinese culture that may date back even further include the domestication of silkworms, the production of ceramic and jade objects, and the use of chopsticks. The classical Chinese written language originated well before 1000 BC and served as an important unifying force in ancient Chinese kingdoms.

Much about ancient Indian worship and philosophy, as well as the structure of Indian society, would be perfectly recognizable to the people of present-day India. Eastern European tribes swept eastward in ancient times; the Aryans who invaded India had a lasting influence on its civilization and culture. The roots of Hinduism and the caste system, both of which still influence Indian society, lie in the ancient Indo-Aryan civilization.

CHAPTER OBJECTIVES

- Identify the factors that gave rise to the early Chinese civilizations.
- Describe the Shang and Zhou dynasties.
- Describe the ancient Indian civilization.

Chapter 4 Time Line

(all dates are BC)

1700	Shang dynasty begins
1500–500	*Vedas* are collected
1400	Pan Geng founds capital city of Yin
1324–1264	Wu Ding's campaigns against Wei and Gui
1150	Zhou dynasty begins
800–550	Aryans settle Ganges River valley
800–500	*Upanishads* are collected
600s	Birth of K'ung-Fu-tzu (Confucius)
563	Birth of Siddhartha Gautama (the Buddha)
400	Development of Indian writing system

China

The core of what later became the unified nation of China developed in the river valleys and deltas, mainly around the Huang He (Yellow) River. Archaeological findings, especially of early bronze artifacts, show evidence of numerous ancient settlements scattered along the Huang He and along the Yangtze to the south. The northern settlements existed in a rather cold and arid climate; the southern climate was much more humid, better suited to farming rice and millet.

Two important geographical factors characterize the early Chinese settlements. First, they were inland rather than coastal. The coastline of the Yellow Sea was farther west in ancient times than it is today, but the early Chinese settlements and cities did not develop along the seacoast. The Chinese settled along the rivers, which they used as highways for transport and communication. Second, China was isolated from the Fertile Crescent and other early civilizations not only by distance, but by topographical features such as deserts and mountain ranges. There is no evidence that the ancient Chinese and the ancient Near East had any knowledge of one another.

The Shang Dynasty

Modern Western history is usually broken up into small units called "reigns," in which we speak of the events that take place under an individual monarch. Because ancient history tended to proceed at a much slower pace, with major changes happening at much longer intervals, we speak of centuries rather than reigns. Traditionally, Chinese history is taught in terms of dynasties rather than individual reigns. The first Chinese civilization for which we have reliable written records is the Shang dynasty, which took power around 1700 BC. The area over which the Shang kings maintained control was a bit smaller than present-day England and included a large number of city-states and settlements. The Shang dynasty lasted more than five hundred years.

Government

Tang was the first king of the Shang dynasty. He and his supporters and family used their military powers to dominate the region; Tang maintained power because of his personal qualities. Written records of the Shang dynasty credit him with wisdom and justice; these characteristics earned him the loyalty of his people.

The Shang civilization resembled the feudal system that arose centuries later in Western Europe. A number of small city-states existed along the Huang He and Yangtze rivers. The clan ruler of each city-state owed his loyalty to the emperor; he paid financial tribute and also provided military support when called on. In exchange, the emperor gave the clan ruler absolute power over his own city-state. Within the city-state, the clan ruler protected his people from attack by outsiders in return for their service.

The loyalty of the clan rulers—in time, many were members of the extended royal family—meant that the Shang king could speedily raise a very large army when necessary. Peasants were required to serve in the military whenever called; the Shang dynasty also commanded an officer corps of young men from the upper social ranks. Peasants served as the infantry, or foot soldiers; the noblemen served as the cavalry, riding horse-drawn chariots and armed with powerful bows. The chariot was the Shang clan's main military advantage over the other tribes.

The superior Shang military led Tang's successor Wu Ding and his queen Fu Hao to victory in a number of military campaigns against various other tribes in the region, notably the Gui and Wei people. Fu Hao actually led troops into combat herself; her tomb is almost the only one of its era that was not looted in antiquity, so all records of her achievements have not been lost.

Society

The people of ancient China were divided into two categories: nobles and peasants. The nobles had special privileges, such as clan membership and protection against corporal punishment. Clan membership was crucial to a person's social position because it conferred special religious standing. Many of the clans were linked to one another, and to the extended royal family, in a network of relationships. The Chinese believed that the king and his immediate family were related to the highest god.

A landowner owned everything on his estate, including the human beings. In effect, the peasants were slaves. They labored in the fields, were drafted into military service whenever necessary, and could be sold or traded if the landowner saw fit. There are almost no written records about the peasants of ancient China.

Religion

As was the case throughout the world until relatively modern times, religion and government were closely intertwined. The Shang kings claimed that they were divinely appointed to rule; in addition, they claimed a family connection to Shang-di, the supreme deity among a variety of nature gods and spirits. The people were less likely to question or defy a claim to power that was based on religion rather than, say, force of arms. One strong warrior might always try to defeat another, but there was no authority superior to that of the gods.

Chinese religion of the era had two aspects. First, the people believed that the gods could affect the harvest, so they must be appeased with sacrifices and ceremonies. Similar beliefs existed throughout the world in all tribal societies that depended on the harvest for their survival.

Second, the Chinese developed a system of ancestor worship that pervades their culture to this day. They believed that the souls of the dead had special powers to bring good or ill fortune to their living descendants. If you showed proper respect for the memory of your ancestors, they would function along the lines of what Westerners call "guardian angels." If you forgot your ancestors or spoke of them with contempt, they would turn nasty and bring you bad luck. To this day, respect for old people and for the dead is a central aspect of Chinese culture.

Writing

As far as records and artifacts can prove, the Shang civilization was the first literate one in ancient China. Shang written records consist of inscriptions on oracle bones and on bronze artifacts. These show that, by the Shang era, the Chinese written language had developed into a vocabulary of at least three thousand characters and that the grammatical rules for this language contain the roots of classical Chinese grammar. The Chinese writing system would later be simplified.

This written language was an important unifying force in Chinese society. The city-states were scattered geographically, so spoken Chinese differed from place to place, but written Chinese was understood the same way everywhere. This had two important effects. First, it fostered the later growth of the bureaucracy that was always needed to manage an empire. Second, it made literacy a stepping-stone to higher rank; a person who could read and write could travel and make himself understood in any part of China and thus could take on any job.

Artistically, the Chinese were highly advanced in the production of ceramics; their porcelain is famous throughout the world to this day. Fu Hao's tomb includes a tremendous number of jade and cast bronze artifacts of great beauty and sophistication.

The Zhou Dynasty

The Zhou tribe came from the west and unseated the Shang dynasty around 1150 BC. Zhou leaders did not make vast changes to Shang culture, religion, or government. Instead, they made various refinements and amendments that defined Chinese culture as it would develop for the rest of history.

The Zhou dynasty remained in power until the second century BC, but it was already substantially weakened by the 700s, when the court was driven eastward all the way to Honan. During the second century, the Qin (Ch'in) dynasty replaced the Zhou. China gets its name from the Qin dynasty (see Chapter 7).

Society and Economics

During the Zhou dynasty, the Chinese civilization developed into a mercantile urban society, resembling Western Europe in the medieval period. The Chinese developed a standardized currency, built cities, and learned to forge iron.

Enough urban remains have survived to tell us that by 500 BC, the Chinese were living in what we can readily recognize as cities, divided like modern cities into neighborhoods on the basis of income and occupation. Aristocrats lived in a particular area of the city. Artisans grouped themselves around another location, which included living quarters for their families as well as a marketplace for manufacture and trade. Farmers tended the fields of crops immediately outside the city walls—all early Chinese cities were walled in for protection.

Early in the Zhou period, the Chinese developed a standardized currency of cowrie shells. The fact of standardized currency is clear evidence of a mercantile economy—one based on the buying and selling of goods. Archaeologists' discoveries of jade, bronze, and ceramic artifacts are also evidence of this type of economy; if there is an artisan class manufacturing goods, then the goods are obviously being bought and sold. In all civilizations of the world, the development of a mercantile economy is a major shift from the simple subsistence farming that characterizes tribal cultures.

The Chinese arrived at the ability to cast and forge iron in the fifth century BC. Extremely high temperatures are required for the forging of iron—this technology did not arrive in the West for the better part of the next nineteen hundred years.

Government and Philosophy

During the Zhou dynasty, a major debate arose over how China should be governed. The feudal system had given rise to a class of powerful clan rulers whose standing posed a threat to the king. If the clan rulers grew too strong, they could band together and defy the king, refusing to pay tribute or to muster an army when commanded. Giving the clan rulers enough power to keep them happy, while at the same time keeping them weak enough not to threaten his own position, called for a tricky balancing act on the part of the king. By around the seventh century BC, this tense situation had created a social and political crisis.

Chinese scholars debated various solutions to the crisis. One group, called the Legalists, argued for a code of laws that would apply equally to all. They believed that such a legal code would naturally give rise to a wealthy, powerful state with a strong central government. The king favored the Legalist position, but the clan rulers raised many objections to it.

The birth of China's most influential thinker in the sixth century BC brought a new voice into the debate. K'ung-Fu-tzu, known in the West as Confucius, was born into the minor nobility and probably rose no higher than a minor official position. In the end, he became a teacher and a scholar. Despite his relatively humble life, Confucius's teachings carried as much weight in Chinese tradition as the teachings of Jesus would later carry in the West. To this day, he is the most important influence on Chinese thought and culture.

Confucius took a conservative view of society and government. He argued in support of the established order, in which everyone had a place. For the established order to function smoothly, all that was needed was for each person to know and keep his place, to do his duty, and to respect traditional culture. Confucius's system of thought relied on personal integrity; integrity would lead naturally to just government and to a wise and benevolent use of authority.

One other major figure in ancient Chinese thought is Lao-tzu, about whom historians know almost nothing—it is not even known with certainty whether he lived during the Shang or Zhou periods. According to tradition, Lao-tzu is the author of the *Tao Te Ching*, a collection of short poems that can be interpreted as advice to princes or philosophy by which all people should live. The basic message of the *Tao* is noninvolvement in the affairs of others; it advocates the wisdom of living as simply as possible and allowing the outside world to take care of itself.

India

Geography played a major role in the isolation of ancient India. The Himalayas, which include some of the world's tallest mountains, blocked access from the north; the other two sides of the triangular peninsula border on the Indian Ocean. This unique geographical location ensured that India could be invaded only from the northwest, through present-day Pakistan; such invasion in the ancient world was rarely successful. The Persian Empire extended only as far east as the Indus River that gave the nation of India its name; even Alexander the Great halted at the Indus River.

The oldest Indian civilization is the Indus Valley or Harappan civilization (see Chapter 1). The people of Harappan were literate, although archaeologists are unable to decipher most of their writing. However, writing seems to have temporarily disappeared from India about 1500 BC, when the Harappan civilization gave way to the Indo-Aryan civilization. Under the Aryans, literacy would not return to India until about 400 BC.

The Aryans (the word means "freeborn" or "noble") originated in Eastern Europe. Many of them settled on the Iranian plateau and would later be identified as Medes and Persians; others pushed farther eastward into the Indus valley. The Aryans were skilled horsemen, equipped with weapons and chariots; it is possible that they deliberately destroyed the Harappan civilization. Since the Harappan civilization seems to have been peaceful, its people would have been no match for an invading race of warriors.

The lack of written Indian sources from 1500 to 400 BC means that much of ancient Indian history is a matter of conjecture. One written source that tells historians something about ancient India is the four collections of hymns and religious rituals collectively known as the *Vedas*. These texts came into existence in oral form and were collected over the centuries, from about 1500 to 500 BC. Because the exact wording of the *Vedas* was of great religious importance, scholars believe that the surviving written version is a very accurate reflection of the original text.

Based on information in the *Vedas*, historians believe that the Aryans eventually expanded as far as the Ganges River, dividing the land mass into a number of small tribal kingdoms. Each one had a tribal leader, or *raja*, and a council of advisors. As this form of government gave way to monarchies, the rajas consolidated their power, eventually becoming autocrats.

Hinduism

The Aryans made two major, linked contributions to Indian culture—the set of religious beliefs and the system of social organization that, together, constitute what eventually became known as Hinduism. To this day, Hinduism is the basis of much of Indian life. Historians believe that Hinduism includes elements that are native to India, mixed with the ideas and beliefs of the invading Aryans. For instance, archaeological evidence suggests that the origins of the Hindu god Siva may lie in the Harappan civilization.

The Vedic religious beliefs that evolved into the Hindu religion are based on concepts of sacrifice. Like most ancient peoples, the Aryans believed in many gods rather than just one. The importance of sacrifice helps explain why Agni, the god of fire, was one of the major Vedic gods; in the ancient world, ceremonial sacrifices were made by fire. In time, Hinduism evolved into a belief in three major gods, or rather three aspects of one god: Vishnu, the god of love; Siva, the god of both protection and wrath; and Brahma, the creator. Hindus also believe in a cycle of rebirth and reincarnation along the path to enlightenment.

The Vedic religious system evolved over time into Brahmanism, which differs from its Vedic roots mainly in its emphasis on the importance of the priests and their role in religious rituals. The major text of Brahmanism is the *Upanishads*, a collection of philosophical meditations on the nature of the universe and the self. It describes Siva as the creator and protector of the universe.

The second aspect of Hinduism is the caste system —the division of every member of society into specific social classes. Like the Aryan religious beliefs, the caste system pervades Indian society to this day. The rules today are less rigid, but the tradition is so ingrained that it maintains immense power over the people.

Originally there were four castes. The first included rulers and warriors; the second comprised only priests; the third included a mix of artisans, merchants, and farmers; and the last was made up of servants and slaves. When the caste system first took shape, mobility between castes seems to have been possible, except for an absolute ban on intermarriage between Aryans and non-Aryans.

Over time, the caste system became more and more detailed, with many more levels being added. Each caste had its own assigned occupations and duties, and contact between members of different castes became more and more rigidly controlled by law. Not only intermarriage, but eating together or even the simplest physical contact was forbidden. A person was born into his or her caste and could not rise into a higher one.

A religion based on sacrifice and a caste system based on duty went hand in hand. These tenets demonstrate that ancient Indian society cared much more for the stability of the community than for the rights of the individual. The caste system did not define rights; it defined god-given responsibilities that each person must carry out so that society would continue to function smoothly. This emphasis on the sacrifice of personal importance in two major human institutions—religion and society—accounts for the fact that lower-caste Indians did not rise up in rebellion as the peasants and slaves in other world cultures so often did. Their religion assured them that at the end of a harsh and thankless low-caste existence, they might well be reborn into a better situation.

Buddhism

Buddhism first evolved as an attempt to reform Brahmanism. Buddhism arose from the ideas in the *Upanishads* but placed a very different emphasis on them.

Siddhartha Gautama, born into the nobility in 563 BC, is known to history as the Buddha (the title means "Enlightened One"). Obeying the teachings of Brahmanism, he left his comfortable existence as a prince to become an ascetic; when this did not satisfy his search for spiritual fulfillment, he turned to meditation. He became a preacher and teacher who offered his followers a "Middle Way" to enlightenment.

The Buddha taught that since all suffering and conflict in the world came from frustrated ambition, passion, or egotism, the elimination of these emotions would lead to contentment and spiritual peace. A Buddhist could eliminate destructive passions by always observing right conduct, speech, thought, and effort. Buddhism also opposed the caste system.

Mahayana Buddhism, the form of the Buddha's teaching that evolved in northern India, spread into Central Asia and thence to East Asia in the second century BC. Ironically, Buddhism would take a greater and more lasting hold in China than in India, where it was largely shouldered aside by Hinduism.

QUIZ

1. The earliest Chinese civilizations developed _____.
   A. in the mountains
   B. along the coast of the Yellow Sea
   C. in the eastern river valleys
   D. on the large islands off the east coast

2. Government under the Shang dynasty is best described as _____.
   A. a military dictatorship
   B. a group of independent, self-governing city-states
   C. a tribal society with a chief and a council of elders
   D. a feudal system in which the lords were loyal to the emperor

3. The Aryan peoples who invaded and settled in India originally came from _____.
   A. China
   B. Eastern Europe
   C. the Mediterranean islands
   D. North Africa

4. The four sets of hymns and religious rituals that form the basis of ancient Indian religion are known as _____.
   A. the *Tao Te Ching*
   B. the *Upanishads*
   C. the *Vedas*
   D. the Buddha

5. All these concepts are of central importance to Hinduism except _____.
   A. the caste system
   B. the cycle of reincarnation and rebirth
   C. the concept of sacrifice
   D. the attempt to control one's passions

6. Which best describes the relationship between the ancient civilizations of China and the Mediterranean?
   A. Their leaders agreed to maintain peace between their peoples.
   B. They had no knowledge of one another's existence.
   C. Their merchants did a brisk business in international trade.
   D. They were constantly at war with one another.

7. **Siddhartha Gautama is an important historical figure because he _____.**
   A. was the first king of the Shang dynasty in China
   B. led the Aryan invaders into India
   C. founded the religion that became known as Buddhism
   D. argued against the Legalist side of debate over Chinese rule

8. **_____ were ethnically related to the Aryans.**
   A. The Egyptians
   B. The Chinese
   C. The Persians
   D. The Indians

9. **Which best explains why historians believe the texts of the *Vedas* are very little changed from the originals?**
   A. It would have been very important to use the exact, correct wording of religious ceremonies and hymns.
   B. The original texts of the *Vedas* date back to the Harappan civilization.
   C. India seems to have been an illiterate civilization under the Indo-Aryans until about 400 BC.
   D. The *Vedas* are almost the earliest written work that has survived from ancient India.

10. **According to the Indo-Aryan caste system, _____.**
    A. a person is born into a caste and cannot rise to a higher one
    B. a person can marry into a higher caste
    C. a person can rise to a higher caste through extraordinary service to the kingdom
    D. a person can choose which caste to join, but then cannot go back on the choice

chapter 5

The Greek Civilization and the Macedonian Empire, 2000–275 BC

The Greek civilization began where the Mediterranean Sea meets the Aegean Sea—an area dotted by a large number of islands. The peninsular and island culture of Greece meant a close relationship with the sea; trading was done by boat, and the Greek navy became the mightiest and most efficient of the era.

Greek culture of the Golden Age (roughly 750 to 400 BC) is the foundation of Western civilization. The Greeks provided the basis of Western art, architecture, literature, science, philosophy, and government. Succeeding civilizations would use and change all these elements, but the Greek foundation consistently shows through the outer layers.

Greek scholars and philosophers believed in the supremacy of human reason—that people could come to understand the workings of the universe by means of abstract thought. This belief is their most important contribution to the development of human society, particularly in the West. Many of the Greek scientific theories turned out in the long run to be mistaken, but this does not diminish the lasting influence of the Greek belief in the supremacy of science and rational thought.

In sharp contrast to the rest of the ancient world, ruled by the principle of the divine right of emperors, Greek civilization featured a new form of government called *democracy*. True popular democracy, of course, has never existed in any nation in history, including the Greek city-states; it is simply not possible for every member of a large community to play an equal part in deciding how it should be run. However, the concept of government by the people is one of the major founding ideals of the modern Western world; the adult citizens of almost all modern states have the right to vote and to participate in their own governments.

The conquests of Philip II of Macedon and his son Alexander the Great both ended Greek civilization and disseminated it as far east as the Indus River. Indeed, Greece would continue to affect the known world of the Mediterranean culturally, linguistically, and politically for many years to come.

CHAPTER OBJECTIVES

- Identify the Greek civilization at its fullest extent.
- Describe society and government during different stages of the Greek civilization.
- Describe the course of major changes in the Greek civilization, including wars.
- Identify the major achievements of the Greek civilization and its important influences on the modern world.
- Describe the rise and fall of the Macedonian Empire under Philip and Alexander.

Chapter 5 Time Line

(all dates are BC)

●	2000	Minoan civilization begins on Crete
●	1450	Mycenaean civilization begins
●	1200	Trojan War

- 750   *Iliad* and *Odyssey*
- 492   Persian Wars begin
- 478   Delian League
- 431   Peloponnesian War begins
- 359   Philip II becomes King of Macedonia
- 336   Philip II is assassinated; Alexander III (Alexander the Great) becomes king
- 334–323 Macedonian Empire
- 323   Death of Alexander the Great

The Greek Civilization

Peoples of the Fertile Crescent probably settled the area we today call Greece as early as 6000 BC. The beginning of an identifiable Greek culture, however, goes back only about as far as 2000 BC with the arrival of the Achaeans. These people came from southeastern Europe, between the Carpathian and Ural mountains—the region we today refer to as the Balkans.

The Achaeans remained on the mainland, eventually establishing trade relationships with the Aegean islands and other settlements in the region. This trade network fostered the eventual supremacy of the Greek language throughout the region.

The earliest Achaean palace dates to about the seventeenth century BC, at the city of Mycenae in the Peloponnese (the southernmost section of the Greek peninsula). This city eventually gave its name to the Mycenaean civilization, when the Achaeans invaded and took over Crete (see "The Mycenaean Civilization" later in this chapter).

Geographically, Greece is rocky, mountainous, and somewhat barren. Its poor soil and hilly topography make it ideal for such crops as grapes, olives, and apricots, and for herding sheep and goats. As in any island culture, fish also became a staple of the Greek diet.

Throughout the centuries of their civilization, most Greeks were subsistence farmers, and the economy relied more on barter than on purchase for coin or currency. The Greek economy was a mercantile economy, meaning that it was based on buying and selling and trade, but it was by no means an economy of mass production. Pottery, jewelry, and other everyday and luxury goods were made by hand, one at a time. The number of artisans was not large.

The Minoan Civilization on Crete

The Minoan civilization arose on the large island of Crete about 2000 BC. Knossos was the main Minoan city; others included Phaistos and Malia. Minoan civilization was quite sophisticated, featuring an absolute ruler, a thriving mercantile economy, and vast palaces.

The king was called *minos*, hence the name *Minoan*. There are numerous ancient legends of King Minos of Crete but no historical evidence of any individual of that name. Historians believe that *minos* was a title, not a person's name. The *minos* was an absolute ruler who identified himself with the gods; the people were entirely subject to his arbitrary will. The magnificent size and scale of the Minoan palaces is clear evidence of Minoan belief in the divinity of their king.

Social classes on Crete at this time included artisans and literate scribes in addition to farmers, fishermen, shipbuilders, and sailors. The artisan class created a steady stream of luxury items for both export and local use; the jars, amphorae, jewelry, and other objects of the period were remarkably sophisticated and beautiful. Archaeologists have discovered troves of written records that testify to the large group of scribes.

Manufacturing and trade were vital to the Minoan economy, because Crete was poor in natural resources, particularly the metals that were necessary for making weapons and tools. Like any island population, the Cretans were superb sailors and shipbuilders. They maintained an extensive trade network throughout the Mediterranean region.

The Mycenaean Civilization

The Achaeans invaded Minoan Crete around 1500 to 1450 BC; they ruled supreme on Crete until about 1200. Their rise to supremacy on Crete coincides with the wholescale destruction of the Minoan cities by fire. Historians have never solved the mystery of whether the Mycenaeans set those fires in an act of aggression.

Mycenaean palaces were more heavily fortified than Minoan ones, and Mycenaean art reflects more warlike themes. However, the two civilizations had many things in common. First was the thriving commercial trade. Both Egyptians and Hittites knew of the Mycenaeans, and Mycenaean art shows definite Egyptian influences—clear evidence of communication between the cultures. Archaeologists have found fragments of Mycenaean pottery throughout the Mediterranean and also on the Black Sea coast. The civilization evidently traded with peoples in Sardinia and Libya; Mycenaean trading ships regularly navigated the Dardanelles Strait (then called the Hellespont). Greek legends of heroes such as Hercules and Jason show that this was a culture of people who sailed, explored, and roamed their known world.

Like the Minoans, the Mycenaeans were a record-keeping society. Archaeologists have discovered huge caches of written records on clay tablets. The earlier ones, written in a script they refer to as Linear A, have not yet been decoded; the later ones, written in Linear B, are mainly accounting documents—lists of figures and inventory totals.

Around 1200 BC, the Mycenaeans attacked the city of Troy in Asia Minor. The Trojan War is the subject of the *Iliad* (see the following section). Historians generally agree that the attack on Troy was probably for the simple reason of greed; it was a fabulously wealthy city and very tempting to take over and loot.

The "Dark Ages"

Soon after the Trojan War, the Mycenaean civilization declined. The years from about 1200 to 800 BC are called the "dark ages" of Greece. Historians still debate the causes of the fall of Mycenaean culture; various authors have argued for natural disasters (the area is prone to volcanic eruptions) or an invasion of hostile outsiders such as the Dorians or the Sea People.

The Dark Ages saw movement and resettlement of peoples all along the eastern banks of the Mediterranean and in the Aegean islands. The Aeolians settled in the northern part of this area, the Ionians in the center, and the Dorians in the south. These various tribal groups were more or less constantly at war with one another.

During this otherwise chaotic era, the religious system of Classical Greece was refined and set in the form we recognize from legend and mythology. It was a polytheistic religion, with one supreme god ruling over a number of gods and goddesses, each one responsible for a particular aspect of the forces that governed life on earth. Aphrodite was the goddess of love, Apollo the god of the sun, Poseidon the god of the sea, and so on. The Greeks absorbed the gods of neighboring cultures into their own belief system: Aphrodite came from the Semitic tradition, Zeus from the eastern Europeans, and Apollo from the Anatolians.

The Greek gods were a family network (for example, Zeus was Hera's husband, Poseidon's brother, and Athena's father). Like any human family, the gods squabbled among themselves. According to Greek belief, the gods could and did interfere regularly in human affairs, either to help their favorites or to harm those of whom they were jealous. If a god considered that a human hero was becoming too bold or arrogant, the god would humble him by bringing him misfortune. Gods could assume human or animal form at will and take part in any activity among the humans—many of the heroes of Greek legend were the offspring of a god or goddess and a human being. The only way to appease the gods and keep them on one's side was through the proper prayers and sacrifices.

The gods and goddesses play major roles in the *Iliad* and the *Odyssey*, epic poems written about 750 BC that tell the story of the Trojan War and its aftermath. These two heroic adventure stories are among the most influential literary works of Western history. Scholars have consistently attributed them to Homer, about whom very little is known except that he was probably Ionian and was active during the eighth century BC. The barbarism and violence evident throughout the *Iliad* and the *Odyssey* reflect the chaotic, brutal Dark Ages in which Homer lived.

Classical Greece: The Golden Age

A new Greek civilization, the Classical Age or the Golden Age, began around the eighth century BC. This Classical Greek civilization featured a form of government entirely new to the ancient world. It was neither an empire nor a centralized state but a large number of independent city-states sharing a common language, a common culture, and eventually a common sense of Greek identity. Examples of unifying factors in Greek civilization included the polytheistic religion, the oracles that all Greeks worshipped, and the Olympic Games in which all the city-states participated. City-states often cooperated in the area of foreign relations.

The Greek city-state was called a *polis*, which gave us the English words *police* and *metropolis*. The capital city of the polis was usually built on a high rock, or *acropolis*, that overlooked the entire city. The reason for this was military defense; battle strategy through the ages teaches the lesson that the army controlling the high ground will win the battle. A weak polis would often find itself dominated by a stronger one.

During this era, the Greeks made a vastly important contribution to the future Western civilization—they created the concept of democratic rule, in which individual citizens were permitted some say in how they were governed.

The word *demos* means "person" in Greek; hence, *democracy* means "rule by the people." Democracy in Greece was by no means universal. First, not every polis adopted this form of government; many were military dictatorships. Second, the only citizens of a democracy who could participate or vote were adult men who owned a certain amount of property. In practice, only about one-tenth of the population of any given polis participated in its government.

Around 750 BC, the Greeks began exploring the Mediterranean and establishing outposts very far from home. Historians believe that they roamed the seas for several reasons. First, a series of droughts and poor harvests probably drove them out in search of food and viable farmland. Second, they wanted to extend their trading network by establishing outposts within reasonable sailing distance and by discovering new markets for their own exports. At its height, the Greek civilization included almost the entire coast of Turkey; all of mainland Greece; Crete; the mouth of the Nile; parts of Sicily, Corsica, and Cyprus; the southern tip of Italy; and stretches of the Mediterranean coastlines of Spain and France. Their settlements also nearly surrounded the Black Sea. All this exploration led to cultural exchange and also to military conflicts.

The polis of Athens is famous as the pinnacle of Classical Greek civilization in its intellectual and cultural achievements. Athens first achieved significance under Solon in the early sixth century with a new law code. The Athenians discovered rich silver mines during the reign of Peisistratus in the second half of the sixth century; this new source of wealth allowed Peisistratus to indulge his imperial ambitions. By extending trade and acquiring new colonies, Peisistratus made Athens the wealthiest of the Greek city-states. Athenian democracy—rule by mutual agreement of the adult men—was fully developed in the last quarter of the sixth century. By this time, all adult men were entitled to attend the assemblies and to vote for their political leaders. This development was significant because it marked the first time in world history that common men were on a politically equal footing with aristocrats—both had the same opportunities to rise to political power and authority.

The Persians and Greeks fought a major war in several stages between 492 and 479 BC. During the mid-sixth century, the Persian Empire took control of all the Ionian city-states; the Persians later occupied Thrace and demanded tribute from all the city-states. The Persians rightly viewed the Greeks as a serious threat to their own supremacy in the Mediterranean. In the end, the Greeks won the Persian Wars and secured their independence. Their victory over the largest empire in the ancient world was primarily due to two factors. First, the Greek—specifically the Athenian—navy was superior to the Persian; Themistocles, the leader of Athens, had built up the Athenian navy into the mightiest in the world. Second, the Persian threat was so alarming that it constituted a unifying factor: the Persian Wars marked the first time the Greek city-states sent forth a united Greek army against an enemy (see Chapter 3).

The Golden Age of Athens was truly launched after the victory in the Persian Wars with the creation of the Delian League, an association of about two hundred city-states who agreed to join forces against any future Persian threat. Specifically, members agreed that they would build and supply a common fleet of ships. Athens took the leading role in the Delian League because an Athenian was commander of the fleet; this was unsurprising since Athens was the strongest polis in the league. Before long, smaller states were contributing money instead of ships to the league, and the system quickly acquired all the trappings of an Athenian empire in which satellite states paid tribute.

Pericles was the most important Athenian ruler of the era. The Persians had burned Athens to the ground during the wars; Pericles oversaw a great era of rebuilding, including the building of the Parthenon. This era of Greek architecture, with its columns, pediments, and relief sculpture, has had an enormous influence on monumental architecture throughout the Western world down to the present day. Athens was equally notable for visual arts, drama, philosophy, and literature. Its playwrights invented tragedy and comedy as we know them today, its lyric poets influenced writers down to the modern era, its philosophers held sway over Western thought for many centuries, and its historians established the method of drawing conclusions from eyewitness accounts and primary sources whenever these were accessible.

Table 5.1 lists the most important and influential authors and intellectuals of the Golden Age of Greece, along with their major literary works.

The cultural and intellectual brilliance of Athens did not make smaller city-states any less restive under the iron grip of its dominance. The most likely rival to Athens was Sparta, a strong military state in the Peloponnese (the southern tip of the Greek peninsula). Sparta gave birth to the English adjective *spartan*, which means "plain and austere to the point of harshness." This gives an idea of Spartan culture, which frowned on comfort, ornament, and luxury while encouraging physical strength and stamina above all other virtues. The Spartan army had proved its superiority in the Persian Wars (see Chapter 3).

Sparta and Corinth allied against Athens, and the two sides began a long series of military squabbles around 460 BC. In 431, the hostility culminated in the Peloponnesian War, which pitted Athens and the Delian League against Sparta and its allies. Sparta had a stronger land army and Athens a superior

Table 5.1 The Golden Age of Greece

Name	Dates*	Field	Major Works
Sappho	630–570	Poet	Lyric poetry (only fragments survive)
Pythagoras	570–495	Mathematician, philosopher	All lost; major ideas survive in the writings of his followers
Aesop	mid-500s	Storyteller	Fables
Aeschuylus	525–456	Playwright (tragedy)	The *Oresteia*
Pindar	522–443	Poet	Odes, lyric poems
Sophocles	496–406	Playwright (tragedy)	*Antigone*
Herodotus	484–425	Historian	*Histories* (of the Persian Empire)
Euripides	480–406	Playwright (tragedy)	*Medea*
Socrates	470–399	Philosopher, teacher	All lost; major ideas re-created in the writings of Plato
Thucydides	460–395	Historian	*History of the Peloponnesian War*
Aristophanes	450–386	Playwright (comedy)	*Lysistrata*
Plato	427–347	Philosopher, historian	*Apologia, Republic*
Aristotle	384–322	Philosopher	*Poetics*

* Dates for Sappho and Aesop are approximate within about fifty years; dates for all others are approximate within a year or two.

navy; therefore, neither side was able to make much headway against the other in the first several years of the war. In 415, Athens attacked the Sicilian city of Syracuse, hoping to rob it of its considerable wealth for use in the continuing fight against Sparta. This strategy backfired when Sparta came to Syracuse's rescue and managed to destroy the Athenian fleet. In 408, the Persian Empire came into the war as Sparta's ally; like the Spartans, the Persians wanted to see Athens defeated. Athens finally succumbed in 404.

Sparta maintained supreme authority among the Greek city-states for only a short time. After the war, Athens began to repair its trade networks and thus recover some of its former prosperity. In 378, Athens and Thebes united against Sparta. Thebes won a major victory against the Spartan army in 371 BC and was the strongest polis until Greece was finally defeated by the rise of the Macedonian Empire.

The Macedonian Empire

The Macedonian kingdom occupied the northern section of the Greek peninsula. It was part and parcel of the Greek civilization and shared the Greek language and culture, but it was so firmly under the control of the Persian Empire that the Athenians and Peloponnesians considered it a barbaric kingdom. In addition, its society was much rougher and more warlike than that of southern Greece. Macedonia did not achieve self-rule or dominance until Philip II's reign began in 359 BC.

Philip II

Philip's goal was to improve the Macedonian army into a powerful weapon that would enable him to expand his kingdom. He instituted strategic innovations and new weapons, such as catapults, extra-long pikes, and battering rams. By 338, he had taken over the neighboring regions of Thessaly and Thrace, which were strategically important because of their harbors. That same year, Philip's army defeated the united forces of Thebes and Athens at Chaerona. Philip was assassinated in 336. His son Alexander—known to history as Alexander the Great—succeeded him.

Alexander the Great

Born in 356 BC, Alexander learned history and philosophy from the Greek genius Aristotle. He soon showed his grasp of military strategy, leading his troops to victory against the Persians, first at Granicus in 334 and again at Issus in 333. Over the next two years, Alexander expanded the Macedonian Empire into Syria, Egypt, and Mesopotamia. By the time of his death in 323, he had taken over a vast empire that stretched from the Danube River in the west to the Indus River in the east.

The conquests of Alexander are historically important because he spread the Hellenistic (Greek) culture throughout Egypt, Turkey, and the Middle East. The empire was politically unified while Alexander lived. After his death, it broke up into smaller kingdoms, but all can accurately be described as Hellenistic—meaning that they were culturally and linguistically part of the Greek civilization. Alexander built new cities throughout the years of his eastward conquering march (at least five were called Alexandria in his honor). These cities served not only as military and trading posts but as seats of cultural exchange. Alexander caused libraries to be built and stocked, thus making

Greek discoveries in mathematics, science, and philosophy available to eastern scholars. The Egyptian city of Alexandria boasted the finest library in the ancient world. It is no accident that some of the greatest scientific and mathematical names in history—Euclid, Archimedes, and Eratosthenes—all worked and studied in Alexandria.

Three main Hellenistic kingdoms rose by 275 BC. Ptolemy and his successors ruled Egypt, while the vast Middle Eastern swath of Macedonia was divided between the Seleucids in the east and the Antigonids in the west. All three kingdoms were eventually absorbed into the Roman Empire (see Chapter 6).

QUIZ

1. **The Peloponnesian War was fought between _____.**
   A. Athens and Sparta
   B. Sparta and Macedonia
   C. Macedonia and Persia
   D. Persia and Greece

2. **Trade was important to the Minoan civilization because Crete lacked _____.**
   A. good harbors
   B. arable land
   C. skilled artisans
   D. metal deposits

3. **The most important difference between Mycenaeans and Minoans was that the Mycenaeans were more _____.**
   A. intellectual
   B. warlike
   C. politically conservative
   D. religious

4. **All of the following were major Athenian playwrights except _____.**
   A. Aeschylus
   B. Aristophanes
   C. Euripides
   D. Herodotus

5. The Greeks believed that human beings could understand the workings of the universe by _____.
   A. collecting data and drawing conclusions from it
   B. drawing conclusions based on abstract thought
   C. studying the great authors of the past
   D. using one's common sense

6. The polis of Sparta is most famous in history for its _____.
   A. military might
   B. economic wealth
   C. cultural brilliance
   D. literary achievements

7. At its height, the Macedonian Empire absorbed all of the following except _____.
   A. Egypt
   B. Greece
   C. Italy
   D. Mesopotamia

8. Alexander the Great is a significant historical figure because he _____.
   A. wrote classic works of philosophy that have influenced scholars down to the present day
   B. presided over a great flowering of architectural, artistic, and cultural achievement
   C. spread Greek culture and the Greek language throughout the known world
   D. wrote two of the greatest epic poems in the history of literature

9. _____ invaded, conquered, and looted the city of Troy.
   A. Philip II of Macedon
   B. Themistocles
   C. The Spartans
   D. The Mycenaeans

10. The three Hellenistic kingdoms that succeeded the Macedonian Empire were eventually conquered by _____.
    A. the Athenians
    B. the Spartans
    C. the Persians
    D. the Romans

chapter **6**

The Roman Empire and the Rise of Christianity, 900 BC–AD 476

The Roman Empire was the most impressive organizational achievement of the ancient world. At its height, it encompassed all of Europe from the Atlantic Ocean to the Rhine and Danube rivers; all the islands of the Mediterranean; Egypt and a broad swath of the North African coastline; and all of Anatolia (Turkey), Israel, Syria, and Jordan. Two political institutions managed this vast area: the bureaucracy and the army. Both were organized and professional beyond anything that had been seen before in the ancient world.

Rome's greatest historical importance lies in the fact that it brought all the Western civilizations together into an economically and politically unified whole that allowed the individual cultures within it to flourish. It is because of Rome that our present-day phrase *Western civilization* has a meaning—it refers to a shared past, a common way of thinking about and living in the world that has its origins in the Roman Empire.

The most likely reason the Roman Empire spread as far as it did and held together as long as it did was its tolerance. Roman rulers made no attempt to force a particular way of life on any of the diverse groups under its authority. The people were only required to obey the law code, pay their taxes, and be loyal to the Roman state. Worship of the Roman gods was mandatory, but it was not an exclusionary religion; people might also worship any other gods they pleased. Even this rule was flexible; when the Jews objected to it on religious grounds, they were exempted.

Rome adopted its mythology, religion, and culture from the Etruscans and Greeks. As a civilization, it lent itself to solving practical problems rather than to abstract thought. The most important original achievements of the Roman civilization were in the areas of law, government, and engineering. In addition, Latin would continue to be the common language of all educated Westerners for a thousand years after the fall of the empire.

Ultimately, Rome was a military civilization. Its greatest rulers came from military backgrounds, the Roman army was responsible for the empire's successful expansion, a large proportion of the male population earned their living as soldiers, and the military was garrisoned throughout the empire.

The introduction and spread of Christianity occurred simultaneously with the fall of the Roman Empire—and contributed to that fall. In the end, Catholicism would spread to all parts of the world and would hold undisputed sway over Europe until the AD 1500s.

CHAPTER OBJECTIVES

- Identify the location of the Roman Empire at its greatest extent.
- Describe Roman government under the republic and under the Caesars.
- Discuss the effect the rise of Christianity had on the Roman Empire.
- Identify the major achievements of Roman civilization.

Chapter 6 Time Line

BC

●	753	Founding of Rome
●	509	Roman Republic begins
●	275	Romans defeat Greeks to take over entire Italian peninsula

- **264–146** Punic Wars (against Carthaginians)
- **49** Gaius Julius Caesar becomes dictator of Rome
- **27** *Pax Romana* begins
- **4** Birth of Jesus

AD

- **284** Diocletian reorganizes Roman Empire into two halves (east and west)
- **324** Constantine becomes emperor; he reunites Roman Empire under one emperor (temporarily) and establishes Christianity as state religion
- **330** Constantine establishes new capital city at Constantinople
- **378** Goths defeat Romans at Adrianople
- **395** Roman Empire officially becomes two separate states
- **410** Goths sack Rome
- **476** Romulus Augustus, last emperor of Rome, is assassinated

Ancient Italy

The Italian peninsula is easily identified on a map because of its distinctive shape—it resembles a high-heeled boot. A long spine of mountains—the Apennines—runs down the center of the peninsula. In the north, where the peninsula meets the European mainland, the land is rich and fertile; in the south, it is rocky and barren, good for growing grapes. Archaeologists continue to find ancient Roman amphorae and wine containers throughout the former empire; even today, Italy is the world's largest wine producer. In ancient times, Italy's position in the middle of the Mediterranean gave it a central role in international trade.

By the ninth century BC, three civilizations flourished on the Italian peninsula. The Etruscans held sway in the north, the Romans controlled the center, and the Greeks established independent city-states in the extreme south, including Syracuse on the island of Sicily (see Chapter 5). The Romans would eventually overpower the other two and control all of Italy.

The Etruscans were not native Italians; historians disagree about where they originally came from. Their roots may lie in Anatolia (Turkey), or they may be descended from the Sea Peoples who roamed the Mediterranean in gangs around 1200 BC (see Chapter 2). There is strong evidence that they came from somewhere in the Near East. Evidence includes their literacy; their skill at all kinds of building projects, from shipbuilding to making jewelry; and the complexity and sophistication of their political systems. Historians believe that the Etruscan civilization was organized into independent cities or city-states that resembled the Greek model (see Chapter 5). Politically, the Etruscans would dominate the Romans until about 500 BC.

The Romans originated among the Italic tribes who are native to the peninsula. These Latin-speaking people organized themselves into free cities, some of which formed leagues for their mutual advantage and security. Rome, the most important city, was built in a hilly area on the banks of the Tiber River, in the spot where it was easiest to cross. Roman mythology assigns 753 BC as the official date on which the city was founded, although it had, of course, existed as a town for some time before that date. The Romans absorbed a great deal from the dominant Etruscan civilization. Roman scribes adapted the Etruscan alphabet to write in Latin, Roman artists and artisans adopted and imitated Etruscan methods and models, and Roman political and military leaders studied Etruscan systems of organization.

The Roman Republic

The first step along the road to Roman supremacy and the Roman Republic was the defeat of the Etruscans. The Etruscans were bound to fall; because their civilization was not politically unified, it was not strong enough to defend itself against a determined challenger.

First the Romans and then the Greeks defeated the Etruscans—the Romans on land in 509 BC, the Greeks at sea in 474. The Greeks were content to maintain control of their established power base in the south; the Romans, more expansion-minded, were thus handed control of the rest of mainland Italy.

The last blow to the Etruscan civilization came about 400 BC with the invasion of the Gauls, a northern European tribe. After defeating the Etruscans, the Gauls moved south and in 390 they sacked Rome. The Romans held out against them, however, and the Gauls eventually retreated north.

The Romans used 509 BC— the date on which they defeated the Etruscans—as the founding date for the Roman Republic. It would last in name until 31 BC, although the republican system of government would, in fact, develop into a dictatorship before that date.

Roman society was divided into two classes based on birth: the patricians (aristocrats) and the plebeians (commoners). The Roman leaders recognized this division when they created their system of government. The highest officers were the two consuls, elected for one-year terms. To be elected consul, a man had to have served in at least two lower-level political offices; this ensured that those in charge of the government would always be experienced leaders. The consuls ruled through the Roman Senate, which contained two categories of officials: senators and tribunes. Only a patrician could be a senator; the tribunes represented the plebeians.

Both Senate and society reflected a balance of power. In the Senate, the tribunes had veto power, and, after 366 BC, one of the two consuls was always a plebeian. Outside the Senate, the plebeians had the power of popular demonstration against the government. In addition, since the mass of the army was drafted from the plebeians, the patricians had an incentive not to alienate them. On their side, the patricians had the power and privileges that accompany wealth in any society.

Women enjoyed some degree of rights and freedoms in ancient Rome. No woman could hold office, but even plebeian women could own property and run businesses (such as taverns or laundries). Patrician women were often very well read and educated, although they usually received their schooling at home. A forceful, intelligent woman from an influential patrician family could wield a high degree of political influence.

Around 450 BC, the Romans developed a civil and criminal law code known to history as the Twelve Tables of Law. It banned intermarriage between patricians and plebeians, thus demonstrating the Roman belief in the necessity of maintaining the separation of classes in society. However, its laws applied equally to all.

Geographical Expansion of the Republic

War with Greece

By about 272 BC, all of Italy was a unified, centrally controlled state under Roman authority. Under Pyrrhus of Epirus, the Greeks fought for ten years to maintain their power base in southern Italy; but despite Pyrrhus's considerable abilities as a commander, the Romans refused to accept defeat and continued the struggle until Pyrrhus eventually withdrew. (Today, the idiom *Pyrrhic victory* refers to an empty victory or one won only at great cost.) In fact, the Greeks achieved a highly significant long-term victory; their culture would reach and influence successive generations because of its adoption by the Romans. Romans would follow the Greek models in literature, fine art, philosophy, and architecture. They also adopted the Greek religion, with its family network of gods and goddesses (see Chapter 5). The Romans used different names for the gods: thus, Zeus became Jupiter, Athena became Minerva, Ares became Mars, and so on.

Punic Wars

Having driven the Greeks out of their Italian stronghold, the Romans turned their attention to the large islands off the Italian coast. At that time, the Phoenicians were centered in the North African city of Carthage and had established large colonies in Sicily and Sardinia (see Chapter 3).

Carthage had originally been an important trading post for the Phoenicians. When the Persians conquered Phoenicia, many Phoenicians fled to Carthage, which grew from a trading post into the center of a new Phoenician empire. From the sixth century BC on, Carthage was the most important center of trade in the Mediterranean; this made it a threat to Roman domination in the region.

Conflict between Carthage and Rome over the control of Sicily eventually escalated into the Punic Wars (*Punic* is Latin for "Phoenician"). In 241 BC, the Romans won the First Punic War, which was largely a naval conflict. The Carthaginians agreed to cede control of Sicily.

The Second Punic War, which began in 218, pitted the great Carthaginian general Hannibal against the Roman army. The Carthaginians had taken over Greek settlements along the east coast of Spain, giving Hannibal a base from which to invade Italy from the northwest, over the Alps. This surprise attack is considered one of the greatest examples of military strategy in history and would be imitated by Napoleon centuries later. Despite its brilliance, it ended in a stalemate, with Hannibal in power in the south and the Romans still in control of their capital city. In 202, Scipio led the Roman troops into Carthage, where they defeated Hannibal.

Fifty years went by before the Third (and last) Punic War. Carthage had begun to show signs of economic and political recovery. This alarmed many Romans, who foresaw an endless struggle for supremacy against Carthage if it recovered its former position of power. The Roman statesman Cato insisted that Carthage must be destroyed; as soon as the Roman troops achieved victory over the Carthaginians, they demolished the city.

The most important effect of the Punic Wars was Rome's unquestioned dominance of the western Mediterranean. No other civilization could possibly match the might of the Roman military, nor the resources of the Roman state. The Roman Empire was not only vast in physical size, it was politically, culturally, and economically unified. The Romans had created the world's most powerful civilization.

Conquest in the East

After the death of Alexander, the Macedonian Empire had broken up into a number of small kingdoms (see Chapter 5). This made the Roman conquest of the region a fairly simple matter for two reasons. First, the successor Macedonian kingdoms were much too small to stand up against the might of the Roman army. Second, there was too much hostility and distrust among these kingdoms for them to unite their forces against Rome. In the end, the entire region, including Egypt, fell under Roman domination. The Ptolemies continued to rule Egypt more or less independently until its final defeat by Rome in 31 BC. Attempts at rebellion in the eastern outposts of the empire always ended in defeat. For instance, Anatolia and Syria rose up against Rome in 89 BC, but the great Roman general Pompey put down the rebellion in 62.

The map in Figure 6.1 shows the Roman Empire at its greatest geographical extent.

The Roman Roads

As the Romans expanded north and east, they built roads, primarily to make it easier and more efficient to move their troops throughout the empire. The roads also eased communication, travel, and trade. The Romans built most of this vast network of roads between the fourth and second centuries BC. It was possible to travel from southernmost Italy, Greece, or Spain to the northern coast of France, and from the Atlantic coast to the Hellespont, without ever leaving a Roman road. The Romans also built roads along the North African coast, on the islands, and in their Near Eastern possessions.

The Romans were the greatest engineers of their time. Their roads were paved with stones, sloping slightly from the center toward both sides to provide for drainage. Trenches carried off the rain and melted snow. Sections of Roman roads and walls exist to this day.

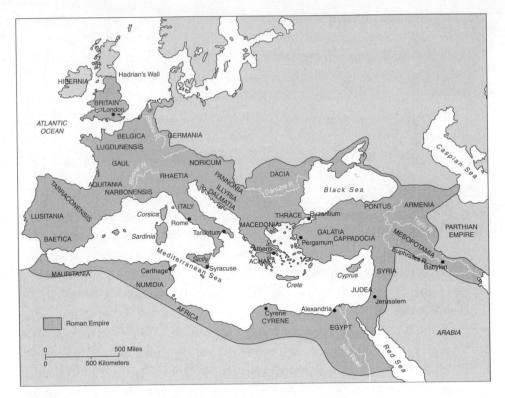

FIGURE 6.1   The Roman Empire at the End of Trajan's Reign, AD 117

Roads were not the only great achievement of the Roman engineers. They also invented concrete, a building material still in use today, and they erected stone bridges that are as strong today as they were when new, two thousand years ago. The aqueducts that brought water to Rome and the sewer systems that managed the city's waste were marvels in their day; it would be many centuries before northern European cities such as Paris and London would have sewer systems to match ancient Rome's.

Soldiers played a major role in the road-building project. Given the size of the empire, a vast army was essential for internal law and order, as well as external defense and attack; untold thousands of men from all parts of the empire joined the army. This took them away from farming the land; thus small independent farms gave way to estate farms that employed slave labor. All ancient civilizations practiced slavery; in the Roman Empire, the typical slave had been taken as a prisoner of war. Roman law gave slaves certain rights; for example, they could earn money, and their status was not permanent. A slave could purchase his or her freedom, and many did.

From Republic to Empire

The Roman Republic found itself threatened from within and without. Internally, political and social instability gave rise to attempts at reform, which pitted the plebeians against the patricians. Externally, military threats from northern Europe and North Africa distracted Roman leaders from the republic's domestic problems.

Political Troubles

Between 137 and 121 BC, tribunes of the Gracchi family called for social and political reforms, including the expansion of voting rights and a more equitable distribution of land. Naturally, this aroused strong opposition among the patricians, who did not wish to lose any of their benefits and privileges. The murders of the Gracchi brothers did not end the calls for reform.

Rome saw massive slave uprisings between about 135 and 71 BC, particularly in Sicily and southern Italy. The gladiator Spartacus led the last of these rebellions, which ended in a crushing defeat for the slaves. In a gruesome spectacle, the bodies of over six thousand of them were nailed to crosses along the Appian Way (the 560-mile paved Roman road that led from Rome to Brindisi).

Military Troubles

Northern European tribes were a constant threat to Rome. Other threats came from North Africa, particularly Numidia. By 101 BC, the gifted general Marius had eliminated these threats at least for the time being. The Romans showed their gratitude by choosing him as First Consul for an unprecedented five-year term.

Marius's first task as consul was to reform the army. Until he took power, soldiers had always been drafted from the peasantry; under his reorganization, military service became a well-paid job. Naturally, recruitment immediately rose and the army grew both larger and stronger, since men now had a powerful incentive to enlist. This change to military organization showed a significant shift of power in Roman society from the patricians to the military.

Marius also extended Roman citizenship to all Italians. Citizenship was highly prized for various reasons, but one of the most important was that citizens were tax-exempt. Only those living in the provinces had to pay taxes. Marius was persuaded to take this step toward democracy by loud protests from southern Italy; he believed that ceding to the demand for citizenship was necessary to prevent full-scale civil war.

The Roman general Sulla, who had achieved military distinction in the eastern provinces, succeeded Marius; the Senate elected him dictator in 82 BC. His close associate Pompey succeeded him in 79, creating the First Triumvirate (*tri* means "three," and *vir* means "man") with Crassus and Julius Caesar. Each man chose his own power base within the empire. Crassus ruled over Syria and the eastern Mediterranean but was soon killed in battle against the Parthians. This left Caesar, then in charge of the army in the province of Gaul, as Pompey's only serious rival for the dictatorship.

Pompey promptly ordered Caesar to return to Rome. A skilled general and a shrewd politician, Caesar knew that he could depend on the loyalty of his troops. With his army behind him, he crossed the Rubicon River that marked the border between Gaul and Rome. This was not only defiance but treason; Roman law expressly forbade a military commander from leading soldiers into Rome. Caesar's move was therefore the equivalent of a declaration of war. The power struggle that followed took the troops all the way to Egypt. Pompey was assassinated and his forces defeated. Caesar returned to Rome, where the Senate named him dictator for life.

Achieving absolute power did not seem to corrupt Caesar; he was a reformer who quickly won the support of the people. Among his most notable reforms was the establishment of the Julian calendar, with its 365-day year and an extra day in every fourth year. The month of Quintilus was renamed Julius in Caesar's honor; similarly, Sextilis was renamed Augustus in honor of the next ruler. Most Western nations used the Julian calendar until AD 1582, when it was tweaked slightly to bring it more closely into line with the solar year.

Caesar's reign was brief. A conspiracy of senators and their supporters, dismayed by the the dictator's exercise of absolute power and wanting a return to the Roman Republic, murdered him in the Senate in March of 44 BC. Since the conspirators had not made a coherent plan to bring about the desired result, civil war broke out among the factions. Caesar's nephew and heir Octavian led one group, Marc Antony the other. The war spread to Egypt, where Antony allied with and married the pharaoh Cleopatra. Octavian's forces defeated Antony and Cleopatra's in 31 BC. Egypt was added to the empire, and Octavian became the first Roman emperor. He ruled under the title Augustus.

The Roman Empire

The Roman Empire was an absolute monarchy—a form of government that has, throughout history, been very dependent on the personality of the monarch. An absolute monarch holds all the power but paradoxically is faced by threats from all sides. The monarch must pacify the nobility (because they constitute the likeliest possible threat to his or her supremacy); ensure the loyalty of the army; run an efficient, centrally controlled administration; and pursue a coherent foreign policy. The shrewdest absolute monarchs of history also realized that it was very helpful to win the genuine loyalty and affection of the common people.

One of the most important decisions Augustus made was to maintain the symbols of the Roman Republic; no doubt the brutal murder of Caesar made him feel it would be prudent to make this gesture toward those who had opposed him during the civil war. The Senate continued to meet and debate and was always spoken of with respect. Maintaining the Senate for its symbolic value was one part of Augustus's policy of pacifying the patricians. He also created new political offices for them, thus giving them moderately prominent roles to play in the government and preventing widespread discontent.

Augustus was a highly skilled administrator. He established a civil-service network whose efficiency in collecting taxes and maintaining law and order has never been equaled. He reorganized the military, calling for a professional standing army with troops garrisoned throughout the empire, to protect it from external threats and internal rebellions.

A glance at the map in Figure 6.1 shows that Augustus was much more interested in maintaining his empire than expanding it. Under Augustus, the Roman Empire featured natural borders such as the Rhine and Danube rivers, which provided strong natural defenses. The empire would remain the same size and shape for four hundred years, apart from the annexation of Britain as far as Hadrian's Wall under Claudius.

Economically, the empire flourished under Augustus. For the first time, all the ancient civilizations of the world—the West, the Near East, China, and India—were involved in international trade (see Chapter 7). This era of peace and prosperity would last until about AD 180—a stretch of nearly two hundred years known to history as the *Pax Romana* (the Roman Peace). It saw major achievements in many of the arts and sciences—Pliny and Ptolemy in astronomy; Livy, Caesar, Suetonius, and Tacitus in history; Cicero in rhetoric and essays; Virgil and Catullus in poetry; and Horace and Juvenal in satire.

Under Augustus, the Roman Empire continued its policy of tolerance— essential in any civilization that was so widespread that it contained a great variety of cultures. Rome required that all people within the empire obey the

Roman law code, pay their taxes, and worship the Roman gods; other than that, everyone might do as he or she pleased, including practicing other religions.

Augustus's early successors were other members of the Caesar family. (Originally a family name with no secondary meaning, *caesar* eventually became the imperial title; it would later become the German and Russian imperial titles *kaiser* and *czar*.) In AD 98, when there was no direct heir to the throne, the senators elected an emperor of their choice; from then until 180, each *caesar* chose his own successor. Peace and prosperity reigned throughout this era.

The year AD 180 marked a return to hereditary succession; unfortunately, the lack of competent heirs ended the era of wise leadership. A series of military takeovers followed, during which no emperor reigned for more than two years. This was known as the period of Soldier Emperors. During this era, a recent series of apparently insignificant events in Israel began playing a decisive role in the eventual downfall of the Roman Empire.

Jews in Ancient Rome

The Jews were the one group within the Roman Empire that absolutely refused to comply with its legal and religious requirements, minimal though these were. Jews protested that their religion forbade them from worshiping other gods or obeying any civil laws that did not accord with their own. Astonishingly, the response of the Roman government was tolerant and flexible; rather than forcing compliance, the Romans created special legal exemptions to meet Jewish demands. The only thing the Romans insisted on was that the Jews remain politically loyal to the state of Rome.

This did not happen. The Jews were never content to pay taxes to what they regarded as a foreign government; in AD 66, they rose up in armed rebellion. The Roman army sacked Jerusalem and destroyed the Temple in 70; in 135, they finally drove the Jews out of Judea and razed Jerusalem to the ground. Even after this, as they settled in small groups throughout the empire, the Jews were allowed to retain their special legal status. They continued to maintain their unique form of worship and observe their own religious laws. Those who had followed the Jewish rabbi Jesus, known as the Christ or the Messiah (both words mean "anointed one" or "chosen one"), began a serious missionary effort to convert Romans throughout the empire to their own beliefs. This gave rise to Christianity, which began as a form of Judaism and which would soon spread through the entire world.

Christianity

Christianity is named for Jesus Christ, the rabbi whose life story is told in the four Gospels—books of the Greek Bible, known to Christians as the New Testament. Scholars believe the Gospels were written thirty-five to seventy years after Jesus's death; although there is no historical evidence to prove or disprove it, historians have generally accepted that the story the Gospels tell is grounded in fact. Through the Gospels' secondhand reporting of his words, Jesus became the single most influential thinker in the history of the Western world.

Born probably around 5 or 4 BC in the town of Bethlehem, Jesus was a commoner descended from King David of Israel. As an adult, he became a rabbi, or teacher, who could fascinate large crowds. His usual teaching device was the parable—he would illustrate a complex theological concept by comparing it to a homely, everyday image that any peasant could understand. This ability of an imaginative thinker to communicate with the common people won him a following in his own day; it may well be the reason his teachings continue to influence untold millions.

Jesus's acclaim among the people alarmed various powerful vested interests in Israel; in the end, he was accused of blasphemy and executed by crucifixion about AD 30. His closest friends and followers believed that he appeared alive again a few days later, which proved to them that he truly was the only begotten son of God, whose appearance on earth had been foretold in the Hebrew Bible. These apostles and those who heard them speak eventually spread the religion of Christianity throughout the world.

Whether Jesus himself intended to found a new religion, or even a new sect of Judaism, is a matter of debate. Certainly, Jesus lived and died an observant Jew who obeyed Jewish laws. His revolutionary contribution to religious faith is that he preached a gospel that was not only relevant to the Hebrew people and their unique culture and traditions but that would also bring eternal salvation to anyone who followed him.

The most influential and important follower of Jesus is Saul, a Jew who underwent a visionary experience, converted to Christianity, and took the new name Paul. Paul became an important missionary, traveling through the eastern half of the Roman Empire and preaching the Gospel. It is due to Paul that Christianity took hold in the empire; it was Paul who spread the belief that Jesus was literally divine. Paul can safely be described as the true founder of Christianity; his writings make up much of the New Testament.

The roots of Christianity lie in Judaism; both believe in the same God. In order to make Christianity appeal to Greeks, however, Paul blended Hebrew beliefs with elements of Hellenistic culture and religion. The Christian concept of the trinity, in which God the Father, Christ the Son, and the Holy Spirit are three aspects of the same divine being, shows the influence of Greek abstract philosophy, as does the notion that Jesus was both fully human and fully divine. One other major difference between the two is that Judaism is not a missionary religion; the Hebrew people have never made any attempt to convert or recruit followers. Christianity owes its success to its missionary tradition.

Like Judaism, Christianity is based on a moral code that claims it is superior to any state government or social organization, a moral code that applies equally to an aristocrat and a peasant or to a master and a slave. Jesus added a new element to this moral code when he gave his disciples a new commandment to add to the original ten—the commandment to love one another. The promise of eternal salvation—that, just as Jesus rose from the dead, all the faithful would enjoy eternal life—and the command to love one another appealed to many people in the warlike world of the late Roman Empire.

Like Judaism, Christianity was an exclusive religion that did not permit the observance of any other belief system. Christians therefore followed the Jewish lead in refusing even to pay lip service to worship of the Roman gods. In consequence, the spread of Christianity helped to bring down the Roman Empire. As small Christian communities throughout the empire began to grow into larger ones, the Roman state showed no particular alarm; the official position seems to have been tolerance, as long as Christians obeyed the civil law code.

Emperor Constantine

The period of the Soldier Emperors ended with the reign of Diocletian, a highly capable administrator who believed that the empire had become too large and unwieldy to manage from Rome. He therefore divided the empire into two halves, each to be ruled by an emperor and an assistant emperor. This system did not survive Diocletian's lifetime; instead of being content as coemperors, each likely successor to power wanted to rule the entire empire.

In AD 324, Constantine won the power struggle and reunited the Roman Empire under his sole authority. The fact that Constantine was a Christian changed the course of history, both for the empire and the future of the new religion.

No individual on earth had as much power as the Roman emperor; now that such a prominent individual gave Christianity his official blessing, it changed from being a minor sect of Judaism into a mainstream religious faith. In order to unify the faith by eliminating the numerous rival forms in which it flourished, Constantine decreed that the only proper form of this religion was the one he himself observed. (The idea that a subject must worship as the monarch did would hold sway over Europe for the next thousand years.) Many Romans converted to Christianity, either from sincere belief or political expediency.

In AD 325, Constantine opened the Council of Nicaea, at which the participants decided on the principles and creeds of Christianity as it would thereafter be practiced. The idea was to eliminate confusion and disagreement over doctrine and to standardize the forms of worship. The Council of Nicaea set forth the rules that Roman Catholics and Greek Orthodox Catholics would follow from that time on. Jerome, one of the most important of the early Church Fathers, translated the Bible into Latin; this edition, known as the Vulgate, would later become the first printed book in the Western world. From 325 until after World War II, Latin would be the language of the Church; it would, in fact, be the common written language of all learned Europeans until the 1500s, when it began to be replaced by the languages Europeans actually spoke in their everyday lives.

In AD 330, Constantine founded a new capital city—Constantinople (now called Istanbul), built on the Bosporus Strait that connects the Black and Marmara seas. Despite the move of the seat of government to the East, Rome remained the most important city in the western half of the empire.

The Fall of the Roman Empire

There were many reasons for the fall of the Roman Empire. First, it was too large to govern effectively from one city. Second, a cultural division had grown up between east and west. Third, the empire was mired in economic troubles. Fourth, it faced serious military threats from the north.

Politically, the reunion of the two halves of the Roman Empire under one ruler proved to be temporary. Instead of working effectively as partners, the eastern and western halves became rivals. When the western empire was threatened by invasion from the north, the eastern empire reacted with indifference.

Culturally, of course, the two halves had different roots. The eastern empire was culturally and linguistically Greek, the western half Latin. These cultures had a great deal in common, but not enough to hold them together as one unified nation-state in the face of all the other factors that destroyed Rome.

Economically, the Roman Empire was no longer prosperous. The soil was overworked and produced smaller harvests; a smaller food supply and fewer goods for export had diminished the state's income. Like all other governments in history desperate to raise money quickly, the empire fell back on raising taxes. In a serious miscalculation, the government established a tax exemption for the wealthy; men could offer their services to the military in lieu of paying taxes. The burden of payment therefore fell on the plebeians, who could least afford it. Naturally, this gave rise to resentment between the social ranks.

Militarily, the state was no longer as mighty as it had been. The infantry legions had always been the backbone of the Roman army; in the early centuries AD, however, the infantry began to give way to cavalry regiments. These were both less efficient and more expensive. Because they were less mobile, they contributed to Rome's military weakness; because they cost more to maintain, they worsened the state's economic crisis. The military solution was to hire mercenaries—paid foreign troops who had no personal loyalty to either their commanders or to the Roman Empire. This combination of Roman military weakness with growing aggression from foreign peoples helped bring down the empire.

The Barbarian Invasions

Between about AD 100 and 500, massive migration took place in northern Europe. A large number of peoples were on the move, usually traveling west and south in their quest for plunder (see Chapter 8). These northern Europeans were generally of a nomadic warrior culture that can fairly be described as far more primitive than the level of civilization the Romans had achieved; hence, the Romans used the catch-all term *barbarians* to refer to them.

The Huns, who originated in the steppes of Central Asia (later Russia), were among the most warlike of all the tribes. As they swept eastward into Europe, they drove other peoples in their path aside. The Goths had established a stronghold around present-day Poland and Hungary; invaded by the Huns, the Goths began to move south. In 378, Goth warriors massacred the Roman army at Adrianople. This marked the final defeat of the Roman army, and resulted in official Roman recognition of a separate Goth state in 382. In 395, the Roman Empire officially broke apart into two independent states, with the eastern half becoming known as the Byzantine Empire. Constantinople was its capital, and it would continue to exist until the 1400s; the patriarch of Constantinople became the metropolitan, the head of the Orthodox Catholic Church.

The Roman Empire in the west was finished, especially after a further invasion that culminated in the sack of Rome in 410. At the same time, other tribes were invading the empire's northern provinces; the Sueves, Burgundians, and Anglo-Saxons were seizing territory and establishing themselves in Spain, France, and Britain (see Chapter 8). The Roman Empire existed only in name from AD 410 to 476, when Romulus Augustus, the last emperor, was assassinated.

QUIZ

1. The Etruscan civilization fell primarily because _____.
   A. it was economically poor
   B. it was ethnically and religiously diverse
   C. it had no standing army or navy
   D. it was not politically unified

2. Under the Roman Republic, the plebeians had all the following powers except _____.
   A. they were represented by the tribunes
   B. they could become senators
   C. they could hold public protests
   D. they could rise to the position of consul

3. The Romans defeated _____ in the Punic Wars.
   A. the Greeks
   B. the Etruscans
   C. the Phoenicians
   D. the Goths

4. What was the primary purpose of the vast network of Roman roads?
   A. efficient movement of troops
   B. speed of communication
   C. ease of travel for merchants and civilians
   D. employment for convicts and slaves

5. **The Gracchi brothers were murdered because they advocated _____.**
   A. social and political reform
   B. a return to the republic
   C. the assassination of Julius Caesar
   D. the division of the empire into two halves

6. **The *Pax Romana* began during the reign of _____.**
   A. Marius
   B. Julius Caesar
   C. Augustus
   D. Constantine

7. **The Roman state allowed the Jews many special exemptions from the rules but insisted absolutely that they must _____.**
   A. pay outward worship to the Roman gods as a matter of form
   B. pay extra-high taxes in exchange for their privileges
   C. serve in the military for a specified term (if male)
   D. remain politically loyal to the empire

8. **Christianity and Judaism are similar in all these ways except _____.**
   A. they both have moral codes that apply equally to all believers
   B. they are both missionary religions
   C. they both believe in the worship of the same god
   D. they are both exclusive faiths that do not allow their followers to worship other gods

9. **Constantine is historically significant because he _____.**
   A. gave official sanction to Christianity
   B. divided the empire into two halves
   C. restored the Roman Republic
   D. brutally put down a major slave rebellion

10. **At its height, the Roman Empire included all these present-day European nations except _____.**
    A. Spain
    B. Portugal
    C. Turkey
    D. Russia

chapter 7

Early Asian Empires, 400 BC–AD 600

During the Qin and Han dynasties, the Chinese emperors established many major precedents that would become constants in Chinese culture. These included a law code, a merit-based civil service, and strong central control of the state. This was interrupted briefly during the Three Kingdoms period, but from AD 589 until the present, China has existed as a unified state.

International trade became a major factor during this era. China, India, Central Asia, and Rome all bought and sold goods from one another. Some merchants traveled along the Silk Road, others sailed across the Indian Ocean or the Arabian Sea. Trade even went as far as the east coast of Africa.

The Indian civilization continued to take shape under the first two Indian empires. Both comprised all of northern India; southern India was still more or less independent, both politically and culturally different from the north. The era began with religious plurality in India but ended with Hinduism having been firmly established as the chief religion in the region. Buddhism had by no means disappeared, however; it was taking firm hold in China and elsewhere in Asia.

The warrior tribes of Central Asia played a significant role in all the ancient civilizations, both eastern and western. Their method can be summed up in one word—*invasion*. Once these fierce, iron-clad warriors invaded any culture, they were very difficult to push back. Eventually, various Central Asian tribes would contribute their part to the stories of China and India and would settle permanently in Europe.

CHAPTER OBJECTIVES

- Describe the Qin dynasty and explain its importance in Chinese history.
- Describe the rise and fall of the Han dynasty and its major successes.
- Compare and contrast the Mauryan and Gupta empires in India.
- Identify the major international trade routes and relationships of the era.
- Describe the culture of the Central Asian steppes.

Chapter 7 Time Line

BC

322–232	Mauryan Empire
298	Death of Chandragupta Maurya
250	Emergence of Buddhism
221	Zheng establishes Qin dynasty; rules as Qin Shi Huang Di, or "First Emperor"
212	Great Wall of China is completed
206	Liu Bang establishes Han dynasty

AD

184–205	Revolt of the Yellow Turbans in China
208–265	Three Kingdoms period
320–550	Gupta Empire in India
589	Sui Yang Jian establishes Sui dynasty

China

✦ The Qin Dynasty

The Zhou dynasty (see Chapter 4) began to collapse in the late 700s BC; the main cause was rivalry from the nearby tribes. By 403 BC, the area of Chinese civilization had expanded, spreading eastward to the coastline, south to the South China Sea, and north to the Gobi Desert. This sprawling civilization comprised several kingdoms. Each had its own army—by the sixth century BC, iron swords and armor had replaced their bronze equivalents—and each had built thick stone and earthen walls for its defense. The seven kingdoms —Seven Warring States—that fought for complete control of China were the Han, Wei, Zhao, Qin, Chu, Yan, and Qi. The Qin (sometimes spelled Ch'in), which had the most powerful and best-organized army, emerged victorious in the struggle about 221 BC. The Qin dynasty barely outlasted its first emperor, but it gave its name to the nation and established certain precedents that would remain constant in Chinese culture and society for centuries to follow.

Zheng, the Qin king, had ruled his kingdom according to Legalist ideas, which advocated a strong, centrally controlled state (see Chapter 4). Zheng would take the same approach to ruling the Chinese Empire. He took the name Qin Shi Huang Di, or "First Emperor," and chose Xianyang on the Wei River as his capital city.

Under Zheng, China cast off its traditional feudal model of government and underwent sweeping changes to the economy, the military, and the state. The purpose of the changes was to create a prosperous, centrally controlled state, in keeping with Zheng's preference for the Legalist way of thinking. Zheng's tomb, with seventy-five hundred life-sized terra-cotta warriors guarding his remains, provides evidence of his grandiose ideas about the exalted position of the emperor.

Economic Changes

Zheng established new taxes to fill the royal treasury; he also oversaw the standardization of weights, measures, and currency. The building of hundreds of miles of roads linked the capital to the provinces. Combined, these measures made trade more efficient and therefore more profitable. Zheng also placed certain major economic activities under state control, including the manufacture of iron and the harvesting and distribution of salt.

Military Changes

Zheng used the military for both expansion and defense. Troops conquered new territory and were stationed in the farthest outposts of the empire to maintain order in case of rebellion. Under Zheng, soldiers were garrisoned as far from the capital as Korea and Vietnam.

Defense was especially necessary in the north; the Xiongnu and other nomadic warrior tribes of Central Asia were a constant threat. To protect his empire from northern invasion, Zheng ordered the filling in of the empty spaces between the walls erected by the individual kingdoms. This mammoth construction project was completed between about 221 and 212 BC. The completed Great Wall of China stretched along the empire's northern border for fourteen hundred miles. It still stands today; the Chinese have maintained and repaired it all along.

Changes to the Government

The Qin dynasty can accurately be described as a totalitarian state, albeit an efficient one—thus exemplifying the positive and negative implications of the Legalist position. On the positive side, Zheng created a modern bureaucracy that could administer a large empire and established a uniform system of writing that enabled local officials to communicate easily with those in the capital. Perhaps more importantly, China was now a unified empire, without the inter-kingdom squabbling that had characterized the Warring States period. Apart from a relatively short era following the Han dynasty (see "The Han Dynasty" in this chapter), China has continued as a unified state down to the present day.

On the negative side, Zheng tolerated no opposition to his government. He literally wiped out all those who spoke out against the government; they were either deported, murdered, or imprisoned. Zheng also ordered the forced relocation of massive numbers of peasants to new territories captured by the army. The impressive system of Chinese roads and the Great Wall of China were built by compulsory unpaid labor.

The repressive policies of the Qin dynasty made it so unpopular that it collapsed soon after the death of Zheng. His successor was weak and ineffectual, and China soon found itself in the midst of a civil war that pitted aristocrats and Legalists against Confucianists and commoners. Liu Bang, a commoner who had risen through the ranks of the army, became the leader of the latter group; he led his supporters to victory in 202 BC and became the first emperor of the Han dynasty under the name Han Gao-zu.

The Han Dynasty

The Han dynasty officially began in 206 BC and lasted until AD 220. Its long tenure was partly due to the great abilities of its first ruler. Gao-zu's first acts in office were to undo some of the iron-fisted Qin dynasty policies; for example, he eliminated tight government controls over the economy. Gao-zu also began choosing his closest advisors on the basis of their qualifications rather than their family connections or their influence. He may well have felt that since he himself had risen from humble beginnings, others should be given a similar chance. A government and civil service based on merit set a precedent that the Chinese would maintain with remarkable tenacity for the next two thousand years.

Emperor Wu Di, who ruled from 141 to 87 BC, was one of the great Chinese civil and military leaders. He centralized the government and supported what can be described as a free-market economy. Militarily, he led many victorious campaigns against the Xiongnu, with the end result that they lost much of their power and thus their ability to threaten China's supremacy.

The Han dynasty saw a series of capable emperors that lasted into the mid-second century AD. Their success can be measured in several ways. First was the establishment of a law code: under the Han rulers, China achieved a legal code modeled on the Wei kingdom law code, first written in the early fifth century BC. Trade also grew throughout the Han era, both within the empire and outside; the establishment of the Silk Road (see "The Silk Road" in this chapter) opened up many new markets for Chinese goods. The standardization of the currency greatly eased trade within the empire. The Zhou period had seen the introduction of iron plows; by the Han period, these improved tools were clearly making the farms more productive. A rise in food production probably led to a rise in population; according to census records, there were 57 million people in the Chinese Empire by AD 2. The first century AD also saw the invention of paper, which would be of enormous importance to world culture throughout the rest of history.

The Han dynasty began to wane in the middle of the AD 100s, due to a number of linked causes. The first was corruption at court. The wise Han emperors of the early dynasty were followed by several incompetent men interested only in extravagance and idle pleasures. Poor government led to the second problem—a major peasant revolt. A religious cult called the Yellow Turbans acquired a substantial following among the peasantry; the fighting went on for twenty-one years, ending only in 205. The government managed to defeat the rebels, only to see the last emperor deposed. The third cause was the collapse of the dikes along the Huang He River, which led to severe floods and a change in the river's course. Widespread loss of property, homelessness, and a major economic depression were the consequences. The Chinese moved south in massive numbers in search of better conditions, and the Xiongnu took advantage of the chaos to assert their independence.

The Three Kingdoms Period

From AD 208 to 265, China was divided into the three kingdoms of Shu, Wei, and Wu; hence, this era is called the Three Kingdoms period. The Xiongnu put an end to a brief period of reunion by sweeping into China from the north, sacking the capital at Louyang in 311, and going on to sack Changan in 316. In 383, however, the Chinese managed to defeat the Xiongnu; they would never again expand into the south. The nomadic warrior culture of the Xiongnu had an important influence on northern China. This region absorbed a measure of Central Asian customs and would remain distinct from the traditional Chinese culture in the south. The influence of Buddhism grew in southern China during this era, which also saw a return to the old feudal system of governing.

The era of disunion and fragmentation ended as abruptly as it began. The Chinese warrior Sui Yang Jian usurped the throne from an infant king in AD 581, ushering in a series of successful military campaigns that ended in the reunion of the Chinese Empire in 589. The Sui dynasty, however, would last only until 618, when the Tang dynasty took power (see Chapter 10).

East-West Trade

The Silk Road

During the second century BC, China began its long history of overland trade with the West via the Silk Road. The Silk Road is not literally one road, but rather the name given to an east-west trade route. The exact path that the merchants followed varied depending on political and military conditions at any given time.

The idea for the Silk Road originated when the Han emperor Wu Di sent an envoy north to visit the Yuezhi, a tribe of warrior nomads who had been driven westward by the Xiongnu. This contact showed the Chinese that there were profitable markets outside China for their luxuries. This was the impetus for establishing the Silk Road, which originated on the Huang He River in the Han capital, Luoyang. It continued westward all the way to Constantinople and

Alexandria, stopping along the way at Persepolis, Palmyra, and Antioch. By the first century BC, the Silk Road was well established.

At this early date, the Chinese were the only people who had learned to manufacture silk; this fabric was, therefore, both rare and highly prized in India and the West. The Chinese sent silk and spices along the Silk Road to India and then to the West. India was already famous as a manufacturer of cotton textiles, as it remains to this day. The Romans sent luxury goods east to Asia along the Silk Road; a load of Roman valuables such as jewelry took up little space in a trader's pack, so the profits were enormous. Central Asians plied their trade in the towns along the route; by 100 BC, for example, Iran was selling horses to China. All the ancient civilizations along the Silk Road used it for trade. Like any trade route, the Silk Road also facilitated the exchange of arts and ideas; Buddhism spread outside of India along the Silk Road.

Other Trade Routes

Overland trade routes were always slow and dangerous: animals might get injured or sick, bad weather could destroy a valuable cargo, and gangs of thieves were never far away from a good source of loot. For trade between Europe and Asia, the Silk Road was the most direct route, but sea trade was less hazardous and more efficient where possible. Of course, ships were always vulnerable to bad weather, shipwreck, and pirates, but the risks on land were greater.

Sea trade routes in ancient Asia crossed the Indian Ocean and Arabian Sea and followed the coasts of China, India, and east Africa. Indian coastal trade dated back as far as the third millennium BC. The sea traders followed the regular cycle of monsoon winds, which blew eastward in the summer and west in the autumn. In the West, Alexandria was the port that saw the greatest amount of shipping to the east and south.

Indian Empires

The Mauryan Empire

By about 500 BC, there were small kingdoms scattered throughout the Ganges River valley. Magadah was the strongest, largely due to its favorable location. It controlled trade along the rivers and also had the advantage of a wealth of natural resources.

In 321 BC, Chandragupta Maurya became king of Magadah. Within about fifteen years, he ruled most of northern India, including present-day Afghanistan.

Historical sources are ambiguous; Chandragupta may have ruled his empire as a monarch or as something more like a president in charge of a bureaucracy. His son and successor expanded the Mauryan Empire far into the south. The third Mauryan emperor, Ashoka, presided over a politically united India, except for the extreme southern tip of the subcontinent.

Ashoka's is the first Indian reign for which there are detailed and reliable written records. The emperor and his royal council ruled supreme over a society based on the caste system. Ashoka commanded the loyalty of a royal army, a bureaucracy, and even a secret police. The reign of Ashoka was an era of peace and prosperity; he made efforts to unify society by stressing ideals of tolerance and respect among his diverse subjects. Ashoka also sent a Buddhist missionary to Tibet, with far-reaching consequences. The missionary converted the king, who then established Buddhism as the state religion. Tibet remains Buddhist to this day.

The unified Mauryan Empire disintegrated into smaller kingdoms after Ashoka's death in 231 BC. Various peoples invaded India from the northwest, although most did not go beyond that immediate area. The general pattern was to assimilate into the local population, which in turn absorbed various cultural elements from the newcomers.

One group, the Sakas, arrived about 130 BC and penetrated much farther into India's interior, eventually gaining control over a vast territory. The Parthians and the Kushans, other Central Asian tribes, followed the Sakas. These groups loosely controlled northwestern India until the third century AD. In the end, the Gupta Empire took over northern India (see "The Gupta Empire" in this chapter).

The Kushan kings claimed to rule by divine right, stating that the king was a manifestation of the god Siva. This would become a fundamental tenet of Hinduism. Although they were inclined toward the Hindu religion, the Kushans were tolerant monarchs. During their era of dominance, their subjects represented all known religions except possibly Judaism.

The Gupta Empire

Chandragupta I (not the same Chandragupta as the Mauryan king Chandragupta) established the Gupta Empire in AD 320. A series of successful military campaigns gave his son and heir Samudragupta control over all of northern India; he became emperor in 335 and would rule for twenty years. The Gupta period was characterized by a religious revival, a shift toward a mercantile economy, and a major flowering in the arts.

At first, the Gupta rulers tolerated the practice of various religions, just as had the Kushan kings; however, a major revival of Hinduism eventually shouldered the other faiths aside. During the same period, Buddhism put down strong roots in China, Japan, Tibet, and Sri Lanka. The Gupta economy became more mercantile as international trade increased. Like all economies before modern times, however, it was still heavily dependent on agriculture.

Artistically, the Gupta Empire is considered the classical era in Indian history; artists, writers, and builders created the classical Indian styles of poetry, drama, painting, and architecture. The Indian poet and playwright Kalidasa, who was active around AD 400, holds the same place in Indian regard as Shakespeare does in the English-speaking world. The great Indian literary classics the *Mahabharata* (an epic poem about war) and the *Ramayana* (a love story of good versus evil) had been told and retold orally since at least 600 BC, but it was during the Gupta Empire that they were written in the versions we know today. The Indians regard the *Mahabharata* and the *Ramayana* in much the same way Westerners regard the Homeric epics and the Bible; they are the most influential literary works of an entire culture.

The Gupta Empire was not politically unified; the government allowed the local rajas to continue ruling their kingdoms within the empire. This system had the advantage of providing a continuum of government and society for the people, allowing everyday business to continue uninterrupted by any major reorganization of the government. The greatest disadvantage to this political decision was that the empire was not a centrally controlled state; instead, it was an empire of small monarchies whose rulers were potential rivals for imperial power.

In the end, the Gupta Empire fell apart from three linked causes. The first was rival claims to the throne from the small kingdoms and among the ruling family. The second was the bickering factions that grew up around the various claimants. The third was a series of popular uprisings that probably began because the government was weak and ineffectual. A civil war resulted from all the chaos, and in AD 510, the Huns took advantage of the situation to sweep into India from Central Asia. They sacked many cities and razed a large number of Buddhist monasteries, thus contributing to the ultimate failure of Buddhism in India. The Huns were so destructive and divisive that they crushed any Indian pretense at empire. Culturally, India remained unified, at least in the north, but politically it was once again a collection of small independent kingdoms.

/ Southern India

Slowly, the culture of northern India began to spread into the south, which for many years had remained largely unaffected by outside events. The scholars of southern India adopted Sanskrit as their universal language (Pali was also spoken throughout the region), and both Buddhism and Hinduism spread through the south. Ambitious leaders in the region began to establish independent kingdoms. Southern India was geographically too far from the Silk Road to use it for trade, but it did profit handsomely from overseas trade with the Roman Empire and also with China and the Southeast Asian islands.

Peoples of Central Asia

From the sixth millennium BC, people had inhabited the steppes of Central Asia—this area includes present-day Mongolia, Russia, and Siberia. The steppes were bleak grasslands in a region whose borders were defined by the Ural Mountains and the Gobi Desert. The climate was harsh, and only the hardiest could survive and thrive in it.

By 4500 BC, the people of the steppes were herding livestock and farming. By 2000 BC, they had learned to ride horses, which quickly acquired central importance in their culture. The combination of mastering horses and learning to work with iron—they were the first people to make wheels with spokes—made them into formidable warriors. The tribes of the steppes were much more fierce and aggressive than the peoples of the ancient civilizations of the Mediterranean, China, and India. Rather than settling in one place and building cities, they roamed in bands, invading and attacking one another and also the settled civilizations on which their lands bordered. There were settlements in the region, especially around the area of the Black Sea, but nothing to resemble the planned cities of China, Greece, or Rome.

The Xiongnu succeeded in invading China and even dominating it at one time. The Huns swept into India in AD 460, but were repulsed; when they tried again after the Gupta civil war, however, they succeeded. The Huns would also invade Eastern Europe and establish themselves there permanently.

Between about 800 BC and AD 100, all these nomadic warrior tribes were on the move westward into Europe, where they would battle the Romans and the European tribes. The Xiongnu migrated both east and west in their attempt to conquer China. Tribes whose territory was already on the southern steppes moved south rather than west; the Parthians swept into the Persian Empire and the Kushans took control of India.

QUIZ

1. All these groups except _____ were nomad warrior tribes from the steppes of Central Asia.
   A. the Huns
   B. the Mauryans
   C. the Parthians
   D. the Xiongnu

2. _____ is an important historical figure because he is considered the greatest of the ancient Indian poets and playwrights.
   A. Samudragupta
   B. Zheng
   C. Ashoka
   D. Kalidasa

3. All of these are measures of the success of the early Han emperors except _____.
   A. the rise in food production
   B. the codification of the laws
   C. the assertion of Xiongnu independence
   D. the establishment of international trade

4. The Han dynasty was immediately followed by _____.
   A. the Three Kingdoms period
   B. the period of the Seven Warring States
   C. the Gupta Empire
   D. the Qin dynasty

5. _____ supported the Legalists in the civil war that arose after Zheng's death.
   A. The aristocracy
   B. The Confucianists
   C. The commoners
   D. The peasants

6. _____ was a major contributing factor that made northern Chinese culture different from southern Chinese culture.
   A. The rise of the Han dynasty
   B. The invasion of the Xiongnu
   C. The fragmentation of the empire during the Three Kingdoms period
   D. The flooding of the Huang He River

7. **Which best describes the Silk Road?**
   A. a fortified barrier between China and the Gobi Desert
   B. a paved road that led from Luoyang to Constantinople
   C. an overland international trade route from eastern China to India and the Mediterranean
   D. a major international market in which silks were bought and sold

8. **Which factor determined the cycle of sea trade between India and Rome?**
   A. military conflicts
   B. monsoon winds
   C. economic fluctuations
   D. royal whims

9. _____ was a major factor in the nomadic warrior culture that developed in Central Asia.
   A. The tendency toward westward migration
   B. The writing of classic works of literature
   C. The planning of sophisticated cities
   D. The ability to ride a horse

10. **The Kushans' major contribution to Hinduism was _____.**
    A. their role in coverting the Tibetan king to Buddhism
    B. their refusal to tolerate other forms of worship
    C. their belief that the king was a manifestation of Siva
    D. their commission of a written version of the *Mahabharata*

PART ONE EXAM

1. During the Shang dynasty, the emperor expected all the following from the clan rulers of the city-states except _____.
   A. political loyalty
   B. religious sacrifices
   C. regular financial tributes
   D. military support

2. Akhenaton was unique among Egyptian pharaohs because _____.
   A. he reunited Upper and Lower Egypt under the rule of one pharaoh
   B. he decreed that Egyptians should worship only one god
   C. he was given a lavish burial
   D. he was religiously conservative

3. The Roman Empire under Augustus and his early successors is best described as _____.
   A. an absolute monarchy run by a highly efficient, centrally controlled bureaucracy
   B. a group of city-states united by a common language, a common religious faith, and a shared cultural heritage
   C. a collection of independent principalities and free cities owing allegiance to one titular monarch
   D. a constitutional monarchy with an emperor as the head of state and a representative assembly that carried out the will of the people

4. China during the Qin dynasty is best described as _____.
   A. a popular democracy
   B. a totalitarian state
   C. a constitutional monarchy
   D. a military dictatorship

5. The geographical expansion of the _____ threatened the supremacy of the Phoenicians.
   A. Egyptian state
   B. Huns
   C. Chinese Empire
   D. Greek civilization

6. **Which best describes the *Vedas*?**
   A. epic poetry about the lives of the gods and goddesses
   B. collections of hymns and religious rituals
   C. philosophical advice to princes and individuals
   D. the early history and legends of a civilization

7. **During the twelfth century BC, Egypt and _____ agreed to a policy of mutual nonaggression.**
   A. the Hittites
   B. the Hyskos
   C. the Libyans
   D. the Persians

8. **The Greeks Herodotus and Thucydides and the Romans Suetonius and Tacitus are significant because of their contributions in the field of _____.**
   A. philosophy
   B. astronomy
   C. history
   D. drama

9. **Alexander the Great is famous in history for his _____.**
   A. military conquests
   B. philosophical essays
   C. epic poems
   D. civil law code

10. **The first human civilizations arose in _____.**
    A. the Americas
    B. the Near East
    C. southern Africa
    D. the Far East

11. **All these causes contributed to the fall of the Gupta Empire in India except _____.**
    A. a series of popular uprisings against the government
    B. rival claims to the throne among the rajas
    C. bickering among the various political factions
    D. the lack of connection between northern and southern India

12. The Legalists of ancient China supported the establishment of a code of laws because _____.
    A. they were concerned about repeated crime waves in the provinces
    B. they believed it was the best way to avoid peasant uprisings
    C. they believed it would lead to a wealthy state with a strong government
    D. they believed it was divinely ordained that society should be fair and just to all

13. _____ was (or were) the most valued of the goods exported by China during the ancient era.
    A. Silk
    B. Ceramics
    C. Jade
    D. Iron weapons

14. The most important contribution the ancient Hebrews made to human civilization is _____.
    A. the tradition of popular revolution
    B. the invention of the copper-tin alloy we call bronze
    C. the belief in one god who created man and woman in his own image
    D. an alphabet in which each character stood for a sound rather than a whole word

15. The most likely reason Buddhism did not become the major religion of India is _____.
    A. it showed the way to achieve spiritual peace
    B. it urged believers to overcome destructive passions
    C. it opposed the caste system
    D. it discouraged belief in the rights of the individual

16. The world's first literary epic is a product of the _____ civilization.
    A. Greek
    B. Chinese
    C. Egyptian
    D. Sumerian

17. _____ won a major victory in the Peloponnesian War.
    A. Athens
    B. Carthage
    C. Rome
    D. Sparta

18. _____ is unique among the ancient civilizations for having a rigid caste system that still exists today.
    A. Rome
    B. India
    C. China
    D. Egypt

19. Many of the Roman emperors came from a background of _____.
    A. law
    B. academics
    C. military service
    D. business and trade

20. Minoan and Mycenaean civilizations had all these things in common except _____.
    A. they were skilled sailors and shipbuilders
    B. they kept extensive written records
    C. they were warrior cultures
    D. they had thriving mercantile economies

21. The first Babylonian Empire is noted for its achievements in all these fields except _____.
    A. civil and criminal law
    B. astronomy
    C. mathematics
    D. abstract philosophy

22. The Greek civilization was finally defeated by the rise of _____.
    A. the Indo-Aryan civilization
    B. the Roman Republic
    C. the Macedonian Empire
    D. the Zhou dynasty

23. The Phoenicians were famous in their own time as _____.
    A. traders
    B. warriors
    C. philosophers
    D. engineers

24. **The philosophy of Confucius embraced all the following ideas except _____.**
    A. the established social order should be maintained
    B. each individual should carry out his responsibilities to his best ability
    C. personal integrity would lead naturally to just government
    D. the worker makes the most important contributions to society

25. **The women of _____ seem to have had greater freedom and opportunity than women in other ancient civilizations.**
    A. Egypt
    B. Akkadia
    C. Babylon
    D. the Indus Valley

26. **How did the invading Huns help Hinduism become the supreme religion in India?**
    A. by converting to Hinduism as they blended with the native Indian population
    B. by destroying many Indian Buddhist monasteries
    C. by sending Hindu missionaries to Central Asia
    D. by encouraging religious pilgrimages along the Silk Road

27. **Attributed to the Ionian poet Homer, the *Iliad* and the *Odyssey* describe _____.**
    A. the fall of Athens
    B. the destruction of Carthage
    C. the conquests of Alexander the Great
    D. the Trojan War and its aftermath

28. **The Assyrians were particularly concerned to maintain a formidable army because _____.**
    A. their empire was geographically vulnerable to invasion
    B. they were a deeply religious people
    C. their economy was based on the production of arms
    D. they had no navy and no knowledge of shipbuilding

29. **_____ is the Roman emperor who officially established Christianity as the state religion.**
    A. Augustus
    B. Caesar
    C. Constantine
    D. Marius

30. _____ can accurately be described as the most influential thinker in the history of the West.
    A. Caesar
    B. Aristotle
    C. Buddha
    D. Jesus

31. The Persians and Medes originally came to the Near East region from _____.
    A. Southern Europe
    B. Eastern Europe
    C. India
    D. China

32. After the death of Alexander the Great, the Macedonian Empire _____.
    A. broke apart into small independent kingdoms
    B. was absorbed into the Greek civilization
    C. began a long war of attrition against the Romans
    D. attempted unsuccessfully to invade India

33. Around 550 BC, the Second Babylonian Empire gave way to _____.
    A. the Assyrians
    B. the Egyptians
    C. the Medes
    D. the Persians

34. In ancient times, India was geographically vulnerable to invasion only from _____.
    A. the southwest
    B. the northwest
    C. the southeast
    D. the northeast

35. Why did the Greeks traditionally build the capital city on the acropolis (highest rock)?
    A. so that its importance would be clear to all observers
    B. so that the ruler could always observe what the people were up to
    C. so that it would be secure from enemy invasion
    D. so that the people would always look up to it

36. **Which best describes the Egyptians' belief about the pharaoh?**
    A. The pharaoh ruled by divine right.
    B. The pharaoh was wiser than all other Egyptians.
    C. The pharaoh was descended from the gods.
    D. The pharaoh was divinely inspired.

37. **The Roman civilization is notable for its original contributions to humankind in all these areas except _____.**
    A. polytheistic religion
    B. engineering and building
    C. republican government
    D. civil and criminal law

38. **_____ made continual attempts to invade China from the steppes of Central Asia.**
    A. The Guptas
    B. The Buddhists
    C. The Indians
    D. The Xiongnu

39. **At its height, the Greek civilization included all of the following territory except _____.**
    A. the mouth of the Nile
    B. the bulk of the Italian peninsula
    C. the coast of the Black Sea
    D. the island of Crete

40. **The _____ emerged victorious in the Persian Wars of the fifth century BC.**
    A. Persians
    B. Phoenicians
    C. Greeks
    D. Romans

41. **Rome fought the Punic Wars in order to _____.**
    A. take control of the entire Italian peninsula
    B. defeat the Greek civilization
    C. push the Roman Empire's boundaries as far north as the Rhine River
    D. defeat the Carthaginian threat to Roman supremacy in the region

42. The greatest legacy of the Assyrian king Sargon II is _____.
    A. his library of ancient works of literature
    B. the luxury objects found in his tomb
    C. the code of laws that bears his name
    D. his establishment of the Aramaic language as the international standard

43. Historians believe that all these groups share a common Eastern European origin except _____.
    A. the Aryans
    B. the Medes
    C. the Etruscans
    D. the Persians

44. All these were major factors in the fall of the Roman Empire except _____.
    A. economic troubles
    B. threats of invasion
    C. natural disasters
    D. cultural divisions between east and west

45. The Middle Kingdom period of Egyptian history ended with invasion and conquest by _____.
    A. the Hebrews
    B. the Sea Peoples
    C. the Hyskos
    D. the Romans

46. The Gupta Empire in India began as the result of _____.
    A. a major religious revival
    B. successful military campaigns
    C. the unexpected death of the emperor
    D. a massive foreign invasion and takeover

47. Before long, the Delian League formed after the Persian Wars became _____.
    A. the basis of a united Greek army and navy
    B. a great empire stretching from the eastern Mediterranean to the Indus River
    C. a popular democracy in which the adult male citizens made the decisions
    D. a group of satellite states subject to Athenian control

48. All of the following internal problems contributed to the fall of the Persian Empire except _____.
    A. lack of organization within the military
    B. weak and incompetent rulers
    C. dissension among the diverse ethnic groups that made up the empire
    D. geographical expansion beyond the government's ability to maintain control

49. Buddhism became the major religion in all the following regions except _____.
    A. Tibet
    B. India
    C. China
    D. Sri Lanka

50. Historians know very little about the ancient Indus Valley civilization because _____.
    A. its people were illiterate
    B. invaders destroyed all its written records
    C. its written records have not yet been decoded
    D. it is too far in the remote past

Part Two

The Settlement of Europe, the Colonization of the Americas, and the Rise of the Ottoman Empire

chapter 8

Europe and the Byzantine Empire to AD 1000

The fall of Rome ushered in the era of Europe. In the beginning, Europe truly was what the Romans called it—a barbarian region. The tribes who settled Europe—Huns, Franks, and so on—would not achieve anything resembling Classical civilization for some time to come. They clung to their origins in tribes of warriors whose idea of political supremacy was to be the most successful at plunder and pillage. This early era in European history is sometimes referred to as the "Dark Ages" to contrast it with the highly sophisticated civilizations of modern Europe.

The Byzantine Empire contrasted sharply with these early European societies. It was a settled civilization like those of the ancient world, with great cities, a fully articulated law code, a high degree of literacy, and even a university—one of the world's very first. Although the Byzantines lost a great deal of territory during this era, the empire would remain a constant for another 450 years. The Byzantine Empire was a Christian state that sent out missionaries to Europe, successfully converting the Slavs and Russians to Christianity. In the late eighth century, Charlemagne of France also converted; thus, Europe was—to some extent at least—religiously unified.

The Dark Ages were an era of conflict, with the barbarian tribes continually struggling for supremacy. In the east, the Slavs became the dominant culture over a mix of Viking, Turkish, and Mongolian elements. In the west, the Germanic tribe of the Franks divided, with the West Franks eventually becoming the French and the East Franks eventually becoming the Germans. The West Franks dominated a mixed culture that included Roman Gauls, Bretons, Belges, Vikings, and a mix of others; the East Franks absorbed Slav elements into their culture.

CHAPTER OBJECTIVES

- Identify the various barbarian tribes and where they settled Western and Eastern Europe.
- Describe the development of the early European kingdoms and empires.
- Discuss the Byzantine Empire.

Chapter 8 Time Line

450	Huns give way to Magyars in Hungary
527	Justinian becomes Byzantine emperor
541	First outbreak of bubonic plague in Europe
750	Vikings begin raids into Europe
768	Charlemagne becomes king of France
800	Charlemagne is crowned emperor of Rome
843	Treaty of Verdun divides France into three kingdoms
867	Basil I establishes Macedonian dynasty in Byzantine Empire
962	Holy Roman Empire is founded (as "Roman Empire")
966	Mieszko of Poland converts to Christianity
988	Vladimir I of Kievan Rus converts to Christianity
997	Magyars convert to Christianity
1053	Permanent schism between Roman and Orthodox churches

Eastern Europe

The Byzantine Empire

As of about AD 500, the Byzantine Empire comprised the entire eastern half of the old Roman Empire, from the Balkans on eastward to Syria, Lebanon, and Israel, including Egypt. Three major influences shaped the Byzantine Empire—Greek, Roman, and Christian. The Greek cultural and philosophical influence was the result of geography; the Byzantine Empire was centered in the Greek half of the former Roman Empire. The Roman influence was legal and political; since what became the Byzantine Empire had been administered from Rome for centuries, its leaders were accustomed to Roman methods of organization. The Christian influence was there from the very beginning, with the conversion of the emperor Constantine (see Chapter 6) and his decree that his subjects would practice his religion. Christianity was the central defining factor of the Byzantine Empire throughout its existence.

Politics and Government

The Byzantine emperor was regarded somewhat differently from the Roman emperor. The Romans had considered their emperor to be himself a god. The Byzantines, on the other hand, believed that their emperor was God's representative on earth.

Just like the Romans and all other successful empires, the Byzantines had a highly efficient bureaucracy and an impressive army. Byzantine civil servants were educated at the University of Constantinople, which was founded in the fifth century. This shared educational background served as a unifying factor across all branches of the civil service. The military featured an intimidating cavalry with great skill at archery. The Byzantines also inherited the Roman skill at architecture, building impressive fortifications.

Below the emperor, the Byzantine aristocracy was divided into three groups: bureaucrats, clergy, and military officers. The bulk of the army was drawn from among the farmers at first; as time went on, however, the Byzantines began relying more and more on mercenaries, just as the Romans had done. Below the aristocracy were the merchants and peasants. Byzantine women had certain legal rights, just as they had under Rome; three even ruled all of Byzantium as empresses. An educated Byzantine woman from a wealthy and powerful family could wield considerable social and even political influence.

The wealth of the empire was based on agricultural production, but it also profited hugely from international trade. Constantinople was on the Bosporus strait, in an ideal geographical position for a port. All ships sailing into or out of the Black Sea stopped at Constantinople. The empire traded with Russia and Africa and even had contact with China. One of the Emperor Justinian's most profitable decisions was to send spies to smuggle silkworms out of the Asian empire. This allowed the Byzantines to begin manufacturing their own silk, which up to that time had been a secret exclusive to the Chinese.

Justinian and his wife Theodora reigned over the empire from 527 to 565. Justinian is best remembered for his expansionist policies. His goal was to reunite the two halves of the Roman Empire, with Constantinople as the new capital. Under the great military commander Belisarius, the Byzantines took back a great portion of the territory they sought. By 533, they had captured the North African coast to the west of Egypt. They recaptured the southern tip of Spain in 552, and by 554 they controlled Italy. However, this was the end of expansion under Justinian. Various stumbling blocks arose. First, Justinian had spent so much money on the military that the imperial treasury was in a condition of grave vulnerability. Second, the Slavs and the Persians had taken up arms and were attacking the Byzantine Empire from the east and north, thus diverting military attention from advancing into the west. Third, the bubonic plague struck the Mediterranean in 541.

The bubonic plague originated in the East and was brought westward on trading ships. Highly infectious, it was spread by flea and rat bites and close contact. Symptoms included raging fever, delirium, aching joints, vomiting, and painful swellings in the armpits and groin. Very little could be done to make a sick person comfortable, let alone cure him or her. Most of the plague's victims died within a week of catching the disease. Plagues would recur throughout the medieval era, taking a heavy toll on the European population again and again.

The early seventh century was an era of bewildering shifts in the boundaries of the Byzantine Empire. Economic crises and foreign invasions characterized the first decade, with Slavs, Persians, and Lombards (from northern Italy) all attacking the empire from different directions. The Persians had the greatest success, taking over most of the empire by the year 626. Heraclitus, who became emperor in 610, persuaded Constantinople's churches to fund a determined military drive to recover the lost territory, a goal achieved by 627. By 636, however, the same territory was in Persian hands once again.

Arabs arrived at the gates of Constantinople in 673 but did not succeed in taking the capital; a second attempt in 717 also failed. The city's heavy fortifications proved more than adequate to protect it. The Byzantines also had better weapons than the Arabs and a great military leader in the person of Emperor

Leo III. In the end, however, the Arabs conquered about half the Byzantine territory.

The Eastern European Slavs also issued serious challenges to Byzantine authority. From the late 500s, Slavic power and influence spread throughout the Balkans and into Greece. At the same time, the Bulgars of Central Asia, who were ethnically related to the Huns, established the kingdom of Bulgaria in the Balkans.

The end result of the era of invasion and conquest was to make the Byzantine Empire a more manageable size, easier to administer and defend. Several historical factors favored continuing Byzantine success in the region. First, the Arab caliphate in the East began to fall apart, breaking into smaller independent kingdoms that constituted a lesser threat to Constantinople. Second, the Byzantines continued to send out missionaries; as the Slavs converted to Christianity, they recognized the authority of the emperor. Third, the population rose for two reasons: the wave of bubonic plagues died out, and new agricultural practices led to larger harvests.

A change of dynasty took place in 867, when Basil I usurped the throne. He rose from peasant origins to a prominent position at the imperial court. After a violent beginning—Basil seized power by murdering a rival and then engineering the assassination of Emperor Michael III—he became an able and intelligent ruler. This began the Macedonian dynasty of Byzantine emperors, so named because Basil I came from the old Macedonian region of Thrace. Between 966 and 1014, Basil II brought the kingdom of Bulgaria and its holdings back into the empire; his methods were so violent that he earned the nickname "Bulgar-Slayer."

Religion

In the Byzantine Empire, the Orthodox Church and the state were mutually dependent and supportive. The entire purpose of the state was to serve as an ideal society on earth, one that carried out all of God's commandments. Therefore, the state supported the Church and ensured it a great many privileges, such as tax exemption. The Church, on its side, supported the state and cast a mantle of righteousness and morality over all its policies and actions—no matter how warlike.

During the first millennium AD, two main forms of Christianity developed: the Roman Church in the west and the Orthodox Church in the east. The differences between the two have to do with doctrine, liturgy, and the authority of the ecclesiastical courts; they are also to some extent by-products of the estrangement that had grown up between the Greek and Latin halves of the old Roman Empire. Each of the two, of course, considered itself to be the true Church, rejecting the practices of the other. The final schism between the two churches occurred in 1053, when Michael, the Patriarch of Constantinople, condemned certain practices of the western Church as blasphemous. To this day, the churches remain separate; we refer to them as the Roman Catholic and Eastern Orthodox churches. During the first millennium, the words *Catholic* and *Christian* are synonymous; the Roman and Orthodox churches wielded enormous power over affairs of state throughout Europe until they were first challenged by new denominations in the 1500s.

Christianity is a missionary religion; therefore, it was part of the overall purpose of the Byzantines to convert all the people of their world to the Orthodox faith. In practical terms, this meant converting the princes or leaders of the various kingdoms and tribes, because, according to custom, the people would worship as their leader worshipped. The Bulgarians converted to Christianity in 870, Mieszko of Poland in 966, and Vladimir I of Kievan Rus in 988. Bohemia also became Christianized in the tenth century. In the mid-ninth century, the great Byzantine missionaries Cyril and Methodius established the Slavic system of writing and translated the Bible into Slavic. Cyril gave his name to the Cyrillic alphabet in which Russian is written.

Rise of the Slavic Peoples in the East

As you read in Chapters 6 and 7, the first millennium AD saw massive westward and southern migration of the tribes of the Central Asian steppes. The Huns eventually settled the land that became the nation of Hungary, to which they gave their name. Around 450, however, the Huns gave way to the Magyars. By that time, the Germanic tribes had moved westward in search of land to call their own.

The Romans referred to these Eurasian invaders of Europe as barbarians, and their point was well taken, given the sharp contrast between the highly developed Roman civilization (a mercantile economy, cities, a sophisticated law code, and a host of literary and artistic achievements) and the early Europeans, who lived very much as their nomad warrior ancestors had done. Early Slavic and Germanic Europe would not achieve anything like the Egyptian, Greek, Roman, or Byzantine level of civilization for centuries to come.

By AD 550 to 600, a variety of Slavs had settled in the Balkans. These linguistically and ethnically related peoples came from the Russian steppes. Some stayed in their native area and are the ancestors of present-day Russians. Others migrated to Eastern Europe; they included Ukranians, Poles, Czechs, Slovaks, and Serbians. The Slavs became the most numerous group in the Balkans, but this region was also home to Turks, Mongolians, Germans, and Vikings. The Slavs remained the dominant culture, absorbing elements of all the others along the way.

Slavic prosperity was based on agriculture and the slave trade. Roman plows and the Roman system of crop rotation, both of which the Slavs acquired around 500, greatly improved the harvests. Lacking a manufacturing or artisan economy, the western Slavs made money by kidnapping eastern Slavs and selling them into slavery in the Muslim world.

Between about 750 and 1054, the Vikings carried out a series of swift and merciless raids into France, Britain, and Eastern Europe. One of these Viking tribes, the Rus, founded the city-states of Kiev (also known as Kievan Rus) and Novgorod; in the end, Muscovy would absorb these states into an ever-expanding Russian empire (see Chapter 13). After the Christian conversion of Vladimir I in 988, Kiev became culturally more Slavic/Byzantine. Viking influence was what gave the Slavs the push to leave their tribal habits behind and develop into a civilization. With a view to acquiring the necessary force to expel the unwelcome Viking invaders, the Slavs began reorganizing themselves along Viking-style political lines; this inevitably led to a more sophisticated degree of social organization and thence to civilization.

In the tenth century, kingdoms began to emerge from Slavic tribal settlements: Poland in 966, Bohemia in 973, and Hungary with the Christian conversion of the Magyars in 997. The Slavs were already linguistically and ethnically interconnected; with their conversion to Christianity, they were now religiously linked to one another and also to the Byzantine Empire. Bohemia was something of an exception to this pattern; its population was Germanic as well as Slavic, and given its comparatively western geographic location, it would be absorbed into the Holy Roman Empire during the medieval era. However, the Slav strain in the culture would triumph in the long run.

Western Europe

The Development of France

The present-day nation of France evolved from Roman Gaul, an area of towns and settlements north and west of the Italian peninsula. As the Roman Empire collapsed, a variety of tribes competed for this region. The Franks achieved political supremacy and gave their name to France.

The Franks were a Germanic tribe that achieved conquest over a mix of peoples, including the Gauls, the Bretons, the Belges, and the Gascons. The Franks were a numerical minority in the region, which is probably the reason that many of the most readily identifiable cultural traits of France are not Germanic. The Roman Empire left its cultural mark on France. Early Merovingian coins are stamped with Roman motifs and Latin captions, the French language is closely based on Latin, and the culture was wine-drinking rather than beer-drinking. Over the centuries, the Franks intermarried with the other local tribes, and, in the end, the mix of barbarian peoples produced a homogenous French culture.

The Frankish tribes included the Salians, the tribe of the Merovingian family that became France's first ruling dynasty. The Bretons came across the English Channel into northern France, and the Gascons from the Pyrenees into southwestern France; these two groups had a high degree of cultural influence in the regions where they settled. At the same time, the Belges were crossing the Channel in the other direction, thus creating something of an exchange of peoples and culture between Britain and France.

The Merovingian Dynasty

The Merovingian dynasty was not a central government like those of ancient Egypt or ancient Rome. It was a number of sizeable kingdoms with a suggestion of cultural and linguistic affiliation.

The system of government was based on an exchange of favors. Warriors swore loyalty and service to King Clovis in exchange for room and board and a share of whatever booty they captured. In time, this system evolved into the feudal system that characterized medieval Europe: the king's vassals would offer military service in exchange for sizeable tracts of land where they would build their own estates. In their turn, the vassals would acquire their own retinues of loyal men, who would take up arms for the lord in exchange for housing and a share of the loot. The land grants given by the king might or might not be permanent. Generally, they were not permanent; the king preferred to retain the ability to revoke them as a check on the power of the vassals. Under careless or lazy kings, of course, the land grants might be permanent in fact.

The Merovingians are an example of the typical level of civilization reached by Europeans during this era. They were descended from nomadic warriors, and their idea of domination and success was not to build cities and learn to read and write but rather to plunder and pillage from other tribes. In time, of course, this violent barbarian culture gave way to literate and highly sophisticated civilizations.

The original power base of the Merovingians was in northern France; Clovis named Paris as his capital city in the year 511. By the end of the sixth century, the Merovingians had expanded south and east, taking over three kingdoms: Aquitaine in the southwest, Burgundy in the southeast, and Austrasia in the northeast.

There are very few written records of Slavic history from this period; the case is somewhat different in France. The *History of Gaul* by Gregory of Tours is an eyewitness account of Merovingian rule, written about 593 to 594. This is the only source for much valuable information about early France, such as the biography of Clothilde of Burgundy.

The Salians gave their name to the Salic Law, the Merovingian legal code that was based on Roman law and originally written in Latin. The Salic Law barred women from ruling France, but it did give them some rights. As in Rome and Byzantium, educated women from powerful families could wield significant influence. In addition, the Church offered a respectable alternative to marriage; women could enter the scholarly world of the cloister and potentially rise as high as the position of abbess in its power structure. Some of these nuns were among the best-educated people of their time.

Burgundian princess Clothilde married Clovis in 492 and persuaded him to convert to Christianity; she was later canonized. From that date onward, France was a Christian nation. As in the Byzantine Empire, church and state worked together as two arms of the same authority. In one example of their close connection, the same internal borders divided France into units of political administration by the state and diocesan administration by the Church.

The Merovingian rulers were eventually overcome because they failed to consolidate France into a centrally controlled state. This would change when the Arnulfing family first rose to power. Their dynasty is called *Carolingian* because so many Arnulfing men were named Charles (*Carolus* in Latin).

The Carolingian Dynasty

By the end of the eighth century, the Carolingian rulers had united all the Franks under one central government. They expanded the Merovingian holdings into a Carolingian empire, conquering the Italian peninsula and expanding as far west as the Elbe River in the north and the Danube River in the south.

On Christmas Day 800, the Pope crowned the French king Charlemagne emperor in an elaborate public ceremony in Rome. He was considered the new hope of a new Roman Empire and a rival to the Byzantine Emperor in the East. Charlemagne is a highly important figure in the early history of Christianity. He spearheaded the Carolingian Renaissance, an artistic and literary flowering that was motivated entirely by the desire to spread Christianity and to better understand its history. He also encouraged the study of Christian texts in Latin and set monasteries full of monks to copy and illuminate manuscripts and devotional works. The Carolingian Renaissance instituted high educational standards for monks and priests throughout France and the standardization of worship services in all parishes. This was not a Classical renaissance but a Christian one.

In 843, the Treaty of Verdun divided Charlemagne's empire among three grandsons. West Francia became the greater part of the modern nation of France, while in East Francia the Germanic culture would dominate; East Francia was eventually absorbed into the Holy Roman Empire (see "The Foundation of the Holy Roman Empire" later in this chapter), which in 1871 would become the nation of Germany. Lotharingia, the central and smallest division, sometimes allied with West Francia and sometimes with East Francia: later, when it developed into the region of Lorraine, it would continue this pattern, serving as a bone of contention between France and Germany for at least four hundred years. This is historically important because it shows that the French and the Germans have a common ethnic, cultural, and historical origin—a fact that both sides acknowledged in the twentieth century, when they put aside centuries of enmity to found the European Union.

By the seventh century, a money economy had already replaced the barter system; there were an astonishing number of mints in Merovingian France. However, the region had slumped economically under Merovingian rule; this was due not to incompetent administration so much as to a variety of other factors (military invasions, bad weather, and a fall-off in international trade). Under the Carolingians, France underwent economic recovery and was poised to play a central role in the bustling mercantile economy that would include all Europe after the year 1000.

By the end of the ninth century, the system of delegating royal authority to the vassals (now called counts, hence the noble title *count* and the administrative division *county*) was breaking down. Those counts who had acquired extensive lands began calling themselves dukes and assuming a greater degree of royal authority than they had ever been granted. With their own armed retinues of vassals, who were much more loyal to the local lord than to the faraway monarch, these dukes were very difficult to control. The kingdom became built up with heavily fortified castles, whose purpose was to protect the duke and his followers not only from foreign invasion but also from regional and local rivals.

Cultural and local divisions deepened; Frankish culture remained strong in the north, while southern France was more culturally Roman. Viking tribes had been sweeping into France at irregular intervals since the 700s. One group had settled Normandy, on the shores of the English Channel, and soon became known as Normans. In 911, after unsuccessfully attacking Chartres and then Paris, the Viking leader Rollo converted his tribe to Christianity and swore loyalty to France, in exchange for permission to settle permanently in the kingdom.

The Foundation of the Holy Roman Empire

Historians like to joke that the Holy Roman Empire was neither holy nor Roman nor an empire. Its story begins in the year 962, when Otto I of the Carolingian dynasty became emperor of West Francia and Lotharingia—in other words, all the land between France on one side and Poland on the other. Otto's inheritance, with only minor border adjustments, would be handed down for the next nine hundred years as a hereditary monarchy.

At first, this culturally Franco-Germanic Christian state was referred to simply as the Roman Empire; Otto assumed the imperial title to enhance his own prestige and to impress upon the world that he was the ruler of all of Christian Europe (quite an exaggeration on his part, as there was extensive Christian territory outside his realm). The name *Roman Empire* also paid tribute to Charlemagne's role as the titular successor to the empire of the Caesars. In the 1100s, Emperor Frederick Barbarossa added the word *Holy* to the name, to distinguish the Christian "Roman Empire" from its pre-Christian predecessor. Of course, the empire was not Roman in any respect; it was well north of the Italian peninsula and its ethnic and linguistic roots were Germanic, Slavic, and Viking.

The "empire" was actually a collection of seven independent kingdoms and counties: Mainz, Cologne, Trier, Rhine, Saxony, Brandenburg, and Bohemia. They were called electorates because the monarch of each one was an elector—that is, he cast a vote in the selection of each new Holy Roman Emperor. In fact, the throne was passed down within the family, as in all other hereditary monarchies, but when an emperor died, the electors met to hold a formal vote on who would be the successor.

QUIZ

1. All these cultures had tremendous influence on the development of the
   Byzantine Empire except _____.
   A. Christian
   B. Egyptian
   C. Greek
   D. Roman

2. The Slavs of southeastern Europe have been connected since the turn of the
   first millennium in all these ways except _____.
   A. ethnically
   B. linguistically
   C. religiously
   D. politically

3. The Merovingians exercised their greatest degree of authority in which section
   of France?
   A. the northwest
   B. the southwest
   C. the southeast
   D. the northeast

4. Expansion of the Byzantine Empire under Justinian halted for all these reasons
   except _____.
   A. the imperial treasury had become all but bankrupt
   B. the churches refused to provide any funding for the army
   C. military threats from the Slavs and Persians
   D. a series of outbreaks of the bubonic plague

5. Which early Slavic kingdom was absorbed into the Holy Roman Empire?
   A. Poland
   B. Bohemia
   C. Kievan Rus
   D. Hungary

6. **Gregory of Tours is historically important because of his contributions in the field of _____.**
   A. architecture
   B. poetry
   C. history
   D. law

7. **The Byzantines claimed that the major purpose of their empire was _____.**
   A. to unite all Europeans under one government
   B. to exist as the ideal Christian society on earth
   C. to restore the Roman Empire to its former glory
   D. to overthrow the Roman Church in the West

8. **Why is it ironic that the French and Germans were enemies for so many centuries?**
   A. because they are descended from the same barbarian tribe
   B. because they are both Christian nations
   C. because they were both once part of the Roman Empire
   D. because they are geographical neighbors

9. **The _____ culture became numerically and culturally dominant in the Balkan region of southeastern Europe.**
   A. Germanic
   B. Hun
   C. Slav
   D. Viking

10. **The Carolingian Renaissance refers to a period of rediscovery of _____.**
    A. Classical artistic styles
    B. Roman military strategy
    C. Greek philosophy
    D. Christian theology

The Rise of Islam, African Civilizations, and India to AD 1000

Islam, the religion that would eventually unify the entire Near East, was founded in the early seventh century. The founding of this new monotheistic religion, which had its roots in Judeo-Christianity, led to an era characterized by conquest and conversion. By the end of the tenth century, a major new religion had taken firm hold on a sizeable region of the world. Islam also brought political changes to the Arab world, which found its tribes unified under one central government for the first time in their history.

It is important to remember that at this point in history, the term *Arab* refers to the ethnic group that is native to the Arabian Peninsula. The peoples of Iran and Iraq, whom we describe today as Arabs, are not ethnically Arabian at all, but Persian. The Muslim Empire that rose during the first millennium took its religion and its official language from the Arabians but was culturally and artistically Persian in many ways. As the first millennium drew to a close, the Muslim Empire became more and more diverse and cosmopolitan, embracing Turkish, Persian, and African elements as well as Arabian ones.

The major African civilizations of the first millennium included Nubia, Axum, and the kingdom of Ghana, in addition to Egypt. Foreign invasion, religious conversion, and international trade are the major themes of these civilizations.

After the fall of the Gupta Empire, the Indian civilization entered a chaotic period of strife among independent kingdoms; this fragmented political status would persist for several centuries. At this point, India resembled medieval Europe, with its feudal system of government and its thriving mercantile economy. Hinduism continued to develop and change, adopting many of the ideas and concepts of Buddhism.

CHAPTER OBJECTIVES

- Discuss the founding of Islam and its main ideas.
- Describe the formation of the Arab Empire.
- Describe African civilizations in the first millennium AD.
- Discuss India after the Gupta Empire.

Chapter 9 Time Line

- 350   Sonike dynasty begins in Ghana
- 543   Nubians convert to Christianity
- 570   Birth of Muhammad
- 572   Persians drive Axumites from Arabia
- 622   The hegira (Muhammad flees to Medina)
- 661   Umayyad caliphate begins
- 700   Beginnings of Muslim trade in east Africa
- 711   Arabs conquer the Indus Valley
- 740   Chola dynasty begins in southern India
- 750   Abbasid caliphate begins
- 753   Rashtrakuta dynasty begins in central India
- 762   Baghdad is founded as new capital city
- 802   Kingdom of Cambodia is established
- 939   Vietnam establishes independence from China

The Birth of the Islamic Empire

The Creation of Islam

Muhammad was born around 570 in Mecca, near the Red Sea coast in present-day Saudi Arabia. Beginning in 610, he underwent a series of visionary experiences in which Allah revealed a new moral code to him, urging the unity of all believers under a common code of law and the worship of Allah as the one God. Muhammad made some converts in Mecca, but his monotheistic message was not popular there and he was forced to flee south to Medina in 622 in an event Muslims refer to as the *hijra* (hegira). Once in Medina, Muhammad had much greater success as a prophet; one possible reason for this is that Medina was home to a large Jewish population who found nothing threatening or unfamiliar in his preaching of monotheism and his emphasis on charity. (Relations between the two groups did not remain cordial; as more and more of Medina fell under the sway of Islam, the Jews were shut out of the city.)

The Teachings of Islam

The Arabic word *Islam* means "surrender or submission to God." The holy book of Islam is called the Quran (Koran). Considered the word of Allah as revealed to Muhammad, the verses of the Quran were collected and written down in Arabic in their final form soon after his death, around 650. The Quran is not only holy scripture; it also forms the basis of the Arab legal system. Muslims also venerate the Sunna, their name for the actual words and teachings of Muhammad.

Islam has five basic requirements of its followers. Known as the Five Pillars of Islam, these are faith, prayer, alms, fasting, and pilgrimage. Faith means exclusive worship of Allah, the one God, and acknowledgment of his prophet Muhammad. Muslims must face in the direction of Mecca and speak five ritual prayers each day in addition to praying at a mosque every Friday afternoon. Muslims are expected to give generously to charity, to fast between sunrise and sunset throughout the month of Ramadan, and to take part at least once in their lives in the annual mass pilgrimage to Mecca. Muslims also take very seriously the concept of *jihad*, which means "struggle"; jihad requires Muslims to work for the good of Islam in all ways, not only or even primarily by taking up arms. (Non-Muslims, particularly Westerners, commonly mistranslate *jihad* as "holy war.")

Islam has its roots in Judaism and Christianity. All three religions are monotheistic and worship the same God; *Allah* is simply the Arabic name for him. Muslims consider Jesus a major biblical prophet, but they do not accept that he was literally the son of God. They believe that Muhammad was the last and greatest of the prophets and that Islam is the true religion prophesied throughout the Bible. Like Christianity and unlike Judaism, Islam is a missionary religion with the goal of converting all peoples to its beliefs. This missionary aspect of the faith is part of what drove the expansionist policies of the early caliphs.

The Islamic Empire

Muhammad was not only a prophet but also an extraordinary political leader. In 630, the Muslims conquered Mecca under his leadership, and by 632, Muhammad had united the entire Arabian peninsula as a unified state for the first time in history.

Muhammad named no successor, which eventually led to strife among his followers. The first four caliphs to follow Muhammad are known to Sunni Muslims as the "righteous caliphs"; all four were related to Muhammad by marriage, blood, or both. After these four, however, internal conflict over the leadership led to civil war and the beginnings of what would become a permanent schism between two Islamic denominations—the majority Sunnis and the minority, fundamentalist Shiites.

The Umayyad Dynasty

Civil war between the Islamic factions culminated in the accession of the first Umayyad caliph, Muawiya, in 661. The Umayyad family ruled from the ancient city of Damascus. They established Arabic as the official language of the culture, and they began minting coins. The economy flourished under their rule, with most of the profits coming from international trade. Under the Umayyads, the Arabian Empire expanded and Islam spread through a sizeable territory. With this large empire came new methods of administration, resembling the Roman and Byzantine bureaucracies. In addition, the building of the Dome of the Rock in Jerusalem issued a direct challenge to both Judaism and Christianity.

The Arabian culture was largely a nomadic warrior culture. Like all nomadic warriors in history, the Arabs survived largely by plunder. When Islam created a unified Arabic realm, it eliminated the possibility of plunder within that realm; Muslims were forbidden to attack and rob other Muslims. The habit of roaming and subduing other tribes, combined with the powerful drive to convert non-Muslims to the new faith, caused the Arabs to expand their sphere of influence.

The Muslims conquered Egypt, Persia, and Syria between 632 and 649. Having conquered Egypt, they proceeded westward along the northern coast of Africa, then crossed the Mediterranean into Spain. They penetrated Europe as far as Poitiers in France; a great battle at this site halted their advance in that direction for good. They would remain in Spain, however, holding sway over the entire Iberian peninsula (except for the extreme northern coastal area) for the next seven hundred years (see Figure 9.1).

There were various reasons for the Arabian success in conquering territory and converting peoples. Throughout the region, there was widespread discontent with current regimes, and people were often glad to exchange unpopular rulers for new ones who might prove more capable and perhaps even more benevolent. Islam preached the equality of all believers and the importance of rule by popular consent; these concepts must have appealed to many people at the bottom of a rigid class structure. Additionally, the Arabs had greater fighting skills than most of the peoples they conquered.

The downfall of the Umayyads was rooted in minority objections to their right to rule; their opponents claimed that they did not rule with the consent of the entire community, which was a serious objection because Islam is based on consensus.

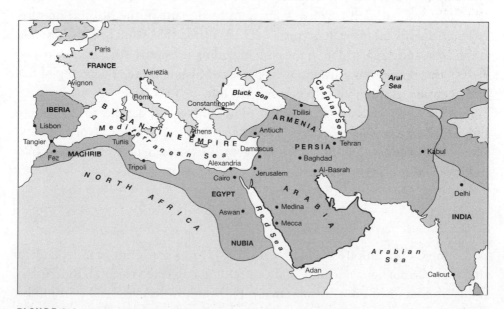

FIGURE 9.1   The Spread of Islam to 750

The Abbasid Dynasty

In 750, Abu-al-Abbas assassinated the last Umayyad caliph and launched a new dynasty, the Abbasids. One of their important decisions was to move the capital from Damascus to Baghdad, at that time a humble backwater on the Tigris River; one effect of this decision was the start of a major cultural exchange between Arabs and Persians. The Persians were converted to Islam, while the Arabs absorbed many aspects of Persian artistic and architectural styles. There was thus assimilation and accommodation on both sides.

Under Abbasid rule, the Arabs enjoyed a growing trade with China and India; Abbasid coins have even been found in Scandinavia, which suggests active trade between these far-apart regions. Trade and cultural exchange led to a broader Arabian understanding of the world beyond the peninsula. A growing curiosity about the ancient world, particularly the Greek world, led to the translation of foreign books into Arabic. In the early ninth century, the Abbasids began buying Turkish slaves to serve as soldiers; a certain term of military service would usually earn a slave his freedom. The Turks were very able warriors—so able that they eventually became the rulers of the great Muslim state known to history as the Ottoman Empire.

Probably because it included such an ethnically diverse population, the Abbasid Empire was cosmopolitan in its outlook. Many of the ruling elites surrounding the caliph were not ethnic Arabians; they were religiously unified, but ethnically and culturally diverse, coming from all parts of the Muslim Empire.

The Abbasid caliphs ruled over a very large area that stretched to Armenia in the west and Afghanistan in the east, including the entire Arabian peninsula. In 750, this region was only about 10 percent Muslim; by the beginning of the tenth century, it was about 90 percent Muslim.

Like the Umayyads, the Abbasids were not universally acclaimed as divinely chosen rulers; they lost territory to local warlords, especially in North Africa. Rival caliphates were set up in Spain, Egypt, and elsewhere, and much of Iraq and Iran was broken up into collections of separate kingdoms.

India

When the Gupta Empire fell in 550, it gave way to a scattering of independent kingdoms throughout northern and central India. By the year 600, the Pushyabhuti dynasty had risen to supremacy. Pushyabhuti leader Harsha would be the last ethnically Indian ruler to try to take over the entire subcontinent; his troops did succeed in conquering the north, but not the south. Harsha's reign was characterized by the production of many great works of Sanskrit literature.

A system that strongly resembled the feudal system of medieval Europe would characterize India from this time until about the eleventh century. At the head of each independent kingdom was a strong military leader. Below him were his retinues of vassals, warriors who paid him financial tribute and served in his army in exchange for his protection. The king and his army would wage war on other kings in the region; when one king had subdued all his neighbors, he became known as a *maharaja*. The history of India at this time is chaotic because no one maharaja ever held onto his power for long. His kingdom would usually collapse promptly after his death, usually because his heirs were incapable of effective administration or managing crises or leading troops into battle. As one kingdom fell, another would rise to take its place.

The Ganges River valley was a rich agricultural region and was therefore considered a prize; several dynasties competed for supremacy in this area during the first millennium. The Rashtrakuta dynasty began a period of rule in 753 in this region. Krishna II, who succeeded to the throne late in the tenth century, was its most notable maharaja. Krishna and his warriors overpowered most other kingdoms in the region, but the Rashtrakutas fell from power almost immediately after his death.

The Huns had invaded India from the north around AD 510 and had remained there ever since. Their descendants, known as the Rajputs, converted to Hinduism in another instance of the typical Indian/Near Eastern assimilation of an invading people into the native culture. In 727, the Rajputs, whose military skills were greatly admired, were formally welcomed into the Hindu warrior caste. They became politically dominant in the region. The Chola dynasty began to rule in southern India in 740; the Cholas' geographical location gave them control of international trade, and they were also notable for their impressive navy. The Pala dynasty of Bangladesh in the northeastern corner of India is notable for being India's only Buddhist dynasty; it began in 750 and would last for three hundred fifty years. The Palas presided over what became a study center for Buddhism that attracted scholars from all over the known world. During this era, however, Buddhism would more or less die out throughout India. As Hinduism evolved, it began to incorporate many ideas and concepts from Buddhism. This can be seen as another instance of a great religion adapting itself to the needs and expectations of the people.

India's guilds and the wealthy merchant families who headed them drove the Indian economy in this post-Gupta era. The merchants occupied positions of great social and political power, similar to the European Medici or Roth-schilds in later centuries. Members of the Indian merchant caste served as the maharajas' bankers, and they often had their own armies. India was something of a hub of international trade, positioned as it was between China and the Near East.

Africa

Archaeological evidence has determined that the *Homo sapiens* evolved on the African continent. People slowly migrated from Africa to Europe and Asia and thence to the Americas. There is no such thing as a unified "African civiliza-tion" or "African culture"; the continent is too large and ethnically diverse and the peoples too widely separated by geographical obstacles, such as the Sahara Desert. There was no shared linguistic or religious bond among the early Afri-can tribes.

The Nubian Civilization

Nubia rivaled its neighbor Egypt in terms of civilization in ancient North Africa. Located on the Upper Nile and occupying the area between Egypt and the Red Sea, Nubia was a literate civilization before 1000 BC with an organized army, skilled artisans, a complex religion, and monumental architecture. The Nubians conquered Egypt and ruled it for a century, only shouldered aside by the Assyr-ians in 671 BC. With a later Egyptian resurgence, the Nubians moved their capital to a safer location at Meroe. Alexander's conquest of Egypt resulted in the Hellenization of both Egypt and Nubia. Around AD 543, Byzantine mis-sionaries converted the Nubian aristocracy to Christianity.

The Axumite Civilization

The Sabeans from the southern tip of the Arabian peninsula (present-day Yemen) sailed across the Red Sea to present-day Ethiopia and established trad-ing posts. These colonizers intermarried with the local African population and the resulting Arab-African cultural tradition eventually emerged as the Axu-mite civilization around 100 BC. Axumite civilization reflected Arabic religion, politics, and farming methods in addition to Arabic writing while also reflecting ethnic and cultural African traits.

Located at the mouth of the Red Sea, Axum was ideally situated to make its fortune in international trade. King Aphilas of Axum even invaded and conquered Yemen to tighten his control on access to the trade routes. The Axumites traded with India, China, and the eastern Mediterranean civilizations, as well as with the tribes of Africa and the Arabian Peninsula.

Around AD 350, King Ezana of Axum converted to Christianity. He then led the takeover of the Nubian capital at Meroe, thus ensuring the continued existence of Axum as a great military power. The Axumites stormed the gates of Mecca in 570 but were repulsed. This show of strength enabled Mecca to become, over time, the greatest Arabian military and economic power. Thus the Christian civilization failed to take what became the holiest city of Islam, and, in the tenth century, the Muslims converted the Axumites. The final blow to Axumite civilization came in 960, when Jewish warriors sacked the city of Axum; the Jews would maintain a presence in Ethiopia until they migrated to Israel in massive numbers in the twentieth century.

The Kingdom of Ghana

The most valuable commodities in western Africa were gold and slaves. As Europe converted more and more into being a money economy, gold became a necessity, and slave labor was a constant in all ancient civilizations.

This foreign desire for gold caused the kingdom of Ghana to rise to prominence around 300 BC. When Islam was introduced in the ninth century, the local Muslim traders and the people of Ghana held aloof from one another, but eventually they began to jell into one society despite their different faiths (the people of Ghana practiced a traditional, polytheistic African religion). In AD 1076, the Berber people sacked the Ghanan capital city of Kumbi, thus ending the prominence of the kingdom.

Sub-Saharan Africa

Historians generally refer to the people of sub-Saharan Africa as Bantu. Probably because they were isolated from the rest of the world by oceans on both sides and the Sahara Desert to the north, the Bantu had little contact with outsiders until the early modern period. Hunter-gatherers at first, they eventually acquired the rudiments of civilization: the ability to cultivate their own food, the skill to fashion iron tools, and the desire to organize their societies in a formal way.

After about 100 BC, the domestication of the camel enabled North Africans and Egyptians to cross the Sahara in search of slaves and hired mercenaries. Camels are essential for crossing large deserts because, unlike horses, they can survive for many days without water; additionally, their feet are soled not with hard hoofs but with soft pads, perfectly adapted for walking and running on sand. Sub-Saharan Africans fought in all the armies of Mediterranean and southern Europe until the Middle Ages. This provides evidence that the Europeans knew of the southern African peoples and their societies and that Europe absorbed at least a smattering of sub-Saharan African culture long before the modern era.

QUIZ

1. _____ was in a favorable trading position because it had large deposits of gold.
   A. The Arabian Peninsula
   B. Ghana
   C. Persia
   D. India

2. Which correctly describes the authorship of the Quran, according to Islam?
   A. Muhammad is the author of the Quran.
   B. Scholars wrote the Quran after Muhammad's death.
   C. The Quran represents the word of Allah as revealed to Muhammad.
   D. The Quran has no known author.

3. The Islamic Empire that arose toward the end of the first millennium converted large numbers of people in all these areas except _____.
   A. Spain
   B. Persia
   C. North Africa
   D. Italy

4. The Rajputs were descended from _____.
   A. the ancient peoples of the Indus Valley
   B. the nomadic warriors of the steppes of Central Asia
   C. the Macedonians
   D. the ancient Greeks

5. **The Five Pillars of Islam include all of these except** _____.
    A. alms
    B. fasting
    C. jihad
    D. prayer

6. **In what way is Islam unlike Christianity?**
    A. Islam does not call for worship of the same God.
    B. Islam is not a missionary religion.
    C. Muslims do not believe in the divinity of Jesus.
    D. Islam does not have scriptures believed to represent the word of God.

7. **Which best describes government in the Indian kingdoms after the fall of the Guptas?**
    A. a feudal system based on an exchange of favors between the lord and the vassals
    B. an autocracy ruled by a succession of hereditary dynasties
    C. a centrally controlled, politically unified state with a large bureaucracy
    D. a representative government that insisted on popular consensus

8. **The African civilization of Axum eventually became present-day** _____.
    A. Saudi Arabia
    B. Egypt
    C. Ethiopia
    D. Ghana

9. **One major cause of the civil war and factionalism that characterized the caliphate after Muhammad's death was** _____.
    A. the Islamic emphasis on conversion of non-Muslims
    B. the political unification of the Arabian Peninsula
    C. the lack of a definitive written version of the Quran
    D. Muhammad's failure to name his successor

10. **The Pala dynasty was characterized by** _____.
    A. its military prowess
    B. its devout Buddhism
    C. its suspension of the caste system
    D. its brevity

East Asian Civilizations to 1000; the Americas to 1500

The Tang dynasty in China oversaw the culmination of many central Chinese customs and traditions, particularly the all-important merit examination for the civil service. China expanded very far into the west under the Tang emperors, only to lose territory near the end of the eighth century. The Tang dynasty saw the invention of printing and gunpowder; these two items would revolutionize the Western world, but not until the technologies made their way westward hundreds of years later.

As very small states in the shadow of a very large one, Japan and Korea absorbed many Chinese traditions—everything from the form of government to the styles of architecture. Japan's distance from the mainland enabled it, over time, to develop its own distinct cultural and political traditions, related to the Chinese but not imitative of them. China would remain more dominant over Korea than over Japan.

Civilization came to South and Central America in ancient times, when the people learned to cultivate maize. This staple crop and the knowledge of how to grow it slowly spread north. Latin America was the location of a variety of civilizations that resembled ancient Mediterranean ones in many ways, such as geographical expansion, the building of cities, the creation of beautiful artifacts and monumental architecture, achievements in mathematics, and autocratic systems of government. The mightiest of the civilizations, the Aztec and Incan empires, fell swiftly with the arrival of the Spaniards.

The North Americans never became civilized in the sense of building cities, becoming literate, or undertaking conquest and expansion. The culture remained traditional and tribal, with small communities that (apart from the warlike Apaches) generally left one another alone. When the Europeans began grabbing North American land after 1500, the people they called "Indians" would have no means with which to fight them off.

CHAPTER OBJECTIVES

- Discuss the major events and trends in Tang and Song China.
- Describe the early history of Japan, particularly its political and social organization.
- Discuss the status of Korea during the period before AD 1000.
- Identify and describe the major civilizations of Mexico and of Central and South America.
- Describe the North American peoples who settled the continent in ancient times.

Chapter 10 Time Line

BC

●	2000	Mound Builders in the Ohio and Mississippi valleys
●	1400	Cult of Chavín
●	1200	Olmec civilization
●	200	Moche civilization
●	100	Establishment of Teotihuacán
		Anasazi culture takes shape in the southwestern desert

AD

●	300	Height of the Mayan civilization
●	618	Tang dynasty begins in China

668	Three Kingdoms period in Korea ends with Silla's victory over Koguryo
735	China concedes Korean independence
794	Heian period begins in Japan
907	Ten Kingdoms/Five Dynasties period begins in China
936	Koryo dynasty reunites Korean principalities
950	Toltec civilization begins
960	Song dynasty begins in China
1200	Aztecs settle in southern Mexico
	Manco Capac settles in Cuzco Valley
1438	Incan Empire
1450–1600	Iroquis Confederacy founded
1503	Montezuma II becomes Aztec emperor

China

The Tang Dynasty

The Tang dynasty embodied the culmination of much of the political and intellectual progress made under the Han dynasty. Tai Zong, who succeeded to the Chinese throne in AD 626, perfected the design of the Chinese government: a three-branch organization of the military, the ministers, and the censors, with the last functioning as the emperor's intelligence service. The emperor was the head of state, but it was the ministers' job to make and carry out policy. The inner court immediately around the emperor became highly liable to corruption under the Tang dynasty; the emperor's closest advisors often squabbled among themselves, typically exercising as much domination over him as they could. Since it was fairly common for a small child to become emperor, this influence could be considerable. The Dowager Empress (the widow of one emperor and the mother of his successor) could also wield considerable power during her son's minority.

The Han had initiated merit examinations for civil service positions; this tradition was expanded and emphasized under the Tang and would reach its final form in the Song era. The exam was designed to test the applicant's knowledge and understanding of Confucianism, his memory of the classics, his calligraphy, and his writing skills. Since it was extraordinarily difficult, it also tested his ability to perform under pressure. This exam would remain a requirement for government employment until 1905, and it had three major effects on the future of Chinese government. First, it created a strong link between government and scholarship; nothing like this existed in the West, where an administrator's practical abilities were of much greater concern. Second, it ensured that the state would maintain Chinese orthodoxy—in other words, Confucianism. This demonstrated a basic theme of Chinese history: resistance to innovation. Third, the examination proved a unifying factor for the administration for centuries to come; everyone who had a government post, whether stationed in remote provinces or in the capital, had the same training and the same scholarly background. Dynasties and emperors would rise and fall, but the makeup of the bureaucracy would remain a constant.

Tang society was divided into three ranks: the extended royal family, the nobles, and the commoners. It was unusual for commoners to move up in rank, although it sometimes happened, particularly as the result of military prowess or by acquiring a great fortune in trade. In theory, the civil service was a meritocracy because it required the passage of the exam; however, it would be all but impossible for a commoner to acquire the scholarly knowledge required to pass the exam.

Buddhism spread throughout the region during the Tang era; by the turn of the first millennium, it had taken firm hold in Korea and Japan. The fact that many Chinese also practiced Buddhism made it something of a unifying factor in the region. However, the Tang did not welcome religious diversity in their realm; the state dissolved thousands of Buddhist monasteries during this era. Since there is also persuasive evidence that the Chinese were tolerant of diversity and even welcomed some degree of it, some historians have speculated that the Tang may have been more concerned with seizing valuable property than with stamping out a belief system.

China reached its greatest geographical expansion to date under the Tang, acquiring control over the Silk Road and establishing protectorates as far west as Samarkand. Changan, the Tang capital, was considerably farther west than earlier Chinese capital cities and was undoubtedly the grandest and most impressive city in the world during this period. All the peoples using the Silk Road came to Changan; it absorbed Turks, Persians, Arabians, Koreans, Japanese, Indians, and peoples from the Southeast Asian kingdoms and islands. All of these various peoples brought in elements and ideas from their own cultures, all of which were assimilated into mainstream Chinese culture. This is particularly true of the Persian influence, since Persia was geographically close to China and thus its traders were the most numerous.

The Tang era was one of tremendous economic prosperity. Control over the Silk Road and the expansion of international trade created great wealth for China. Good harvests were another major reason for the economic surge. It was also an era of impressive artistic and cultural achievements; the manufacture of fine ceramics and other luxury goods was both aesthetically desirable and economically profitable, since these objects were highly valued by foreign customers. Chinese culture dominated the East Asian region.

The Tang army remained supreme in the region until the disastrous year of AD 751, when they lost two major battles. At the Battle of Talas River, the armies of the Abbasid caliphate took over Afghanistan, expanding the Muslim Empire as far as the Indus Valley. After the battle, the two sides agreed on a permanent border between the Tang and Abbasid empires. Another battle took place in the south, against the independent kingdom of Nanzhao; perhaps as many as sixty thousand Chinese soldiers fell in this battle.

Another heavy blow against the Tang state came in 755, when the military commander An Lushan led a rebellion against the emperor. Tens of thousands of Chinese supported him. Although the government eventually managed to put down the rebellion, it was severely and permanently weakened. This weakness was demonstrated in 787 when the Tibetans marched into Changan and sacked it; in 791, they struck again, defeating the Chinese near Beshbaliq. After this time, the Tang languished in power; provincial governors usurped much of their authority. The last Tang emperor was deposed in 907.

The Chinese population grew enormously in the Tang era—so much so that it began to impoverish the land, and this process continued gradually over the following centuries. As the country grew more and more crowded, land was divided into to more and more plots—with the plots, of course, becoming smaller and smaller. This meant even greater poverty and struggle for the subsistence farmers who made up the great majority of the Chinese population.

The Song Dynasty

The end of the Tang era ushered in a period of political disunity known in northern China as the era of the Five Dynasties (Liang, Tang, Zhin, Han, and Zhou) and in southern China as the era of Ten Kingdoms. China was not reunited under one government until AD 960, when general Zhao Kuang-yin founded the Song dynasty. He became its first emperor, ruling under the title Emperor Taizu until his death in 976.

Song China was geographically much smaller than Tang China, due to losses in the west. The Song faced continual military threats from the north, which caused them to withdraw to a more secure location farther south, establishing their capital in the coastal city of Hangzhou. The Central Asian states of Jin and Liao, ruled respectively by the Juchen and the Khitan, invaded northern China again and again; by 1127, the Juchen had overrun northern China. Khitan troops repeatedly attacked the Korean kingdom of Koryo; in 1011, they succeeded in establishing military rule. Within a decade, however, the Koreans rallied and decimated the Khitan armies.

The Chinese had invented paper in the second century AD and printing under the Tang dynasty. By the Song era, they had become probably the world's first culture to use paper currency. They were also printing books seven hundred years before the West acquired the technology; books were in great demand among the elite because of the intensive study required before taking the civil service exam. However, printed books did not result in near-universal literacy, as would happen in Europe. First, the Chinese language was written in characters, not in an alphabet of individual letters; this presented special problems for printing, because while Western alphabets generally have twenty-five or thirty letters, there are thousands of Chinese characters. Second, these special printing requirements meant that books remained expensive, out of the reach of the great mass of Chinese people. Books in the West, on the other hand, would remain affordable even by those who had small incomes.

Around AD 850, the Chinese invented gunpowder—another innovation that would not reach the West for centuries to come. However, the Chinese used gunpowder for fireworks and to exorcise demons in religious ceremonies; for whatever reason, they did not put it to military use. China had a history of military conquest and expansion, so guns would certainly have been useful. The traditional Chinese resistance to new practices and new ways of thinking may be the reason they did not develop guns.

Japan

Historians have drawn some useful parallels between Japan and Britain. Both are groups of large islands off the coast of a continent. Both are so near to the continent that their histories were unavoidably intertwined (although Japan is quite a bit farther from Korea than Britain is from France). At the same time, each island nation's geographical detachment from the mainland enabled it to maintain a certain degree of isolation from continental affairs. Britain was rarely invaded, and the last time was with the Norman Conquest of 1066; Japan was never successfully invaded at all, although it was heavily bombed and then occupied by foreign troops in 1945. All these factors significantly affected the development of Japan (and Britain).

Archeological evidence suggests that people migrated from China and the Korean peninsula to Japan in neolithic times. By the early centuries AD, Japan was showing all the signs of being an established civilization, complete with a religious system, a privileged warrior class, and an emperor (or empress) whom the people believed was descended from the sun goddess. The massive royal tombs, most notably that of the emperor Nintoku, who reigned at the turn of the fifth century, provide evidence of the Japanese reverence for the ruler.

From the beginning, the Japanese emperor played a more symbolic than political role; thus, the Japanese tradition is distinct from that of almost all other nations, where the monarch is the most powerful figure in the government. This imperial detachment from actual governing developed early in Japan's history and has remained a constant. This purely symbolic role probably accounts for the unique stability of the imperial dynasty; the Yamato family had established its power by the sixth century, and the current Japanese emperor is a direct descendant. No other ruling family in the history of the world has remained on a throne for so many centuries. There is no bar in Japanese law or custom to a female ruler; the first Japanese empress was Suiko, who acceded to the throne in AD 592.

Although China influenced Japan in many fundamental ways (see "The Yamato Period" and "The Nara Period" in this chapter), the position of the emperor was an exception. The Japanese believed that the emperor's divinity was hereditary and could not be questioned; therefore, the Chinese pattern of one dynasty replacing another would never occur in Japan. This belief in the importance of a person's birth extended to the Japanese aristocracy; the Japanese did not accept the Chinese idea of merit-based examination as a condition of government employment. In Japan, political conflict would consist of influential families jockeying for influence over the emperor and the court. In general, Confucianism took much less hold on Japanese ways of thinking than it did on Korean.

Positions in the Japanese civil service were reserved exclusively for the hereditary nobility, who received landed estates and tax exemption in return for their services to the government. These great landlords, in their turn, extended various protections and privileges to their tenants, who paid them in rent and in unswerving loyalty, ready to provide any type of service the landlord might command. These landlords soon acquired all political power in Japan; the most important social and political unit was the clan, or extended family network. Absolute loyalty to the clan was an article of faith with the Japanese. Clans used all available means to rival one another for power—everything from arranged marriages to assassination. Because Japan was so much smaller than a vast state like India or China, control over all of it was much more feasible. Therefore, the aim of all the powerful clans was to acquire so much influence at court that they themselves would rule the country (although, of course, the emperor would remain the titular head of the government).

The Yamato Period

The Yamato family used a combination of military power, diplomacy, and dynastic marriages to become the dominant clan and claim the imperial throne. Exactly when the first Yamato was recognized as emperor is a matter of debate, but the family was securely established on the throne by the late sixth century.

China was, of course, the dominant culture in East Asia and had a lasting influence on the development of Japan. The Chinese system of writing came to Japan during the Yamato period; Confucianism and Buddhism were also introduced to Japan at this time. Prince Shotoku, whom the Empress Suiko appointed as her regent in AD 593, sponsored several study missions to China, encouraging his envoys to observe and note Chinese ideas and social and political customs. As a result of his envoy's reports, Prince Shotoku oversaw the centralization of the Japanese government and is credited with the authorship of the Seventeen-Article Constitution. This document, written in AD 604, is Japan's first written constitution; it is strikingly different from the Western concept of such a document, as it lays much more stress on the moral behavior required of the ministers than on their exact duties and qualifications for office.

Prince Shotoku was an educated Buddhist and encouraged the spread of Buddhism throughout Japan; it proved quite compatible with the traditional Japanese religion, called Shinto. In fact, the scholar Saicho would unite the two into one religion during the Heian period. Shintoism had none of the features of the Near Eastern religions—no written scriptures, no identifiable founder, and no codified rules. Shintoism involves the worship of local or personal gods at the appropriate shrines; hence its compatibility, like Chinese ancestor worship, with more formalized religions.

The Nara Period

Japanese political, social, and religious customs crystallized in the Nara period, which lasted from about AD 710 to 784; the traditions established in this era would pervade Japan until the nineteenth century. The period is named for the capital city, which featured impressive and beautiful buildings in the Chinese architectural style.

The Fujiwara Clan

The wealthy and powerful Fujiwara clan rose to prominence in the ninth century, achieving a stifling influence over the imperial family. Several members of the Fujiwara family had married into the royal family; these close family connections allowed the Fujiwara lords to exercise considerable political influence over the emperor.

Fujiwara Mototsune was appointed as regent to a child emperor in 877, after having served in an important political post. Mototsune soon established himself as a dictator, taking all the power of the state into his hands; a highly capable and strong-willed man, he remained the sole ruler of Japan until his death in 891.

The Fujiwara would remain in power until the end of the twelfth century; historians consider that many of them were able and talented governors. Fujiwara Tokihira, who held the post of senior statesman at the turn of the tenth century, issued a series of edicts that show a serious, balanced attempt—although an unsuccessful one—to reform provincial corruption. The Fujiwara established many important themes of Japanese governing practice during their supremacy, including the importance of loyalty to one's clan and the custom of rising in the social and political scale by patronage. They also firmly established the tradition of court intrigue, scheming, and manipulation that was to characterize Japanese political history for centuries to follow.

The Heian Period

The Fujiwara oversaw the Heian period of Japanese history, which began in AD 794 with the move of the capital to Nagaoka; considering the location to be ill-omened, the court moved in 804 to Heian (present-day Kyoto). The Heian period would last into the twelfth century; the political stability of Fujiwara supremacy led to prosperity and peace. The Heian period was a high-water mark of Japanese literature, art, and culture, and an era of courtly sophistication.

Korea

Korea's geographical location accounts for much of its early history. Because it lay between China and Japan, it served as a connection between the two; many aspects of Chinese culture, such as Confucianism and Buddhism, first reached Japan through its trade and communications with Korea and with Korean traders and scholars. Because Korea bordered on China, but was only a fraction of China's size, it was politically subordinate to China for much of its history. Korea also absorbed Chinese culture and customs; Confucianism pervaded Korean traditions as it did Chinese.

By 57 BC, Korea was organized into three kingdoms: Silla in the southeast, Paekche in the southwest, and Koguryo in the north. In AD 660, Silla crushed Paekche, then went on to defeat Koguryo in 668. The Koguryo general Tae Cho-yong established the new state of Bohai in the northwest, and the Koreans built a wall that constituted a border between the two.

In 735, China conceded Korean independence; until that time, Korea had been a tributary state, making regular payments to China and promising political loyalty. The separation between the two was peaceable, characterized by frequent travel and trade. Silla had organized its government along Chinese lines, with an absolute monarch ruling over provincial officials and a central bureaucracy. In the ninth century, the Korean parliament became stronger as the king became weaker, leading to the fragmentation of the kingdom into several principalities. The northern principality of Koryo, established in 918, united all the principalities under one rule in 936, thus restoring a unified Korean state. Korea takes its name from the kingdom of Koryo. The Koryo dynasty would remain in power until 1392.

The Americas

Latin America

Land and Climates

The name *Latin America* is an anachronism for describing the era before colonization, but historians tend to use it for convenience, rather than writing out "Mexico and Central and South America." The name *Latin America* comes from the fact that the entire area speaks the Latin languages Portuguese and Spanish, Spain and Portugal being the conquering powers throughout the region.

Latin America has three main geographical features: its mountains, its plains, and its rain forest. Mexico is covered by highland plateaus that lie between the eastern and western ranges of the Sierra Madres. The Andes Mountains run the length of South America's west coast. The highest peaks of the Andes are in Peru; they are among the highest mountains in the world. The southern plains of South America provide land for farming and raising cattle. The rain forest, which occupies most of the Amazon River Basin, is the largest in the world. The Amazon River begins in the Andes and flows four thousand miles eastward to the Atlantic Ocean.

Human beings are not native to the Americas; they migrated there from somewhere else. Scholars believe that nomadic Asian peoples crossed a land bridge (long since underwater) from Siberia to Alaska, probably migrating in search of food. Some of these ancient immigrants settled in Alaska, while others continued to move south and east, eventually settling all the habitable areas of the Americas. This may have happened as early as 40,000 BC or as recently as 15,000 BC; the oldest human remains yet discovered in North America date from about 14,000 BC.

Early Civilizations of Mexico

American civilization became possible around 2700 BC, with the cultivation of maize, or corn; the ability to grow a staple crop eventually led to a surplus of food, a rise in population, and the organization of a society. The first known civilization in the Americas, the Olmec, developed along the Gulf Coast of Mexico around 1200 BC. This was an ideal area for farming because rivers frequently flooded, thus providing irrigation. The Olmecs also supplemented their diet with fish. They were a relatively sophisticated people, developing a calendar and carving giant stone heads, some of which weighed several tons. They built large stone courts on which to play ball games; the Olmec made their balls from rubber, which grew in abundance in the region.

The Zapotecs settled in southern Mexico, in the present-day state of Oxaca. They had developed a writing system by 500 BC. Monte Alban, their capital city and home to thirty thousand people, featured stone buildings, large plazas, and ceremonial pyramids.

Teotihuacán was an even larger city than Monte Alban. Located just northeast of modern Mexico City, Teotihuacán was home to one hundred twenty-five thousand people at its height. From about 100 BC to AD 750, this city flourished as the most important political, religious, and economic power in Mexico. At the city's center was a broad boulevard called The Street of the

Dead; prominently located along this central avenue was what we would today call the central business district. It featured the city's administrative building (the Ciudadela), its religious temples (the Pyramids of the Sun and Moon), and its largest market. The residential areas were stone apartment buildings surrounding the city's center.

Society was divided into three ranks. The largest group was the farmers, who went outside the city every day to work their land. The next group included artisans, builders, merchants, and warriors. The highest rank comprised the priest-rulers who governed the city.

Mayan Civilization

The Mayan civilization, which occupied all the land between the Yucatán peninsula and Guatemala, flourished from about AD 300 to 900. It was not a unified empire but a number of independent city-states or kingdoms linked by a common language and culture. The king occupied the top place in the Mayan social pyramid; the priests and hereditary nobles, many of whom played prominent roles in the government, came next. Artisans and merchants ranked below the nobility, followed by the peasants, laborers, and slaves.

The Mayan religion was polytheistic, as were most religions in the ancient world. Priests performed daily rituals to please the gods, who were believed to control the weather. The Mayans built huge pyramids as temples to the gods, decorating them with murals depicting historical scenes or legends.

The pyramids and murals were only two examples of the Mayans' remarkable achievements in the arts and sciences. Their 365¼-day calendar was the most accurate in the world at that time. Their writing system used glyphs to represent words and symbols. Like the Romans, the Mayans were outstanding engineers and road builders; Mayan roads linked the city-states, easing trade and communication.

The success of the Mayan Empire was based on agriculture. The Mayans cleared forests and built raised fields on which they sowed their crops; because the fields were raised, drainage was good even when too much rain fell. Historians have interpreted the available evidence to calculate that a good Mayan harvest could feed twenty thousand people.

The Toltecs

The Toltecs, an ethnically mixed group that included refugees from Teotihuacán, dominated central Mexico from about AD 950 to 1200. Tula, the Toltecs' capital city, was located about forty miles from modern Mexico City.

A farming and trading people with a sophisticated religious system, Toltecs worshiped a god called Quetzalcoatl, meaning "plumed serpent." The quetzal, a South American bird, symbolized the sky, while the coatl, or snake, stood for the earth. *Quetzalcoatl* therefore symbolized a union of earth and sky. Teotihuacán's Temple of the Plumed Serpent includes carved friezes and paintings of Quetzalcoatl. In the tenth century, a Toltec priest called Ce Acatl Topiltzín became identified with the god Quetzalcoatl. Topiltzín became a recluse and eventually disappeared from his kingdom. Aztec leaders would claim that they ruled by right of their descent from Topiltzín. The Toltecs and Aztecs always believed Topiltzín Quetzalcoatl would return; this belief brought disaster to them when the first Europeans reached Mexico. Having no understanding of where these people had come from, with their bizarre (in Aztec eyes) clothing and facial features and their incomprehensible language, the Aztecs accepted them as divine rather than recognizing them as invaders.

The Aztec Empire

The Aztecs moved into the central plain of Mexico around AD 1200. Their capital city was Tenochtitlán on Lake Texcoco in central Mexico. They settled there in AD 1324 on the appearance of an eagle perched on a cactus growing from a rock—a sign the prophets had promised them they would find.

By the mid-1400s, the Aztecs had developed a unified empire with one ruler. Aztec policy was based on conquest and expansion; warriors invaded the city-states surrounding their capital, forcing the conquered people to pay them tribute in gold or in kind (usually maize, tobacco, or precious stones). They took many prisoners of war, enslaving some and using others for the ceremonies of human sacrifice that were central to the polytheistic Aztec religion.

Because the land around Lake Texcoco was swampy and difficult to farm, the Aztecs had to use their ingenuity. They invented a remarkable system of floating farms called *chinampas*—large rafts made of reeds covered with a layer of earth. The reed platform provided excellent drainage for the crops.

In the Aztec Empire, both girls and boys were educated. They studied civics, history, and religion in addition to the use of weapons (for boys) and the arts of healing (for girls). Aztec women had certain rights; they could own property and enter certain professions, such as midwife, weaver, priestess, or musician.

/ Early Peoples of Peru

Ancient Peru, on the Pacific coast between Chile and Colombia, was home to the Incan Empire, which became the most powerful in Latin America up to the time of the European conquest. However, the Incan civilization was not the first in the region. The cult of Chavín was a religious movement that lasted from about 1400 to 400 BC. The followers of Chavín left no written records, but archaeologists continue to study their architectural ruins and works of art. These include stone or adobe temples decorated with carvings or paintings of animals—jaguars, serpents, and caimans (a type of alligator)—and images of Chavín gods.

The Moche civilization emerged about 200 to 100 BC. This was a military culture that controlled a vast area of land. The Moche were skilled engineers, building roads, irrigation systems, and canals that brought water from the mountains to the valleys. As is the case with the cult of Chavín, only artistic and architectural remains of the Moche have survived. Unlike most ancient American art, Moche portraits are realistic representations of individuals. Moche murals, figurines, and other works of art show people from every level of society involved in a wide variety of activities. Historians believe that the Moche civilization collapsed around AD 900 from economic failure, which may have been caused by changes to the climate.

The Incan Empire

Little beyond legend is known of early Incan history. Most accounts state that around AD 1200, Manco Capac and his brothers and sisters traveled a few miles southwest of their home in the town of Pacaritambo to settle in the valley of Cuzco. Manco Capac is considered the first Inca ruler.

The Incas held the valley by force of arms, attacking and conquering adjoining lands, until by AD 1438 they had taken over the entire Cuzco valley. Led by Prince Inca Yupanqui, the Incas fought and won a decisive battle against invaders from the south. Inca Yupanqui took the name Pachacuti and became the first of the great Incan emperors. Under Pachacuti's rule, the Incas built their capital city of Cuzco, expanded their empire, and subdued all other peoples in the region.

The Incan government was a hereditary monarchy. The emperor was the chief male member of the ruling family, and his successors were his direct descendants. Each of the four quarters of the Incan Empire had its own governor. Members of the extended royal family and the nobility filled these posts, as well as most other important government offices. They were considered the only purebred Incas and comprised the highest social rank. The Hahua Incas, nobles from the outlying provinces, filled any remaining high offices. Hahua were considered Incas by adoption and ranked below the purebred Incas. Below them were the lower-ranking provincial nobles, who ruled the large estates and the people who worked the land on them. Lowest of all in the social scale were the artisans, traders, workers, peasants, and slaves. Incan society was not mobile; a soldier might rise in rank, or a servant might become a royal favorite, but most Incans died in the same social position in which they were born.

The Incan government provided an unusual degree of social services, including food, clothing, and public feasts on holidays. However, it was authoritarian, requiring travel permits and maintaining strict laws about dress.

Pachacuti's son, Topa Inca, succeeded him in AD 1471. Within five years, Topa Inca had greatly expanded the empire. His soldiers conquered the Chimú, the only serious remaining threat to Inca supremacy in the region. Conquest brought cultural exchange, with Chimú artists influencing Incan artistic styles and methods.

Huayna Capac succeeded his father Topa Inca in AD 1493. He abandoned Cuzco to fight wars in the north, and his long absences created difficulties at home. Rivals for power began gaining followers. When Huayna Capac and his heir both died in 1527, it was apparent that others would have to fight for the throne. Atahualpa, one of two rival brothers, won the conflict after a bloody war. He was the last of the independent Inca rulers before the Spanish conquest of Latin America.

The planned city of Cuzco was designed in the shape of a puma, or mountain lion, an animal sacred to the Incas. A fortress temple was built at the head of the puma, and the residential buildings and palaces were laid out in a grid along the shape of its body. Houses were built in groups around rectangular or square enclosures. Four highways, one leading to each of the four quarters of the Incan Empire, originated in Cuzco's central plaza. Because the region was mountainous, many Incan roads were built in a zigzag pattern rather than going straight up the steep grade of the slope. This meant that the army would be able to march farther, as climbing the gradual slope of the zigzag path takes much less energy than marching straight up a steep hill.

The Incas undertook many other building projects. They were highly skilled architects, able to build stone walls that needed no mortar to hold them together. They built roads, highways, and palaces, including Pachacuti's estate Machu Picchu. This palace remained unknown except to locals until 1911, when American historian Hiram Bingham stumbled upon it. High in the Andes, Machu Picchu provides a breathtaking record of Incan civilization.

The empire's well-built roads made the postal system possible. Runners called *chasqui* carried messages along the roads. Every three miles, they would come to a rest house where they would pass their message on to the next runner. Soldiers on the march could also stop to refresh themselves at these rest houses. Despite the remarkable level of their artistic and architectural achievements, the Incas had no writing system; therefore, the runners had to carry the messages in their memories. If the message involved numbers or amounts of money, a runner might carry a *quipu*—a long string to which several smaller strings were tied. Knots, different colors of string, and methods of twisting the strings indicated different numbers or amounts.

The Incan religion, like many other ancient religions, was polytheistic, with gods who represented and controlled various aspects of nature—thunder, the sun, the moon, the earth, and the sea. The sun god was the special patron of the Incas. Their chief god was Viracocha, whom they considered the creator of their people. In addition to the gods, the Incas believed in nature spirits called Huacas. Any unusual natural phenomenon, such as an oddly shaped rock, indicated the presence of a Huaca.

The emperor Pachacuti was the first to organize the Incan system of beliefs into a state religion. He ordered temples built to all the major gods. Under his rule, the Incas developed a specific calendar of religious festivals, most of which were tied to important seasons in the farming year, such as planting and harvesting. Their chief religious concern was to pray to the gods for good health and a good harvest.

North America

The area that became the United States and Canada developed very differently from Latin America. Pre-Columbian North America had no unified empires, no cities, no writing systems, and no palaces. Instead, it had a number of small civilizations that survived by hunting, gathering, farming, and a minimal amount of trading with one another. Society remained largely tribal. These early North Americans adapted themselves to the local climates, developing a wide variety of cultures, languages, styles of dress and architecture, and belief systems.

These early cultures lacked many of the key ingredients of civilization. They were not literate, they did not develop money economies based on trade, and they were subsistence farmers and hunters. However, they developed complex belief systems and created impressive and beautiful examples of art and architecture. For example, the southwestern Anasazi used adobe bricks to build what resemble modern apartment buildings, such as the famous Cliff Palace in present-day Mesa Verde, Colorado. They also dug large, shallow pits and built domed log roofs over them; these *kivas* were used for ceremonial gatherings and important meetings. The Pueblos built small adobe towns around central plazas that looked to the invading Spaniards exactly like their own small towns—*pueblos*—at home. To this day, the Pueblo are renowned for their beautiful pottery, of which many ancient examples still exist in museums.

The first Americans developed a variety of belief systems. The Pueblo religion was largely based on prayers for a good harvest—crucial to survival in the harsh Southwestern climate. Pueblos worshipped *kachinas*—spirits of ancestors who return to earth in the forms of plants, animals, or people. They held *kachina* dances to honor these spirits, believing that they had the power to heal the sick and to bring rain.

The early Navajo and Apache were hunters who used bows and arrows to hunt and harpoons to spear fish. They followed the herds on which they depended for food. Over time, the Navajo turned more and more to farming and grew more and more settled. The Apache, on the other hand, did not abandon their nomadic warrior culture until they were forced to by the encroachment of the United States government on their lands in the nineteenth century. Unable to survive on hunting alone, the Apache often raided settled villages, stealing food, livestock, and other supplies. In Apache culture, the courage and skill it took to make a raid successful were highly valued.

The Mound Builders of the Mississippi and Ohio river valleys are named for the structures they built. Among the first people to settle in this fertile area were the Adena, who arrived in the valley about 2000 BC. The Adena built mounds of dirt over the graves of their leaders and chiefs, burying bodies close together and adding another layer to the mound with each burial. Archaeologists have found copper, silver, and mica ornaments, jewelry, pottery, and pipes in these graves. The Adena and their descendants, the Hopewell, were famous for their artistic skills.

Not all mounds were built to honor the dead. The Great Serpent Mound, built two thousand years ago and still standing in Ohio, is in the shape of a snake uncoiling itself, showing its wide jaws and sharp teeth. The Adena and Hopewell built many mounds to honor animals or animal spirits. The Mississippi people, who settled farther south, built temple mounds as well as burial mounds. Some of these earthen pyramids reach a height of 100 feet. Archaeologists have found many tools and ornaments made of clay, shell, marble, copper, and mica inside the pyramids, with decorative motifs such as skulls, bones, weeping eyes, and images of death. The Mound Builders died out in the seventeenth century; historians speculate that crop failure or war were the most likely causes.

The Iroquois of present-day New York State are historically remarkable for the Iroquois Confederacy—probably the world's earliest example of an international (or rather intertribal) peacekeeping organization. The Iroquois are a nation that comprises several tribes, including the Mohawk, the Onondaga, and the Huron. Unlike most tribes, the Iroquois often fought among themselves; their common language and culture and their geographical proximity frequently led to conflict over territory or hunting grounds.

Historians are not certain of the exact founding date of the Iroquois Confederacy; most agree on a time frame of AD 1450 to 1600. Hiawatha of the Onondaga and Deganawidah of the Huron envisioned a council of elders and chiefs from each Iroquois tribe; the council would discuss issues of importance to their people and settle disputes. The tribal chiefs embraced the plan, agreeing to meet regularly under the Great Tree of Peace, which symbolized a healthy mind and body, compassion for others, and physical strength and civil authority. These principles would balance one another and bring about a stable and lasting peace.

Five Iroquois tribes participated: Mohawk, Seneca, Onondaga, Oneida, and Cayuga. (The Tuscarora would join the confederacy later.) Each nation had its own council. The women of each tribe nominated the chiefs, taking polls among their relatives so that everyone's opinion was heard. In effect, the chiefs, called *sachems*, were elected by popular vote. The sachems' most important duty was to maintain peace within the confederacy, basing their decisions on the welfare of the people. Sachems were cautioned against losing their tempers or making hasty judgments. They could be removed from office if they committed crimes or missed too many council meetings.

The Mohawk and Seneca chiefs, called the Elder Brothers, were the first to debate any question that came before the council. They would reach an agreement, then explain their decision to the Oneida and Cayuga chiefs—the Younger Brothers. If they disagreed, the question would be taken to the Onondaga chief for a final decision. If they agreed, the Onondaga chief still had the power to adjust their decision to conform with the Great Law of the Iroquois.

QUIZ

1. Which of these made civilization possible in Latin America?
   A. the European conquest
   B. the development of writing
   C. the ability to cultivate maize
   D. the mild climate

2. _____ is the author of Japan's first written constitution.
   A. Fujiwara Mototsune
   B. Prince Shotoku
   C. Fujiwara Tokihira
   D. Empress Suiko

3. The Incan Empire is unique in history as a complex empire that did not have _____.
   A. a foreign policy of expansion and conquest
   B. absolute monarchs
   C. a system of writing
   D. hereditary right to rule

4. The Khitan people of Central Asia invaded and conquered _____ in the early eleventh century.
   A. China
   B. Japan
   C. Korea
   D. Persia

5. An Lushan is historically significant for _____.
   A. leading a major uprising against the Tang emperor
   B. sacking the capital city of Changan
   C. sending envoys to China to learn about its culture
   D. being the first empress of Japan

6. Which tradition learned from China had the least influence on Japan?
   A. hereditary monarchy
   B. Confucianism
   C. Buddhism
   D. the Chinese writing system

7. **What was the major long-term consequence of China's rise in population?**
   A. the enlargement of the army
   B. the division of China into several kingdoms
   C. the impoverishment of the land and the peasantry
   D. the revocation of the civil service exam

8. **The Chinese invented all of the following except _____.**
   A. the printing process
   B. paper
   C. gunpowder
   D. the pendulum clock

9. **The kingdom of _____ overcame the other Korean kingdoms in the seventh century.**
   A. Bohai
   B. Koguryo
   C. Paekche
   D. Silla

10. **Which best defines the Iroquois Confederacy?**
    A. a popular democracy
    B. a parliamentary legislature
    C. an intertribal peacekeeping organization
    D. a nation of several tribes

11

The Rise of the Turks, 1000–1500

The beginning of the second millennium saw the rapid rise to international power of the Turks—the universal name for the peoples descended from the nomadic warrior tribes of the steppes of Central Asia. The Turks are ethnically and culturally related to one another, hence it is reasonably accurate to use the same designation for all of them.

Geography and environment were the forces dictating the Turks' development as herding and roaming peoples. The steppes were grasslands that were not conducive to farming or permanent settlement because there were few sources of fresh water and very little rainfall. The Turks were always on the move with their herds because if they stayed in one place for too long, the animals would have eaten all the grass.

Persians, Arabians, and Egyptians had great respect for the Turks' skilled horsemanship and their fearlessness in battle, often enslaving them or hiring them as mercenaries. Because the concept of slavery in the medieval Near East was very different from the racism and insistence on total subordination that would characterize North American slavery in the nineteenth century, Turkish slave soldiers had the potential to rise high in the army. Military life encouraged communication, mass gatherings, and bonding among the troops, and, of course, it also provided them with weapons, clearly defined leadership, and the habit of discipline. By the early eleventh century, the Turks were using these assets to seize power from their masters. By 1500, Turks ruled Egypt, southeastern Europe, the Near East, and India.

The ancient Greeks had lost to the Romans on the battlefield, but Greek culture remained supreme under the Roman Empire. In the same way, the Arabians gave way to Turkish military might, but the Turks continued to practice the Arabian religion of Islam throughout the region.

The armies of Western Europe united against the Turkish Muslims in a series of military expeditions called the Crusades. The Christians briefly took over the eastern Mediterranean, but they recognized defeat at the hands of the Turks before 1300.

CHAPTER OBJECTIVES

- Characterize the Turks, including their origins and their culture.
- Identify the various states that fell under Turkish domination between 1000 and 1500.
- Describe the causes and outcome of the Crusades.

Chapter 11 Time Line

- 1055   Turks take Baghdad
- 1071   Battle of Manzikert
- 1095   First Crusade
- 1146   Second Crusade
- 1187   Saladin takes Jerusalem
- 1188   Third Crusade
- 1198   Fourth Crusade
- 1217   Fifth Crusade
- 1250   Mamluk sultanate begins in Egypt
- 1258   Mongols sack Baghdad
- 1291   Mamluks capture Acre
- 1354   Ottomans invade Balkans

- **1363**   Tamerlane becomes khan at Samarkand
- **1389**   Ottomans take over Balkans at Battle of Kosovo
- **1453**   Ottomans take Constantinople

The Turks in Persia and Egypt

As the turn of the first millennium approached, the Abbasid caliphate went into a steep decline, suffering several crushing blows to its political and even its religious authority. The region remained largely Islamic, but with an important change in Persia—an era of Shiite supremacy began that continues to this day.

The Buyids of Persia were rivals to the Abbasids, partly as a matter of political and territorial competition and partly because they were Shiite Muslims. The Buyids captured Baghdad, the Abbasid capital, in 945. Under Buyid rule, the Abbasids remained in their royal place in the hierarchy, but only as puppets of the Shiite scholars who took most of the high political and administrative offices. This placed all the strands of Persian social, political, and legal authority in Shiite hands (see Chapter 16).

The Oguz Turks, Sunni Muslim converts, invaded the Iranian plateau in 1038 and reached Baghdad in 1055. Their victory ended the reign of the Buyid dynasty and began the reign of the Turkish Seljuks. The Oguz troops went on to defeat the Byzantine army at Manzikert in 1071. This loss is historically important for three reasons. First, it clearly spelled disaster for the Byzantine Empire; warfare between Byzantines and Turks would drag on for a while, but the Byzantines would never recover their supremacy in the region. Second, it inspired the Byzantine emperor to turn to the pope in Rome for assistance; this led to a call to arms from the Church in the West and brought the Crusaders to the East to fight the Turks (see "The Crusades" in this chapter). Third, the Battle of Manzikert marked a turning point in the region. From this time on, Turkish dynasties would replace the Arabian and Western European ones that had ruled supreme until then.

The Seljuk ruler, Malik Shah, found himself in control of a Sunni empire that stretched from the eastern shore of the Bosporus through Persia to the steppes. Malik Shah himself ruled over the central core of this empire, installing other members of the Seljuk family as sultans in the outlying provinces. Malik Shah had a dominant personality; the combination of this and his generosity in rewarding his nobles and commanders allowed him to maintain supreme control over all until his death in 1092. The Seljuk dynasty remained in power for a time, losing control of Syria by 1117, eastern Iran by the 1150s, and western Iran by 1194. However, the family would continue to flourish in Anatolia until the thirteenth century. The Iranian-Turkish Ghurids ruled eastern Iran from about 1150 to 1204, when they were defeated in battle.

The Abbasids also lost Egypt, where the Shiite Fatimids established a dynasty in 909. They founded the city of Cairo as their capital. Many of the Kurdish soldiers in the Egyptian army threw their support to Saladin, founder of the Ayyubid dynasty; under his leadership they overthrew the Fatimids in 1171 (see "The Crusades" below). The Ayyubids were Sunni Muslims; therefore this change of dynasty restored Sunni authority in Egypt. Around 1250, the Mamluks—Turkish slave-soldiers and mercenaries who made up the great bulk of the Egyptian army—rose up against the Ayyubids. The Mamluk Turks staged a palace coup in Cairo, thus establishing themselves as the rulers of Egypt. They would remain in power until 1517.

In 1059, the Fatimids took over Baghdad, but their reign over Persia was brief; it had waned by the end of the eleventh century, due to provincial rebellions and palace coups.

The Crusades

The Crusades were a series of European military expeditions against Islamic power in the Near East. Both Christians and Muslims would claim that these were holy wars; the Muslims were defending their territory against the Christian heathens, while the Christians were trying to retake once-Christian territory from the Islamic heathens. From a modern perspective, of course, these wars were territorial and political struggles, with the cloak of a religious imperative thrown over them as a rallying point and a justification.

The Crusades began when the Byzantine emperor appealed to the pope for aid in the long, losing struggle against Turkish aggression. Realizing that success in battle against the Muslims would add significantly to his and the Church's prestige, the pope agreed to raise an army that would sail east from the major port cities of Venice and Genoa. Motivated by a variety of forces, thousands of Europeans answered the call. First, the mass of knights and vassals had an absolute obligation to serve their lords; they had no choice but to accompany their lords on the Crusades if so ordered. Second, the call to arms had come from the Church; that meant the Crusade would be considered a holy pilgrimage that would earn the soldiers official forgiveness for any sins they committed. Third was desire for a share of the plunder; the Crusaders were well aware that there were great riches and valuables to be seized in the East. Last was the common human sense of adventure and the desire to see new places.

The First Crusade embarked from Europe in 1095; it resulted in the establishment of four Christian states in the eastern Mediterranean. These were Jerusalem, Tripoli, Antioch, and Acre—fundamentally the same territory that comprises present-day Syria, Lebanon, and Israel. The taking (the Christians considered it retaking) of Jerusalem was symbolically the most important victory, because Christians believed that the site of Jesus's grave should be in Christian hands.

The primary reason for the success of the First Crusade probably lies in the squabbling and conflict among the various Turkish ruling factions. Malik Shah's descendants ruled Aleppo and Damascus, but they were at daggers drawn with one another and with all other rulers in the region. However, the Turks managed to hold off the troops of the Second Crusade, which ended in 1148 with the European failure to take Damascus.

The turning point of the Crusades came in 1154, when the Turk Nur al-Din, who had by then succeeded to the throne of Aleppo, annexed Mosul and Damascus. When the Christian king of Jerusalem sent troops into Egypt to defeat the Fatimid dynasty, Nur al-Din sent his general Saladin after them. Saladin and his followers quickly defeated the Europeans; in 1171, they proceeded to overthrow the Fatimids, thus establishing the Ayyubid dynasty in Egypt and restoring Sunni Muslim rule.

A few short years after Nur al-Din's death, Saladin overpowered his rivals and installed himself as Nur al-Din's successor. In 1187, he and his troops defeated the Crusaders in a battle near the Sea of Galilee. A determined attack by King Richard I of England at the head of the troops of the Third Crusade nearly defeated Saladin in 1189, but after Richard fell in battle, the Europeans were forced to acknowledge that they had been beaten. The Europeans lost the Fifth Crusade in 1221; seventy years later, the Mamluks captured Acre, ending the era of Christian rule in the Near East.

The Turks in India

Mahmud, an Afghani Turk, began to lead raids into India around the year 1000. In short order, he annexed Punjab and Sind into his own realm, which he ruled from Afghanistan. Although Mahmud cast his conquests in a religious light as an attempt to convert more people to Islam, the Indians were more inclined to believe that his sole motive was plunder of their jewels, gold, and artistic treasures. Although Mahmud showed no desire to live in India as its emperor, he clearly appreciated its culture; he kidnapped a number of Indian artisans and architects and took them west to work for him. Mahmud left an army of occupation behind him, headed by the Hindu Indian general Tilak.

Many Muslims had come into India from the northwest over the previous three centuries, and, like other foreign populations, had been assimilated into the larger Indian culture with little fuss or disruption. Indians generally opposed Mahmud, however, because he imposed Islam on their country as a by-product of military conquest.

Mahmud died in 1030; India remained undisturbed by further invasions for more than fifty years, until Shahab-ud-Din of the Ghurids (Iranian Turks) rode in from the northwest and overthrew Mahmud's empire. Prithvi Raj, the Hindu king of Delhi, defeated the Ghurids and drove them back west, but they returned one year later. By the late 1100s, the Ghurids were securely installed in Delhi, but only for a short time. They were soon superseded by a new wave of invaders from Afghanistan.

By 1211, the Afghanis had established a Turkish Muslim sultanate in Delhi. It would quickly expand to embrace all of northern India. By 1335, it ruled supreme over the entire Indian subcontinent apart from three tiny patches, one at each corner of the great triangle of the peninsula.

The Afghani Turks were Indo-Aryans, ethnically related to those who had invaded India in ancient times. This fundamental kinship with the population allowed them to be more readily accepted and assimilated into India than their Ghurid predecessors. The Turks brought their religion and culture with them; under their rule, India became religiously Islamic, culturally Persian, and politically and administratively Turkish. The invaders showed no racial or religious scorn for their new subjects, and intermarriage between Muslim court officials and Hindu women was frequent. Even sultans married high-caste Hindu women.

The Delhi sultanate lasted until 1398, when it abruptly fell before the advance of the great conqueror Timur, usually referred to in the West as Tamerlane (a corruption of "Timur the Lame," a taunt the Persians used against Timur after he was injured on the battlefield). A native of the steppes of Central Asia, Tamerlane rose through the military ranks to become khan at Samarkand in 1363. One of history's most successful and brutal military conquerors, Tamerlane led his troops into Persia, India, Mesopotamia, Syria, and Anatolia; he had conquered all of these lands and states by 1402. His descendants would continue to rule Iran and Turkestan for another century, although the rest of the empire he acquired would fall into other hands long before that.

/ The Turks in Byzantium

After the Oguz Turks defeated the Byzantine army at Manzikert, they pushed on to Syria and Palestine, which they occupied by 1078. They reestablished Sunni ideology in the region. As of the late thirteenth century, a number of Turkish tribes were occupying the Anatolian highlands. Osman, who proved to be the strongest of the tribal leaders, founded the Ottoman dynasty in 1281.

Throughout seven centuries of steady warfare and continual attacks, the Islamic forces had never managed to take Constantinople; its fortifications were too strong for the weapons that existed in the early medieval period. With the development of artillery, however, the Turks finally succeeded in their objective. Constantinople fell to the Ottomans in 1453, marking the end of the Byzantine Empire and the beginning of the slow transition from Greek to Turkish cultural supremacy in the region. The change of Constantinople's name to Istanbul is symbolic of this turning point in history. The Ottomans would go on to take over most of the Balkans. By 1517, they had absorbed Syria and Egypt into their new empire, and in 1538, they conquered the Arabian Peninsula (see Figure 11.1). These victories set the seal on the domination of Turkish Muslims over Arabian Muslims until after the Arab Revolt of 1916.

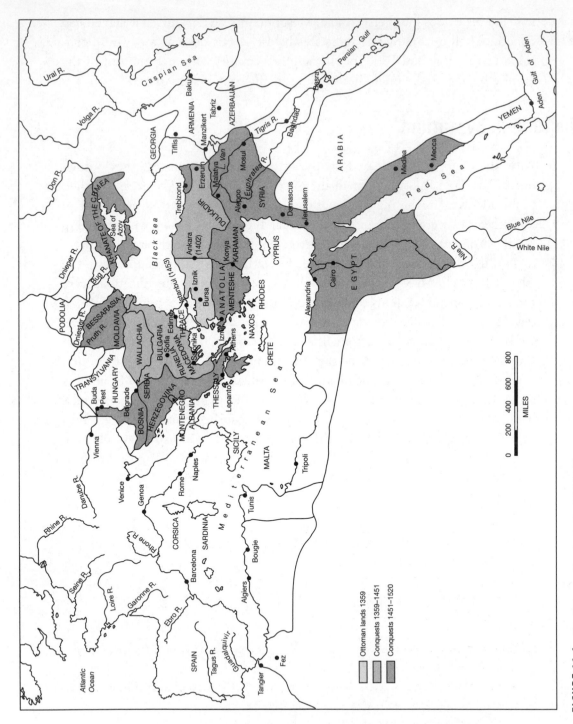

FIGURE 11.1   The Ottoman Empire in the Mid-1500s

QUIZ

1. Participants on both sides described the Crusades as _____.
   A. attempts to expand an empire
   B. wars of political aggression
   C. defensive territorial wars
   D. holy wars against the heathens

2. The Arabians' _____ was their most important and lasting contribution to the history of the Near East.
   A. religion
   B. language
   C. artistic style
   D. political structure

3. What finally enabled the Ottoman Turks to take Constantinople in 1453?
   A. political weakness in Byzantium
   B. the development of artillery
   C. military reinforcements from the West
   D. a strong power base in Egypt

4. As a result of the First Crusade, the Europeans temporarily established Christian kingdoms in all these present-day states except _____.
   A. Egypt
   B. Israel
   C. Lebanon
   D. Syria

5. The Ayyubid conquest of Egypt in 1171 restored _____ authority there.
   A. Christian
   B. pagan
   C. Shiite Muslim
   D. Sunni Muslim

6. One probable reason for the Indian acceptance of the Afghani sultanate that ruled from 1211 to 1398 was _____.
   A. the ethnic relationship between the Afghani Turks and the ancient Indians
   B. the Afghani Turks' willingness to convert to Hinduism
   C. the Turks' decision to dismantle the caste system
   D. the Turks' military successes in the Near East

7. _____ is historically important as the founder of the Ayyubid dynasty.
   A. Mahmud
   B. Osman
   C. Saladin
   D. Tamerlane

8. All these except _____ are probable motives for Western European knights and vassals to join the Crusades.
   A. desire to earn forgiveness of their sins
   B. obedience to the commands of their lords
   C. greed for valuable prizes and plunder
   D. desire to emigrate permanently to the Near East

9. _____ ensured that the ancient Turkish tribes of the steppes would establish a migratory herder culture.
   A. The physical environment
   B. Military threats from outside
   C. Religious imperative
   D. Scientific discoveries

10. As a result of conquest, Turkish culture began to replace _____ culture in the eastern Mediterranean after about 1450.
    A. Arabic
    B. Egyptian
    C. Greek
    D. Roman

Medieval Europe, 1000–1500

The Middle Ages was a chaotic era in Western Europe, as the warrior tribes began to settle down into kingdoms and to develop systems of government. A feudal system prevailed for centuries before giving way to a system of hereditary monarchy, which usually contained some element of a balance of powers between the monarch and the legislature. In the High Middle Ages—in some places, well into the nineteenth century—the monarch would retain the upper hand.

The High Middle Ages was a period of constant military struggle between France and England. In 1066, the Normans invaded and conquered England; the ethnically French Plantagenet dynasty would take the English throne in the 1100s and hold it until 1485. The two kingdoms fought over territory for many decades until England at last ceded its claims to any territory on the mainland.

The most important event in English history during this era was the signing of the Magna Carta, or "Great Charter." This document is remarkable for its declaration that the monarch is not above the laws of the realm.

Two important factors made the Renaissance that began around 1350 a great turning point in European—and world—history. One was the rediscovery of the Classical era, the great age of Rome and to a lesser extent Greece. The second was the questioning of teachings of the Catholic Church as great scholars began to study subjects other than theology, the development of movable type made printed books widely available, and literacy rates rose. Cultural exchanges led to the study of ancient texts unaffected by Church tradition. This trend of reading on one's own and questioning the Church's accuracy and authority would eventually lead to the Reformation, the Scientific Revolution, and the Enlightenment.

CHAPTER OBJECTIVES

- Describe the feudal system that prevailed throughout Western Europe in the Middle Ages.
- Describe the balance of powers in medieval government and society.
- Analyze the political struggles within England and those between England and France.
- Explain the historical importance of the Italian Renaissance.

Chapter 12 Time Line

●	1066	Norman Conquest of Great Britain
●	1211	Frederick II becomes Holy Roman emperor
●	1215	Magna Carta
●	1226	Louis IX becomes king of France
●	1305	Avignon Papacy begins
●	1338	Hundred Years' War begins
●	1348–1350	Black Death
●	1438	Council of Florence
●	1455	Johannes Gutenberg publishes the Vulgate Bible—the first book in Europe printed with movable type
●	1459	War of the Roses begins
●	1485	Death of Richard III; Tudor dynasty begins in England
●	1495–1498	Leonardo da Vinci, *The Last Supper*
●	1508–1512	Michelangelo, Sistine Chapel ceiling
●	1511	Erasmus, *The Praise of Folly*
●	1513	Machiavelli, *The Prince*

Medieval Society and Government

The feudal system that developed in Western Europe bore no resemblance at all to the sophisticated, centrally controlled political system of the Roman Empire. It was much more similar to systems that prevailed in China and Japan.

As the Western European tribes fought one another for supremacy, one lord would usually emerge as the strongest and would become the king of an entire realm. However, he did not have anything like the power of the Roman emperors or the Egyptian pharaohs. Instead, the king was only the chief lord among many others.

A loyal retinue of warriors surrounded the medieval monarch. Their relationship was based on an exchange of favors: the warriors gave the king their loyalty and their military service, and in return, he provided them with titles and large land grants. Each of these large estates duplicated the structure of the monarchy. The landlord ruled supreme; he offered his own retinue of knights housing and payment (usually in kind rather than in money), and they gave him their loyalty and military service in return.

The feudal system was held together by oaths of loyalty—an oath being considered a binding legal contract. The obligations were binding on both sides: just as the vassal was obliged to obey commands and to serve the lord, the lord was obliged to protect the vassal and provide for his welfare. The same duties and responsibilities existed in the upper ranks between the monarch and the lords who served him.

Conflict was inherent in the feudal system. On one side, the monarch naturally wanted to control the realm and command the obedience of all his subjects. On the other side, the landlords held so much independent power on their estates that they were reluctant to bow down too low to the king—even though all sides agreed that the king ruled by divine right. Over time, the balance of power would tilt in the monarch's favor, but throughout the Middle Ages, the feudal system prevailed.

The feudal system contained the roots of representative government. In England, the barons were required to attend an annual council; this eventually developed into the British Parliament. Because the kings of England and other nations depended on the lords for military service, they had to allow them some say in matters of policy. Once the state had a standing army of its own, this obligation would disappear and the rise of absolute monarchy would become possible.

Money was another factor in the balance of feudal power. The thriving mercantile economy of medieval Western Europe meant that the merchants were the most prosperous class; it was the merchants who had money to spend and to lend. It was quite common not only for lords but also for kings to turn to merchants for loans. The Medici family of fifteenth-century Florence is only one example of a merchant family that gained enormous political power by lending money to highly placed officials.

One last factor in the medieval balance of power was the Catholic Church, which had spread throughout Western Europe by the eleventh century. The Church was the most powerful institution of the day, much more so than any individual monarch. The pope could excommunicate any king who disputed his official position on any issue; this threat was always effective and would persist until the mid-1500s. The Church was also the source of highly trained, literate men of the sort kings always needed in their governments, another factor in the alliance between the Church and the state that prevailed all through the Middle Ages.

A person's social rank in medieval Europe—peasant, merchant or artisan, nun or priest, scholar, aristocrat—was generally determined by birth. Some of these classes overlapped; for example, the clergy and the nuns were largely drawn from the ranks of the nobility. There was a certain degree of social mobility in medieval Europe, however; a commoner of great ability, especially a man, could rise to prominence in politics, in the Church, or as a military leader. Monasteries and convents, which could be found throughout Europe, became centers of scholarly study, culture, and social services such as medical care.

The great universities of Europe—Bologna, Paris, Oxford, Cambridge, Salamanca, Padua, and so on—were founded between about 1000 and 1300. These were educational centers where young men would go to seek the higher learning that was considered essential for those intending to enter the Church. By the time of the Renaissance, the universities had gone well beyond theological offerings; they had developed into places where scholars could study the seven liberal arts (*liberal* from the Latin *liberus*, or "free man," whose proper education this was in ancient Rome). The liberal arts consisted of grammar, logic, rhetoric, arithmetic, music, geometry, and astronomy. The general name for this course of study was *humanism*—which meant something very different from the secular connotation this term has today (see "Humanism" in this chapter).

England and France

In its formative years, what became the nation of England was a mix of peoples: Roman Britons, Celts, Angles, Saxons, and after the early 800s, Vikings and Danes as well. The Anglo-Saxons would eventually dominate all the other groups except in Ireland, where the Celts would become the strongest group.

Like Germanic tribes on the mainland, English tribes spent their time raiding one another in the struggle for supremacy. In the late 400s, a brilliant Briton military leader vanquished the Saxons in a series of battles. The legends of King Arthur are based on this man, whose name is lost to history.

Religious and political unity came to England slowly. Christianity took firm hold on England during the 600s; Archbishop Theodore of Canterbury convened the first council of a united English Church in 672. Only in 829 did England become a unified political entity under King Egbert. In 1016, the Danish monarch Canute annexed England into the Danish Empire. Canute had great ability as an administrator, and his division of England into counties persists to this day.

The major political event in early medieval England occurred in 1066, when the Normans crossed the English Channel from France and defeated King Harold; this event is known as the Norman Conquest. It is documented in one of the most unusual primary sources in existence—an embroidered textile known as the Bayeux Tapestry. This 230-foot-long linen banner, first exhibited at the Bayeux Cathedral in 1077, is embroidered with scenes of the military campaign and the Norman victory, with accompanying embroidered narration in Latin—the style of the whole work reminds many contemporary viewers of a graphic novel or a film storyboard. No one knows for certain who commissioned the Bayeux Tapestry, nor the names of the women (almost certainly nuns) who embroidered it; it is a unique and valuable record of the contemporary view of events.

From 1066 until the 1300s, France and England would be culturally and politically intertwined, as English kings married French princesses and the two realms struggled over territory. The Saxons were quite hostile to the conquerors at first, but William the Conqueror won them over with generous land grants, ensuring that those he treated well would abandon any thoughts of an anti-Norman conspiracy.

In 1154, Henry II inherited the English throne through his mother Matilda. He founded the Plantagenet dynasty, which would rule England until 1485. Henry's wife Eleanor had inherited the entire French kingdom of Aquitaine.

This inheritance, plus the Norman heritage from William the Conqueror, made the English believe that their kings had the divine right to rule France as well as England.

In 1200, King John—universally agreed to be among the very worst monarchs in English history—angered the king of France, who promptly claimed all the mainland territory that had been disputed between the two kingdoms. In one of many instances of poor judgment and outright corruption, King John made no effort to reclaim these lands. The English barons came to believe that John would have to be forced to rule in a proper manner, since he would not or could not do so on his own.

The barons drew up a document known to history as the Magna Carta, or "Great Charter." Together with the English Bill of Rights of 1689, this document serves as England's only written constitution. The Magna Carta is remarkable for its time; it declares that the monarch is not above the laws of the realm and that the subjects have certain individual rights, such as freedom from oppression and the right to speedy justice in the courts. The Magna Carta establishes the right to a fair trial by jury and outlaws unreasonable taxes. John was forced to sign the Magna Carta in 1215.

In 1337, an era of territorial and political struggles broke out between England and France; the fighting went on for so long (albeit only intermittently) that the conflict is called the Hundred Years' War. It ended in 1453 with a French victory and with England once and for all confined to its island kingdom. One of the most remarkable individuals in history played a significant role in the Hundred Years' War. Jeanne d'Arc (called Joan of Arc in England) was a peasant girl who heard heavenly voices that gave her remarkably specific advice on how to rescue the hapless French king and expel the English troops from the mainland. Her predictions were so accurate that she soon gained access to the highest military commanders and even the king; by 1429, still in her teens, she found herself dressed in armor and leading troops into battle. Amazingly, the French troops rallied behind her; they considered her little short of a saint and obeyed her commands with enthusiasm. In 1431, the French factions who opposed her betrayed her; she was sold to the English as a prisoner of war, tried, and executed. The detailed trial transcripts have proved to historians on all sides that her execution was judicial murder under the guise of a trial. Jeanne d'Arc was officially canonized by the Catholic Church in 1920.

In 1459, two factions of the Plantagenet dynasty began a long struggle for supremacy. The War of the Roses pitted John, Duke of Lancaster (whose emblem was the white rose), against Richard, Duke of York (whose emblem was the red rose). Both represented branches of the Plantagenet family. Whenever the branch currently in power produced a weak or incompetent monarch, the other side would seize the opportunity to stage a coup to unseat him. The wars went on intermittently until 1485, when Richard III, the last representative of the Yorkists, fell in the Battle of Bosworth. Henry VII, whose connection to the House of Lancaster was tangential at best, became the first of the Tudor kings.

Spain

It was only toward the end of the Middle Ages that Christian armies began to drive the Muslims out of the Iberian Peninsula. During the 1400s, the expansion of the Spanish military led to success in this venture. This retaking of the lands that would eventually become the nations of Portugal and Spain is known as the *Reconquista*. In 1492, the Spanish army completed the *Reconquista* by capturing Granada, the last Muslim stronghold.

The Renaissance

The two-hundred-fifty-year period of European history that ended the Middle Ages and ushered in the modern era is called the Renaissance because it marked a return to the values of the Classical era. A variety of conditions gave rise to the Renaissance. First, the Black Death decimated Europe, striking down almost half of the population. Second, survivors of the plague began migrating to the cities, causing them to grow and prosper. This prosperity, in turn, meant that wealthy citizens had disposable income to spend on culture and the arts. Third, the perfection of the printing process brought about the possibility of near-universal literacy and education.

The Renaissance in Italy

The earliest stirrings of the ideas that would make historians label this era "the Renaissance" occurred in the Italian city-states. Several factors were responsible. First, Italy was the location of the Roman Empire, whose great artistic and intellectual achievements became so important to the era. It was natural that the Italians would be the first to celebrate the cultural past that could be seen, touched, and studied literally on their very doorsteps. Second, Italy was enjoying a period of great economic prosperity. This meant that there were enormously wealthy families who had money to spend on major artistic and architectural projects. Third, the Catholic Church, which was headquartered in Rome, had begun to depend financially on wealthy Italians like Cosimo de' Medici. This financial dependency gave these wealthy businessmen and politicians a certain amount of power over Church policies. Fourth, Italy's geographical location continued to make it a place of cultural and intellectual exchange.

The Black Death

The Black Death is the name given to a severe epidemic of bubonic and pneumonic plague that spread across Europe from about 1348 to 1350, killing 30 to 60 percent of the population. The loss was highest in cities, where people were crowded together in unsanitary conditions; the populations of Florence, Paris, and London were cut in half. The death rate was comparatively lower in isolated rural areas, where there was less chance of infection.

Naturally, this was a time of terror throughout Europe. Medical science was at a primitive stage, and no one understood where the disease had come from or what caused it. Many people believed it was a sign that the world was coming to an end. People turned to the Church for help, as it was the universal authority of the time. However, the Church could do nothing to combat the epidemic. Priests who cared for the sick caught the plague and died like anyone else.

The Black Death helped to bring about the Renaissance in a number of ways. First, survivors began moving to cities looking for work as the disease receded. Cities grew larger as a result. Second, so many workers and artisans had died that those who were left found that their services were in greater demand. Third, people began to doubt that the Church was as omnipotent as it had always claimed to be. If it was so helpless in the face of real disaster, what power did the Church really have?

The Church in the Renaissance

The Renaissance marked a turning point in the Catholic Church's position in Western Europe. It was during the Renaissance that the Church began its long, gradual loss of authority over all aspects of human society and behavior. A number of factors besides the Black Death played into this loss of faith in the Church. One was the challenge of the secular authorities, such as the powerful merchant families of Italy. Another was the Church's own encouragement of the Classical revival; a third was its sponsorship of cultural exchanges that led to Western European study of Greek and Near Eastern texts and ideas. Last, the availability of printed books in Europe after 1450 meant that more people were reading; as they read, they fell into the habit of thinking for themselves rather than simply accepting what the Church fathers told them.

Beginning in 1414, the Church sponsored a series of councils in the hope of repairing the Great Schism and then reuniting the Roman and Eastern Orthodox churches, which had split in the year 1053 (see Chapter 8). It failed in the latter goal; in fact, it only succeeded in weakening the Church's authority by making the exchange of ideas possible. The Council of Florence of 1438, funded in part by the Medici, saw a gathering of scholars and officials from Greece, Ethiopia, Russia, Cairo, and Trebizond. It was an unprecedented cultural exchange between East and West. Scholars traded books and manuscripts and debated and discussed science and philosophy While the Eastern guests admired new Italian works of art and architecture, the Western hosts pored over texts by Euclid, Plato, and Aristotle to which Westerners had had no access since ancient times.

Politics and the Economy

Since the fall of the Roman Empire, Italy had not been a unified nation; rather, it was a collection of politically independent city-states with a common ethnic, cultural, religious, and linguistic heritage. Wealthy middle-class families ruled these states; grabbing and holding political power was the best way to further their business interests.

Florence was especially important among the city-states during the 1400s because it was enjoying a period of economic prosperity. The Medici, a stupendously wealthy family of bankers and importers who ruled Florence, used and invested its money in two areas. The first was patronage of the arts; the Medici sponsored many of the most significant artistic achievements of the period. The second was loans to the Church. By being the Church's banker, the Medici gained a significant amount of influence over Church policies. Strong family ties to the papacy gave the Medici virtual control of Rome as well as Florence. In the 1480s, a Medici married the son of Pope Innocent VIII. In 1513, Giovanni de' Medici became Pope Leo X.

Table 12.1 shows the most prominent members of the Medici family and their major achievements.

Table 12.1 The Medici Family

Name	Political Achievements	Contributions to the Arts and Letters
Cosimo de' Medici (1389–1464)	Sponsorship of the Council of Florence in 1438	Built up family library into one of the largest and most important in Europe
Lorenzo de' Medici (Lorenzo the Magnificent) (1449–1492)	Organized army against Turkish invasion in 1480 Arranged marriage between his daughter and the son of Pope Innocent VIII	Founded academy for artists in Florence Patron of Michelangelo Accomplished poet Continued to add to family library
Giovanni de' Medici (Pope Leo X) (1475–1521)	By 1512, had returned Medici family to power lost in 1494 Became Pope Leo X in 1513 United central Italian states politically	Ordered and oversaw reconstruction and restoration of the Vatican and St. Peter's Basilica in Rome, including major contributions by Michelangelo, Bramante, and Raphael

Machiavelli

Niccolò Machiavelli, born in Florence in 1469, remains a highly influential political thinker. His most famous work is a short discourse titled *The Prince*. Published in 1513, *The Prince* explains how to gain and hold absolute political power. (In an obvious bid for employment, Machiavelli dedicated *The Prince* to Giuliano de' Medici.) What made the book so revolutionary was its frank assertion that a prince should not hesitate to act treacherously or dishonestly in order to keep his power, nor be swayed by considerations of ethics or religion. Machiavelli's realistic approach to politics is as relevant today as it was in his own time; it would have a profound effect on European diplomacy for the next several centuries.

Michelangelo

Born in Florence in 1475, Michelangelo Buonarroti is one of the towering figures of art. He achieved great fame in his own lifetime and forever after as a sculptor, architect, painter, and poet. The frescoes Pope Leo X commissioned him to paint on the ceiling of the Vatican's Sistine Chapel constitute Michelangelo's greatest claim to fame. From the historian's point of view, the Sistine Chapel ceiling is most notable for its mix of biblical and Classical elements. Michelangelo set aside twelve large, prominent spaces for portraits of ancient prophets of the birth of Jesus, treating biblical prophets and pagan sibyls equally in terms of placement, size, and scale. There is no evidence that either the artist or the patron saw any incongruity in this. Given that the Sistine Chapel was at the very heart of the headquarters of the Catholic Church, and that the Church itself sponsored the project, this alone makes it clear that Renaissance Europeans had no sense that these elements were contradictory.

The ceiling frescoes show a clear break with medieval artistic traditions in their style as well. The figures are heroic in size and scale, bursting out of frames that cannot contain them. They are portrayed in a great variety of poses, from every angle and point of view—a complete break from the medieval style. These figures also show that Michelangelo had a thorough knowledge of anatomy; the depiction of the bones and muscles beneath the skin is perfectly accurate. The faces reveal recognizable emotions that make the frescoes a celebration of the human being. All these elements make the Sistine ceiling a product of the Renaissance. Sixteenth-century art historian Giorgio Vasari later wrote that the Sistine ceiling "restored light to a world that for centuries had been plunged into darkness."

The Perfection of Printing

Woodblock printing had been invented in China before AD 700 and remained the main method of printing on cloth and paper for centuries. This method, however, was not practical for printing multiple copies of long texts. Movable type, in which each block was an individual letter or character, made the process much more efficient. Printers first tried movable wooden type but soon turned to metal because it was much more durable.

Like all other Asian inventions, the technology of printing eventually traveled westward. Europeans were producing printed textiles and fabrics by the twelfth century. When paper became widely available in the West around 1400, they began trying to develop an efficient method of printing texts on it. German artisan Johannes Gutenberg achieved the first and best success at movable-type printing in Europe around 1453. He invented the modern printing press and also arrived at a combination of metals that made his type the clearest and most durable—his recipe continued to be used until digital printing became near universal around the beginning of the twenty-first century. The first European printed book was the Vulgate Bible, often called "the Gutenberg Bible" in honor of the printer.

The development of movable type and the printing press in China did not lead to any sweeping cultural changes; Chinese books remained luxury items for the wealthy (see Chapter 10). In the West, however, the impact of this technology was truly revolutionary. Printing may be the single most important innovation of the millennium. The widespread availability of printed books led directly and swiftly to a rise in literacy. For the first time, literacy and knowledge were not exclusive to priests and wealthy people but came within the reach of everyone, because Western books were affordable across all social classes. For the first time, texts (including the Bible) became available in the languages people actually spoke, not just in Latin.

Humanism

The humanist course of study that became common at European universities during the Renaissance focused on the seven liberal arts—grammar, logic, rhetoric, arithmetic, music, geometry, and astronomy. The scholars studied Roman texts, which were both easier to understand than Greek ones (Latin was quite familiar to all educated Europeans and was, in fact, the basis of Spanish, Portuguese, French, and Italian) and more readily available, since the heart of the Roman Empire had been right there in Rome. Only time, travel, and cultural exchange would bring Greek manuscripts to the West for study.

Humanist scholars of the Renaissance focused their interest on the human being as a unique individual, with his or her own way of thinking about the great questions of philosophy and the meaning of life. All of this, however, was firmly in the context of the human being as God's creation, with all human achievement being dedicated to God's glory. In this era, the word *humanism* did not have the secular connotation it has today.

Desiderus Erasmus, born in Rotterdam in 1466, is probably the best known of the humanists. Erasmus's work shows that he embraced both biblical and Classical studies. He published a Latin translation of the New Testament in 1516 and also completed translations and scholarly commentaries on Classical texts, including the works of Plutarch and Seneca. He corresponded with most of the great European scholars of his day and was widely regarded as the hub of the intellectual world.

QUIZ

1. All of these factors tended to mitigate the power of the medieval monarch except _____.
   A. the loyalty of the knights and vassals to their lords
   B. the authority of the pope and the Catholic Church
   C. the debts most monarchs owed to wealthy merchants
   D. the founding of universities

2. _____ is an important historical figure because he perfected the process of printing books with movable type.
   A. Michelangelo Buonarroti
   B. Cosimo de' Medici
   C. Martin Luther
   D. Johannes Gutenberg

3. What happened during the Norman Conquest?
   A. France successfully invaded England.
   B. The English converted to Christianity.
   C. France defeated England in the Hundred Years' War.
   D. Jeanne d'Arc was executed and later canonized.

4. What was the cause of the War of the Roses?
   A. a struggle for power over French territory
   B. a family struggle for the English throne
   C. a struggle for Spain between Christians and Muslims
   D. a struggle among the barons to depose King John

5. The Magna Carta is an early instance of the official recognition of _____.
   A. citizens' individual rights
   B. a three-branch government with a balance of powers
   C. abdication by a hereditary monarch
   D. the divine right of kings

6. Vassals promised _____ to the lord in exchange for his protection.
   A. rent and taxes
   B. prayer and fasting
   C. obedience and service
   D. political support

7. Humanism included the study of all these branches of higher learning except _____.
   A. astronomy
   B. logic
   C. music
   D. philosophy

8. The Medici family ruled _____ for most of the fifteenth century.
   A. Rome
   B. Florence
   C. Italy
   D. France

9. _____ wrote a political treatise stating that princes should not hesitate to commit unethical acts in order to hold onto their power.
   A. Jeanne d'Arc
   B. Johannes Gutenberg
   C. Desiderus Erasmus
   D. Niccolò Machiavelli

10. The most important effect of the Council of Florence was _____.
    A. the official reunion of the Roman and Orthodox Catholic churches
    B. a major exchange of books and ideas among Eastern and Western scholars
    C. Pope Leo X's decision to restore the Vatican and St. Peter's Basilica
    D. the publication of the first Bible printed with movable type

Medieval Asia, 1150–1600

Many of the Turkish tribes of the Central Asian steppes had ridden into Europe and the Near East; their success at conquest was legendary. At the same time, their cousins the Mongols were applying the same military techniques to Asia. By the early 1200s, the Mongols held sway over almost all of the Asian continent.

Such a large empire was bound to disintegrate, and the Mongol Empire did not survive Genghis Khan's death. It split into four smaller khanates, none of which was able to maintain control of its territory. In the western khanates, the Turks pushed the Mongols out; in the eastern khanates, native Russian and Chinese rulers asserted themselves and took, or retook, control of their own realms.

The Mongols twice attempted to invade Japan but failed both times; severe storms defeated them in both cases. Meanwhile, the Japanese established a feudal society under military rule that would last until 1867.

CHAPTER OBJECTIVES

- Identify the Mongol Empire at its greatest extent.
- Identify the four smaller khanates and explain what became of them.
- Describe the early Russian Empire.
- Describe the important trends in China under the Ming dynasty.
- Describe the government and society of medieval Japan under the early shogunates.

Chapter 13 Time Line

●	1156–1185	Civil war in Japan
●	1192	Minamoto Yoritomo establishes first shogunate, moves capital to Kamakura
●	1206	Temujin becomes Genghis Khan ("Universal Ruler") of Mongol tribes
●	1260	Khanates of former Mongol Empire become independent states
		Kublai Khan establishes Yuan dynasty in China
●	1281	Mongol invasion of Japan crushed by *kamikaze*
●	1335	Muromachi shogunate begins
●	1368	Emperor Taizu begins Ming dynasty in China
●	1369	Tamerlane conquers Chaghatai khanate
●	1380	Russians defeat Tatars in Battle of Kulikovo
●	1388	Yi dynasty begins in Korea
●	1405	Death of Tamerlane and end of his empire
		Fleet of two hundred ships departs China on study mission
●	1446	Koreans begin using phonetic alphabet
●	1467–1477	Onin War in Japan
●	1480	Ivan III withholds tribute from Akhmat Khan; Battle of Oka
●	1515	Portuguese establish trading post in Macao
●	1590	Toyotomi Hideyoshi reunites Japan under central rule

| | 1590s | Korea launches world's first ironclad ships |
| | 1600 | Tokugawa Ieyasu founds Tokugawa shogunate |

The Mongol Empire

The Mongols (also called Tatars or Tartars) were people of the steppes of Central Asia (present-day Mongolia), ethnically related to the Turks. The Persian word *tatar* means "mounted messenger," referring to the fact that the Mongols practically lived on horseback. The English common noun *tartar* means "violent person"; this came about because of the Mongols' historic reputation for military discipline, brutality, and iron-fisted dealings with the peoples they conquered.

Like all the other peoples from the northern steppes, the Mongols lived in a nomadic warrior culture in which military skills and horsemanship were of central importance. One respect in which these cultures differed from settled civilizations was social mobility; in a warrior tribe, one's position in the hierarchy depended largely on one's own character and abilities. An orphan named Temujin had such extraordinary skills as a military leader in the constant intertribal warfare that he attracted more and more followers. By 1206, the Mongols had proclaimed him Genghis Khan (a title meaning "world leader") and had united under his sole leadership.

Genghis Khan was not quite literally the ruler of the whole world, but on his death in 1227 he was master of almost the entire Asian continent. The Mongols controlled all the inhabited land between the Pacific Ocean and the mouth of the Danube River, apart from India, eastern Anatolia, and the extreme northern latitudes of Russia. This was by far the largest empire the world had yet seen.

The key to Genghis Khan's continued success lay in his management of the army. He chose his generals carefully, both for their military skills and their personal loyalty to him. Under his command, the Mongol army was notable for its insistence on discipline. Genghis Khan also adopted legal, financial, and writing systems for his realm, and, like all emperors, claimed that he had divine approval for his rule.

On Genghis Khan's death, his empire was split into four smaller khanates, one for each son as was the custom with Mongolian inheritances; one Great Khan would have supreme authority over all the realms. Infighting among the sons of Genghis Khan led to the end of this system; by 1260, the four khanates were four independent kingdoms. The Ilkhanate covered the Anatolia/Persia region, the Golden Horde comprised what would later become the Russian Empire, the Chaghatai khanate included Tibet and the western end of the Silk Road, and the Khanate of the Great Khan was China.

The Ilkhanate

Genghis Khan's descendant Huelegu had conquered and sacked Baghdad in 1258, thus ending the rule of the Abbasid caliphate. The next step was to expand into Egypt, but the Mamluks in power there were also fierce fighters from the Central Asian steppes, and the Ilkhanate army could not make any headway against them. The two sides agreed that the Euphrates River would be the permanent border between their realms, although this did not prevent continual attempts on both sides to invade the other until about 1320. The Ilkhanate would collapse in the wake of civil wars after 1335.

The Chaghatai Khanate

From 1299 until 1308, the leader of the Chaghatai khanate made repeated attempts to invade India, but the Delhi sultanate was able to withstand all the attacks. In 1369, the Mongol khanate fell to Tamerlane and his troops (see Chapter 11).

The Golden Horde and the Russian Empire

The Golden Horde lasted somewhat longer; under Mongol rule, the Russian princes had to pay annual tributes to the khan but were more or less left to the details of governing on their own. Despite this degree of autonomy, the early Russian princes wanted nothing more than to overthrow the Mongols and rule their own realm.

The principality of Muscovy, with the city of Moscow at its center, became the core of the Russian Empire by a combination of geographical and political factors. Muscovy had no natural borders to define it or to protect it from invasion. This explains its conquering mentality: Moscow could maintain its position of power only by remaining constantly on the attack. Successful attacks gave the rulers of Muscovy control over major rivers, which were essential for transportation and trade. The policy of conquest and expansion also enriched the royal treasury because it meant a larger population paying tax to the crown. In addition, Moscow unified Russia by consolidating power into the hands of one prince.

Moscow's ruling family, the Danilovitch, was abler and more shrewd than ruling families of the other principalities. Several important dynastic marriages allied Muscovy and the other principalities. Family connections, territorial annexation, and a common belief in the Eastern Orthodox faith helped to unify the various states into one empire.

The major goals of the early Russian princes and czars were fourfold. First, they wanted to break away from the stranglehold of Tatar authority. Second, they wanted to consolidate power into the hands of one absolute monarch, with a capital city as a central power base. Third, they wanted the central government to control all the elements of society, from the boyars (hereditary nobles) through the peasants. Last, they wanted to expand the empire both eastward and westward for strategic and trade purposes.

Prince Dmitri, known to history as Dmitri of the Don, led the Russian army against the Golden Horde in the Battle of Kulikovo in 1380. The Russian victory was a major blow against Mongol authority in Russia. The khan agreed to recognize Moscow as the central Russian authority and to allow the princes of Moscow to appoint their own successors. In 1450, Vasili II declared that only his own direct heirs would rule after him. This constituted a major step in the process toward unified central rule of Russia.

Vasili II and his successors carried out a policy of expanding the army by offering land to anyone willing to serve the state in the military. These land grants were made for life, and most of them could be passed on to the landowner's heirs. With such a powerful incentive, many men joined the ranks of the army, including hereditary princes, boyars, and wealthy nonnoble families. (In Russia, the title *prince* does not necessarily refer to a member of the royal family; it is a title of the higher nobility similar to the English titles *duke* and *earl*.) Peasants and other commoners were required to serve their community in proportion to the local population.

In 1469, Ivan III, Grand Prince of Moscow, married Zoe (sometimes called Sophia) Palaeologos, niece of the Byzantine emperor. Zoe's cultural and family background was to have a major influence on the style of the Russian court, which gained a great deal of ceremony and pomp with her arrival. Ivan and Zoe made the Byzantine double-headed eagle the official emblem of the Russian state; by adopting this symbol, Ivan declared himself the last defender of the Eastern Orthodox faith, in the wake of the fall of Constantinople to the Turks and the failure to reunite Orthodox and Roman Catholicism at the Council of Trent. The final blow to the Golden Horde came in 1480, when Ivan III withheld tribute from the Mongols and the two armies confronted one another from opposite banks of the Oka River. Neither side attacked; this stalemate was only resolved when the Mongols withdrew. This was the end of the Golden Horde and the beginning of the Russian Empire.

The Russian emperor was an absolute monarch—far more of an autocrat than any Western European ruler at this period of history. The emperor had advisers, usually drawn from the boyars and the upper clergy, but these men had no power or privileges other than what the emperor chose to grant them. Nor did the Russian government have any form of popular representation. The emperor truly was the state.

Russia's climate and geography were major obstacles to the formation of a prosperous mercantile middle class such as existed in Italy and other European nations in the early modern period. The countryside was bleak and barren, and the weather was often bitterly cold; these factors combined to make travel difficult. Travel meant trade; without frequent travel, trade did not become an important part of the local economy. Nor did Russia enter into trade or cultural exchange with the rest of Europe until somewhat later in its history.

With travel so difficult, and with the population as widely scattered as it was, a typical Russian estate provided for all its own needs. This contrasted with the economic system in use in Western Europe, where people either bartered or sold their surplus crops or livestock to obtain necessities and luxuries they could not produce themselves.

The Great Khanate and the Yuan Dynasty

Kublai Khan inherited the Khanate of the Great Khan and soon established the Yuan dynasty in China. By 1279, he had conquered the entire Chinese Empire. The Chinese officials and bureaucrats did their best to come to terms with their new foreign rulers, working to imbue them with Chinese culture and customs; however, this attempt met with only mixed success. Kublai Khan generally preferred to hire non-Chinese to government posts; the famous Italian traveler Marco Polo was among his appointments.

The Yuan period was one of slow decline, ending abruptly in 1368 in a peasant uprising. The rebel leader crowned himself Emperor Taizu and founded the Ming dynasty. It is justly famous as a high-water mark of Chinese culture and civilization and was to be the last of the native Chinese dynasties.

China: The Ming Dynasty

Under Taizu, the government reestablished various Chinese traditions that the Yuan had dropped, such as the Confucian civil service examination and the national census that determined tax assessments. There were attempts at land reform, but these resulted in the ownership of larger and larger parcels of land by fewer and fewer landlords. This began a practice of sharecropping, in which the tenant farmer sublet land to subsistence farmers.

The Ming government sent out a study mission of two hundred ships under Admiral Zheng in 1405. By the time the fleet returned in 1433, it had traveled widely, ranging as far as the Horn of Africa, the Persian Gulf, Mecca, and Aden as well as stopping at ports in India, Ceylon, and throughout Southeast Asia. The ships came back stuffed with a variety of treasures, including plants and seeds of nonnative crops that would alter Chinese agriculture: pineapples, yams, potatoes, maize, tomatoes, and beets. These new crops drew on mineral resources in the soil that had lain idle, while other minerals had been completely used up. New harvests were good and food production rose, altering the national diet and the national landscape in the process. The Chinese were also experimenting with new irrigation and farming techniques that came from the West. All of this led to a steady population growth, after millions had died of bubonic plague and the effects of Mongol brutality during the era of Mongol rule.

With agriculture booming, the Chinese economy prospered. The Chinese port of Shanghai saw a brisk trade with the Japanese city of Nagasaki, almost geographically opposite. In addition, in 1515, the Portuguese established their first Chinese trading post at Macao, which became a major southern port city, as did Canton and Quanzhou. Spain and the Netherlands followed suit with trading posts of their own. The Chinese exported sugar, silk, ceramics, cotton, paper, and tea; they generally insisted on silver in exchange, because European products did not interest the Chinese. This influx of silver, naturally, led to even greater prosperity.

The Ming dynasty was notable for a flowering of literature, including long prose narratives. Ming porcelain was world famous, highly prized by both foreign customers and wealthy Chinese; in many Western languages, all fine ceramics are called simply "china" in tribute to the culture that produced those of the finest quality. Chinese innovations in decorative arts and design would prove very influential on Western tastes; many Western porcelain factories, in fact, imitated Chinese styles and patterns. Of course, the Chinese invention of gunpowder and the printing press would revolutionize the West (see Chapter 12).

The year 1500 marked the beginning of the end of the Ming dynasty. Like all absolute monarchies, China depended for success on the personality of its emperor, and after 1500 the Ming emperors were, without exception, incompetent or weak. Many preferred enjoying the luxuries of royal privilege to the duties of administration. Court corruption contributed its share to the problems, while rampant tax evasion impoverished the treasury. A short-lived attempt at tax reform failed. By the mid-1520s, the peasant uprising had become an annual event. Somehow, the Ming dynasty would cling to power for another century; two probable reasons for this are the continuity provided by the Confucian-educated bureaucracy and the inherent Chinese respect for tradition.

Japan

As the twelfth century began in Japan, the Fujiwara clan was on the decline and the aristocracy was on the rise. Japan was beginning to acquire an administrative and social system that bore a striking resemblance to the feudalism of medieval Europe. Powerful provincial warlords commanded armies, protecting them and seeing to their welfare in exchange for their service and loyalty. These retinues of soldiers were not a national army, loyal only to the state, but rather a number of independent provincial armies whose only loyalty was to their own lord, or *daimyo*. During this era, even Buddhist temples maintained armies for their own security against robber bands.

In 1156, a series of rebellions culminated in an all-out civil war between the Taira and Minamoto clans. War ended in 1185 with a brief assertion of power on the part of the emperor. In 1192, however, Minamoto Yoritomo established the first shogunate, stripping the emperor of any pretense of an official role beyond the purely symbolic.

The Japanese word *shogun* literally means "military commander"; the Western term *generalissimo* is more or less the equivalent. When referring to the head of the Japanese government between 1192 and 1867, however, *shogun* means "military dictator." With the beginning of the Kamakura shogunate, Japan became a military society and would remain so until after World War II. Despite the shogun's assuming the powers that would belong to the monarch in almost any other nation, the Japanese emperor was in no personal danger of assassination or exile. The Japanese had a deeply ingrained belief in the importance of heredity and in the holiness of the emperor's person; no shogun, however powerful, could possibly become emperor.

The Kamakura period, which would last until 1335, is named after the new capital city rather than the new shogun's clan. The period oversaw another important aspect of the Japanese military culture; the development of *bushido*, which literally means "the way of the warrior." Japan's warrior class was called the *samurai*, and *bushido* referred to the complex honor code and also the military skills required of them. The most famous aspect of the samurai honor code is the belief that it was a man's duty to die with honor if a military defeat or personal scandal meant he could no longer live with honor. Ritual suicide by the sword was considered an honorable death and was a fairly common occurrence in medieval Japan.

Around the end of the twelfth century, a new form of Buddhism, known as *Chan* after an Indian word for "meditation," developed in China and made its way to Japan, where it was pronounced "Zen." Eisai and Dogen were considered the most important of the Japanese Zen masters. Zen Buddhists observe strict monastic discipline, and they believe that enlightenment comes in an epiphany—a sudden realization—rather than gradually.

In 1274, the Mongols attempted to invade Japan. Nature intervened and swept them out to sea. In 1281, they made another attempt; this time, the Mongol fleet was destroyed after several weeks of fighting by a severe windstorm, or *kamikaze*. Understandably, the Japanese regarded these storms as miracles. The nation would not be invaded again until the nuclear bombings of 1945 and the entrance of the Allied army of occupation after the Japanese surrender.

The Ashikaga shogunate came to power in 1335; it is sometimes called the Muromachi shogunate, since the Muromachi were an individual family within the greater Ashikaga clan. This shogunate lasted until 1573, maintaining the policies of the Kamakura period. The shogunate weathered a period of bloody civil war; the Onin War lasted from 1467 to 1477. The end result was total fragmentation of authority, as the individual *daimyos* became autonomous leaders of their own armies in their own regions. They even began to arm their peasants, which, of course, created the potential for uprisings. Society did not settle down after the Onin War ended; rather, it gave way to an era of the *daimyos'* small armies staging raids on one another, as had happened during the formative years of the Western European kingdoms in the earlier medieval period. Despite political and social chaos, the Muromachi period is culturally notable for the rise of *noh* drama and the perfection of the ritual tea ceremony.

The Azuchi-Momoyama period began in 1573; it was named for the castles of two leaders, Oda Nobunaga and his successor Toyotomi Hideyoshi, both of whom strove to restore peace to Japan. Hideyoshi, born a peasant but able to rise through the military ranks to become a warlord, finally reunited Japan under one central authority in 1590. He reorganized the land distribution and tax system and took the weapons away from the peasants, creating an immovable social barrier between samurai and peasant.

Hideyoshi died in 1598. His general Tokugawa Ieyasu founded the Tokugawa shogunate in 1600 and established the new capital at Edo (now called Tokyo). Ieyasu was officially proclaimed shogun in 1603.

Korea

By 1259, the kingdom of Koryo found itself under Mongol subjugation like the rest of Asia. In 1388, General Yi Song-gye founded the Yi dynasty, which would last until Japan annexed Korea in 1910.

The Koreans were the first in the world to print entire books with movable metal type, perhaps as early as the 1200s. The world's oldest surviving book printed with movable metal type is a Korean guide to Buddhism published in the late 1300s. The introduction of a phonetic alphabet resulted in a swift rise in the literacy rate in Korea. One other important Korean invention was the ironclad ship; when the Japanese attempted to invade Korea in the last decade of the sixteenth century, the Korean ironclads were able to repel them.

QUIZ

1. _____ was a key factor in preventing the rise of a prosperous mercantile class in Russia.
   A. Orthodoxy
   B. Geography
   C. Politics
   D. Absolutism

2. Many Russian nobles joined the military in the 1400s because _____.
   A. they believed it was their duty
   B. they were eager to show their loyalty to the throne
   C. they were required by law to serve
   D. they were given hereditary titles to land

3. Under Genghis Khan, the Mongols failed to conquer or subdue _____.
   A. China
   B. India
   C. Persia
   D. Korea

4. During the Ming dynasty, all of these contributed to the growth of the Chinese population except _____.
   A. the planting of crops that were new to the country
   B. the use of new irrigation techniques
   C. the reestablishment of the civil service examination
   D. the profits from international trade

5. Why did the Ming government send out a fleet of two hundred ships in 1405?
   A. to fight a naval war against the Mongols
   B. to conquer Japan, Korea, and the Southeast Asian kingdoms
   C. to establish Chinese colonies in the West
   D. to make friendly contacts throughout the region

6. What was the result of the Onin War in Japan?
   A. The emperor was restored to political supremacy.
   B. The Muromachi shogunate was established.
   C. The *daimyos* began an era of competition among their own armies.
   D. The Mongols attempted to invade Japan.

7. **A Japanese shogun is most closely comparable to _____.**
   A. a constitutional monarch
   B. a high-ranking officer
   C. a military dictator
   D. a prime minister

8. **The world's oldest surviving book was printed in _____.**
   A. China
   B. Korea
   C. Japan
   D. India

9. **All these except _____ helped to weaken and eventually topple the Ming dynasty in China.**
   A. widespread famine and drought
   B. weak and idle emperors
   C. repeated peasant uprisings
   D. corruption surrounding the court

10. **The early Russian princes and czars had all these goals except _____.**
    A. to pass important land distribution and tax reforms
    B. to drive the Mongols out of Russia
    C. to establish a hereditary, absolute Russian monarchy
    D. to expand the Russian Empire

chapter **14**

European Reformation and the Age of Absolute Monarchy, 1500–1750

The Reformation is the name given to the era in which thousands of Christians abandoned the Catholic Church to join new Christian denominations. In 1517, the birth of the Lutheran Church put an end to the thousand-year supremacy of the Catholic Church. By 1600, thousands of Europeans were worshiping in Protestant churches: Lutheran, Calvinist, and Anglican. In response, the Catholic Church made serious efforts to reform itself from within.

The era that began with the Reformation and ended in the 1700s has been called the Age of Absolute Monarchy in Europe. Because governments were passed down within families, and because legislative assemblies were either weak or nonexistent, it was an era of autocratic monarchs whose decisions could generally not be questioned, challenged, or overturned other than by violent means. The success or failure of an absolute monarchy depends largely on the monarch's personal abilities.

The Thirty Years' War (1618–1648) ended the dominance of Europe's powerful Hapsburg family and began an era of French domination. It also ushered in a period in which states completed the long process of centralizing their governments, becoming what we recognize today as modern nations. The war was fought over many issues. It was a religious war fought between Catholics and Protestants, with much bitterness on both sides. It was a war of two powerful families, the Catholic Hapsburgs and the Protestant Wittelsbachs. It was a political war in which nations fought for territorial expansion and to gain stronger positions in the balance of European power.

CHAPTER OBJECTIVES

- Define the term *Reformation*, and explain its importance in European history.
- Identify the major Protestant denominations, and explain how and why each one came into being.
- Identify the various monarchs of Europe during the era, and discuss their strengths, weaknesses, and major decisions.
- Identify the causes of the Thirty Years' War, and describe the major provisions of the Peace of Westphalia.

Chapter 14 Time Line

●	1516	Charles I becomes king of Spain
●	1517	Luther publishes Ninety-Five Theses
●	1521	Diet of Worms
●	1534	Act of Supremacy declares Henry VIII Supreme Head of the Church of England
●	1540	Society of Jesuits is founded
●	1541	Calvin establishes theocracy in Geneva
●	1545–1563	Council of Trent; Catholic Reformation (Counter-Reformation)
●	1555	Peace of Augsburg
		Philip II becomes king of Spain

- **1556**   Ferdinand I becomes Holy Roman Emperor
- **1558**   Elizabeth I becomes queen of England
- **1588**   British defeat of the Spanish Armada
- **1598**   Henry of Navarre becomes king of France; issues Edict of Nantes
- **1617**   Ferdinand Hapsburg becomes king of Bohemia; revokes Letter of Majesty
- **1618**   Defenestration of Prague; Thirty Years' War begins
- **1619**   Ferdinand II elected Holy Roman Emperor

                 Bohemians crown Frederich Wittelsbach as king, deposing Ferdinand
- **1629**   Edict of Restitution bans Protestantism throughout the Holy Roman Empire
- **1635**   France declares war on Spain
- **1643**   Louis XIV becomes king of France
- **1648**   Peace of Westphalia; Thirty Years' War ends
- **1740**   Frederick II becomes king of Prussia

The Protestant Reformation

The rise of Protestantism had multiple causes, including a growing realization that the Church was not as powerful as it had claimed; a rise in secular political power; and the perfection of the printing process, which stimulated a rise in literacy. The spark that finally pushed people into widespread, open rebellion against the Church was the trade of indulgences for financial contributions to the Church.

The Catholic Church functioned on a system of the forgiveness of sins. When a person sinned, he or she confessed and received absolution in exchange for some form of penance, such as repeating a certain number of prayers or doing good work in the community. A sinner who was granted an indulgence did not have to go through such a penance; an indulgence was an official promise that the Church forgave earthly punishment for sins already committed. The first indulgences were granted to soldiers who had fought in the Crusades, as forgiveness for sins committed in the course of war. Of course, God might still choose to punish sins after death; the Church could only forgive earthly punishment.

The practice of granting indulgences quickly became corrupt. Both the Church and its agents, most notably Johann Tetzel in Germany, grew greedy for money and began offering indulgences in exchange for financial donations. People were assured that if they donated money, their sins would be forgiven—not only on earth but also after death. They were also told that they could buy heavenly forgiveness for family members who were already dead.

The idea that one could buy forgiveness for sins with money—or that the Church could preempt God's power to forgive sin after death—deeply offended many devout Catholics. The most notable of these was Martin Luther.

Martin Luther

The German-born Martin Luther was a noted theological scholar and a devout Catholic. His Ninety-Five Theses, which appeared in 1517, were propositions for debate that questioned and criticized many aspects of the Catholic Church, including a prominent and harsh reference to the sale of indulgences. The Ninety-Five Theses were printed and widely circulated, impressing many readers with their logic. When the pope ordered Luther to recant his criticisms of the Church on pain of excommunication, Luther refused. Summoned before a diet (official assembly) at the German town of Worms, he again refused to recant. Accepting an offer of protection from the Elector of Saxony, Luther continued to write and publish; to his own astonishment, he soon realized that instead of bringing about reform in the Catholic Church, he had founded a new denomination.

The most important idea behind Lutheranism is the notion that salvation depends on faith. Each believer must read, study, and understand scripture for himself or herself—in effect, each soul would serve as his or her own priest, instead of relying exclusively on an ordained priest to interpret the word of God. Luther translated the Bible into German, making it possible for ordinary Germans to read it for themselves. Hand in hand with this went Luther's conviction that worship services should also be conducted in the language of the people, not in Latin. Luther also advocated a simple worship service, since he believed that communion with God took place in an individual's heart and mind; outward show had no spiritual significance. These ideas and reforms appealed to thousands of Germans.

Several of the German princes became enthusiastic Lutherans as well. They had a financial motive as well as a spiritual one; making Lutheranism the state religion meant a state takeover of all Catholic land and property. Despite the financial incentive, however, many princes remained devoutly Catholic.

At first, the Holy Roman Emperor tolerated Lutheranism. As it spread, however, various groups began using it as a basis for social and political revolt. In 1529, the emperor decreed a ban on Lutheranism. It was during this period that the term *Protestant* first came into use, describing the Lutheran princes and people who *protested* against the emperor's decree. War eventually broke out between the German states over this issue. In 1555, the Peace of Augsburg settled the matter by declaring that each German prince could determine the religion of his own state.

John Calvin

Scholarly Frenchman John Calvin came to believe, as Luther had, that the Catholic Church needed reform. When Calvin spoke out on this issue, however, he found himself so unpopular in France that he fled to Switzerland. Here, he eventually acquired so much power and influence that many historians describe the city of Geneva as a theocracy—a state ruled by the church.

The central idea of Calvinism is predestination—the belief that God predetermines everything that will happen on earth. Human beings were marked for salvation or damnation at birth, and no amount of faith or good deeds can earn salvation. Calvin argued that those who were saved would naturally perform good works and lead exemplary lives; therefore, all believers must live this way because it was one sure sign that they were among the saved. Calvinism made church attendance mandatory, encouraged simplicity in dress, and forbade many forms of enjoyment such as dancing, singing, and playing cards.

Despite its harsh rules and its intolerance of other forms of worship, Calvinism gained many converts. Calvin's followers spread his ideas and practices throughout Switzerland, the Netherlands, and France. John Knox transported many of Calvin's ideas home to Scotland, where the religion was called Presbyterianism after the *presbyters*, or elders, who ruled the church. In 1560–61, Parliament made Presbyterianism the state religion of Scotland.

France as a state was not sympathetic to the Reformation. The French monarchs sided with the Catholics throughout a series of civil wars fought from 1562 to 1598, helping to ensure that Protestantism could not establish itself securely. Thousands of Huguenots (French Protestants) were massacred, and many more fled France to settle in Holland, Belgium, or England.

When the Calvinist Henry of Navarre became Henry IV of France in the 1580s, he converted to Catholicism. This was an act of political expediency;

Henry's main goal was to strengthen the monarchy, so he sided with the religious majority. In 1598, Henry issued the Edict of Nantes, which established Catholicism as the state religion of France and its territories but allowed Protestants to worship as they saw fit, without molestation. This ended the French civil wars of religion. Henry was enlightened enough to understand that tolerance in the matter of private worship would lead to domestic accord in the population and would therefore benefit the kingdom.

Henry VIII and the Church of England

The Anglican Church (also called the Church of England) is unique in history. First, it was created solely for political reasons, not religious ones. Second, it was the most sweeping assertion of secular authority in the history of Europe up to that date.

Lacking a male heir, King Henry VIII dreaded possible rival claims to the throne and a return to the civil wars of the 1400s. He was also personally tired of Queen Catherine, who was older than himself and past the age of childbearing. Therefore, Henry petitioned Pope Clement VII for an annulment of his marriage. The king had fallen in love with the young lady-in-waiting Anne Boleyn, who seemed likely to provide him with healthy children. (Ironically, only one daughter of their marriage would survive; Henry would have to marry yet again in order to produce a son.)

When the pope refused Henry's request, the king named loyal court official Thomas Cranmer the new Archbishop of Canterbury. Archbishop Cranmer granted Henry his annulment and then married him to Anne Boleyn. When the king and the archbishop were excommunicated, the British Parliament passed the Act of Supremacy (1534), which acknowledged the king as the Supreme Head of the Church in England. With one stroke, Parliament thus created a new Christian denomination and eliminated any future papal involvement in British affairs. The British monarch now had the same authority over England that the pope had over the rest of Europe. No secular government had asserted such power in a thousand years.

It is important to note that the king did not create the Anglican Church with a wave of a royal scepter. Instead, the duly elected representative government passed the Act of Supremacy according to the laws of the land. Thus, Henry VIII had some right to claim that the English people and the government fully supported his desire to break away from the Catholic Church.

In a clear sign that Henry's action had been politically and not spiritually motivated, the Anglican Church continued to hear confessions and celebrate mass in the same manner as the Catholic Church. Under Henry's son and successor Edward VI, the clergy introduced various reforms, such as permission for priests to marry. In 1549, Archbishop Cranmer published *The Book of Common Prayer*, which contained the prayers and proper forms of all Anglican services—in English, not Latin. During the next century, the status of the Church of England varied according to the personal faith of the monarch.

The Counter-Reformation

Meanwhile, the Catholic Church had become well aware of the need to reform itself from within. Reform proceeded slowly, by fits and starts. Some popes felt a genuine need to reform corrupt practices; others hoped to reclaim Protestants who had left the Church; still others stubbornly refused to support any changes.

Pope Paul III, who supported reform, called for a council of high-ranking Church officials to meet in the city of Trent to devise a plan. Due to strong opposition from within the Church, the Council of Trent did not meet until 1545 and took more than fifteen years to reach any conclusions. In the end, it supported all doctrines that Protestants had criticized, banned the sale of indulgences, and required the founding of hundreds of new seminaries for the education and training of priests.

Paul III and several of his successors supported reform. In 1542, Paul created the Congregation of the Holy Office of the Inquisition to supervise the Roman Inquisition, whose job was to try people accused of heresy. The Roman Inquisition generally assessed penalties such as fines or public whippings; those convicted of serious heresy could be sentenced to life imprisonment. When the Inquisition handed a prisoner over to secular authorities, it meant the person would almost certainly be executed. The Inquisition began as a sincere attempt on the part of reformers to root out heresy, but despite their good intentions, it eventually became a byword for torture and terror.

Pope Paul IV was a particularly strict reformer. He eliminated the practice of simony (the sale of Church offices), streamlined the Church bureaucracy, and oversaw the publication of the *Index of Forbidden Books*. This document listed all books that were off-limits to Catholics because of their corrupting influence. Not content with banning the books, the Church also burned thousands of copies. Owning a copy of a forbidden book made the possessor liable to punishment under the Inquisition.

In 1540, the Spaniard Ignatius Loyola gained papal approval to found the order of the Jesuits. While recovering from wounds received in battle, Loyola had vowed to emulate the simplicity and humility of Jesus. He took vows of poverty, wore the simplest clothing, and spent his days serving and helping the poor. He and his followers lived simply and chastely, preferring to convert non-Catholics rather than resort to the bullying techniques of the Inquisition. Eventually, their missionary ambitions would take them far beyond Europe's borders. Jesuit schools offered the best education then available to children in Europe; pupils from all income levels and all ranks of society were welcomed and treated equally. The activities of the Jesuits and other similar orders, such as the Ursulines and Capucines, helped to counteract the effects of the Protestant Reformation and to strengthen and improve the Catholic Church as an institution.

The Age of Absolute Monarchy in Europe

In the early modern era, European rule was a family affair rather than an official form of government as we understand government today. National borders changed with bewildering rapidity as monarchs died and passed their authority and their lands on to their children. Kings, princes, and electors of Europe ran their territories in much the same way that a lord ran his estate. The territory was considered to be similar to private property; the king owed his subjects his protection in return for their obedience.

Spain

Isabel and Ferdinand

As of the *Reconquista* of the late 1400s, Spain was not a unified nation, but a collection of principalities. The two strongest were Aragon in western Spain and Castile in eastern Spain. In 1469, Ferdinand of Aragon married Isabel of Castile, uniting the crowns and consolidating Spanish power. Both were monarchs in their own right, but since Isabel was female, she considered it politically expedient to share some of her authority in Castile with Ferdinand. On his side, Ferdinand had no reason to share his authority in Aragon with Isabel.

The major goal of the Spanish monarchs can be summed up in one word: control. Control over the nobility would make their position on the throne secure. Control over the population would prevent any threats of uprising or civil war. Control over the other Spanish provinces would unite the kingdom and give the monarchs greater power and authority in Europe.

Control of the Nobility

Relations between the Spanish monarchy and the aristocracy were based on an exchange of favors for loyalty. Isabel and Ferdinand offered the nobles salaried offices, titles, rewards for military service, and grants of land that they could pass on to their heirs. In exchange, the Spanish nobles were remarkably loyal to the throne, with no incentive to alter a system that brought them rich rewards in return for relatively little effort.

Control of the People

In 1478, Isabel and Ferdinand established the Spanish Inquisition, which reported directly to the monarch rather than operating under the authority of the Church. The Spanish Inquisition's purpose was to ensure that the people lived and worshiped as observant Christians. The monarchs believed that if the people all shared the same faith, there would be less cause for civil unrest, conflict, and possible uprisings.

Many Muslims still lived in Spain, and the peninsula also had a substantial Jewish population. In 1492, all Jews were ordered to convert or leave Spain; in 1499, the same order was issued against Muslims. Many Jews and Muslims converted, not wishing to give up home, friends, livelihood, and family. However, converts were still objects of suspicion. By Spanish law, it was a crime to practice any non-Christian religion, even in the privacy of one's own home. If someone observed that the Jewish converts next door never ate pork, for example, the neighbor could denounce the family to the Inquisition on suspicion of practicing Judaism. The Inquisition would arrest such people, then use a variety of interrogation techniques to find the facts. In cases of high crimes, the inquisitors used torture, which had been standard under the Roman laws on which the Inquisition was based. The Inquisition was an enormously effective royal tool for maintaining control by means of fear.

Control of the Lands

In 1492, Isabel turned her attention to finding a viable sea route to Asia. Her sponsorship of the first voyage of Christopher Columbus marked the beginning of the cultural exchange between Europe and the Americas After Isabel's death in 1504, Ferdinand annexed provinces in Italy and France and even expanded as far as Oran in North Africa.

Isabel and Ferdinand cemented or established important foreign alliances by arranging dynastic marriages for their children. Princess Catherine of Aragon married Arthur of England; when he died, she married his younger brother Henry, who would rule as Henry VIII. Princess Juana married Philip the Handsome, son of Holy Roman Emperor Maximilian I. By birth, Philip would inherit all the considerable Hapsburg lands in central Europe; he was also the likely successor to his father as Holy Roman Emperor.

Charles I

After King Ferdinand's death in 1516, his grandson became King Charles I of Spain. He also inherited all Hapsburg lands in central Europe, which put him in possession of more territory than any one individual had ever ruled in Europe. At first, Charles was much more interested in the Holy Roman Empire than in Spain; when his Spanish subjects interpreted his long absences as disrespect and rebelled, Charles returned to Spain. His sisters married heirs to various thrones in Denmark, Hungary, Portugal and France, creating or solidifying alliances between Spain and these European states. In 1519, he was elected Holy Roman Emperor, making him simultaneously Charles I of Spain and V of Germany.

A devout Catholic like all the Spanish monarchs, Charles engaged in a series of costly and ultimately futile wars to try to wipe out Protestantism and reunite Europe under the Catholic faith. With the Peace of Augsburg of 1555, which established that each elector in the empire could choose the religion of his own state, Charles abdicated. He turned the Holy Roman Empire over to his brother Ferdinand and abdicated the throne of Spain in favor of his son Philip, who would rule as Philip II.

Philip II and the Fall of Spain

By the 1550s, Spain boasted a thriving wool industry, a powerful navy, a stable aristocracy, religious unity (albeit enforced), and great wealth coming in from the American colonies. In addition, Philip's close family ties to several European rulers created strong national alliances for Spain.

Philip established Spain's first national capital in the city of Madrid, chosen for its double advantages of a central location within Spain and its insignificance among Spanish cities. The choice of a more established center of learning or culture such as Seville might easily have created resentment among the cities that were passed over.

Unlike Henry IV of France, who had converted for reasons of political expediency, Philip had no religious tolerance in his nature. He refused to allow the practice of any religion except Catholicism anywhere in his realms, including the distant American colonies.

The Holy Roman Empire

Ferdinand I was officially named Holy Roman Emperor in 1556, after the abdication of his brother Charles. Because Charles had concentrated his attention on Spain, Ferdinand had, in fact, already been ruling the Austrian Hapsburg lands for thirty years. He was king of Bohemia and Hungary as well as Holy Roman Emperor.

Ferdinand's major foreign-policy goal was to withstand the constant threat of Ottoman invasion. In 1529, the Turks, under Suleiman the Magnificent, laid siege to Vienna. The next seventeen years saw repeated Turkish invasions that the Austrians managed to repel. In 1547, a peace treaty divided Hungary into three zones: Royal Hungary under Ferdinand's rule, Transylvania under its own rule, and the rest—the largest share—under Ottoman Turkish control.

Ferdinand ruled over a diverse population that included ethnic Germans, Czechs, Poles, and Hungarians, both Lutherans and Catholics. Ferdinand believed that the only way to manage such a varied population was to maintain a centrally controlled, efficient civil service. He established three councils of government: one executive, one administrative, and one judicial. He retained the loyalty and cooperation of the great landlords by allowing them most of the responsibility for day-to-day government at the local level. He also allowed his subjects freedom of worship; Ferdinand realized that no government would ultimately succeed in dictating the personal faith of its subjects.

Ferdinand I had laid the foundations of a united Austrian state. Although he divided his lands among his sons on his death in 1564, Austria would emerge from the Thirty Years' War as a relatively strong, unified empire.

England

Queen Mary

In 1553, Mary Tudor became queen of England, succeeding her half-brother Edward VI. A Catholic herself, Mary restored Catholicism as the state religion; in 1554, she married Philip, who would soon rule Spain as Philip II. The marriage was highly unpopular in England because Philip was Catholic, foreign, and had a son from a previous marriage who might inherit the English throne.

Mary was given the nickname "Bloody Mary" for the number of Protestants who were executed during her reign. By her order, between two hundred fifty and three hundred Protestants were executed or burned at the stake; however, due process of English law was observed in all these cases. The accused were tried in court and executed.

Mary reigned for only a short time; she was well past her youth when she became queen, and she was not physically robust. She died childless in 1558 and was succeeded by her half-sister Elizabeth, daughter of Anne Boleyn.

Queen Elizabeth

Like her father Henry VIII, Elizabeth had a thoroughly pragmatic attitude toward both statesmanship and religion. She restored Anglicanism as the state religion but was tolerant for a monarch of her era; she believed that faith was a personal matter and should not be dictated by the crown.

Elizabeth knew that monarchs could be overthrown or assassinated, and she knew that Mary's reign had not inspired the people with confidence in a woman's ability to govern. With the goal of a long, peaceful reign over loving subjects, she cultivated popular goodwill as a matter of policy. She was highly successful; two of her people's nicknames for her were "Gloriana" and "Good Queen Bess."

Elizabeth was only twenty-five when she became queen; her youth, attractive looks, and high spirits made her a likely candidate for marriage. Philip II of Spain and Henry III of France both proposed to her. However, Elizabeth's single status was highly useful to her as a diplomatic tool, because any king considering marrying her was forced to maintain good relations with England. In fact, she never married; when she died in 1603, the Tudor dynasty ended and the crown passed to her Stuart cousin, James VI of Scotland.

The most significant event of Elizabeth's reign was the British defeat of the Spanish Armada—the armed fleet. Acts of English piracy on the high seas—and Elizabeth's open approval of them—infuriated Philip II of Spain; he thus decided to attack England and wipe out the Royal Navy. In 1588, the 130 ships of the Spanish Armada sailed toward the English Channel. The Armada looked very impressive and intimidating, but the English navy was more technologically advanced; its smaller, lighter ships were better armed and easier to maneuver.

The English had loaded a number of battered old ships with explosives. In the darkness, the few sailors on board these ships steered directly toward the Armada, lit the explosives, and jumped overboard once the course was set and the ship was well alight. When the Spaniards saw these burning ships bearing down on them, apparently by magic, they panicked. The Spanish captains created a veritable stampede of fleeing ships. When a fierce storm blew up, the English knew they had won. This battle marked the end of Spanish supremacy in European history.

Elizabeth gave her name to the Elizabethan Era, which is also called the English Renaissance because of its great flowering of literature and the arts. This period lasted from about 1550 to 1650, encompassing the reigns of both Elizabeth and James I. Playwright and poet William Shakespeare (c. 1564–1616), who can safely be called the most important English-language writer in history, was active in London theater during Elizabeth's reign. His colleagues included Christopher Marlowe, Ben Jonson, John Webster, and John Ford. Poets John Donne and John Milton, organist and composer Henry Purcell, and painter Hans Holbein were other notable creative artists of the era.

Elizabeth's cousin and successor, who ruled as James I of England, made his own major contribution to the English Renaissance when he commissioned the best scholars of the time to compile a new translation of the Bible. Published in 1611, the King James Bible may be the single most influential work in the history of English literature. It inspired generations of English and American writers and statesmen, and countless idioms of everyday speech come from its pages. Scholars and historians agree that although more technically accurate English translations of the Bible have appeared since, none can rival the beauty, majesty, and poetry of the King James version.

France

Louis XIV

In 1643, a five-year-old child was crowned Louis XIV of France. He would reign until his death in 1715. Known to the world as the Sun King, Louis was perhaps the most absolute of the absolute European monarchs of the seventeenth century. He chose the sun for his symbol because it was the source of all light and life on Earth.

Like all the monarchs of his era, Louis believed in the divine right of kings. This was not a theory to him but a reality by which he lived and ruled. Louis considered that he and the state of France were one entity. He had no intention of ceding any of his power to the aristocracy, the Church, or the common people of France.

Domestic Policy

King Louis XIII's chief minister of state had been the highly able Armand Jean du Plessis de Richelieu, a member of the minor French nobility who had become a cardinal in 1622. As the king's chief minister, Cardinal Richelieu's goal was to make France the most powerful nation in Europe. To him, this meant above all that the government should be placed firmly in the hands of the king and his ministers. Accordingly, Richelieu discouraged representative institutions. His successor Jules Mazarin, also a cardinal, became Louis XIV's chief minister. Both were hardheaded men with great common sense who excelled at the politics of realism as described by Machiavelli in *The Prince*, and neither believed in a strong central authority. Louis XIV never once convened the Estates-General, which was France's titular (although powerless) legislative assembly; he and Mazarin preferred to govern without their advice or interference. During Louis's reign, opposition to the king was considered treason; even had the Estates-General met, the deputies would have had no power to do anything other than agree with whatever the king wanted. After the death of Mazarin in 1661, Louis served as his own chief minister rather than summoning the Estates-General.

The reign of Louis XIV saw numerous construction projects. The building of the Canal du Midi (1665–1681), which connected the Mediterranean Sea and the Atlantic Ocean, was important for trade and an impressive feat of engineering for the time. The crown also pursued an aggressive tariff policy that discouraged imports and bolstered French luxury industries such as the textile industry. Louis hired architects to oversee the restoration/remodeling of the Louvre and the building of Versailles, the king's "retreat" 14 miles outside of Paris. An enormous palace with endless corridors of mirrors, marble, and gold leaf, Versailles became a major symbol of the king's absolute power; it also symbolized the dominant role France played in Europe in the seventeenth and eighteenth centuries.

Louis required all French aristocrats to spend part of each year at Versailles. In the short term, this policy prevented them from conspiring against the crown. In the long term, it weakened the all-important bond between estate owners and their tenants. Instead of living on their estates and managing their land and their people, the nobles spent half their time at Versailles; the money that should have been spent on maintaining and improving their estates was wasted on court finery and travel expenses. Louis did not know it, but he was helping to lay the groundwork for the French Revolution.

Louis XIV also helped to lay the foundation for the eighteenth-century Enlightenment. The crown was the most important patron of arts and letters in France. Investigation, learning, and publication in the arts and sciences flourished under official state sponsorship with the establishment of the French academies of letters, science, and the arts. Not since the Renaissance had artists enjoyed such a degree of official protection. This helps to explain why the Enlightenment was centered in France.

The Fronde was a series of uprisings and rebellions in the Paris-Bordeaux region over the issue of new taxes Mazarin levied on the people to pay for debts run up during the Thirty Years' War. Since the state controlled the army, which had greatly expanded during the war, the rebels were doomed from the start. The Fronde was crushed in 1652.

Foreign Policy

Louis XIV conducted a series of wars in the hope of strengthening France's position in Europe. On the whole, his wars were not successful. He expanded French territory on the northern front, but he also supported the losing side in the struggle for the English throne. Meanwhile, military spending drained the French treasury of money. This last would have serious consequences under Louis's successors. When the king's grandson Philip was crowned Philip V of Spain, all the nations of Europe rose up in alarm; a close alliance or official union between France and Spain would completely upset the delicate balance of European powers. In the end, Philip V agreed that France and Spain would never unite as one kingdom.

Prussia

The history of Germany as a nation-state really began in 1640, when Frederick William Hohenzollern became king of Brandenburg-Prussia (later known simply as Prussia). The king took several important steps to consolidate his power. First, he enlarged and strengthened the standing army, ensuring its loyalty to the throne. Second, he achieved control over the *junkers*—Prussian hereditary nobles—by giving them administrative duties. Third, he began to lay the groundwork for uniting all the territories he had inherited under his sole control.

In 1688, the elector's son became King Frederick I of Prussia. For twenty-five years, he maintained the modern state his father had created. His son Frederick

William I, who succeeded him in 1713, continued to streamline the bureaucracy of government. He also lavished money and attention on the army, which soon became a fighting force admired and envied by all Europe. Although the army did not spend much time on the battlefield during this period, it was an intimidating and impressive symbol of the power of the Prussian state.

In 1740, Frederick II, who became known to history as Frederick the Great, was crowned king. Always fascinated by military strategy, Frederick would prove a highly effective ruler. His daring foreign policy was dictated by Prussia's geographical position. Because Prussia was in the middle of Europe, it was surrounded on all sides by other nations, making it vulnerable to invasion at any time. Frederick's solution to this dangerous situation was twofold. First, he built up such an impressive, efficient army that other nations hesitated to attack him. Second, he himself struck aggressive blows to enlarge his territory and intimidate his neighbors.

The Austrian province Silesia was rich in natural resources, which Prussia lacked. Since Austrian Empress Maria Theresa was new to the throne, Frederick believed Austria was at its most vulnerable. His invasion of Silesia paid off in 1745 when he agreed to recognize Maria Theresa as empress and her husband as emperor in exchange for Silesia. The result of this was to elevate Prussia's position among European nations; Prussia and Austria were now considered equally strong German powers.

Frederick's reign also revealed the influence of the Enlightenment on his thinking. He stressed the importance of merit in the ranks of the civil service, raising the standards for admission. He expanded freedom of speech, promoted education, and reformed the legal system. Although the Prussian state was overwhelmingly Protestant, Frederick did not hinder Catholics from observing their faith. He also developed something of a friendship with the French philosopher Voltaire, entertaining him at court.

By the time Frederick died in 1786, Prussia had become a strong, centralized state. It formed the core of what would, in the following century, become a unified Germany.

The Thirty Years' War

The Thirty Years' War is the name given to a series of religious and political wars fought in the Holy Roman Empire from 1618 to 1648. In religious terms, Catholics and Protestants struggled for ascendancy. As of 1600, three of the empire's seven electorates were Protestant, while the other four were Catholic.

Catholics and Protestants hated one another as a matter of course; within the Protestant portions of the empire, Calvinists loathed Lutherans, believing that they were far too lax in their approach to religion.

In political terms, two prominent ruling families each tried to dominate the other. The two most important and influential ruling families in the Holy Roman Empire were the Wittelsbachs and the Hapsburgs. As of 1600, there was religious dissension within each family, although the Hapsburgs were mainly Catholic and the Wittelsbachs were mainly Protestant. One major figure emerged in each family in the early 1600s: Ferdinand Hapsburg, elected king of Bohemia in 1617 and Holy Roman Emperor two years later, and his rival Frederich Wittelsbach.

The Bohemian War, 1618–1620 and 1621–1623

A 1609 document called the Letter of Majesty had extended the rights of Protestants within Bohemia. The result was a mostly Lutheran landed gentry whose members resented being controlled by Catholic officials in the civil service. When the Catholic Ferdinand Hapsburg was elected king of Bohemia in 1617, he revoked the Letter of Majesty, thus earning many enemies among the wealthy and powerful Lutherans. Hostilities came to a head one day in Prague Castle, when a group of discontented Lutherans threw several of the hated Catholic civil servants through the upstairs windows onto a compost heap in the courtyard below. This event, called the Defenestration of Prague, marked the start of a major Protestant uprising in Bohemia. In the end, the Protestants deposed Ferdinand and replaced him with Frederich Wittelsbach in 1619.

Ferdinand, of course, fought back against the Protestant defiance. By this time he had succeeded to the throne of the Holy Roman Empire; this gave him a much greater position of power from which to fight for control of Bohemia. The Catholic electorates and free cities within the empire supported his cause. The Protestant armies under King Frederich fared badly against the Catholic armies, led by Maximilian of Bavaria. In 1620, the Catholic side won a decisive victory at the Battle of the White Mountain. Frederich hastily decamped to the Hague in Amsterdam, abandoning the Bohemians to a brutally enforced program of reconversion to Catholicism.

The Swedish War, 1630–1634

In 1628, Ferdinand decreed that all Protestant landowners in Inner Austria must leave the country, turning over their property to the state. Many of them converted to Catholicism to avoid banishment. In 1629, Ferdinand signed the Edict of Restitution, which banned Protestantism throughout the Holy Roman Empire. It also stated that any originally Catholic lands and property be restored to the Church.

Ferdinand did not realize that the time for such high-handed conduct had passed into history. Instead of meekly obeying his edicts, his Lutheran and Calvinist subjects united against him as their common enemy. In fact, not even Ferdinand's fellow monarchs and ministers of state sympathized with him. The Lutheran nation of Sweden immediately made preparations to march into Germany and fight for the Protestant side. Even Catholic France considered the ban and the Edict of Restitution reactionary and dangerous. For the moment, however, the French bided their time.

Gustav II Adolph, who had become king of Sweden in 1611 at age seventeen, entered the Thirty Years' War with an eye to expanding the Swedish empire by picking up new territory on the Baltic Sea. If Sweden could take over all the land around the Baltic, it would be able to control the trade routes, an enormous advantage over other nations in the region. In 1631, Gustav led his troops to a major victory over veteran General Count Johann Tilly's imperial forces at Breitenfeld, near the town of Leipzig. Gustav then formed alliances with most of the Calvinist leaders in areas such as Brandenburg. Over the course of the next year, Gustav and his forces marched south, progressing in triumph all the way to Munich. Gustav fell at the battle of Lützen in 1632. Despite this disaster, Sweden's great generals maintained the advantage on the battlefield.

Franco-Swedish War, 1635–1648

As a Catholic nation, France should have been the natural ally of Ferdinand II in his attempts to impose Catholicism on his subjects. The chief French minister of state, in fact, was a cardinal of the Catholic Church. However, France fought on the Protestant side and played a decisive role in the Hapsburgs' defeat. France's goal, like that of most other European nations of the time, was to strengthen its own position by keeping its neighbors as weak as possible.

The Holy Roman Empire and the Hapsburg family had always been a thorn in France's side. Geographically, the empire occupied a very strong central position on the continent. In addition, the Austrian Hapsburgs were related to the Spanish royal family and had been acquiring more and more authority in the empire. Cardinal Richelieu wanted to avoid a strong, united German state under Hapsburg rule, with Spain as its powerful ally; France's position between two such strong allied nations would be very shaky and vulnerable.

France's intervention on the Protestant side indicates that religion was by no means the central issue in the Thirty Years' War. Richelieu's position as minister of the Church took second place to his position as minister of France. Cardinal Mazarin shared Richelieu's point of view and supported his policies.

The decisive Swedish military successes inspired Richelieu to offer them substantial monetary support. French troops finally joined the fighting in 1635. The combined French and Swedish troops continued to win victories for the next ten years.

By 1644, Gustav's daughter Kristina was old enough to rule Sweden in her own right, assisted by the canny advice of her chief minister Axel Oxenstierna. Sweden was also fortunate in having some brilliant generals who achieved an impressive series of military victories. The Swedish army had reached Bavaria by 1646 and Prague by 1647; by the terms of the Peace of Westphalia in 1648, Sweden annexed several important territories.

Results of the Thirty Years' War

The Peace of Westphalia cemented the work begun under Ferdinand—the creation of a unified Austrian nation-state, which would, before long, become the Austro-Hungarian Empire. The Hapsburgs would continue to rule Austria into the twentieth century.

Provisions of the Peace of Westphalia

- Restored borders within the Holy Roman Empire to their 1624 locations
- Revoked the Edict of Restitution
- Gave Alsace to France
- Recognized Switzerland and the Netherlands as independent nation-states
- Made Bavaria, Prussia, Saxony, and Wurttemberg self-governing, independent states within the Holy Roman Empire
- Created a unified Austrian Empire, including Bohemia, Moravia, Silesia, and parts of Hungary

Since the war had been fought entirely within the Holy Roman Empire, the Germans suffered most from the violence. Of a total ethnic German population of about 17 million, historians agree that between 3.5 million and 7 million died; additionally, millions of acres of farmland were laid waste, and foreign troops released from combat duties roamed the countryside, looting and murdering. German unification, which had seemed possible in the early 1600s, was set back for some time to come.

With north central Europe devastated by the war, France emerged as the dominant nation-state. It would remain Europe's greatest power until Napoleon's defeat at Waterloo in 1815. The Holy Roman Empire would continue to exist on paper, but the emperor would have only nominal authority. Four of the electorates—Prussia, Bavaria, Saxony, and Wurttemberg—were made independent, self-governing states owing pro-forma allegiance to the emperor; the others were made part of the Austrian Empire.

The Peace of Westphalia was the result of the monarchs and ministers gathering together—the first time this had happened in European history. The nations agreed to recognize one another's sovereignty and to create and maintain a balance of power that would prevent future wars. The Peace of Westphalia was thus an important first step toward recognizing that affairs of state could be settled around a conference table rather than on the battlefield.

QUIZ

1. _____ marked the end of a period in which Spain was a dominant European power.
   A. The conquest of Granada
   B. The death of Queen Mary
   C. The defeat of the Armada
   D. The marriage of Ferdinand and Isabel

2. The officials of the Spanish Inquisition reported directly to _____.
   A. the Church in Rome
   B. the military
   C. the monarch
   D. the civil courts

3. What was one practical reason for the Spanish government to insist that all the people must practice the same religious faith?
   A. to avoid the need for popular elections
   B. to avoid the possibility of domestic conflict
   C. to keep the monarchs more securely on their thrones
   D. to maintain the union of Aragon and Castile

4. What explains Elizabeth I's belief in the importance of her subjects' personal affection?
   A. The people were more likely to vote for a popular monarch.
   B. The people were less likely to rise up against a popular monarch.
   C. The people would not pressure a popular monarch to marry.
   D. The people would not support the policies of a popular monarch.

5. Charles V abdicated as Holy Roman Emperor in the wake of _____.
   A. the conquest of Granada
   B. the defeat of the Armada
   C. the marriage of his son Philip
   D. the Peace of Augsburg

6. Most of the fighting in the Thirty Years' War took place in _____.
   A. France
   B. the Holy Roman Empire
   C. Italy
   D. Spain

7. _____ emerged from the Thirty Years' War as the dominant power in Europe.
   A. England
   B. France
   C. Spain
   D. Sweden

8. France's primary reason for entering the Thirty Years' War was _____.
   A. to weaken its hostile neighbors Austria and Spain
   B. to help its most prominent Catholic ally defeat the Protestants
   C. to end the threat of Swedish expansion on the continent
   D. to stimulate an economic recovery at home

9. What did the Edict of Restitution state?
   A. It settled the terms of surrender among the Holy Roman Empire, France, and Switzerland.
   B. It replaced Ferdinand II with Frederich as king of Bohemia.
   C. It banned Protestantism throughout the Holy Roman Empire.
   D. It allowed each elector to decide the official religion of his own state.

10. Louis XIV required the hereditary nobles to attend him every year at Versailles because _____.
    A. he wanted to prevent them from conspiring against him
    B. he wanted to consult them regularly about government policy
    C. he wanted be able to raise the army on a moment's notice
    D. he wanted their protection in case of a peasant uprising

PART TWO EXAM

1. All these religions worship the same God except _____.
   A. Buddhism
   B. Christianity
   C. Islam
   D. Judaism

2. What was the result of the 1281 Mongolian invasion of Japan?
   A. The Mongols defeated Japan and established a military dictatorship.
   B. The Mongols were crushed by a severe storm
   C. The Japanese defeated and enslaved the Mongols.
   D. The Japanese were converted to Islam.

3. The subjects of the Byzantine Empire believed that the emperor
   was _____.
   A. the direct descendant of God
   B. the earthly manifestation of God
   C. God's representative on Earth
   D. God's chief prophet

4. The Khitan peoples of the Central Asian steppes briefly conquered _____
   in the early eleventh century.
   A. China
   B. India
   C. Korea
   D. Japan

5. Which one is not a barbarian tribe that established itself in early medieval
   Europe?
   A. Franks
   B. Bretons
   C. Anglo-Saxons
   D. Etruscans

6. **The examination required for employment in the Chinese civil service tested the candidate's knowledge of _____.**
   A. Chinese history
   B. Confucianism
   C. geography
   D. accounting

7. **The Holy Roman Empire is best described as _____.**
   A. an absolute monarchy run by a highly efficient, centrally controlled bureaucracy
   B. a group of city-states united by a common language, a common religious faith, and a shared cultural heritage
   C. a collection of independent principalities and free cities owing allegiance to one titular monarch
   D. a constitutional monarchy with an emperor as the head of state and a representative assembly that carried out the will of the people

8. **Which best describes the difference between Sunni Islam and Shiite Islam?**
   A. Shiites are more secular than Sunnis.
   B. Shiites are more fundamentalist than Sunnis.
   C. Shiites and Sunnis disagree about whether Muhammad was a true prophet.
   D. Shiites are more tolerant than Sunnis of non-Muslims.

9. **Which event happened simultaneously with, and helped to cause, political unification of the Arabian peninsular tribes?**
   A. the founding of Islam
   B. the founding of the Ottoman Empire
   C. the rise of the Turks in Egypt
   D. the fall of the Roman Empire

10. **_____ is considered the single event or action of the Church that sparked the Protestant Reformation.**
   A. The granting of indulgences in exchange for financial contributions
   B. The interrogation policies of the Roman Inquisition
   C. The insistence on conducting Church business and services in Latin
   D. The lack of education demonstrated by many parish priests

11. **During the reign of Justinian, the Byzantine emperor expanded into all of the following areas except _____.**
   A. the Italian peninsula
   B. the Iberian peninsula
   C. the North African coast
   D. the Central Asian steppes

12. **The Mayan civilization was characterized by all of these except _____.**
    A. an accurate 365¼-day calendar
    B. a complex writing system
    C. military conquest
    D. major public-works projects such as roads

13. **The Mongols and _____ come from the same region and are therefore ethnically related and culturally similar.**
    A. Indians
    B. Persians
    C. Koreans
    D. Turks

14. **What was the major purpose of the Iroquois Confederacy?**
    A. to expand Iroquois territory by diplomatic means
    B. to set prices for trade with tribes of other nations
    C. to settle disputes among the member tribes
    D. to conduct religious ceremonies

15. **The frequent ritual suicides among the samurai show that in Japan, a very high value is placed on _____.**
    A. obedience
    B. loyalty
    C. personal honor
    D. military skill

16. **The primary cause of the migratory lifestyle of the peoples of the Central Asian steppes was _____.**
    A. the lack of plentiful sources of fresh water
    B. fear of the Chinese military
    C. the demands of their complex religious system
    D. their desire to enlarge their empire

17. **Which Western European nation was largely a Muslim caliphate until the 1400s?**
    A. Britain
    B. France
    C. Italy
    D. Spain

18. _____ was more responsible than any other factor for making the Tang Chinese capital of Changan the most magnificent city of its era.
    A. The degree of education in the Chinese bureaucracy
    B. The volume of international trade
    C. The rise of literacy throughout China
    D. The development of new printing techniques

19. All of the following led major military assaults against the Byzantine Empire in the seventh century AD except _____.
    A. the Chinese
    B. the Persians
    C. the Arabians
    D. the Slavs

20. The Ottoman Empire was politically _____.
    A. Arabic
    B. Greek
    C. Persian
    D. Turkish

21. The Incan Empire is unique among the vast empires of early civilization because the Incans _____.
    A. had no army
    B. did not read or write
    C. did not build cities
    D. lacked a complex belief system

22. Which best describes the effect of Ivan III's marriage to Zoe Palaeologos?
    A. Russians converted to the Eastern Orthodox religion.
    B. The Russian court became more cosmopolitan.
    C. Ivan III became the emperor of Byzantium.
    D. Ivan III defeated the Golden Horde.

23. _____ were the main military rivals of the Ilkhanate, established in Anatolia after the fall of the Mongol Empire.
    A. The Mughals of India
    B. The Mamluks of Egypt
    C. The Axumites of Africa
    D. The Yuan dynasty of China

24. The establishment of the Abbasid capital in Baghdad led to a major cultural exchange between the Arabs and the _____.
    A. Egyptians
    B. Moroccans
    C. Persians
    D. Greeks

25. Many Russian nobles joined the military in the 1400s because _____.
    A. they believed it was their duty
    B. they were eager to show their loyalty to the throne
    C. they were required by law to serve
    D. they were given hereditary titles and land

26. Which best describes the Hundred Years' War?
    A. a struggle for the English throne between two major factions
    B. a territorial struggle between England and France
    C. a religious war between Protestants and Catholics
    D. a religious war between Christians and Muslims

27. _____ staged repeated raids into Western and Eastern Europe from the eighth to the eleventh centuries.
    A. The Byzantines
    B. The Slavs
    C. The Vikings
    D. The Franks

28. Between 1192 and 1867, the supreme ruler of Japan was called _____.
    A. the emperor
    B. the shogun
    C. the samurai
    D. the *daimyo*

29. _____ characterized Japanese society during the 1400s.
    A. Frequent military strife among the warlords
    B. Peace and prosperity
    C. Major geographical expansion
    D. Destructive foreign invasions

30. **The political organization of India between the fall of the Gupta Empire and the rise of the Delhi sultanate is best described as _____.**
   A. a centrally controlled state ruled by an autocrat
   B. a group of independent warlords fighting for supreme power
   C. a theocracy ruled by the large caste of Hindu priests
   D. a military dictatorship controlled largely by the national army

31. **The absolute monarchs of the seventeenth and eighteenth centuries consistently granted major privileges to _____ as a means of defusing possible disloyalty or opposition.**
   A. the military
   B. the pope
   C. the hereditary nobility
   D. the wealthy merchant class

32. **In the tenth century, the Slav states of Eastern Europe were linked in all these ways except _____.**
   A. ethnically
   B. linguistically
   C. militarily
   D. religiously

33. **Western scholars of the fourteenth and early fifteenth centuries primarily studied Roman texts instead of Greek ones because _____.**
   A. Greek texts were not as well written as Roman
   B. Greek texts were scarcer and harder to understand than Roman
   C. Greek texts were older than Roman
   D. Greek texts showed a different way of thinking than Roman

34. **_____ was the dominant culture of the Far East during the first millennium.**
   A. China
   B. Japan
   C. Korea
   D. Tibet

35. **In 1500, Turkish peoples ruled all these areas except _____.**
   A. Arabia
   B. India
   C. Egypt
   D. Spain

36. **The primary natural resource of the kingdom of Ghana that brought it great wealth by 300 BC was _____.**
    A. diamonds
    B. gold
    C. coal
    D. timber

37. **Which best describes international trade under the Ming dynasty in China?**
    A. The Chinese exported manufactured goods in exchange for foreign silver.
    B. The Chinese exported silver in exchange for manufactured goods from abroad.
    C. The Chinese bartered their crops for manufactured goods from abroad.
    D. The Chinese exported their manufactured goods in exchange for foreign crops they could not grow themselves.

38. **The Crusades happened for all these reasons except _____.**
    A. because the Byzantine emperor requested military aid from the pope
    B. because the pope was eager to enhance his prestige
    C. because the Arabians wanted to convert the Christians to Islam
    D. because European Christians were eager to earn forgiveness for their sins

39. **The new religion Martin Luther founded in 1517 was characterized by all of these except _____.**
    A. simple worship services conducted in the language of the people
    B. encouragement of each believer to read and study the Bible on his or her own
    C. the belief that a person's salvation depended on the sincerity of his or her faith
    D. a strict insistence on proper behavior, simple clothing, and no frivolity

40. **In the wake of the Russian victory at Kulikovo in 1380, the khan _____.**
    A. permanently abandoned Russia
    B. recognized the court of Moscow as the seat of Russian authority
    C. cracked down harder than ever on Russian attempts at autonomy
    D. published a new, punitive code of laws

41. **The _____ settled and dominated the regions that eventually became the nations of France and Germany.**
    A. Franks
    B. Greeks
    C. Vikings
    D. Gauls

42. What was the usual result when a small child became emperor of early medieval China?

A. A popular uprising would overthrow the dynasty and install a new one.

B. The people closest to the throne would all try to influence policy in their own favor.

C. The empire would break up into a nation of independent warring kingdoms.

D. The Chinese capital would be moved to a new city.

43. The Abbasid caliphate expanded as far east as _____ at its greatest extent.

A. the Yangtze River valley

B. the Ganges River valley

C. the Indus River valley

D. the Nile River valley

44. The most likely reason for popular rebellion against the Yuan dynasty is that _____.

A. the Yuan showed no respect for the privileges of heredity

B. the Yuan tried to convert all of China to Buddhism

C. the Yuan were ethnically and culturally foreign

D. the Yuan worked hard to maintain old Chinese traditions

45. Which major geographical obstacle isolated the peoples of southern Africa from the rest of the world until relatively modern times?

A. the Amazon River

B. the Nile River

C. the Gobi Desert

D. the Sahara Desert

46. King Henry VIII of England decided to break with the Catholic Church because _____.

A. he believed that the Church needed reform

B. he was angry over the Church's practice of granting indulgences

C. he could not obtain a divorce from the Church when he wanted to remarry

D. he wanted church services conducted in the English language

47. The Mexican civilization of Teotihuacán is best described as _____.

A. an independent city-state

B. the capital city of an empire

C. a collection of rival kingdoms

D. a nation comprising several ethnically and linguistically related tribes

48. **The most important effect of the 1438 Council of Florence was _____.**
    A. the official reunion of the Roman and Orthodox Catholic churches
    B. a major exchange of books and ideas among Eastern and Western scholars
    C. Pope Leo X's decision to restore the Vatican and St. Peter's Basilica
    D. the publication of the first Bible printed with movable type

49. **France became a Christian realm with the conversion of _____.**
    A. Charlemagne
    B. Clovis
    C. Gregory of Tours
    D. Otto I

50. **Many Turks ended up in the Islamic Empire because _____.**
    A. they were fleeing religious persecution in their homelands
    B. their fighting ability made them desirable in the Arabian armies
    C. they repeatedly failed to conquer the Chinese Empire
    D. they hoped to establish trading posts in the West

Part Three

World History in the Modern Era

chapter **15**

European Exploration and Colonization, 1500–1700

At the end of the 1400s, European monarchs began sponsoring voyages of exploration beyond the known world. Their purposes were fourfold: trade, conquest and expansion, religious conversion, and curiosity. The primary reason for their stupendous success can be summed up in one word: guns.

Europeans had long been trading with Asia, but the overland routes were slow and fraught with the twin dangers of violence and robbery. Since transport of goods by water was much easier, more efficient, and less hazardous, governments hoped to find navigable sea routes to Asia.

The second motive was conquest and expansion. European nations tended to maintain aggressive foreign policies, constantly attacking one another in order to acquire valuable territory and expand their power bases. A larger population meant more revenue for the crown in taxes, more income for the Catholic Church in tithes, and more soldiers in the army. Therefore, three of the most powerful branches of society—the court, the clergy, and the military—were united in the desire to explore the seas and lands beyond Europe in the hope of establishing colonies that would make them richer and stronger than their neighbors.

The third motive, religious conversion, was a product of the universal Christian belief that non-Christians were heathens and that it was a Christian's duty to save their souls from eternal damnation. Just as a nation is politically and economically stronger with a larger population, a church is stronger with more believers. This made the European churches eager to send missionaries to Asia, Africa, and the Americas to bring more souls into the fold.

The last motive, and a very powerful one, was a sense of adventure and curiosity—the urge to find out what lay beyond the horizon and the willingness to take the risk of finding out. This urge has characterized human beings since the beginning of civilization, and is responsible for all scientific discovery and technological achievement. Just as the modern explorations of outer space could not have been accomplished without the fundamental human desire to see and learn about the unknown, the sixteenth- and seventeenth-century voyages of exploration could never have happened if a number of brave souls had not wanted to find out what was on the other side of the ocean.

Although the Chinese had invented gunpowder centuries before, no guns in the world could match those that the Europeans had developed by the 1500s. One of the most important axioms to understanding history is that in any conflict, the side with the greater firepower always wins. The Asians had much less sophisticated guns than the Europeans, and the Africans and the North and South Americans had no guns at all. This is almost certainly the main reason the Europeans were able to impose their will on the peoples of the other continents.

CHAPTER OBJECTIVES

- Identify the motives that led European nations to begin exploring the world beyond Europe.
- Describe where the various European states established trade relations and colonies.
- Identify the major figures of the era and match each person to the geographical area he explored.

Chapter 15 Time Line

- **1487**   Bartholomew Diaz rounds Cape of Good Hope
- **1492**   Spanish-sponsored voyage of Christopher Columbus crosses Atlantic; begins cultural exchange
- **1497–1499**   Vasco da Gama reaches India
- **1513**   Portuguese reach Southeast Asia
- **1517**   Portuguese reach China
- **1539**   Hernando de Soto explores southeastern North America
- **1565**   Pedro Menéndez de Avilés founds St. Augustine on Florida coast
- **1585**   Sir Walter Raleigh establishes English colony on Roanoke Island, Virginia
- **1595**   First Dutch voyage to Southeast Asia
- **1602**   Dutch East India Company
- **1603**   French establish Canadian colonies
- **1754–1763**   French and Indian War; Seven Years' War

Exploration of Africa and Asia

Portuguese Exploration and Trade

Portugal's long stretch of Atlantic coastline and its proximity to Africa placed it in an ideal geographical position to lead Europe into the age of exploration. The Portuguese Prince Henry's passion for ships and sailing gave him the nickname "Prince Henry the Navigator" and made him the ideal sponsor for voyages of exploration. Prince Henry oversaw and paid for the development of the caravel, a light, fast sailing ship. He sponsored exploratory voyages to western Africa and employed skilled cartographers to record the results. Henry's own considerable skills in navigation were hugely beneficial to the Portuguese fleet.

During the late 1400s, Portuguese explorers made a series of voyages along the west coast of Africa. Their purpose was to gather information and perhaps to set up trading posts; at this time, there was no attempt at invasion or conquest. In 1486, the Portuguese entered Benin, finding it a sophisticated and wealthy civilization. In 1487, Captain Bartholomew Diaz and his crew, blown off course during a storm, stumbled accidentally on a viable water route to the East—by rounding the southern tip of Africa.

In 1498, Vasco da Gama became the first European to reach India by sea. He learned two facts of major importance on this first encounter. First, the Indians would sell but not barter; European goods held little appeal for them. Second, the Portuguese would have to drive Arab traders out of the Indian Ocean if their own trade ambitions were to succeed. When da Gama returned to Europe and sold a shipload of Indian pepper for sixty times what it had cost him, it was clear that the thunderstorm that sent Diaz's ship off course had been a great stroke of good economic fortune for Portugal.

A small nation with a small population, Portugal was interested in trade rather than in conquest and expansion. Its goals were entirely commercial—to establish permanent trading posts and to make money. The first Portuguese trading post was in Calicut at the southern tip of India. By 1510, the Portuguese ousted the Arab traders and established their own presence in Malacca (on the Malay Peninsula) and Goa, on India's west coast. Arab traders would continue to operate in the area but on a smaller scale; they were especially successful in continuing their trade with Venice, to which their ships had easy access via the Adriatic Sea.

During the 1540s, Portugal became the first European nation to make direct contact by sea with Japan, and by the 1550s, the Portuguese had set up trading posts in China and throughout the Southeast Asian islands. In addition to purchasing Asian goods for export to Europe, the Portuguese made a handsome profit by carrying goods between Asian nations that traded with one another, such as China and Japan.

Only after 1570 did the Portuguese attempt to colonize Africa as Spain had colonized South America. The Moroccans and Ethiopians resisted their first attempts, but the Portuguese persisted, eventually establishing some communities along the Zambezi River. The story was different in Angola, where Portugal founded the port of Luanda in 1571 and the city of Benguela in 1617. Europeans generally referred to Angola as "Portuguese West Africa." During the nineteenth century, Angola was a colony like any other European colony; the conquerors set up and ran the government, while the natives found themselves at the bottom of the social and political hierarchy.

/ Dutch Trade

Like Portugal, the Netherlands was a small nation that had concentrated on economic activity rather than on foreign policy. By 1600, the Dutch had developed Europe's most substantial sailing fleet. The first Dutch voyage to the East took place in 1595; it returned more than two years later with a cargo that made huge profits, showing the Dutch that shipping trade in this area was financially viable.

It was not long before the Dutch gained the upper hand over the Portuguese in trade with the East. The Dutch had larger ships; in addition, they did not carry guns, so there was more room for cargo. They also had superior trade goods to offer the Indians and Chinese in exchange for their wares.

In 1602, the Dutch East India Company was founded. It sold shares of stock and offered investors a regular return on the profits. As the Portuguese had done before them, the Dutch earned a large profit not only on trade between Asia and Europe but also by serving as carriers of goods in the lively inter-Asian trade.

On the European mainland, Spain was trying to subdue the Netherlands. Since Portugal and Spain were allies, this gave the Dutch the excuse to attack Portuguese ships and strongholds in the East. By the mid-1600s, when Spain finally recognized Dutch independence, the Dutch had ousted the Portuguese from all their trading posts in the Indian Ocean, Indonesia, and the China seas.

The Dutch also challenged Portuguese interests in Africa. Between 1632 and 1652, the Dutch captured three major ports: Elmina on what became known as the "slave coast," the Angolan port of Luanda, and Cape Town on the southern tip of the continent.

The Slave Trade

Slavery had existed in parts of Africa since ancient times, just as it did in all ancient civilizations. The usual rule in the ancient world was that prisoners of war became slaves; since wars were most often fought with neighboring states or tribes, slavery did not necessarily mean finding oneself in an utterly foreign setting or culture. In some ancient civilizations, slaves had certain rights; they could marry, earn money, and even buy back their freedom.

The European trade in black African slaves, however, was very different from anything that had gone before. For one thing, it was based on racism, a concept entirely or largely absent from ancient concepts of slavery, which were the result of conquest. Secondly, it involved the notorious "middle passage," as the journey across the Atlantic Ocean was called. Eyewitness testimony by survivors describes conditions of unbelievable filth and misery below decks on the slave ships, with people crammed into every available inch of space and deprived of light, fresh air, and sanitary facilities. Most Africans who were kidnapped and sold into slavery had no understanding of what was happening to them, which made the experience all the more nightmarish. Historians have estimated that the death rate on the middle passage was as high as 10 percent per shipload of Africans.

Africans themselves became enthusiastic collaborators in the slave trade; Europeans paid them large sums of money to round up their victims. Because the African culture was tribal, Africans had no particular loyalty to people of other tribes, and thus no qualms about participating in the slave trade. From the mid-1700s until the slave trade died out, most African slaves were shipped across the ocean to work, usually in the worst and hardest jobs available, in the American colonies.

The vast majority of African slaves came from what the traders called the "slave coast"—the coastal area of present-day Ghana, Ivory Coast, and Nigeria. The trade in slaves was so brisk for a time that the populations of these areas were decimated. The major European participants in the slave trade were Britain, France, the Netherlands, and Portugal.

Exploration to the West

Spanish and Portuguese Exploration

The race for American colonies and the continuing cultural exchange between the Americas and Europe began in 1492, when Christopher Columbus arrived in the Caribbean in a fleet of three ships. Columbus, an Italian sponsored by the Spanish monarchy, had sailed forth looking for the elusive trade route to India and China. He reasoned that since the world was spherical, one should be able to reach the East by sailing west. There was only one flaw in his theory: the Americas and the Pacific Ocean lay between Europe and Asia. Europeans were ignorant of the existence of this great land mass.

In his four voyages to the Caribbean, Columbus claimed Cuba, Hispaniola, Antigua, and the Bahamas for Spain, establishing a base of operations for the Spanish explorers who followed him. The islands are called the West Indies because Columbus never realized that he had not, in fact, reached India; the misnomer *Indians* has stuck to the earliest inhabitants of the Americas ever since.

Columbus's voyages are historically important because they connected two parts of the globe that had had no previous contact. His safe return to Europe showed the various monarchs that by sponsoring explorers, they could establish colonies and expand their power bases abroad. Missionaries were also pleased at the discovery that there were whole societies of people they could try to convert to Christianity.

In 1513, Vasco Núñez de Balboa sailed to Panama, crossed the isthmus, and became the first European to see the Pacific Ocean. In 1519, Ferdinand Magellan of Portugal sailed all the way around South America and continued on to the west. Magellan died in the Philippines, but thirty-five of his crew returned safely, having circled the globe. This voyage established that it was indeed possible to reach Asia by sailing west.

Between 1519 and 1531, the Spaniards defeated the mighty Aztec and Inca armies of Mexico and Peru. The great wealth they seized fired the imaginations of explorers such as Juan Ponce de León and Hernando de Soto, who sailed to North America in search of similar wealth. These men are known to history by the romantic name of *conquistadors*, a word that celebrates their adventurous spirit and undoubted bravery while minimizing the fact that they were motivated by greed and behaved brutally to those whose lands they invaded.

The conquistadors explored the Southeast and Southwest regions of North America, failing to find any evidence of gold. None of them realized at the time that the wealth of North America was in its natural resources: timber, fruit, vegetables, a temperate seasonal climate, and fertile land.

In 1565, Pedro Menéndez de Avilés established the first permanent European colony in North America when he founded the city of St. Augustine, Florida. The Spaniards began to settle Texas in the late 1600s and California in the mid-1700s. At one time, Spain claimed almost two-thirds of what is now the United States.

By the 1770s, Spain was reaping an enormous profit from its colonies. The Spaniards had organized their territory into the viceroyalties of New Spain and Peru, which were broken down into smaller, locally administered units. Spain controlled the wealth of the colonial gold and silver mines, with the crown taking a one-fifth share of the profits. In addition, the colonists could not trade on their own; they could only accept import of Spanish goods.

The Spaniards and Portuguese exploited the native populations for the purposes of labor. Conditions were little better than chattel slavery at first; like all people in positions of economic power throughout history, the masters and owners paid the workers as little as possible and curtailed their freedoms as much as they could. Under political and religious pressures from Europe, and thanks in large part to the protests of the influential Catholic missionary Bartolome de las Casas, working conditions eventually improved somewhat.

European invasion was catastrophic for the native populations of Mexico and South America. Their empires were destroyed; their cultures all but obliterated; and their people enslaved in backbreaking, dangerous jobs in mines and plantation fields. The South American population dropped drastically after the invasion; many were killed in armed conflict, but the vast majority succumbed to European diseases like smallpox. Never having been exposed to these diseases, the Americans had no natural resistance. With the native workforce dying by the thousands, the Spaniards had to find another source of labor. The solution turned out to be the African slave trade (see "The Slave Trade" in this chapter).

French Exploration

The French began their voyages to America for business reasons: they wanted to expand the fur trade. Giovanni da Verrazano in 1524 and Jacques Cartier in 1535 were the first Frenchmen to explore any part of North America. It took until 1603 for the French to establish their first American colony, when a party of fur traders traveled west to Canada. Samuel de Champlain went with the party as their mapmaker. He mapped the St. Lawrence River and the Atlantic coast. Champlain founded the towns of Port Royal and Quebec. He established friendly relations with the Algonquin and Huron Indians; this friendship led to an important alliance of forces during the French and Indian War.

In 1615, Champlain became the first European to see the Great Lakes. This area became the hub of the French fur-trading industry. As the French prospered, they explored farther south. They settled parts of Ohio and sailed down the Mississippi River to the Gulf of Mexico, where René-Robert Cavelier, Sieur de La Salle founded the colony of Louisiana.

English Exploration

The earliest English voyages to the West were made in search of a trade route to Asia—the elusive "Northwest Passage." In 1497, John Cabot landed on the coast of Maine, becoming the first European since Leif Eriksson (a Norseman who had reached the coast of Canada about five hundred years earlier) to see North America. It was Cabot's voyage that assured Europeans that they had stumbled across a new continent: America was clearly not Asia.

Cabot never returned from a second voyage. His son Sebastian followed him in 1508, reaching the entrance to Hudson Bay. In 1509, Henry Hudson found the mouth of the Hudson River and followed it north to Albany before he realized it led north, not west. On a second voyage, Hudson drove his crew farther and farther west through a network of islands north of Canada. Terrified for their lives in the unknown, frigid waters, Hudson's crew marooned him and turned the ship back east toward safety.

England's interest in acquiring colonies arose when Elizabeth I realized that Spain and France were establishing a foothold in the Americas. During the 1560s, English pirate ships began venturing into the Atlantic to capture Spanish cargoes. Cousins John Hawkins and Francis Drake were especially successful; Drake became the first Englishman to sail around the globe and was knighted on his return to England in 1580. This gesture on the queen's part was one of the sparks that set off the great naval battle with the Spanish Armada in 1588.

England joined the North American land grab by sending Sir Walter Raleigh west in 1584 to claim a large territory that included the present-day states of Virginia, West Virginia, Maryland, and the Carolinas. Raleigh named the terri tory Virginia in honor of Elizabeth the Virgin Queen.

Raleigh and his companions established a colony on Roanoke Island, off present-day North Carolina. A second group of settlers sailed west for Roanoke the following year, led by John White, who immediately returned to England for supplies. When White sailed back to the colony in 1590, he found no trace of the settlement he had left behind. No one knows to this day what became of the settlers of Roanoke.

This failure did not discourage the English from trying again. Their first success was the Chesapeake Bay colony of Jamestown, founded in 1606. By 1638, England had founded seven colonies along the Atlantic coast. As the American population grew, the colonies began to expand westward, carrying out the commands of their royal charters.

The effect of the British conquerors on the American Indians was quite unlike the effect of the Spanish conquerors on the South Americans. The Spaniards dominated and exploited the South Americans, imposing the Spanish language and culture on them; thus, in Latin America, the story was one of enforced assimilation. The British, on the other hand, after the early, friendly contacts turned sour, treated the American Indians as a hostile foreign population. There was no attempt at religious conversion, cultural exchange, or assimilation; rather, the British—later the Americans—simply shoved the Indians aside, encroaching farther and farther onto Indian lands.

/ The Seven Years' War

Conflict broke out between the British and French in the 1750s, when each side wanted to stop the other from expanding its North American territory. In the United States, the ensuing war is called the French and Indian War; in Europe, it is known as the Seven Years' War. Together, the two wars are often referred to as the Great War for Empire.

The battle in the colonies took place in the Ohio River valley, in the vicinity of present-day Pittsburgh. British and American troops (with the Americans led by a young man named George Washington) fought French troops and their Indian allies.

In Europe, Britain and Prussia banded together against France and Austria. Soon Sweden, Russia, and various small, independent states in central Europe joined the war on the French side. The goal of this alliance was to invade and defeat Prussia. In the end, Prussia was able to hold its ground against invasion and conquest, thanks to the strength of its British ally.

The fighting in the colonies ended in 1761. The peace treaty of 1763 ceded all French territory east of the Mississippi River (except New Orleans), plus Canada, to Britain. To prevent an immediate British takeover of the entire continent, France ceded all its territory west of the Mississippi to Spain.

Britain had gained a prize of enormous value in natural resources and a prosperous colonial economy. However, Britain had spent vast sums of money on the war and now needed to tax the colonies to pay for it. In the end, of course, this British attempt to force the colonists to bear the burden of the war debt led to the colonies' declaration of independence from Britain and the creation of the United States of America. Britain surrendered in 1781 and withdrew from North America except for its connection with Canada, which would become an independent nation in 1867.

QUIZ

1. _____ became a major Portuguese colony in Africa.
   A. Angola
   B. Ethiopia
   C. Ghana
   D. Morocco

2. _____ is an important historical figure because his voyage west initiated a major cultural exchange between Europe and the Americas.
   A. Jacques Cartier
   B. Christopher Columbus
   C. Hernando de Soto
   D. Sir Walter Raleigh

3. Which European nation was the first to establish colonies in North America?
   A. England
   B. France
   C. Portugal
   D. Spain

4. Their _____ enabled the Dutch to supplant the Portuguese in Asian trade.
   A. larger ships
   B. stronger military
   C. more-enlightened monarch
   D. earlier success

5. Spanish explorers were initially disappointed with North America because they failed to find _____.
   A. fertile land
   B. Indians
   C. gold
   D. fresh water

6. Britain and France clashed over _____ in the French and Indian War.
   A. alliance with the Indians
   B. sea routes to Asia
   C. supremacy in the slave trade
   D. North American territory

7. **All these European nations were major participants in the African slave trade except _____.**
    A. Britain
    B. France
    C. Italy
    D. Portugal

8. **The 1497 voyage of _____ assured Europeans they had found not "the Indies" but a new continent.**
    A. John Cabot
    B. Christopher Columbus
    C. Giovanni da Verrazano
    D. Pedro Menéndez de Avilés

9. **Portugal was in an ideal position to explore the African coast because _____.**
    A. it wanted to build up its colonial empire
    B. it was the most powerful nation in Europe
    C. it was geographically close to Africa
    D. it could always count on support from Spain

10. **Portugal's most important goal on its voyages to Asia was _____.**
    A. establishing trade relations
    B. annexing territory
    C. military conquest
    D. converting the Asians to Christianity

chapter 16

Russia and the Great Muslim Empires, 1500–1858

The earliest Russian princes and czars had achieved several important steps toward the ultimate goal of creating a state that could take its place among the great nations of the world. When Ivan III withheld tribute from the Tatars in 1480, Russians finally achieved control of their own nation; they have held that control to the present day.

The sixteenth to eighteenth centuries saw major changes in Russia. Both Peter I and Catherine II made great efforts to introduce Western European elements into the Russian culture, with some degree of success. Both continued the imperial tradition of expansion, adding important new territory to what was becoming the world's largest single nation.

The Islamic world reached its zenith of splendor during this era. The Ottoman Empire, the Mughal Empire in India, and Safavid Persia were all remarkable for their cultural achievements: the world marveled at their literature, architecture, painting, and textiles. Their economies were prosperous; their leaders were generally capable or even brilliant men; and their societies flourished.

This state of affairs, however, disintegrated as quickly as it had arisen. Between 1500 and 1850, Western Europe made major strides forward into the modern world; the era was a time of technical inventions, political and social progress, an international Enlightenment, and enormous achievements in literature and the arts. At the same time, the Islamic world stagnated. The printing press is just one example; the first European printing press dates from 1455, but the Muslim empires did not acquire this technology until 1727. Another example is the pendulum clock—an everyday household item in Europe while still a luxury item and a curiosity in India. The Muslim world seemed unable to leave the medieval era behind. After the eighteenth century, this region would not play a significant role in world history for over two hundred years.

CHAPTER OBJECTIVES

- Trace the progress of Russian expansion under the czars through Catherine the Great.

- Compare and contrast sixteenth-century Russian government and society with Russia under the later czars.

- Describe the establishment, height, and decline of the Mughal Empire in India.

- Discuss Safavid Persia and the Ottoman Empire and their relationship to each other.

Chapter 16 Time Line

1480	End of Tatar authority in Russia
1501	Shah Ismail founds Safavid dynasty in Persia (Iran)
1514	Ottomans conquer Mesopotamia
1520	Suleiman the Magnificent becomes Ottoman emperor
1526	Battle of Panipat; Babur founds Mughal Empire
1547	Ivan IV is crowned czar of All the Russias
1571	Battle of Lepanto; Ottoman navy defeated
1587	Abbas I becomes emperor of Persia
1598–1613	Time of Troubles in Russia

- 1613   Mikhail Romanov becomes first Romanov czar of Russia
- 1682   Peter I becomes czar of Russia
- 1703   Founding of St. Petersburg, Russia
- 1707   Death of Mughal emperor Aurangzeb
- 1762   Catherine II becomes empress of Russia
- 1858   Britain annexes India

The Expansion of the Russian Empire

Ivan III

The real beginning of the history of Russia as a nation-state dates to 1480, when Ivan III withheld the annual monetary tribute to the Tatars (see Chapter 13) and asserted his own authority as the supreme ruler of Russia. He thus began the tradition of autocracy that would be a recurring theme throughout Russian history. In 1493, for instance, Ivan forced the kingdom of Lithuania to grant him the title "lord of all Rus." He also began using the title *Czar*, a Russian form of *Caesar*. Symbolically, the use of the imperial title reinforced Ivan's claim that he was descended from the Caesars and that after the fall of Constantinople, the New Rome, Moscow had become "the Third Rome," the center of the world. Officially, however, he remained Grand Prince of Moscow.

Ivan's marriage to Zoe Palaeologos, niece of the Byzantine emperor, stimulated a degree of cultural exchange with the West during Ivan's reign. Ivan established diplomatic relations with Western nations, and an exchange of embassies took place. Russians were curious about Westerners but also contemptuous of them because they were not Orthodox Christians; Europeans no doubt felt similar emotions toward the Russians, whose society seemed to them both more exotic and more primitive than their own. Ivan hired several Italian architects and artists, notably Petrus Antonius Solarius, to rebuild the Kremlin. This complex of buildings was at the heart of Moscow, featuring a large open plaza surrounded by four strikingly beautiful cathedrals and the czar's mansion. The entire Kremlin was protected by strong walls.

Under Ivan, Russia expanded into an empire more than three times the size of the original Grand Principality of Muscovy. Ivan III took control of Novgorod and its territories, which included vast tracts of land to the northeast and northwest of Muscovy. Vasili II, who succeeded Ivan in 1505, added the

Baltic province of Pskov and the province of Riazan on the Oka River. Access to these bodies of water was important for trade, since it was much easier to transport quantities of goods by water than overland.

Ruling a larger empire brought with it both advantages and disadvantages. A substantial rise in population meant a larger army and greater revenue from tributes and taxes, but a larger population was more difficult to control and monitor. A larger bureaucracy became necessary in order to take care of the routine of governing at the local level. Because most of the empire was geographically far from Moscow, a great deal of everyday authority remained in the hands of local officials, which invited corruption on a large scale since there was no oversight. The harsh Russian climate made travel slow and difficult, the postal service was unreliable, and local officials were generally free to carry out or ignore their responsibilities as they saw fit, without any fear of inspection or reprimand by superiors.

Ivan IV "The Terrible"

Born in 1530, Ivan IV succeeded to the imperial throne at age three. He became known in Russia as *Ivan Grozny*, which has traditionally been translated into English as "Ivan the Terrible"; a more accurate translation is "Ivan the Formidable" or "Ivan the Awe-Inspiring." Ivan proved his strength and determination as soon as he turned thirteen; he asserted his authority over the boyars in a manner that struck terror and awe into everyone. Four years later, he became the first Russian ruler to have himself crowned czar of All the Russias. (Ivan III had used the title *czar* only in his private correspondence.)

The boyars created chaos in the government until Ivan was old enough to assume power; this early experience taught the czar that they were quite likely to quarrel among themselves, conspire against him, and overthrow him if they could. Distrusting the boyars, Ivan concluded that he must rule as an autocrat. He chose advisers he felt were personally loyal to him as the head of the state. Partly to counteract the boyars' resentment at having their traditional authority taken away, and partly to protect his own place on the throne, Ivan also passed the first laws restricting mobility of the peasant class. Similar actions taken by his successors would eventually lead to their becoming serfs—the literal property of their noble landlords, with few rights of their own.

Over a nearly forty-year reign, Ivan IV conquered the last remaining Tatars and extended Russia's eastern border far beyond the Volga River, taking over a swath of territory stretching from the Caspian Sea in the south to the Arctic Ocean in the north. With the Tatars finally crushed, the way was open for expansion to the Pacific Ocean.

Under Ivan, the large Russian army began improving in quality. His predecessors had enlarged the army but had not trained it. Under Ivan's rule, military commanders created specialized divisions, such as musketeers and artillery.

The Fall of Ivan IV

Russia's strong czar collapsed during the second half of his reign. His behavior grew more and more eccentric: in 1581, for example, he struck and killed his son and heir Ivan in a fit of rage in front of several witnesses. Historians believe that Ivan IV suffered from paranoia, severe mental illness, and possibly also a spinal disability that meant constant physical pain.

Everyone close to the throne could see that Ivan the Formidable was no longer capable of ruling, but there was no peaceful means of deposing him. Russia was an absolute monarchy with no legislative or representative assembly, no constitution, no balance of powers, and no apparatus in the government for replacing an unstable or incompetent czar.

In 1564, Ivan mapped out an area covering about half the czardom and decreed that he would rule this area as his personal absolute kingdom. He created a bureaucracy for his new realm, confiscated land and property at will, and dismissed and executed any authority figures he saw as a threat. Ivan also formed the *Oprichnina*, an organization of secret police whose members were called *oprichniki*. The *oprichniki* were officially civil servants; in fact, they were murderous thugs, responsible to no one but Ivan, with total authority to crush anything they saw as opposition to the czar's authority. The *oprichniki* would operate until 1572. Creating a climate of fear and secrecy, they proved ruinous to the stability of Russian society, and Ivan was finally persuaded to disband them. The once-formidable czar died in 1594.

Time of Troubles

Hereditary rule had been the law in Russia since 1450, but Feodor I, Ivan IV's son, was the last of his family. When he died in 1598, a council of six hundred boyars, clergy, and military officers elected Feodor's able brother-in-law Boris Gudonov, who had ruled in fact, although not in name, since Ivan IV's death. His election began an era known in Russian history as the Time of Troubles—a period of chaos on many levels. First, Boris was not a popular ruler. Second, there was social unrest within the Russian population. Third, there was a struggle for power among a variety of candidates for the throne. Fourth, fighting broke out among the armies of Sweden, Poland, and Russia as part of the struggle over who would rule the Russian Empire.

Boris Gudonov

Boris was an intelligent and capable ruler, but he had many enemies. For one thing, he had been an *oprichnik*, and his wife was the daughter of the leader of this feared and hated gang. For another, many people suspected him of having murdered Feodor's younger brother Dmitri, who had been discovered stabbed to death in 1591 in a mystery that historians have yet to solve. In addition, the boyars opposed Boris's plans to reorganize the administration and make it more efficient; they preferred to cling to the privileges and personal advantages they enjoyed in an inefficient system.

In 1601, Russia faced widespread crop failure and famine. Thousands of peasants were on the move, some seeking new land that might yield something to eat, others looking for work that would pay wages in the cities. By 1603, the czar had to muster the army to put down rebellion among the peasants and other members of the poorer classes.

The Struggle for Power

After the death of Boris in 1605, Russia reverted to the days before Vasili II, when power was taken by violence and conquest rather than inheritance. The situation was ripe for the appearance of a strong leader, but although several men tried to grab power, none could hold onto it.

In 1601, the first claimant appeared, declaring that he was Dmitri, Feodor I's younger brother. According to his story, the body identified in 1591 as Dmitri's had been someone else's; he, the real Dmitri, had been smuggled out of Russia and grown up in safety. (The claim was false; historians believe the False Dmitri to have been a Russian nobleman.) Despite a triumphal march into Moscow in 1605, with thousands of Poles and Cossacks in his train, the False Dmitri could not maintain power, and the boyars, who had never believed his claim of royal birth, murdered him in 1606. The boyar Vasili Shiuskii then assumed power, with the support of his fellow nobles. He succeeded in putting down a major peasant uprising but was eventually forced out of power.

The Invasions from the West

In 1607, Poland supported the claims of a second "False Dmitri" and established a rival Russian government in the Upper Volga region. The early success of this group forced Shiuskii to summon Swedish mercenaries to help him put it down. However, Shiuskii soon found himself trying to fight both the Poles and the Swedes, both of whom saw strategic advantages in opposing him. Poland and Russia began discussing the possibility of a Polish czar in exchange for an end to the fighting, but there were loud outcries of anger in the Orthodox Church against this plan, since the Poles were not Orthodox. In the end, a national uprising led to the election of a new Russian czar, sixteen-year-old boyar Mikhail Romanov, in 1613. His direct heirs would rule Russia until the Revolution of 1917.

Peter the Great

The most important of Mikhail Romanov's successors was Peter I, who became known to history as Peter the Great. In 1682, when they were young children, Peter and his brother Ivan were named dual monarchs; their older sister Sophia would serve as regent until the boys grew old enough to rule. In 1689, the nobles ousted Sophia from power. On Ivan's sudden death, Peter became the czar; he would rule Russia until his death in 1725.

Peter was characterized by genuine intellectual and scientific curiosity. He also had a dominant personality and believed in absolute rule with a very heavy hand. These two qualities of the czar's character had a decisive effect on Russia's development during the seventeenth century.

Peter was fascinated by European culture. In 1697, he left his homeland to tour Europe, disguised as a commoner (albeit a commoner with a large retinue of advisers and servants!). Given that the czar was six feet, six inches tall—a true giant in an era when people were much smaller than they are today—his disguise fooled no one. However, he enjoyed his ability to speak directly with commoners of all types and even to share their heavy manual labor, as he could not easily have done had he traveled in a more ceremonious style.

Peter planned to turn Russia into a modern nation that would take its place beside the great states of Europe. He began requiring Western administrative practices and Western efficiency from the civil service. He acquired an impressive personal library and oversaw the first Russian translations of a large number of French, English, and German books. He introduced Western-style dress to replace the traditional Russian costumes; his most famous innovation was a law against beards, decreed because European fashion dictated a clean-shaven face for a man. Since Orthodox doctrine required believers to wear full beards, and since a beard was welcome protection against frostbite during the bitter

Russian winters, Peter was eventually persuaded to exempt priests from the no-beard policy.

The Russian army reached a new high of two hundred thousand troops under Peter's rule. By 1721, he had annexed Estonia, Livonia, and part of Sweden. In 1703, Peter founded a new capital city at the mouth of the Gulf of Finland, naming it St. Petersburg after himself. Peter would use this beautiful city much as Louis XIV used Versailles; he required the boyars to attend him there during part of every year and forced them to pay for its construction.

When Peter died in 1725, his widow assumed power, ruling as Catherine I. After her death, a power struggle ended in the coronation of Peter II in 1762. It quickly became apparent that mental and emotional instability made Peter II incapable of ruling. His German wife Catherine assumed power when he died suddenly; historians agree that she either murdered him or ordered her followers to do so.

Catherine II shared Peter the Great's ambitions for Russia. She continued Peter's policy of westward expansion; between 1769 and 1774, Russia gained territory along the Danube River and a port on the Black Sea. A child of the Enlightenment, Catherine introduced Russians to Western music, art, literature, and philosophy. She corresponded with the French philosopher Voltaire. She founded and supported a number of institutions that would improve society, including a major hospital and a medical school, and led a campaign for inoculation against smallpox. She supported education for girls and young women and opened Russia's first public library. She reformed the legal code to limit the torture of prisoners and expanded religious freedoms.

Like other absolute monarchs, Catherine understood the need to protect her position by controlling the aristocracy. She took two major steps to keep the nobles content with their lot. First, she exempted them from taxes. Second, and partly in response to a major peasant uprising, she granted them absolute control over their serfs. With the loss of many important freedoms, including the right to move, the serfs in effect became slave labor. Their status would not improve until the 1860s.

The Late Ottoman Empire

The sixteenth and seventeenth centuries saw the height of the Ottoman Empire; before the end of the era, the empire would begin its final decline. The Ottoman Empire had many things in common with the Roman Empire at its height. These included a high level of cosmopolitanism, ethnic and religious diversity, tolerance, an active mercantile economy, and a highly organized and powerful army.

The prosperity of the Ottoman civilization was based on two things: the agricultural activity of the peasants and the mercantile activity of the trading and artisan class. The vast expanse of the empire ran the gamut from farms to highly sophisticated cities populated by a lively mix of Greeks, Syrians, Jews, and Armenians. Records show that in the year 1600, Constantinople was home to seven hundred thousand people—far larger than any Western city at the same date.

History shows that any empire with a diverse population must practice tolerance if it is to succeed for any length of time. The Ottomans were no exception to this rule; they permitted freedom of religious worship and they did not practice ethnic discrimination. Many men who were neither religiously Muslim nor ethnically Turkish held high political office or military rank and could acquire great wealth and high social position. The ranks of the legendary Ottoman army, the Janissaries, were filled with Christians— many were born to slaves and selected in childhood to attend the rigorous military training program. A slave child who was thrust into the army in this way would earn his freedom after a specified term of service.

For the first half of the sixteenth century, the Ottomans were fortunate in their rulers. Under Selim I, the Turks defeated the Persians at the Battle of Chaldiran in 1514, and in 1517, they went on to conquer Syria and Egypt. Under Suleiman I, known to history as "the Magnificent," the empire would arrive at its artistic and cultural high point. The greatest achievements in the arts were in the field of architecture; Suleiman's chief architect Sinan, who had spent his youth as a Janissary, designed hundreds of buildings. Istanbul (formerly Constantinople) was considered perhaps the most beautiful city in the world at this time. The Ottoman artists followed Persian models in painting and manuscript illumination, creating objects whose beauty amazes people to this day.

The Ottoman Empire was religiously tolerant; although it was a Muslim state, it contained sizeable Orthodox Christian and Jewish minorities. Had it not been for this policy of tolerance, Orthodox worship would have existed only in Russia. Instead, a common religion would prove to be a powerful tie between Russia and its fellow Slav states in Eastern Europe, once those states became independent.

Suleiman modernized the Turkish army and reorganized the government and the courts into a more efficient administrative structure. He also continued the Ottoman tradition of expansion; the Turks took Belgrade in 1521. The Janissaries demonstrated their efficiency in 1526 when they slaughtered twenty thousand Hungarian soldiers in battle and took control of a substantial portion of territory—an event that Hungary has never forgotten.

In 1529, the Ottomans tried again to establish a gateway into Western Europe, laying siege to Vienna. They failed but would try again—and fail again—over a century later, in 1683. Meanwhile, they did succeed in adding Aden, Algeria, Tripoli, Tunis, and Yemen to the empire. Despite a crushing naval defeat at Lepanto, they continued to enjoy freedom of movement in the Mediterranean.

Trade thrived in the Ottoman Empire, which had been a crossroads between West and East for centuries. Many Turks, particularly among the Jewish and Christian communities, worked as trading agents for Western European companies. Because of its geographical position, the Ottoman Empire blocked overland European access to Asia.

Safavid Persia

Shah Ismail seized power in Persia from the White Sheep Turks in 1501, thus founding the Safavid dynasty, which was to prove the zenith of the Persian civilization. His origins are obscure: some historians believe the Safavids were of Turkish descent, while others interpret the available records differently and claim an Iranian-Kurdish origin for the dynasty. (Kurdistan, of course, includes both Iranian and Turkish territory.)

Ismail's main contribution to the history of Safavid Persia is his imposition of Shiite Islam on what had been a largely Sunni Muslim civilization. The Safavids did not necessarily or always impose the Shiite belief system on the people with a heavy fist; rather, there was a long process of cajoling, conversion, persuasion, and inspiration mixed with force. Ismail's action would have serious long-term implications, as it laid the foundation of Shiite fundamentalism; in the short run, it drew a sharp distinction between Shiite Persia and the Sunni Ottoman civilization. Shiite beliefs were an inseparable aspect of the Persian culture and society; thus, Ismail's action in converting the state affected it in all ways, not just in terms of religious worship.

The most notable of the Safavid rulers was Abbas the Great, who succeeded to the throne in 1587. His forty-five-year reign marked the cultural and artistic height of the Persian civilization. Abbas established his capital at the city of Isfahan; at its height, the city was home to one million people and was the greatest of the Near Eastern centers of wealth, trade, sophisticated culture, and architectural beauty.

Persian culture dominated the region throughout this era, and the skills of its artisans were famous throughout the world. Persian rugs, tiles, ceramics, and woven textiles were highly prized in the West. Persian miniature painting, especially in manuscript illumination and illustration, became the standard imitated by both Indian and Ottoman painters; even today we continue to marvel at the delicacy, brilliant color, and detail of the Persian miniatures. Persian poetry and prose held the same place in Near Eastern scholarship and esteem that Greek and Latin held in the West. Persian was the language of educated people throughout the region and was the common language of diplomats and statesmen.

In 1622, Abbas managed to shoulder aside the Portuguese, who had established their presence in Ormuz in 1507 as traders. British merchants eventually took advantage of the Portuguese absence to establish their own base.

A long series of weak rulers followed Abbas; the Ottoman Turks took advantage of this situation to move in and take Baghdad in 1638. In 1639, the Peace of Zuhab established a permanent frontier between the Ottoman and Persian civilizations; this boundary line survives as the border between present-day Iran and Iraq.

In 1664, invasion threatened Persia again in the shape of Cossack raids from the north. At the same time, Russian missionaries entered the city of Isfahan. Russian ambassadors arrived in 1708 and again in 1718; these visits turned out to be a portent of danger. By 1719, the Persians were fighting off the Afghanis; in 1721, the last Safavid emperor abdicated and the Afghani leader Mahmud took the throne. This ended the era of Shiite supremacy in Persia, at least for the moment. The Russians returned in 1723, this time on a mission of conquest rather than diplomacy. Russia seized Derbent and Baku and, in 1724, made an agreement with the Ottoman Turks to carve up Persia between them.

The Mughal Empire

The Mughal Empire (also spelled "Mogul" and "Moghul") began in India in 1526 with the invasion of Babur of Kabul (Afghanistan). Babur was descended from Timur on his father's side and from Genghis Khan on his mother's; it is not surprising that he, too, left his mark on world history. Babur was noted for his military genius and his intellectual abilities; he was the author of a notable autobiography. Although Babur was ethnically Mongolian, he identified himself as Turkish, having grown up in a tribe that had absorbed aspects of Mongol, Persian, and Turkish culture.

When Babur and his troops invaded India from the northwest, they found it relatively easy to take over for three reasons. First, the government of Delhi was weak, largely due to an ineffective sultan. Second, the Mughal invaders had better and more modern artillery than the Indians. Third, Babul's military strategy was highly effective, employing a mix of tactics. Mongol warriors, riding fast horses and armed with bows, were a force to terrify any enemy; their archery skills combined with modern guns and Ottoman Turkish strategy made them an unbeatable fighting force.

The Indians called the new dynasty the Mughal Empire because *Mughal* is the Persian word for *Mongol*. Before his death in 1530, Babur expanded his new empire eastward into the Bengali region. His son and successor Humayan lost some of this territory to Afghani invaders but won some of it back in 1555. Humayan's son Akbar then took power and extended the Mughal Empire throughout all of India north of the Deccan plateau.

A Muslim power had now taken control of a Hindu nation. Just as the Aryans had assimilated into Indian culture in ancient times (see Chapter 4), the Muslims also adapted themselves to their new surroundings rather than arbitrarily imposing their culture on the conquered people. India's culture absorbed Muslim, Turkish, and Mongol elements, blending them with Hinduism and the caste system, so that the resulting Mughal Empire fused elements of both worlds.

Akbar's Reign

Akbar ruled the Mughal Empire from 1556 to 1605; his reign is considered the zenith of that empire and perhaps of Indian history. Akbar's most important contribution to India was that he acted as a unifying factor for its diverse elements; both Hindu and Muslim communities felt that the emperor respected them and acknowledged their importance. The fact that Akbar married a Rajput Hindu princess served as a symbol of the religious tolerance for which he became famous.

Both Hindus and Muslims had a major role to play in Akbar's government, which he and his able ministers remade into a strong centralized state. Muslims served Akbar in the highest rank of the government, as *mansabdars* (service nobility); Rajput Hindu chieftains were also considered members of the imperial aristocracy, but, although they ranked below Muslims, they were technically independent of imperial authority. They ruled over the commoners and lower-caste Indians in the provinces.

Many Indians converted to Islam during the Mughal era. As a religion that preached brotherhood, Islam contrasted sharply with the Hindu belief in rigid social castes. A person might be despised as a low-caste Hindu, but his status might improve significantly if he converted to Islam. Of course, political expediency was another powerful motive for conversion; many Indians probably believed it would be prudent to profess the same religion as the emperor. Although Hindus and Muslims did not intermarry (Akbar's own marriage was a rare exception to this rule), they did mix both socially and in business matters. This applied only to men; it was during the Mughal era that the tradition of *purdah*—keeping women virtually imprisoned in their homes—took hold.

The Mughal Empire was economically prosperous, thanks to two things: a vast annual surplus of food from the fertile river valleys and a thriving international trade in both natural resources (indigo, spices, diamonds, and precious metals) and manufactured goods (textiles, jewelry, and luxury items). The government managed its finances with notable skill. Historians even agree that the tax system under Akbar was fair to the peasants—a highly unusual claim for any society to be able to make!

India underwent a magnificent artistic renaissance during the Mughal era. The Persian influence on the traditional Indian artistic styles and methods created a culture of real gorgeousness, especially visible in Mughal architecture, miniature painting, and manuscript illumination. The Taj Mahal, India's most famous building, dates from this era; it is widely considered the most beautiful work of architecture in the world. The Mughal era also produced popular songs that are still familiar throughout India today, four hundred years after they were composed.

After Akbar's death, fifty uneventful years went by. His two immediate successors were not brilliant men, but both were wise enough to maintain the splendidly functioning, prosperous empire that Akbar had left them. In 1658, however, Aurangzeb inherited the throne of India. His reign ushered in the rapid decline of the great Mughal Empire.

The Empire in Decline

Aurangzeb waged a number of long and costly wars. He succeeded in adding southern India to the empire, but only at the price of ruining the national economy. His changes to the administration robbed it of its famous efficiency. He raised taxes to pay for his wars, thus earning the hatred of the peasants; from 1699 onward, India underwent a very rare period of peasant uprisings, some of them very large-scale.

Southern India was still almost entirely Hindu and did not welcome the sudden Muslim takeover from the north. Exhibiting what might be referred to as a form of Indian nationalism against foreign rulers, the Hindu Marathas resisted the most fiercely of all. Under their leader, Shivaji, they formed guerilla-style bands and were highly successful in many campaigns against the Mughal forces. Attempts to bring the Maratha into Mughal society failed; unlike the Rajput Hindus, the Maratha came from peasant stock and could not be tempted by promises of what they regarded as empty aristocratic titles and privileges.

Unlike Akbar, Aurangzeb did not incline toward religious toleration to begin with, and the opposition of the Hindu Marathas only cemented his prejudice. His policies became rigidly anti-Hindu, thus undoing much of the goodwill and tolerance that had characterized Indian society under Akbar.

The situation was ripe for foreign invasion, with the Mughal leadership clearly in disarray. The Persians, Afghanis, and British all invaded India in their turn.

The Persian Invasion

The Persian invasion came first in the person of Safavid emperor Nadir Shah. Nadir and his troops sacked Delhi in 1739. Although it seemed that control of the country would be the next easy step, this was as much as Nadir was able to achieve. Historians agree that he was a great general but a poor ruler. He was assassinated by one of his own officers in 1747. The Persian invasion did have two important consequences. First, the last Mughal emperors in Delhi would rule only in name; like the Roman emperors after the Goth invasion, they would only be puppets. Second, the invasion marked the final separation of Afghanistan and India into two separate states.

The Afghan Invasion

The Afghan invasion came in 1761. By this time, the Marathas had become so strong, it seemed likely they might overthrow the emperor in Delhi and usher in a new dynasty. However, they met their match at Panipat, where they faced the Afghan army under Ahmad Shah Durrani. After a crushing defeat, the Marathas scattered, becoming a confederation of small kingdoms in western and central India.

The British Invasion and Conquest

European invasions of India grew out of the trade relationships that had been developing since the beginning of the 1500s. During the 1600s, the British East India Company established something of a trade monopoly with India. Belatedly realizing that it was missing an economic opportunity, France formed the French East India Company in the 1700s. Hostility and resentment between the two companies broke out in 1744; during the Seven Years' War, the British drove France from India. As of 1765, Britain controlled Bengal.

The collapse of the Mughal Empire allowed Britain to take over the entire nation from its power base in Bengal. This was a slow process, not completed until the annexation of Punjab in 1849. Many Indians resisted the British takeover, most famously during the Sepoy Mutiny of 1857. (*Sepoy* is an Indian term meaning "soldier.") When sepoys rose up against their British commanders at Meerut, it touched off a wave of other mutinies and popular rebellions in central and northeastern India. Reistance was swiftly crushed, in part because the Indians did not present a united front to the British. In 1858, the East India Company was dissolved and Britain formally annexed India. British civil servants and military officers would occupy India until after World War II, although not in great numbers.

Unlike the earlier Aryan and Muslim invaders and conquerors, the British made no attempt to assimilate with the conquered culture. Perhaps because British society was also based on class, they did seem to understand the caste system—they fit into it perfectly, as a new caste that was higher and more privileged than any of the others.

The British takeover and occupation had mixed effects on India. On the positive side, English became the one common language in a nation where hundreds of dialects were spoken; Britain also introduced Western ideas of education and women's rights to India. On the negative side, the British maintained an attitude of racial and cultural superiority throughout their stay in India, which the Indians naturally found both objectionable and unjustified, given that their culture, literature, and art long predated the Anglo-Saxon. Relations between British and Indians would be characterized by mutual suspicion and mistrust throughout the occupation.

QUIZ

1. **The Janissaries repeatedly failed to capture _____ for the Ottoman Empire.**
   A. Athens
   B. Constantinople
   C. Isfahan
   D. Vienna

2. **Boris Gudonov contrasted with his predecessor czars because _____.**
   A. he was chosen by election
   B. he was a capable and strong leader
   C. he drove the Tatars out of Russia
   D. he tried to establish control over the boyars

3. **Mughal emperor Aurangzeb was notable for his _____.**
   A. religious intolerance
   B. literary skills
   C. philosophical musings
   D. military triumphs

4. **Babur of Kabul is a notable figure in history for all these reasons except _____.**
   A. he was the author of an extraordinary memoir
   B. he was descended from both Timur and Genghis Khan
   C. he persecuted his Hindu subjects
   D. he led many successful military campaigns

5. **The Maratha Hindus were impossible for the emperor to defeat because _____.**
    A. they had superior weapons
    B. they used guerrilla warfare tactics
    C. they outnumbered the royal army
    D. their allies were more skilled and reliable

6. **Despite his mental instability, Ivan IV continued to rule because _____.**
    A. he remained stronger than any of the rival claimants to the throne
    B. the Orthodox Church remained loyal to him
    C. he murdered his son and heir
    D. the system of government contained no procedure to remove a czar from office

7. **Shiite supremacy ended in Persia when _____ overcame the last of the Safavid emperors.**
    A. the Ottomans
    B. the Russians
    C. the Afghanis
    D. the Egyptians

8. **During the Time of Troubles, Poland hoped to _____.**
    A. take over the Russian Empire
    B. gain territory from Russia
    C. establish formal diplomatic and trade relations with Russia
    D. convert the Russians to Roman Catholicism

9. **The literature and art of _____ was the most influential throughout the Muslim world.**
    A. the Greeks
    B. the Persians
    C. Mughal India
    D. the Ottoman Turks

10. **Peter the Great's main reason for dictating changes in Russian fashion was _____.**
    A. to modernize Russian society and culture
    B. to intimidate the boyar class
    C. to encourage Russians to travel to the West
    D. to strengthen his personal popularity among his subjects

17

Western Revolutions in Science, Industry, and Thought, 1550–1900

The Scientific Revolution and the Enlightenment came about as a direct, although not immediate, result of the Renaissance and Reformation. During the Renaissance, many ancient Greek and Latin texts came to light and were seriously studied for the first time in centuries. Scholars learned ancient discoveries in mathematics, astronomy, and philosophy that had been suppressed or dismissed by the Catholic Church. The Renaissance also encouraged individual scholars to question the Church's teachings. The perfection of the printing press made the widespread dissemination of old and new knowledge possible. Finally, the Reformation loosened the stranglehold that Christianity had maintained on thought for centuries.

The Church saw the Scientific Revolution as a threat for two reasons: it changed *what* people thought and, more importantly, *how* they thought. The increase in human knowledge of the workings of the universe that occurred during the Scientific Revolution was the product of experimentation—of scientists making observations, taking notes, studying their data, and developing theories and conclusions based on what they perceived with their five senses. The Catholic Church was naturally hostile to a process that threatened its own supremacy over what people thought; Church officials did not want to change the centuries-old system in which its own scholars and teachers interpreted the world in accordance with their faith and insisted that the people accept this interpretation rather than thinking about the matter for themselves.

The great thinkers—called *philosophes*—of the Enlightenment applied this same scientific process of critical thinking to social and political problems. They believed in the perfectibility of humanity and society; their goal was a peaceful, prosperous world in which ignorance, greed, and tyranny had no place. For nearly a century, the *philosophes* wrote, argued, debated, and taught that all people were born free and equal and that individuals should be able to make their way in the world as reasonable beings with a right to decide how and where they wished to live. In the end, they brought about—at least in part—the new world they had imagined; their teachings led directly to major revolutions in British North America and in France.

The Industrial Revolution demonstrated a third way of using the process of observation and experimentation—by applying it to the mechanical challenges of manufacturing and agriculture. Throughout the eighteenth and nineteenth centuries, new machines appeared with bewildering rapidity. They permanently altered the pace of human life in the Western world and shifted the economy from a basis in agriculture to a basis in mass production and consumption.

CHAPTER OBJECTIVES

- Describe the major achievements of the Scientific Revolution.
- Discuss the European Enlightenment and its major causes and effects.
- Explain the significance of the Industrial Revolution in Britain, the United States, and continental Europe.

Chapter 17 Time Line

- **1543** Copernicus's *De Revolutionibus* argues that planets move around the sun

- **1577** Tycho Brahe proves that comets are astral bodies

- **1609** Johannes Kepler discovers that planets move in elliptical orbits
- **1610** Galileo observes moons of Jupiter
- **1633** Roman Inquisition forces Galileo to recant
- **1637** Descartes publishes work on analytic geometry
- **1654** Christiaan Huygens invents pendulum clock
- **1687** Isaac Newton publishes *Principia Mathematica*
- **1698** Thomas Savery invents first steam engine; improved in 1763 by James Watt
- **1748** Montesquieu publishes *L'Esprit des lois*
- **1759** Voltaire publishes *Candide*
- **1762** Rousseau publishes *Contract social*
- **1787** Edmund Cartwright patents steam-powered loom
- **1793** Eli Whitney invents cotton gin
- **1830** Opening of Liverpool and Manchester Railway
- **1871** Trade unions become legal in Britain

The Scientific Revolution

The ancients, first in the Middle East and then in Classical Greece and Rome, had made great strides in mathematics and the sciences. In medieval Europe, however, any scientific teachings that conflicted with the Bible were rigorously suppressed and denounced as heresy. The Scientific Revolution that took place from about 1550 to 1700 would change this.

Scientists had always had ideas about how the universe worked; this was nothing new. The Scientific Revolution was something new because for the first time, scientists had the means of testing their ideas through direct experiment and observation. The telescope, for example, made it possible to see the heavens up close and observe how the planets moved through space. The technology of printing made it possible to publish and share new knowledge, creating a scientific community of scholars who corresponded, shared, and discussed their ideas.

The Scientific Revolution was an era of major discoveries in astronomy, physics, and mathematics. Perhaps even more importantly, it both demonstrated and encouraged a major shift in the human thought process. In the past, people believed what the Church told them—that the universe worked according to divine whims that were beyond human understanding. With the Scientific Revolution, people began to see the universe as a machine that worked according to fixed laws that human beings could discover and understand.

It is important to remember that the Scientific Revolution did not denounce God or religious faith. Rather, it suggested that God had created the universe and set it in motion according to certain laws, which scientists now had the technology to observe and articulate. God was considered similar to a watchmaker who designed and built a watch, wound it up, and left it to run on its own.

Major Figures of the Scientific Revolution

Copernicus

Nicolaus Copernicus was born in 1473 in Torun, Poland. He studied the works of Ptolemy and Aristotle, who agreed that the Earth was at the center of the universe and that the other heavenly bodies traveled around it. The Church espoused Aristotle's theory because it showed that humankind, God's supreme creation, had its proper place in the center of the universe.

Copernicus came to believe that Aristotle and Ptolemy were wrong. He suggested that the sun was at the center of the universe, with the planets orbiting it in irregular circular paths. In 1543, Copernicus published his thoughts and discoveries in a book called *De Revolutionibus*.

Brahe

Copernicus's theories had been more or less guesses, but Tycho Brahe, born in 1546 in Danish territory, was fortunate enough to have a wealthy patron who provided him with a fully fitted observatory. Here, Brahe conducted direct experiments in astronomy—the first in Europe for many centuries. His observations told him that while the sun and moon traveled around the Earth, the other planets orbited the sun. Like Copernicus, he could not understand why the planets' apparently circular orbits were not regular.

Kepler

Brahe's assistant, the German Johannes Kepler, used mathematics and direct observation to show that the orbits of the planets were regular ellipses, not irregular circles. Kepler also proved that the planets orbited the sun at different speeds. His greatest work was *On the Motion of Mars*, published in 1609; it soon appeared on the Holy Office's *Index of Forbidden Books*.

Galileo

Astronomy took a giant leap forward with the discovery of the telescope, first patented in the Netherlands in 1608. Scientists had grasped the concept of the magnifying lens during the 1300s but had used the knowledge only to manufacture everyday items like eyeglasses. Only in 1608 did a scientist create a lens of a high enough magnification to view objects a tremendous distance away

Born in Pisa in 1564, mathematics and engineering professor Galileo Galilei was the first to make extensive use of the telescope to study the planets. In 1610, he saw that Jupiter had its own moons in orbit around it, just as the Earth had a moon. This discovery alone proved that Earth was not the center of the universe around which all other objects orbited. Galileo also observed that, contrary to Aristotle's assertion that all heavenly bodies were perfect, smooth spheres, the surface of the Earth's moon was craggy and irregular. When Galileo published his discoveries, most of Europe's intellectuals eagerly accepted them—with one major exception. By disproving Aristotle's theories, Galileo made an enemy of the Church.

Galileo's *Dialogue on the Two Great Systems of the World*, published in 1632, discussed theories about planetary orbits and tides. The Roman Inquisition charged him with defying a ban on writing about Copernican theory, despite documentary evidence that he had the required permission. The Inquisition sentenced Galileo to deny the validity of his own discoveries, then placed him under custody of the liberal Archbishop of Siena, who encouraged him to continue working and writing. In effect, Galileo remained under house arrest until his death in 1642. He was free to study, experiment, and write, although it proved difficult (not impossible) to find publishers in the face of a Holy Office ban on anything he might produce. Within the next few years, Galileo's works spread throughout Europe in various translations and editions.

Defending his own writings in his later personal correspondence, Galileo argued that God had given human beings the ability to observe and reason. What people could see and understand with their five senses must be the truth; for instance, that planets moved around the sun. He argued that if this appeared to conflict with the Scriptures, then human understanding of the Scriptures must be at fault.

Newton

Isaac Newton of England revolutionized scientific thinking with his discovery of the principle of gravity—the single, constant force in the universe that attracted objects to one another, both on Earth and in the heavens, and maintained each heavenly body in its place relative to all the others. Newton realized that gravitational force could be calculated mathematically; he was the first scientist to apply calculus to astronomy.

Before Newton, Europeans had understood the universe as operating by divine whims that they could not hope to understand; after Newton, they understood it as operating by fixed, comprehensible laws. For the first time, an understanding of the world could be based on human reason and experience, not on faith.

In Newton's view, the law of gravity was a divine creation, and he was, therefore, honoring God by revealing His divine plan. Unfortunately, the Catholic Church could not accept this view; as it had always done, it reacted to independent intellectual endeavor with suspicion and hostility. In a sense, the Church was right to recognize the threat posed by scientific discovery; since science proved that the Church had been teaching an inaccurate theory of the structure of the universe, *all* Church teaching was called into question. The Scientific Revolution permanently weakened the place the Church held in popular regard.

The Enlightenment, or the Age of Reason

In the wake of the Scientific Revolution came the Enlightenment, a period of intellectual achievement that lasted for approximately a century, from the English Revolution in 1689 to the French Revolution in 1789. The Enlightenment is also called the Age of Reason. The Scientific Revolution had introduced a new thought process to the West; during the Age of Reason, intellectuals applied that way of thinking to social and political questions. They argued against political and religious tyranny, against a fixed hierarchy of social ranks, against censorship, and against chattel slavery. They argued for freedom—freedom of individual thought, freedom of the press and the arts, freedom to have a say in one's own government, and freedom to rise in the world according to merit rather than birth.

The Enlightenment was centered in France, then the dominant power in Europe. Its major figures were a highly varied group, representing several different nations and fields of study and coming to a variety of conclusions about human life, society, civilization, and philosophy. What united them was their common way of thinking—the habit of applying the same reasoning process to the problems and questions of their age. The Enlightenment thinkers are called *philosophes*—a French term that is best translated "critical thinkers."

The Enlightenment marked a break with the past in two major ways. First, the Middle Ages and the period that followed had generally been a time of pessimism, or at best resignation. People made the best of the world on earth only in the hope of achieving something better after death. By contrast, the Enlightenment was an era of optimism, in which the *philosophes* believed that reasoning and knowledge—if properly applied—could solve the problems of society.

Second, human society had always accepted that human beings were God's creation. People had always dedicated their endeavors to the glory of God and had prayed for God's assistance when going into battle or danger. This attitude even persisted during the Scientific Revolution. During the Enlightenment, the *philosophes* began openly questioning the relevance, if not the existence, of God; they focused on human achievement as the product of a particular individual's merit and honored that person rather than God.

Major Thinkers of the Enlightenment

Montesquieu

Charles-Louis Secondat, Baron de Montesquieu, was born in 1689 in the Gironde region of southwestern France. His two most famous works are the *Persian Letters* (1721) and *The Spirit of Laws* (1748).

Many scholars consider the *Persian Letters* to be the book that began the Enlightenment. It is in the form of a collection of letters written by two fictional Persian travelers in Europe, who observe and comment upon French society, government, and customs. Montesquieu used this format to make some pointed, although veiled, criticisms of the despotism that prevailed at this time in France. The book was a great success, going through several editions in a single year.

The Spirit of Laws is a work of serious political theory; unlike the *Persian Letters*, it does not make its points under the guise of fiction. This was the first book to advocate a balanced government made of different branches—executive, legislative, and judicial—each of which had some power over the others. Montesquieu believed this separation of powers was the best way to avoid the autocracy that he felt was corrupt and harmful to society. The work also examined the roles of major social institutions such as the Church, which lost no time placing it on the *Index of Forbidden Books*. The book, however, was widely read and highly influential; fifty years after Montesquieu's work appeared, the government of the United States was organized along the lines he had suggested (see Chapter 18).

Voltaire

Born in Paris in 1694, François-Marie Arouet was educated by the Jesuits. Around 1718, he coined the pen name *Voltaire*, by which he was known for the rest of his long and productive life.

Voltaire's *Letters on England* (1733) describe what he considered an ideal society, one that supported its artists and men of letters while allowing its citizens to worship as they saw fit. This praise of England implied severe criticism of the very different conditions in France, where *Letters on England* was banned. Voltaire continued to publish both fiction and nonfiction and kept up a voluminous correspondence with all the great thinkers of his age. In his short novel *Candide* (1759), he lampooned many of the worst aspects of European society—government, military life, and religion. The novel concludes that "one must cultivate one's garden"—in other words, one must use one's intellectual and philosophical skills to solve real, practical problems in a practical way.

Rousseau

Jean-Jacques Rousseau, born in 1712 in Geneva, Switzerland, was in many ways the odd man out among the *philosophes*. Rousseau believed passionately in the importance of each person as a unique individual, for both his emotional and intellectual qualities; his stress on the emotions leads historians to consider him the father of the Romantic Movement in literature and the arts.

In *The Social Contract* (1762), Rousseau described his ideal society. Because social structure created false ideas of inequality, based on birth rather than merit, Rousseau believed that it was inherently evil. Without an imposed social structure, human beings would follow their nature and would relate to one another in benevolence rather than self-interest. This notion of the "noble savage" seemed ludicrous to many of the other *philosophes*, who believed that education was the key to a better society.

Diderot

Denis Diderot was born in 1713 in the town of Langres in northeastern France. His most important contribution to the legacy of the Enlightenment is the *Encyclopédie*. Its seventeen volumes of text were published from 1751 to

1765, and a further eleven volumes of plates were completed in 1773. The *Encyclopédie* was an attempt to sum up all human knowledge in one place. It included articles by all the greatest thinkers and writers of the age (including Voltaire, Rousseau, and Diderot himself) on a variety of topics: science, technology, crafts, mathematics, art, religion, music, and history. The purpose of the *Encyclopédie* was to enlighten the ignorant—to provide ordinary people with information that everyone, as a sentient being in the world, should know. The *philosophes* believed strongly that ignorance was the enemy of society. Therefore, educating the common people was one of the most basic and important ways to improve the world.

The Industrial Revolution Begins in Britain

The Scientific Revolution had solved many of the mysteries of the heavens, and the Enlightenment applied its methods to the solution of societal ills. Beginning around 1700 and lasting through the end of the nineteenth century, the Industrial Revolution used a similar thought process of observation, trial, and error to improve manufacturing and farming methods.

The Industrial Revolution began in Britain because the geographical and social conditions were most favorable there. Geographically there were three contributing factors. A network of rivers and canals made it easy to transport goods, an abundance of coal made it possible to stoke the factory furnaces, and isolation from the continent protected Britain from invasion during the Napoleonic wars. Socially and politically, Britain was stable. The constitutional monarchy functioned well; the banking system was prosperous; and the population was thrifty. Small business owners tended to invest their profits, and businesses owners could vote; this connected the interests of industry to those of government.

Changes in Farming

The British agricultural industry adopted farming methods that had proven highly successful in the Netherlands—planting a different crop in the same field each year and planting a variety of different crops at once. Crop rotation permitted the soil to renew its own resources, since each type of plant drew different minerals from the soil; and planting several crops increased the likelihood of a good harvest, since even if one crop failed, others might still thrive.

In 1701, Jethro Tull perfected a seed drill that could be harnessed to a horse. As the horse walked down the field, the drill sowed the seeds neatly and uniformly; this improved on the efficiency of sowing by hand. Food production increased 300 percent over the course of the eighteenth century in Britain; pioneering agricultural ideas like Tull's seed drill played a major part.

Until the eighteenth century, small farming had always been permitted on open fields, regardless of who owned the actual land. This made it possible for villagers throughout Britain to grow enough to feed their families. This practice came to an end in the 1700s with the enclosure movement, in which large tracts of privately owned land were fenced in for the owner's exclusive use. The landowner's purpose was to consolidate his fields for large-scale farming, which had become hugely profitable thanks to improvements in farming methods. Enclosure forced villagers to move to the cities looking for wage-earning jobs. This urban migration provided the factories with a steady supply of workers. In this way, agriculture played a major role in industrialization.

Changes in the Textile Industry

Major changes in the British textile industry began in 1733, when John Kay invented the flying shuttle. When Edmund Cartwright perfected the first steam-powered loom in 1787, the weaving and spinning process took another giant step forward toward mass production. Thomas Savery developed Britain's first steam engine just before 1700. In 1705, Thomas Newcomen improved Savery's design. In 1763, James Watt improved the Newcomen engine. By the late eighteenth century, all the mills and factories in Britain were steam powered. It was steam power that made the first railway locomotive possible; later, coal powered the engines.

The Railway

In 1830, the Liverpool and Manchester Railway opened, marking a major change in European society. For the first time, people could move over land faster than a team of horses could run. The railroad could transport large quantities of goods quickly and efficiently over land; this reduced shipping costs, which in turn created larger markets and greater demand for goods.

As demand rose, production increased. Owners built more factories and hired more workers. The railway proved popular and profitable, and within fifty years, British workers were driving engines all over the country. By 1880, technology had progressed so much that the trains were moving at three times their 1830 speed.

The Industrial Revolution in the United States

The Industrial Revolution in America began in 1793 with the invention of the cotton gin. This machine could process as much cotton in one day as a thousand slaves; Southern planters found that it multiplied their profits tenfold. The invention of the steamboat, which could sail upstream against the current, made it possible to move huge boatloads of cotton north, giving rise to the textile industry in New England.

Slavery had begun to decline; it had been outlawed in the North and was proving unprofitable in the South. With the invention of the cotton gin, slavery suddenly became profitable again, both for Southern plantation owners and Northern textile-mill owners. The rise in profits made some Northerners begin to drop their outspoken objections to slavery. However, the North did not want the South to expand its political power base, and a slowly growing number of Northerners continued to object to slavery on ethical grounds.

Between 1815 and 1819, the Great Migration saw record numbers of Americans moving westward into Illinois and Indiana. Improved transportation helped make this possible. The National Road, which also served as an important trade route, even provided flatboat connections that allowed settlers to travel downriver into the Mississippi valley.

The Bessemer process converted iron ore into steel. Both the Englishman Henry Bessemer and the American William Kelly discovered this process in the 1850s. It led to a rise in steel production that enabled the creation of stronger railroad tracks, trains, bridges, and machines and engines of all types.

The Industrial Revolution in Europe

The European continent lagged behind Britain in industrial development for several reasons. First, the French Revolution and the Napoleonic wars had caused a major economic upheaval. Second, the European powers were more likely to fight one another than to make trade agreements. Third, tariffs restricted free trade among European nations. Last, voting rights were very rare on the European continent; hence, the middle class, which supported industrialization, had much less power and influence.

The European Industrial Revolution began in the tiny, coal-rich nation of Belgium. British production techniques found their way across the English Channel to Belgium with relative ease; from there, industry slowly spread throughout Europe. The form industrialization took on the continent depended largely on the location of natural resources. For example, Spanish and French sheep were not the same variety as those in England, so the engineers in that region modified their looms to suit their wool, which was different in texture and quality.

By 1848, several major railways crisscrossed Europe, particularly in Germany, northern France, and Austria. By 1870, it was possible to travel all the way to Russia by train. The railway linked the industrialized areas and proved a great aid in shipping and international trade.

By 1860, Britain's industry was entirely modernized. On the continent, Belgium, France, and Switzerland had made the most progress toward mass production. Things would change in the second half of the century; by the outbreak of World War I in 1914, Germany had surpassed the rest of Europe, including Britain, in production.

/ Labor Relations

The Industrial Revolution changed the manner of production. It did away with the model that had existed in Europe for centuries and replaced it with a new one.

In the past, work had been done slowly and by hand, without mechanized tools. Items were produced in small quantities. Workers considered themselves artisans because of their level of individual effort and the unique qualities of their products. With the development of factories, the process of manufacturing changed: dozens of workers labored together to manufacture large quantities of identical items as quickly and cheaply as possible. Taking the time to make something perfect was discouraged because it was not cost-effective.

Factory owners and managers were concerned with only one thing—making the greatest possible profit. Safety regulations, reasonable working hours, and fair wages would all subtract from the company's profits. Therefore, owners spent as little as possible on their workers and demanded as much as they could get away with—and they could get away with almost anything, because they had all the power. Owners could fire anyone at any time for any reason; workers were easily replaced.

The work week lasted six days, with Sunday, the Christian Sabbath, being the only day of rest. A workday generally lasted at least twelve hours, with perhaps twenty minutes for lunch. Wages were kept at starvation levels; women and children were hired in great numbers because they earned even less than men. Parents put their children out to work at age five or six; there was no thought of sending them to school. Machinery was dangerous to operate at the best of times, and the long hours meant that workers were often too exhausted to move as quickly and carefully as was necessary for safety. Compensation for a workplace injury depended entirely on the owner's generosity. All workers were exposed to dangerous levels of industrial pollution.

Governments soon realized that factory conditions were not reasonable or humane and that an ignorant and poor social underclass was being created. There was undeniable evidence that the owners would not pay fair wages or provide decent working conditions unless they were forced. The British government was the first to argue for regulation—the only guarantee that workers would be treated fairly.

Social reformer Jeremy Bentham and economic theorist John Stuart Mill argued that if one person's situation was bad, the entire community was that much weaker; if one person's situation improved, the entire community was that much stronger. According to Bentham and Mill, it was in everyone's economic interest to treat others fairly and ethically. This way of thinking suggested that both owners and workers had a mutual interest in maintaining cordial relations, because a factory in which workers and owners were both content with their situation would be more profitable. Bentham and Mill proved highly influential during the late Industrial Revolution.

During the nineteenth century, trade unions (called labor unions in the United States) began to form as workers realized that together they could shut down a factory simply by going on strike—walking off the job so that the factory would sit idle and the owner could earn no profits. Trade unions became legal in Britain in 1871, in France in 1884, and in Germany after 1890. In the United States, workers began to form labor unions as early as the 1830s, although the movement became much stronger in the 1870s.

In all nations and regions, owners were bitterly opposed to trade unions. They argued that workers' demands were too high, painting a picture of union workers as lazy people who wanted a luxurious standard of living without effort. History shows that this picture is grossly distorted; workers have generally argued for reasonable hours, reasonable safety conditions, and wages that would allow them to support their families in reasonable comfort. Of course, owners were prone to consider any decrease in their profits "unreasonable"— and higher wages, shorter hours, and improvements to lighting and safety came out of the profits.

The Industrial Revolution changed the European economy, raising personal income and bolstering international trade. In northern Europe, the average person quadrupled his or her income between 1830 and 1910; even in the Balkans, the least industrialized region of Europe, individual income more than doubled. A major period of expansion in the nineteenth century (see Chapter 19) created new markets for European goods and provided industrial nations with new sources of the raw materials they needed to keep their factories running.

QUIZ

1. **The Scientific and Industrial Revolutions and the Enlightenment share which of the following?**
   A. the approval and support of the Church
   B. the design of new systems of government
   C. the process of critical thinking and experimentation
   D. the invention of new solutions to major social problems

2. **_____ is an important historical figure because he realized that the planets moved in regular elliptical orbits around the sun.**
   A. Tycho Brahe
   B. Johannes Kepler
   C. Galileo Galilei
   D. Isaac Newton

3. **Which best describes the social philosophy of John Stuart Mill and Jeremy Bentham?**
   A. Individuals should always do what they think is best for themselves.
   B. Individuals should always do what they think is best for others.
   C. If one person's situation improves, the whole community is that much better off.
   D. If one person's situation deteriorates, the rest will gain from that person's loss.

4. **What argument did Galileo make in support of his discoveries about the planets when the Church refused to accept them?**
   A. that what could be observed by the human eye must be the truth
   B. that Church fathers had no right to make pronouncements about astronomy
   C. that other intellectuals and scientists agreed with his findings
   D. that he had used the finest scientific instruments of the day

5. **Church officials were hostile to the discoveries of the Scientific Revolution because _____.**
   A. the discoveries were not the result of proper experimentation and study
   B. the scientists who made the discoveries were all Protestants
   C. they objected to the scientists' expressed disbelief in God
   D. these discoveries contradicted and disproved what the Church had always taught

6. **The term *philosophe* is best translated as _____.**
   A. scholar
   B. critical thinker
   C. student
   D. intellectual

7. **Which statement is true of all the *philosophes* of the Enlightenment?**
   A. They were all French.
   B. They all supported and agreed with one another.
   C. They all shared a common way of thinking.
   D. They were all knowledgeable about mathematics and science.

8. **Industrial development in Europe depended most on which factor?**
   A. availability of natural resources
   B. availability of workers
   C. proximity to the railroad
   D. topography and climate

9. **The most important source of power for a wage worker in a factory was _____.**
   A. membership in a trade union or labor union
   B. the ability to vote in national elections
   C. ownership of stock in the company he or she worked for
   D. the ability to rise in the company through promotion

10. **Which best describes what the *philosophes* hoped and believed the future might hold for humankind?**
    A. They believed that the world would end in a great war among all nations.
    B. They believed that society might become peaceful, prosperous, and happy.
    C. They believed that there was no possibility that society would ever improve.
    D. They believed that society would succumb to despotism.

chapter **18**

Political Revolutions in the West, 1688–1815

Between 1688 and 1789, the West saw three major political revolutions: one in England, one in America, and one in France. These three revolutions demonstrated a turning of the tide in the West, ushering in an era of steady progress toward representative government that would continue into the nineteenth century.

The Glorious Revolution of 1688 was preceded by fifty years of violent conflicts between the monarch and the legislature, during which Protestants in the British Parliament refused to give way to the demands of Catholic kings with absolutist tendencies. For the first time, a British monarch was executed by due process of law; this led to England's only military dictatorship, an extreme experience that proved that the nation's true bent was the middle ground of a moderate hereditary monarchy and a strong legislature. The Glorious Revolution ushered in a new era of individual rights and constitutional monarchy and ensured that Catholicism would never again take firm hold on the nation.

The American Revolution of 1776 to 1783 pitted the British colonies against their parent nation. The great geographical distance between England and

North America made British interference sporadic and halfhearted and allowed the colonists great freedom to rule themselves. When England wanted to force the colonies to pay for the French and Indian War by taxing them without their consent, the colonists rebelled, arguing that they were British citizens and that the Magna Carta guaranteed them the right to representation in their own government. The ensuing war for independence pitted raw American volunteers against the highly disciplined and professional British army—but the Americans put their experiences of fighting the Indians to good use and won the war. The United States Constitution became a model of balanced representative government.

The French Revolution of 1789 was the most chaotic of the three. It saw the commoners rising up in rebellion against a conservative, overprivileged, extravagant monarchy and aristocracy. Overthrowing the monarchy proved easy, although violent, but the French floundered in their attempts to create a republican government to replace it. In the end, they succumbed to a military dictatorship, which would not be overthrown until all the nations of Europe united against the dictator.

The Napoleonic era saw an attempt by one man to take over all of Europe. His impressive string of military conquests led to the alliance of the other great powers against France. In 1815, Napoleon was finally defeated, and the European leaders created the first international peacekeeping organization.

CHAPTER OBJECTIVES

- Describe the conflicts that led to the Glorious Revolution in England.
- Describe the issues that led to the American Revolution.
- Discuss the historical influences on the United States Constitution.
- Describe the causes of the French Revolution.
- Explain how Napoleon rose to and fell from power in France.
- Explain and analyze the Congress of Vienna and its actions.

Chapter 18 Time Line

●	1629	Charles I disbands the British Parliament
●	1642	Charles I leads troops against Parliament
●	1649	Charles I executed

- **1654–1658** Oliver Cromwell rules England as Lord Protector
- **1660** Restoration of British monarchy
- **1688–1689** Glorious Revolution; English Bill of Rights
- **1764** Sugar Act
- **1765** Stamp Act
- **1770** Boston Massacre
- **1774** First Continental Congress meets in Philadelphia
- **1775** Battles of Concord and Lexington
- **1776** American colonies declare independence from Britain
- **1781** British surrender to U.S. Army at Yorktown
- **1788** Estates-General meet for the first time since 1614; Tennis-Court Oath
- **1789** **14 July** Parisians storm the Bastille

  August Declaration of the Rights of Man and of the Citizen
- **1793** Louis XVI and Marie Antoinette executed; Reign of Terror
- **1804** Napoleon declares himself the Emperor of the French
- **1808–1814** Peninsular War
- **1812** Russians defeat French; French retreat from Moscow
- **1814** Napoleon abdicates; exiled to Elba
- **1815** Battle of Waterloo; final defeat of Napoleon

  Congress of Vienna

The Glorious Revolution of 1688

The Glorious Revolution was the result of tension between the British Parliament and the monarch, which began to simmer during the early 1600s. Through the reign of James I, Parliament's major purpose had been to grant the monarch any funds necessary to carry out affairs of state such as wars. When the Catholic Charles I succeeded his father, the House of Commons balked at carrying out this traditional duty; most of the members opposed Catholicism and were not willing to allow a Catholic king to behave like an autocrat. When Parliament refused to allow the king to raise funds without its permission, Charles acceded to their demand—but disbanded Parliament as soon as the funds were granted. The legislative assembly would not meet between 1629 and 1640.

Archbishop of Canterbury William Laud and the king tried to standardize the rules and rites of all the Anglican congregations. Scotland reacted to this by starting a civil war to defend its right to practice Presbyterianism; this forced Charles to reconvene Parliament to request funds to send troops against Scotland. Parliament took advantage of the situation by passing a series of laws designed to weaken absolutism. The legislature also imprisoned and executed Archbishop Laud.

In 1642, Charles I led an armed attack on Parliament, initiating a civil war that lasted until 1649. Oliver Cromwell, a member of the House of Commons, led the parliamentary forces; with the aid of his considerable military ability, Parliament's troops defeated the monarch's. Later, Cromwell's soldiers conquered both Scotland and Ireland.

Parliament voted to abolish the monarchy, the House of Lords, and Anglicanism as the state religion. In 1649, Charles I was put to death; his teenage sons Charles and James fled the country, eventually finding their way to Holland and safety. The execution of the king by due process of law marked a major defeat for the tradition of absolute monarchy and ushered in the modern era of republican government.

When Parliament refused to pass certain reforms, Cromwell disbanded it. In 1654, he became the only military dictator ever to rule England, under the title Lord Protector. Like other British monarchs before him, Cromwell imposed his own religious faith on his kingdom. A follower of a strict form of Calvinism called Puritanism, Cromwell closed all theaters and saloons because they invited and encouraged what he considered sinful behavior. His government did not come down harshly on Anglicans or Lutherans, but Catholics were forced to practice their faith in secrecy.

In 1658, Cromwell's son Richard succeeded him but proved ineffective. With the blessing of Parliament, Charles I's eldest son was brought back from Europe and crowned Charles II in 1660. Despite Charles II's great popularity, Parliament was by no means willing to give up any of its new power. As often as not, Parliament opposed the king's attempts to assert his authority. It was clear that in England, the days of absolute monarchy were over and that

England was definitively a Protestant nation that would never again welcome a Catholic ruler.

At the end of Charles II's life, the succession to the throne once again sparked parliamentary concern. Charles's heir was his brother James—a devout Catholic. A sizeable parliamentary faction proposed an Exclusion Bill that would bar any Catholic, including James, from the throne. The first British political parties formed in the debate over the bill, with the Whigs for it and the Tories against it. The bill failed to pass both houses, and James II succeeded to the throne on his brother's death.

James's harsh anti-Anglican policies made the Whigs and Tories unite against him; when his wife gave birth to an heir to the throne, who would ensure Catholic rule for another generation, they agreed that the monarch must be deposed and replaced. The best candidates appeared to be Mary, James's grown daughter by an earlier marriage, and her husband, William, *stadholder* (hereditary ruler) of the Netherlands. Deputies from Parliament invited William and Mary to rule England jointly. They arrived in England in 1688. James fled to France without a shot being fired, and the Glorious Revolution was won.

The most important result of the Glorious Revolution was the passage of the English Bill of Rights in 1689. Its two main goals were first, to unite the people and their monarch once and for all under the same state religion, and second, to balance the government by giving Parliament certain important rights over the monarch. The Bill of Rights stated that no Catholic could rule England and no British monarch could marry a Catholic. Parliament felt that this step was necessary to avoid any more of the civil wars that had torn the island apart ever since the days of Queen Mary.

Parliament reinforced its own authority by declaring that it must meet every year. This ensured that the legislative assembly could step in and assume power if the monarch proved irresponsible or incapable. Parliament also assumed other major legislative functions: from this time on, the authority to suspend laws, maintain a standing army, and impose new taxes rested with Parliament, not with the monarch.

In 1707, England and Scotland were officially incorporated as one nation, known as the United Kingdom of Great Britain.

The American Revolution

At the time it occurred, the American Revolution was unique in history as the first instance of a colony declaring its independence from the nation that controlled it. The issue that sparked the American Revolution was that of taxation without representation.

Conflicts with Parliament

The Americans were subjects of the British crown but had no specific representation in Parliament. This was a matter of distance and geography. Even if Parliament had created seats for American members, the mails were too slow and the distance too far for effective representation. Men living in England simply could not keep in close enough touch with the colonies to represent their concerns on an everyday basis.

Parliament's solution to the problem of colonial representation had been to allow the Americans a great deal of leeway to govern themselves. The laws of each colony were different, as all had been settled at different times, but each had a constitution, a governor, and a legislative assembly elected by those who had the right to vote—adult men, including free Africans, who owned the requisite amount of property.

The end of the French and Indian War, fought between France and Britain in the colonies over territorial expansion, brought about a crisis in British-American relations. First, Britain ended the war heavily in debt with no ready means of payment. Second, British territory acquired in the war would have to be guarded against enemies who might move in and lay claim to it. This meant that Britain would have to maintain a standing army in the colonies for the first time. Third, Parliament felt that victory provided a perfect opportunity to strengthen its authority over the colonies.

The Sugar Act

As far back as 1650, Parliament had passed the first of the Navigation Acts, which set forth the rules governing trade within the North American colonies and between the colonies and other nations. Because the Navigation Acts resulted in higher prices for imported goods and fewer opportunities to export goods, Americans rarely obeyed them. Colonial legislatures refused to pass laws putting a stop to smuggling as a simple matter of economic profit. The British felt that enforcing the import duties mandated by the Navigation Acts would swiftly and easily pay off their war debts. Parliament therefore passed the Sugar Act of 1764, instituting a tax on imported molasses and inspections of ships and assessing penalties if captains did not accurately report their cargo or pay the tax. Captains accused of smuggling would be tried in the admiralty courts, which had no juries.

The Americans opposed the Sugar Act for financial and political reasons. Financially, paying the duty on molasses would bankrupt the merchants, and the process of inspection would impede the efficiency of shipping within the colonies. Politically, the Sugar Act infringed on two of the colonists' ancient rights as British citizens—the right not to be taxed without their own consent and the right to a trial by jury. Both these rights were set forth in the Magna Carta (see Chapter 12). Colonial protests took the forms of official letters to Parliament, rioting in the streets, and boycotts of British goods. Parliament was forced to lower the new tax; accepting the lowered tax as a trade regulation, the colonists grudgingly agreed to pay.

The Stamp Act

The Stamp Act of 1765 mandated the use of an official stamp on most paper goods sold or issued in the colonies—newspapers, legal and property records, and so on. It also charged a tax for the use of the paper, and appointed a stamp inspector for each colony. Since this was an outright tax rather than a trade regulation like the Sugar Act, the colonies refused to accept it. Political leaders from nine colonies, meeting in New York as the Stamp Act Congress, agreed on a policy of active resistance. The people formed activist groups called Sons and Daughters of Liberty and attacked the stamp inspectors, damaging their property, hanging them in effigy, and insulting them in newspaper articles. Meanwhile, William Pitt and Benjamin Franklin presented the colonies' case before Parliament. Both men argued that according to law and tradition, British citizens could not be taxed without their consent. Parliament repealed the Stamp Act but insisted that all citizens in the empire were "virtually represented" in Parliament and that parliamentary authority over them was absolute.

The Townshend Acts

In 1767, Parliament tried again to raise money from the colonies through the Townshend Acts, which taxed all imported paint, paper, glass, and tea. Parliament hoped to pass the Townshend Acts off as trade regulation rather than taxation, but the attempt failed. Political activist Samuel Adams of Boston sent a circular letter to the governments of all the colonies, laying out the reasons for colonial objection to the Townshend Acts. Soon there were riots in the city streets again, most notably in Boston. Conditions grew so unsafe that British officials in Boston asked General Gage, head of the standing army, to send troops to the city to help maintain order.

The Boston Massacre

On the night of March 5, 1770, tension between the soldiers and citizens erupted into what became known as the Boston Massacre—a highly inflated name for what actually happened, which consisted of a mob of colonists throwing stones at British sentries. The British fired into the crowd in self-defense, and, in the ensuing melee, five people were killed. An engraving by Bostonian silversmith Paul Revere portrays the British as brutal aggressors and the Bostonians as helpless victims—a distortion of the facts eagerly embraced by the Americans (Figure 18.1). Copies of the engraving circulated all through the colonies very shortly after the event and played a significant role in uniting the colonists against Britain.

The Boston Tea Party

The colonial boycott of British goods, specifically tea, meant that merchants of the British East India Company stood to lose a fortune. The tea that they suddenly could not sell was sitting in warehouses rather than shipping out to sea. When the merchants begged Parliament for help, Parliament agreed to lower the price of the tea so that even with the tax it would be the best bargain on

FIGURE 18.1   The Boston Massacre (engraving by Paul Revere)

the market. The Americans recognized this move as an attempt to manipulate them into paying a tax that they opposed on principle.

On November 27, 1773, the *Dartmouth* sailed into Boston harbor with a cargo of East India tea. No dock worker in Boston was willing to help unload it. On their side, the merchants who had purchased the tea refused to allow the *Dartmouth* to leave the port until the tea was unloaded and the duty paid. To prevent this, the Sons of Liberty decided to unload the tea themselves— into Boston Harbor. Disguised as Indians, about two hundred patriots stormed aboard the *Dartmouth*, hacked open the wooden crates of tea, and dumped them into the sea, cheered on by a great crowd of Bostonians on the docks. The disguise was necessary because the destruction of property was certainly a crime and might have been construed as treason.

The Coercive/Intolerable Acts

News of the "Boston Tea Party" reached Britain in January 1774. Parliament agreed that Boston must be harshly punished as an example to other colonies that might be tempted to defy parliamentary authority. Parliament promptly passed a series of acts that became known in the colonies as the "Intolerable Acts" (see Table 18.1).

Table 18.1 The Intolerable Acts

Name of Act	Provisions	Effect
Boston Port Act	Closed the port of Boston until Boston agreed to pay East India Company for *Dartmouth* cargo	Banned Boston from importing foreign goods and exporting to other nations
Massachusetts Government Act	Members of legislature to be appointed by king; no longer popularly elected	Revoked Massachusetts Charter of 1691; forbade town meetings for which governor had not given permission
Administration of Justice Act	No royal official committing a capital offense could be tried in Massachusetts	Made it more likely that soldiers would get away with violence against citizens
Quartering Act	Colonists must provide food and housing for British soldiers on demand	Robbed citizens of the right to privacy and security in their own homes
Quebec Act (passed later in 1774)	Changed system of government for Canada; disbanded representative assembly and revoked right to trial by jury	Suggested to American colonists that their own assemblies would soon be disbanded and their rights revoked

The First Continental Congress

In response to requests for support from Massachusetts, leaders from all the colonies except Georgia agreed to meet in Philadelphia to take steps to secure colonial rights. All the colonies felt threatened by the pattern of British oppression. By October, this First Continental Congress had debated and approved a document called the Declaration and Resolves. This document had several provisions. First, it stated that since the colonists were not represented in Parliament, it had no authority over them; they were entitled to elect their own local governments. Second, the colonies would immediately cut off trade with Britain and boycott all British goods until the Intolerable Acts were repealed and the standing army disbanded and sent back to Britain. Third, each colony would establish its own militia for defense against the British army.

Congress debated whether to break completely away from Great Britain or to resolve their differences with the mother country and remain part of the British Empire. The delegates agreed to meet again in May if London did not respond positively to their concerns. Before that date, however, fighting broke out in Massachusetts.

The Fighting Begins

The people of Boston deeply resented the presence of a standing army in peacetime. In response to the presence of the British soldiers—known as "redcoats" for the distinctive scarlet color of their uniforms—all the towns near Boston formed their own militias and began stockpiling weapons for use against the enemy, if necessary. The Boston militia chose the village of Concord as a good location for the magazine. When the British army learned of the magazine, General Gage decided to send troops to take the weapons. They would surprise Concord by arriving quietly, after dark.

On the night of April 18, 1775, when the British began their march toward Concord, the watchful colonists spread the word to the militias. The redcoats and minutemen faced one another for the first time as enemies on Lexington Green. The Americans, outnumbered by more than fifteen to one and unused to military discipline, were confused and disorderly. A shot rang out, then another and another. Each side later claimed that the other fired first. No historian has ever been able to discover the truth of the matter; no one will ever know who fired the first shot of the American Revolution.

Having chased the rebels away, the British marched on toward Concord, where the militiamen met them at Concord Bridge. A second skirmish ended when the British commander ordered a retreat to Boston. The militiamen surrounded the city, laying siege to it with the intent of starving the redcoats into surrender. As soon as the news spread, thousands of Americans marched to Boston to support the siege. Soon the militiamen outnumbered the redcoats by about five to one; the British had no choice but to wait for help from outside.

The Battle of Bunker Hill

The Second Continental Congress met in Philadelphia on May 10, three weeks after the Battles of Lexington and Concord. Congress formally created the Continental Army and chose George Washington as commander in chief.

In June, British General Burgoyne brought reinforcements to Boston and planned an attack on the Americans from the high ground overlooking the city. The watchful Sons of Liberty discovered the plan and informed the American troops. On the night of June 16, American commanders General Putnam and Colonel Prescott led a thousand soldiers to Bunker Hill, the location that gave its name to the ensuing battle. A last-minute change of plans moved them to nearby Breed's Hill, where they dug trenches and built a barricade. When the sun rose the next morning and the British saw what had happened, they fired on the Americans, who held their ground. In the ensuing battle, the British gained control of the heights but lost more than twice as many men as the Americans.

Common Sense

"We have it in our power to begin the world over again." With these simple words, a pamphlet called *Common Sense* boldly suggested that America should become an independent nation as soon as possible. Author Thomas Paine's concerns were much broader than the specific conflict between Britain and its colonies. His argument in favor of independence was as follows: Any system of government was at best a necessary evil, but a hereditary monarchy was the worst system of all because monarchs ruled by the accident of birth. If the Americans declared their independence from Great Britain and adopted a new, democratic system based on merit rather than birth, other nations would follow their example. *Common Sense* was widely read by ordinary people as well as by political leaders and was highly influential in the debate over independence.

Most colonial assemblies declared their support for independence from Britain. Some individuals, however, believed that reconciliation was still possible. Congress signed two important documents at this time. The Olive Branch Petition was a direct appeal to King George III to bring about peace between Parliament and the colonies. The Declaration of the Causes and Necessity of Taking Up Arms took the opposite view, closing with the words: "We most solemnly declare that we will preserve our liberties, being with one mind resolved to die free men rather than to live slaves."

The Colonies Declare Independence

In June 1776, Richard Henry Lee of Virginia rose in Congress and read this resolution: ". . . that these united colonies are, and of right ought to be, free and independent states; that they are absolved from all allegiance to the British Crown; and that all political connection between them and the state of Great Britain is, and ought to be, totally dissolved."

This resolution was America's actual declaration of independence from Britain. The much-more-famous Declaration of Independence, written in the following weeks, had a different purpose. Looking back in 1823, its author Thomas Jefferson described that purpose: "To place before mankind the common sense of the subject, in terms so plain and firm as to command their assent."

The Declaration of Independence clearly shows the influence of the European Enlightenment on the people of America. It refers to "self-evident truths" and "unalienable rights" that the Americans believed the British government denied them. It explained that when government was unjust to its people, the people had both the right and the duty to overthrow it. It described in detail the "injuries and usurpations" Britain had committed against the colonists. It concluded with the text of Richard Henry Lee's resolution. After three days of fierce debate, the amended declaration was approved and the Virginia resolution carried unanimously. The most contentious passage had been a reference to slavery as "cruel war against human nature"; as a compromise, the Northern delegates agreed to remove the passage so that the slaveholding Southern delegates would vote for independence. The British colonies were now the United States of America.

The Revolutionary War

The American Army

Few of the American soldiers had any military experience. They served on a voluntary basis and were paid no salaries. The British army was very different: it was a highly trained and disciplined regular army full of experienced veterans. It was clear that the two sides were unequally matched. The only American advantage was knowledge of the terrain and the willingness to fight in Indian fashion, by ambush; the British, reared in the tradition of armies facing one another on open ground, considered this cheating.

Africans and Indians took part in the war on both sides. The British governor of Virginia tempted hundreds of African slaves with a promise of freedom in exchange for military service; hundreds more fought on the side of the Americans. The Indians, skilled fighters valuable to both sides, supported whichever side seemed most likely to respect their own rights. Women served in the combat zone and behind the lines as spies, nurses, cooks, and laundresses; they took up guns when the necessity arose. At least one woman, Deborah Sampson, disguised herself as a man and served in the army.

The Battles

After the siege of Boston, the British marched south, planning to take over New York City; this takeover would cut New England off from the rest of the colonies, allowing the British army to crush both sections in turn. Thousands of mercenaries from the German state of Hesse were sailing across the Atlantic to reinforce the British troops.

In Brooklyn, the British army attacked the Americans from two sides at once, driving them across the river in retreat. This might have led to a decisive British victory, but a failure to follow up the attack allowed the American troops to reach New Jersey safely. Christmas night of 1776 found the Americans in Pennsylvania, just across the Delaware River from the British camp in New Jersey. The Americans took advantage of the Hessians' Christmas celebrations to slip quietly across the river and attack them at dawn. This successful surprise attack, known to history as the Battle of Trenton, inspired many of Washington's troops to reenlist and many more volunteers to join up for the first time.

By the end of September 1777, the British were riding through the streets of Philadelphia. In October, General William Howe led the British to victory in the Battle of Germantown. After this loss, the ragtag American army settled at Valley Forge for the winter, much of which they spent drilling under Frederich von Steuben. This Prussian military veteran had befriended Benjamin Franklin in Paris and sailed west to take part in the war; he drilled the Americans on a daily basis, transforming them into a sharp and disciplined fighting force. In February, France formally allied itself with the United States.

In the spring of 1778, the two armies met in an open battle on the fields at Monmouth, New Jersey. There was no clear victory for either side, but the British learned that the Americans were formidable opponents even in traditional European-style warfare. Meanwhile, the American troops in New York had forced a British surrender at Saratoga.

In December of 1778, the British army began a determined attack on the Southern colonies. Since the American army had left the South largely undefended, British commanders Cornwallis and Clinton thought they could easily conquer the South and then march north, taking control of each colony as they passed through it. By the spring of 1781, the British had captured Georgia and won a great victory at Charleston, South Carolina. However, the Americans defeated them in North Carolina, and the British generals decided to march on to Virginia. By this time, the French allies had arrived in the United States. The Americans and French soon cornered General Cornwallis and his troops at Yorktown, Virginia. Completely surrounded and running out of ammunition and food, the British surrendered in mid-October, ending the war.

The Peace

The 1783 Treaty of Paris granted the United States its independence, along with all the lands between the Atlantic coast and the Mississippi River and between the Great Lakes and Florida. In return, the United States agreed to repay any debt owed to Britain.

The New American Government

While the fighting was raging on the battlefields, the individual states began writing new constitutions for themselves, and leaders in Congress worked to create a government for the new nation. Establishing a new government took some time; the type of government was the subject of fierce debate among the political leaders. The earliest attempt at a written constitution was called the Articles of Confederation, ratified in 1781 by all thirteen states.

The Articles of Confederation had a number of serious deficiencies. First, they left far too much power with the states. Second, they did not create a national executive or a judicial branch. Third, they did not give Congress the power to collect taxes. All national governments must collect taxes; they are a necessary source of revenue that a nation must use to pay for services such as an army. This was especially crucial to the fledgling United States because it was at war at the time the Articles were written. Without the ability to collect taxes from the states, Congress had grave difficulty in paying the officers and supplying the soldiers.

Unable to force the states to help pay for the costs of the Revolution, Congress found itself with a huge war debt when it was over. When states belatedly began assessing taxes to help pay the debt, the people rebelled, believing that Congress was just the British Parliament all over again. Political leaders such as James Madison and George Washington began speaking out against the Articles, urging that Congress try again and this time create a stronger central government, one that had real authority to administer the states. By 1787, it was clear that this was essential if the new nation were to succeed. Delegates from all the colonies except Rhode Island met in Philadelphia at a Constitutional Convention to write what became the U.S. Constitution.

The Constitution

The delegates agreed to discard the Articles of Confederation and start afresh. They had many interests to try to balance. First, small and large states must be fairly represented. Second, state and national governments must fairly share their governing powers. Third, individual rights must be protected. Fourth, issues such as slavery, the Indian population, and territorial expansion must be addressed. In every area, compromise was the only solution; each state had to give up something it wanted so that the final product would be reasonably fair to all.

There were several important historical influences on the Constitution in its final form. The first was the influence of the Roman Republic (see Chapter 6), with its Senate and consuls. The second was the British government, with its tradition of representation and individual rights that dated back to the Magna Carta. The third was the ideas of the Enlightenment philosophers Locke and Montesquieu, who argued for the separation of powers in the government and the rights of the citizens to have a say in how they were ruled. The fourth was their own experience of government within the colonies, which had always run well and prosperously under similar systems of representative government.

These influences led Congress to design a federal government with a balance of powers among its three branches. The executive branch would have a president elected for a four-year term. The legislative branch would be a bicameral Congress; one house would represent the states according to population, while the other would represent all states equally. The judicial branch would consist of a Supreme Court. Each branch would have certain powers over the other two.

Many Americans were dismayed by the fact that the Constitution ignored the subject of individual rights; however, the required nine states did ratify the document. After the first national elections, Congress drafted a Bill of Rights that set forth many important freedoms and privileges of ordinary citizens. These ten amendments were ratified in the year 1791.

Apart from the brief split between North and South in the American Civil War of 1861 to 1865, the American system of government endures to the present day, unchanged in its essentials.

The French Revolution

The French Revolution had a number of direct causes. First, the eighteenth-century Enlightenment gave birth to new ideas about the equality of man (see Chapter 17). Second, the Glorious Revolution in Britain proved that a limited monarchy was a workable system, and the American Revolution provided a unique example of a republican government founded on the idea, if not the practical reality, that its citizens were equal under the law. Third, the combination of unchecked government spending and a series of poor harvests caused rising prices, higher taxes, and food shortages, which led to popular demonstrations and demands for reform. It was the combination of all these things that made the French Revolution happen when it did.

The King Convenes the Estates-General

The most important obstacle to reform in French society was the conservative nature of the monarchy. At a time when France needed a strong, practical leader, Louis XVI was timid and weak. His marriage to Austrian princess Marie Antoinette did nothing to strengthen his position with his subjects, as Austria and France were old enemies. His dismissal of many experienced government ministers signaled an end to attempts at reform and angered the common people.

Unable to solve France's economic crisis, Louis was forced to convene the Estates-General, which had not met since 1614. This poor excuse for a legislative assembly, which had never been much more than a rubber stamp for royal decrees, was divided into three categories by social status. The First Estate was comprised of priests, the Second of hereditary nobles, and the Third of peasants and *bourgeoisie*—the French middle class that included intellectuals, artists, merchants, and businessmen. The Third Estate represented millions more people than either of the others, but representation was not proportional—each of the three estates had one vote. Since members of the First and Second estates were tax-exempt, they always voted against reform; thus outnumbered on every vote, the Third Estate had the least power and influence over national policy even though it represented the greatest number of French citizens.

The Birth of the National Assembly

Change finally came about because there were important bonds between many members of the First and Third estates. First, many of the clergy were commoners, not nobles. Second, many of them were badly off financially; like members of the Third Estate, they were aware of the desperate need for reform. The Third Estate eventually persuaded the First to collaborate on establishing a new government. Calling themselves the National Assembly, the deputies met on an unused tennis court and swore what became known as the Tennis-Court Oath, vowing not to part company (thus preventing possible conspiracy, desertion in the ranks, and betrayal) until they had established a new government.

Louis XVI agreed to the National Assembly's demands for individual liberty, freedom of the press, and tax reform. Under protest, he also signed measures such as equal eligibility for office and reform of the social hierarchy. Reform was coming, but not soon enough to satisfy the people of Paris; on the morning of July 13, they took to the streets in fury, breaking into shops and stealing the goods, especially guns and ammunition. The uprising succeeded because the forces of law and order joined in; the palace guards of the Louvre and all the soldiers quartered in Paris, who suffered as much as anyone else from the scarcity of food and the inflation, threw in their lot with the commoners.

The Storming of the Bastille

On July 14, the people marched on the Bastille, which had served as a state prison under Louis XIV and was a hated symbol of tyranny, injustice, and oppression. In addition to the symbolic value of destroying it, the Parisians wanted the weapons that were stored inside. By early afternoon on what has since been known as Bastille Day, the prison had given way. The Parisians freed all remaining prisoners, commandeered the store of weapons and ammunition, and took brutal revenge on the chief magistrate and governor. They hustled them into the streets, turned the angry mob loose to almost literally tear them to pieces, then rammed their severed heads onto sharp pikes and paraded them through the streets in triumph. The rioting in Paris was duplicated throughout the countryside, featuring looting, arson, and even wholesale murder of hated aristocrats. It was not long before the mobs turned their anger directly against the royal family.

In October, the women of Paris marched on Versailles, armed with a motley collection of sticks and kitchen knives and with thousands of members of the National Guard at their backs. Waving the new French flag of red, white, and blue—the tricolor—the soldiers escorted the royal family back to Paris, where they were kept under guard. The king attempted to escape but was recognized and recaptured. Many members of the hereditary nobility fled to England or Austria; the months of mob violence convinced them that they would soon have to pay with their lives for their ancestors' centuries of privilege.

The End of the Monarchy

The National Assembly created a founding document for the new French republic. The Declaration of the Rights of Man and of the Citizen resembled the American Declaration of Independence. It called for a society based on equal treatment for all; freedom of speech, of the press, and of religion; the right to own property and to resist oppression; and the supremacy of just and reasonable laws that would treat all citizens equally.

The National Assembly had intended for Louis XVI to rule as a constitutional monarch with limited legislative powers, but the king's attempted escape made them change their minds. It appeared that Louis could not be trusted to play the role they had imagined for him but would more likely try to restore an absolute monarchy if he were allowed his freedom. After some debate in the National Convention—the new government of 750 popularly elected deputies—the king was declared a traitor to the Revolution and executed in January 1793. By December, nearly two hundred more would take the same journey to the scaffold.

Many members of the National Convention belonged to one of two informal political clubs: the radical Jacobins or the moderate Girondins. The working people of Paris, called *sansculottes* (meaning literally "without breeches"; breeches were tight-fitting trousers worn by fine gentlemen, whereas working men wore comfortable, loose-fitting trousers), supported the Jacobins, whose price-fixing and food rationing put an immediate end to the worst of the food shortages. The Jacobins soon found themselves gaining power in the convention; the Girondins lost all political power when a mob of *sansculottes* attacked them in their meeting place. In effect, this brought about one-party rule in France.

The Reign of Terror

By June 1793, the Committee of Public Safety, established by the National Convention and headed by Maximilien Robespierre, had acquired complete authority over the government and thus over the people. A lawyer and a Jacobin, Robespierre had supported the execution of Louis XVI.

Under the committee's rule, France underwent a period of violence known to history as the Reign of Terror, or just "the Terror." During this period, anyone denounced for crimes against the state was imprisoned, hastily tried, and taken to the guillotine for execution. Crimes against the state included saying or writing anything that criticized the Revolution. In most cases an accusation was enough—no concrete evidence was necessary—and private conversations were as much of a crime as public statements. Anyone who showed sympathy for an "enemy of the state" could also be imprisoned and executed.

Many of the aristocrats who had not already left the country were guillotined as well, Queen Marie Antoinette among them. Fortunately, this disgraceful episode was short lived. By March 1794, public sentiment turned against the Terror; ironically, Robespierre was among the last to be guillotined.

With the end of the Terror came the downfall of the Committee of Public Safety. The National Convention had become the common enemy of all the factions—royalists, Jacobins, and moderates. It was clear that the National Convention would have to give way to some strong central authority more capable of taking control. When the deputies of the National Convention realized in October 1794 that it was only a matter of time before the Parisians rose up against them, they appealed for help to the army, which was then under the command of Napoleon Bonaparte.

The Rise of Napoleon

Born in Corsica in 1769, Napoleon had been educated at a French military academy. His extraordinary ability in mathematics and geography made him excellent officer material. In 1794, Captain Bonaparte led a successful attack against Austria and was promoted to the rank of general. Charged with controlling the mob in Paris in 1794, Napoleon decided to threaten it with grapeshot—clusters of small musket balls fired from cannons at point-blank range. The ensuing incident, known to history as a "whiff of grapeshot," effectively ended the threat against the National Convention. This efficient, if brutal, handling of the emergency marked Napoleon as a figure of major importance in France. He was soon leading the army to victorious campaigns in Italy and

Austria. Despite a failed campaign in Egypt, he returned to Paris in 1799 to loud popular acclaim.

By the time of Napoleon's return, the National Convention had given way to the Directory—yet another failed attempt at creating a strong, functional legislature. The Directory had no strong leader and no internal agreement about how to shape a new government. Many ideas that had ruined the National Convention returned in the Directory. It took all political rights away from members of the Second Estate who had returned to France after the Terror. It arrested and deported hundreds of members of the former First Estate. Rather than permitting religious freedom, it tried to do away with religion altogether by suppressing the Catholic Church. The Directory found itself unable to agree on provisions for a constitution. The leaders of the Directory soon realized they would have to try again to form a workable legislative assembly.

Because Napoleon was the acknowledged head of the military forces, the Directory turned to him again for help in controlling the mobs of Paris as it tried to form a new government. Over November 9 and 10, 1799, the Directory fell and was replaced by a body of three consuls, one of whom was Napoleon. He quickly became First Consul, the only one with any real power.

Napoleon Rules France

Napoleon began his rule of France by organizing its bureaucracy along military lines, with specific rules and a clear chain of command. Napoleon improved the division of France into *départments* (similar to British or American counties), created France's first national bank and public school system, and reestablished the Catholic Church by concordat with the pope in 1801. To Napoleon, this was strictly a practical matter; he had no religious convictions of his own, but he perceived that his subjects' Catholic faith and heritage was too important to them to jettison.

Using the work of the National Convention as a starting point, Napoleon revised and finalized France's new law code, which went into effect in 1804. The Code Napoleon set forth the basic rights of the citizens, noting that its laws would apply equally to all.

In August 1802, in an election of sorts, Napoleon was chosen First Consul for life. In 1804, he declared himself hereditary Emperor of the French for life, ensuring that he could pass on his title to his sons. In effect, France had exchanged one absolute ruler for another.

Napoleon's Military Career

From 1800 to 1809, Napoleon was spectacularly successful on the battlefield. (See Figure 18.2.) During this period, he pursued the same military strategy in every case: to identify and attack the enemy's weak point and never to be forced onto the defensive.

In 1805, Napoleon's Grand Army was on the march against Austria, which had formed an alliance with Russia in the hopes of preventing future French invasions. Napoleon soon forced the Austrians to surrender; he then marched east to defeat the Russians under General Kutuzov at Austerlitz. The ensuing Treaty of Pressburg replaced the Holy Roman Empire with the French-controlled Confederation of the Rhine. This was the high point of Napoleon's military career.

By 1808, France was fighting Spain. The French invaded and subdued Portugal, then moved into Spain to overthrow its monarchy. The Grand Army imprisoned the ruling Bourbon family and installed Napoleon's brother as king. This provoked the Spanish to rise up in a burst of angry nationalism against the invaders. Britain then sent troops to aid Spain and Portugal; the Duke of

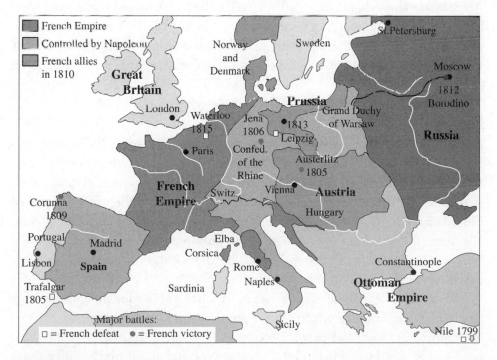

FIGURE 18.2 The Napoleonic Wars

Wellington, commander of the British army, was placed in charge of the allied forces. Unlike Napoleon, Wellington preferred to fight on the defensive, which led to a long war of attrition.

Meanwhile, Napoleon had decided to invade Russia over disagreements with Czar Alexander I. With the French army fighting on the Iberian peninsula, Napoleon gathered an army from territory controlled by France. By June 1812, some six hundred fifty thousand troops—Germans, Poles, Austrians, and Italians—had marched to the Russian border.

Crossing the barren plains of Russia in intense summer heat took a terrible toll on Napoleon's troops. The land provided no shade trees, no crops, and few sources of fresh water. Unable to scavenge much to eat or drink, the soldiers began falling dead by the side of the road. Eventually, they started killing and eating their own horses.

After the Battle of Borodino in September, in which Napoleon lost fifty thousand men, Kutuzov ordered his troops to retreat toward Moscow. When the Russians reached the capital, they evacuated and burned it; when the French arrived, they found no food and little shelter. By October, Napoleon acknowledged that the French would have to return to the West. The Grand Army began the long retreat—only to realize the Russians had turned and were pursuing them. Thousands of Grand Army soldiers died in the retreat. The remnants of the army crossed the border in December. Meanwhile, the Peninsular War was clearly lost. Facing enormous military defeat on two fronts, Napoleon abdicated in 1814.

Napoleon's Final Defeat

Louis XVI's brother now became king of France, ruling under the name Louis XVIII (on Louis XVI's execution, his young son had automatically become Louis XVII but was never seen again after the Terror; he almost certainly died in prison). The king banished Napoleon to the small Mediterranean island of Elba. Persuading himself that he was the only man who could save France, Napoleon quietly escaped Elba with seven hundred soldiers, arms, and money. This small army was soon strengthened by the addition of a French infantry battalion encountered on the road north.

When the news of Napoleon's escape reached the leaders of Europe, they reacted swiftly and in concert. Wellington was placed in command of British, German, Dutch, and Belgian troops, while General Blücher and the Prussians would stand by to help him. Facing two armies about ninety miles apart, one in Belgium and the other in Germany, Napoleon decided to attack from the center and eliminate each army in turn. However, Wellington outsmarted Napoleon by taking up position on the high ground above the fields of the town of Waterloo. After a long day of fighting, the French were defeated. This battle ended the Napoleonic era and finished Napoleon's public career. "Meeting one's Waterloo" is still today an idiom that signifies failure. The British declared Napoleon a prisoner of war and banished him to the South Atlantic island of St. Helena, where he died in obscurity in 1821.

The Congress of Vienna

The leaders of Europe met in Vienna in September 1814 to restore the balance of power that had been so drastically upset by the conquests of Napoleon. The work of the Congress of Vienna was briefly interrupted when Napoleon returned from Elba, but the leaders resumed work after the Battle of Waterloo and completed their task by June 1815.

Each nation was represented at the Congress of Vienna by a monarch or a prominent military or political figure, as follows:

- Austria—foreign minister Prince Klemens von Metternich
- Britain—foreign secretary Viscount Castlereagh; Duke of Wellington
- France—foreign minister Charles Talleyrand
- Prussia—chancellor Prince Karl August von Hardenberg
- Russia—Czar Alexander I

The leaders had two main goals—to restore the balance of powers among nations and to make sure that balance was maintained in the future. First, they redrew and restored boundary lines, making Napoleon's conquered territories independent or, according to the principle of compensation, giving them to one of the four major powers—Austria, Britain, Prussia, and Russia. Second, they agreed to contain future French aggression by supporting the unification of the German states into one strong nation. By 1819, nearly forty German states had formed the German Confederation, temporarily under the presidency of Austria. Third, the Great Powers agreed to create the Quadruple Alliance, which would meet as often as necessary over the next twenty years to see that the terms of the peace were carried out and to discuss any matters of international concern that might arise. This early attempt at an international peacekeeping organization failed in the long run; its first meeting was also its last. However, its goals were important because they showed the trend that diplomacy was taking in history. Peace conferences after major international wars would occur again in the twentieth century, and serious international peacekeeping efforts would be undertaken again.

QUIZ

1. **What was the purpose of the First Continental Congress?**
   A. to raise a standing army and appoint a commander in chief
   B. to establish a unified central government for the colonies
   C. to declare independence from Great Britain
   D. to discuss opposition to the Intolerable Acts

2. **The French Legislative Assembly decided against establishing a constitutional monarchy because _____.**
   A. the king refused to rule jointly with the legislature
   B. the radical and republican deputies outnumbered the monarchists
   C. Louis XVI proved by his attempted escape that he could not be trusted
   D. the people of Paris were determined that the king should be executed

3. **An alliance with _____ made it possible for the Third Estate to establish a new government.**
   A. Louis XVI
   B. Maximilien Robespierre
   C. poor members of the First Estate
   D. members of the Second Estate

4. **Northern delegates agreed to strike a passage referring to slavery from the American Declaration of Independence because _____.**
   A. they did not believe it was the right time to free the slaves
   B. they supported the institution of slavery
   C. most of them were slaveholders
   D. they wanted the Southerners to vote in favor of independence

5. **As a result of the Glorious Revolution, _____ gained supremacy in the British government.**
   A. the monarch
   B. the clergy
   C. Parliament
   D. the common people

6. **Napoleon signed a concordat with the pope and restored the Catholic Church in France because _____.**
   A. he was a devout Catholic
   B. he was afraid of the power of the pope
   C. he believed that a traditional form of worship was important to the people
   D. he wanted to maintain the French clergy in a position of power

7. **Why did Parliament view religious issues in England with such great concern?**
   A. because religious tensions had often led to civil wars
   B. because many members of Parliament were clergymen
   C. because Parliament wanted to abolish the monarchy
   D. because the British people were religiously tolerant

8. **The American idea for a government of three branches, each with power over the other two, originally came from _____.**
   A. ancient Rome
   B. medieval Britain
   C. the Enlightenment
   D. colonial custom and experience

9. **The English Bill of Rights was passed as a result of _____.**
   A. the Restoration
   B. the Glorious Revolution
   C. the English Civil War
   D. the Exclusion Bill

10. **Why did the delegates to the Congress of Vienna recommended German unification?**
    A. because Prussia had played a significant role in defeating Napoleon
    B. because Britain and Prussia were allies
    C. because a united Germany would balance France as a strong central nation
    D. because there had been too much warfare among the German states

chapter 19

Asian Empires 1600–1815; Late European Colonization

The Ming dynasty fell to a popular uprising in 1644; this made way for the Manchu of northeastern China—Manchuria—to move in and seize power. The Manchu would rule as the Qing dynasty until 1911. After a chaotic forty-year period that ended with their triumph over all their political rivals, the Manchu proved to be able rulers in many respects. They made every effort to maintain as many native Chinese traditions as possible, which provided continuity to China's history and culture.

The Tokugawa shogunate that took power in Japan in 1600 had one overall goal—control. Tokugawa Ieyasu and his successors intended to bring peace and stability back to a country that had been torn by violence and war for many years. As a means to this end, the shogunate closed the ports of Japan to all outsiders (apart from minimal contact with Chinese and Dutch traders) and banned all Japanese from leaving the country. This isolation from the rest of the world would continue for the better part of the next two hundred fifty years.

The motives for European colonization in Africa and Southeast Asia were fourfold. First, the European powers expected economic profits from their colonies, many of which were rich in the natural resources and raw materials—including human beings—necessary to keep European factories going. Second, no European nation wanted to grant supremacy to the others; as long as one nation was establishing overseas colonies, other nations would follow suit simply to maintain a balance of power. Third, Christian churches that had steadily been losing power and influence in Europe saw the colonization of Africa and Asia as a splendid opportunity for missionary work. Fourth, the sense of racial superiority that characterized Europeans made them feel it was their responsibility to impose their culture on peoples they regarded as uncivilized or inferior.

CHAPTER OBJECTIVES

- Describe the rise to power of the Manchu Qing dynasty in China.
- Characterize government, society, and culture under the Tokugawa shogunate.
- Describe European colonization and conquest in Southeast Asia and Africa.

Chapter 19 Time Line

●	1600	Tokugawa Ieyasu founds Tokugawa shogunate
●	1637	Ban on foreign travel for all citizens of Japan
●	1641	Dutch trading post moved to island of Deshima, Japan
●	1644	Manchu Qing dynasty begins in China
●	1795	Founding of Baptist Missionary Society
●	1848	France annexes Algeria
●	1850	Britain gains control over India
●	1852	Boers (Dutch) establish South African Republic
●	1854	Boers establish Orange Free State

- **1880**   France establishes protectorate in Congo
- **1882**   Britain establishes protectorate in Egypt
- **1884**   European nations meet at Berlin and agree on division of Africa
- **1886**   Britain takes Burma
- **1887**   France conquers Indochina (Vietnam)
- **1898**   Britain conquers Sudan; establishes control of Hong Kong

Manchu Qing China

The Manchu are from the northeastern region of China, just north of Korea; historically, this region was called Manchuria after its people. Today it comprises the three Chinese provinces Heilongjiang, Jilin, and Liaoning. This region was the source of a number of serious military challenges to China during the early Middle Ages. The Juchen, who ruled what was then called the state of Jin, in fact overran northern China in 1127 (see Chapter 10). The people of Manchuria are Mongols, but unlike most peoples of the steppes, they lived in an agricultural and mercantile society.

Manchurian leaders had by no means given up the idea of conquering the Chinese Empire. During the early 1600s, they actively recruited disgruntled and disaffected Chinese officials and scholars who might help them overthrow the Ming and whose support and advice were actively helpful in the Manchu's adoption of a Chinese-style political structure. As time went by, the Ming began to recognize a serious rival for power in the Manchu.

The Manchu began to move in 1629, breaching the defenses of the Great Wall under their leader Hong Taiji. Manchu troops soon occupied the Chinese cities of Luanzhou, Qianan, Yongping, and Zunhua. In 1631, Hong led another successful military campaign against the Ming garrison city of Dalinghe, laying siege to it and eventually using Portuguese-made cannon to bring down its heavy, fortified walls.

The Manchu succeeded in taking over China in 1644 in a series of violent events. A major rebellion ended with the suicide of the last Ming emperor and the fall of Beijing to the rebel leader Li Zicheng, who declared himself the first emperor of the Shun dynasty. It swiftly became clear that Li and his administration were no better than bullies and thieves; in consequence, Ming army commander Wu Sangui traveled to Beijing to execute the emperor. Li saved himself temporarily by fleeing the capital; he remained on the run until 1645, when a band of soldiers killed him. Li's inglorious exit from Beijing gave the Manchu their opportunity to seize power in China. They would be known as the Qing or Manchu Qing dynasty and would remain in power until 1911. Hong Taiji had died in 1643, leaving his six-year-old son to become the first Qing emperor.

Security on the imperial throne did not happen immediately; in fact, it would take some forty years before the Qing were able to triumph over all their rivals for power. One of the first edicts they issued caused a serious religious and cultural affront that might, with better organization on the part of the protestors, have ended their conquest as soon as it began. In 1645, the order came forth that all Chinese men were to adopt the traditional Manchu hairstyle known as the queue: a shaved forehead in front and a long braid in back. From the Chinese point of view, altering one's natural physical appearance by shaving one's hair was disrespectful to one's parents, an unheard-of affront; additionally, they felt that Chinese should stick to Chinese traditions, not adopt Manchu ones. Some Chinese, especially those living in the highlands, took up arms in protest against wearing the queue.

The period between 1645 and 1683 saw a series of rebellions, both politically and culturally motivated. One rebellion in the Yangtze River delta of central China resulted in the massacre of tens of thousands of Chinese. By 1683, however, the Qing had eliminated their political rivals and crushed the rebellions and could begin governing their new realm in earnest.

As foreign rulers, the Manchu trod carefully, taking to heart the furious reaction against their queue edict. They worked hard to ally the interests of the provincial nobility with the Beijing bureaucracy so that neither group would feel secondary to the other. The gentry were, of course, the source from which the bureaucracy was culled; they were also revered authority figures throughout the provinces. The Qing pacified any tendency the nobility might have toward opposition by respecting and defending their property rights and by suppressing any peasant challenges to the landlords' power.

The Manchu provided as much continuity as they could from the Ming era, retaining political and societal structures that had worked well for many generations. The era was one of prosperity and expansion as well as cultural and ethnic diversity. In 1760, the addition of Manchurian and Siberian territory more than doubled the size of the empire.

Tokugawa Japan

The Tokugawa period of Japanese history is remarkable as perhaps the only instance in world history when a nation withdrew absolutely from foreign affairs, literally closing its borders to all outsiders for the better part of two hundred fifty years.

Tokugawa Ieyasu and his successors closed the ports in an attempt to gain greater control over Japan and to end the long era of civil wars, violence, and unrest. From their point of view, there were several challenges to their supremacy. These were political, social, and intellectual.

The Tokugawa moved the capital from Heian to Edo (present-day Tokyo), which was the location of their own family stronghold, an impressive fortress complex. The shogun ruled as a military dictator, although he paid lip service to the notion that all his authority came from the emperor. From time to time, the shogun would appoint a prime minister, although this office was frequently vacant. A council of six senior and six junior elders served as the shogun's cabinet, providing advice when asked. A large bureaucracy collected taxes and administered society. The last element of the Tokugawa government was the secret police, who spied on people throughout the country, reporting any instances of rebellious behavior or speech.

The political system under the Tokugawa gave a great deal of independent power to the *daimyos*, who were all but autonomous on their own estates in the provinces. To counteract their formidable political powers, the shogun required all *daimyos* to pay long, extended visits to Edo; during their periodic visits home to the country, they were forced to leave their families behind. This enabled the shogun and his court to keep an eye on the *daimyos*, to weaken them politically, and to prevent them from conspiring to overthrow the regime. At the same time in faraway France, Louis XIV was practicing a similar system of enforced attendance at court on the French aristocracy (see Chapter 14).

Having to maintain a second household in Edo could cost up to a quarter of a lord's income; this severely weakened him financially, creating a further check on the power of the *daimyos* as a class. Their enforced spending kept the overall Japanese economy healthy, as it benefited the shopkeepers, restaurant owners, innkeepers, and makers and sellers of luxury goods. With money flowing abundantly in the cities, especially Edo, a trend of urban migration began; thousands of provincial Japanese moved to the cities and towns in search of financial opportunities.

In previous times, the Japanese had generally rejected Confucianism. Under the Tokugawa, however, Confucianism became the approved philosophy. Its support for maintaining tradition and social order and its emphasis on submission to authority fit perfectly with the Tokugawa goal of maintaining a stable, peaceful society. Of course, the code that the Tokugawa advocated was a Japanese brand of Confucianism; it placed more emphasis on heredity and less on individual merit, and it embraced many of the ideals of Buddhism.

According to the guidance of Confucian ideals, the Tokugawa government established a strict, hereditary caste system that divided all Japanese into four classes: the samurai, the peasants, the artisans, and the merchants. The samurai, the hereditary nobility, were considered the highest rank. The peasants ranked second because they produced food; this meant that they deserved great respect. (This was theoretical and abstract, of course; in reality, the peasants were the poorest class and led the harshest and most miserable lives.) Artisans ranked immediately below peasants because they too were producers, although the manufactured goods they produced were considered of secondary value compared to food. The merchants, who produced nothing, were lowest on the social scale; paradoxically, they were also the wealthiest.

The entire Japanese economy was based on the rice harvest. The *daimyos* paid their samurai in rice; the samurai made cash money by selling off the surplus to the merchants, who became even wealthier as they sold the same rice to the people in their turn. With every transaction, of course, the price rose.

Forced into an expensive way of life, the *daimyos* and the samurai soon found themselves borrowing money from the merchants, which enabled the merchants to gain power and influence over them. The class barriers began to break down to some extent; a marriage between a samurai and a merchant would provide money to the one and prestige to the other.

The Tokugawa period was one of outward peace and serenity but inward tensions. The peasants were respected in theory, but, in fact, they carried almost the entire tax burden of the nation on their shoulders. The merchants were wealthy and powerful, but they had no social standing and no political power. The nobility were privileged, but a warrior class in a nation that plays no role in foreign affairs is forced to remain idle. Even Confucianism contributed to the unease. If one thought through the Confucian ideals to their logical conclusions, then the shoguns were not legitimate rulers; they had usurped the imperial authority and, therefore, society should refuse to obey them.

Japan had had a moderate amount of contact with the Western world before the Tokugawa era. Spanish, Portuguese, and Dutch traders had all created trading posts on the Japanese islands, and a considerable number of Jesuit missionaries were working in Japan by 1600. The Tokugawa regarded Christianity as a subversive force in Japanese society, perhaps because of its moral code that treated people equally, regardless of their social rank.

Persecution of the Christians began under the Tokugawa; deportation or execution became the fate of all of them. The Spaniards were forced to leave the country in 1624. A massive Christian uprising, in which thousands of Japanese participated, began in 1637 and continued into 1638; the shogun crushed the rebellion, ordered all the rebels executed, and threw the Portuguese traders out of Japan in the belief that they had aided the rebels. The failed rebellion effectively wiped out Christianity in Japan; ordinary Japanese Christians either converted or faced execution.

The Dutch traders disavowed any desire to convert the Japanese to Christianity and were therefore allowed to maintain their presence in the country. However, the shogun decided that they must move from their long-standing location on Hirado to somewhere more confined. He ordered the construction of the man-made island of Deshima in the harbor; in 1641, the Dutch moved from Hirado to Deshima, where their contact with Japanese citizens was strictly regimented. Chinese traders also maintained a limited economic relationship with Japan, but they too were restricted to Deshima and treated as possible sources of Western corruption.

One other way to prevent any foreign influence from contaminating Japan was by banning foreign travel. In 1637, the Tokugawa forbade all Japanese citizens from leaving the country and denied reentry into Japan to any Japanese who were already abroad. The shogun also banned the construction of any large ships such as other countries used for international trade.

Foreign influence did seep in, of course. Government bans on contact did not eliminate curiosity about the West, interest in studying new ideas, or the desire to see Japan take its place among the great nations of the world. Through approved contact with the Dutch traders, some Japanese could always get news and information about the West. By 1720, social tensions and other forces made the shogunate lift the ban on importing Western books and studying new foreign ideas (except Christianity, which was still banned). The Japanese even experimented with new Western technologies; this would ease industrialization under the Meiji emperor (see Chapter 21).

Artistically, the Tokugawa period was a golden age, especially in theater, poetry, and the visual arts. This era saw the development of *bunraku*, a Japanese form of puppet theater in which puppeteers were visible onstage but dressed entirely in black to show that they were "invisible." The puppets they manipulated, initially small and simple, became very large and elaborate over time. *Kabuki* theater, a much more spectacular and gaudy variety than *noh*, also became popular at this time. Because *kabuki* was considered bawdy and vulgar, the government banned participation by female dancers and actors (this was not unique to Japan; there were no female actors in sixteenth-century England either).

The samurai Matsuo Bashō changed the course of poetry in Japan during the mid-seventeenth century. Bashō was the greatest master of haiku, a three-line, seventeen-syllable poetic form that, up until then, had been considered purely a source of amusement for both writers and readers. Bashō ennobled the haiku, using the form to create simple verbal images of nature—a butterfly on a leaf, a frog splashing in a pond—that were thoughtful, beautiful, and evocative.

The era also saw the development of the woodblock print, a Japanese style that is internationally popular to the present day. The prints were especially well received in Japan because prints, unlike oil paintings, are not unique; they exist in multiple copies and are therefore much less expensive. Woodblock prints were art that the masses could afford. The style of the day was to capture moments of city life: people running across a bridge during a storm, a cat gazing out from a perch on a windowsill, shoppers jostling one another at a market stall. Hokusai and Hiroshige were the most notable practitioners of these woodblock prints in the 1600s.

The Tokugawa shogunate created a Japanese society that was highly regimented, accustomed to obeying decrees and submitting to authority. It was a society in which everyone had a place and was obliged to do his or her duty.

Southeast Asia

With the exception of Siam (present-day Thailand), nearly all the islands and kingdoms of Southeast Asia were under European sway by the outbreak of World War I in 1914. Most of the colonization took place after 1870, although Britain and the Netherlands began the process earlier in the nineteenth century.

During the early 1800s, Britain used its power base in India to open up trade with China, exporting Indian opium in exchange for Chinese tea. By the end of the nineteenth century, trade deficits would reduce China to the status of a second- or third-rate power (see Chapter 21). Thanks to the strength and fighting skills of Indian troops, Britain took over Burma and Singapore; Singapore was important for the protection of British shipping lanes, and Burma was ruled by an ambitious dynasty that threatened British supremacy in the region.

The Dutch won a power struggle on the island of Java in 1830. They gained huge profits by purchasing Javanese crops (sugar, coffee, and tea) very cheaply and selling them in Europe at much higher prices.

France was also active in Southeast Asia, invading Vietnam in 1858 and establishing a colony there, despite resistance from both Vietnam and China. By 1884, the French had established protectorates in Annan and Tonkin; three years later, they took over Cambodia. The French administered the area as the Union of Indochina. This region was valuable for its natural resources of rubber, timber, and rice.

The Takeover of Africa

On the eve of World War I in 1914, almost the entire continent of Africa was under European rule. The only exceptions were the independent nations of Ethiopia on the Red Sea and tiny Liberia on the Atlantic coast.

Europeans regarded Africa as a literal and figurative economic gold mine. Literally, the sub-Saharan portion of the continent had extensive resources of gold (and diamonds). Figuratively, Africa was a repository of natural resources that Europe could not provide for itself, such as rubber and a variety of minerals. Africa boasted a variety of climates, but many regions of the continent were ideal for the cultivation of cotton, coffee, and cocoa—all highly valued in Europe.

Europe had made enormous profits from the slave trade before the mid-1700s. Although European nations did not use African slave labor on the continent, they did carry shiploads of slaves to their colonies across the Atlantic. Millions of Africans—many sold to the traders by Africans from rival tribes—were kidnapped, transported, and sold into labor in the cotton or sugarcane fields of the Caribbean islands, Latin America, and the southern United States. Britain alone shipped more than three million Africans across the ocean.

African tribal culture was centuries old by the time the first Europeans made contact with the continent. The continent was not culturally homogenous; it was home to a large number of tribes who spoke different languages and had a great variety of customs. However, none of these was recognizable to a European as a civilized culture. European invaders of Africa behaved exactly as they had in the Americas in the 1500s: they conquered with their superior firepower, imposed their own culture and language on the native peoples, and exploited them.

In most cases, the Africans were simply not prepared for the European aggression. In some cases, Africans even welcomed Europeans as potential allies against their traditional local rivals. Africans were prone to accommodate the Europeans, rarely risking an all-out armed confrontation that they had no hope of winning due to their lack of sophisticated arms. However, they found many means of both passive and active resistance—everything from nonpayment of tributes and taxes to full-scale rebellion. European control was much more present in urban areas than in the countryside; additionally, many areas of Africa were largely inaccessible without a modern transportation network, which took some time to build. Therefore, European occupation had relatively little effect on thousands of rural Africans.

Christian missionaries began playing an active role in Africa around the late 1700s, with the Baptist Missionary Society being founded in 1795. The men and women who traveled to Africa did not merely spread the gospel; they provided practical, down-to-earth help in a number of areas. First, they brought medicines and medical help. Malaria, which was spread by mosquitoes, was (and still is) epidemic throughout most of southern Africa; the missionaries brought and distributed quinine, which helped to combat it. Second, they held classes for children and adults, teaching them to read and write—not just in European languages, but in their own. Unlike the more secular colonizers, the missionaries lived among the people, ate the same food, and worked hard to learn the native languages. It was the missionaries who were responsible, in many cases, for creating written forms of many of the African languages for the first time. This creation of a whole class of literate, educated Africans would prove crucial in the drive for African self-determination and independence that began after World War II. Third, the missionaries used what influence they had to try to persuade the Africans to discontinue some of their cruelest traditional practices, such as human sacrifice, slavery, and polygamy.

Olaudah Equiano, also known by the name of Gustavus Vasa, was a slave who survived the middle passage (see Chapter 15), gained his freedom as an adult, and wrote an important slave narrative. Equiano traveled to Britain in the early 1800s and became a well-known public speaker on the issue of abolition. It was partly due to his efforts that Britain finally acquired the moral sense to outlaw the slave trade in 1807.

Between 1858 and 1869, the French built the Suez Canal across a narrow neck of Egyptian land; this connection between the Mediterranean and Red seas was to prove of major importance for communication, transport, and trade. The British seized the canal from the French in 1875 and, soon after, established virtual control over the Egyptian government—largely for the sake of maintaining control of the canal. Britain also established itself in Nigeria and in the southern region in a colony it named Rhodesia (present-day Zambia and Zimbabwe).

Britain, France, Belgium, Germany, Italy, and Portugal all established a major presence on the African continent; Spain established one small colony on the Atlantic coast (see Figure 19.1). The Dutch settled in South Africa, where they established the Cape Colony; the British took over the area during the Napoleonic wars. The Boers, as the Dutch South Africans were known, established the South African Republic and the Orange Free State (named for the royal house of Orange) in the mid-nineteenth century. The British eventually drove the Dutch out in the Boer War, and South Africa was made a British dominion.

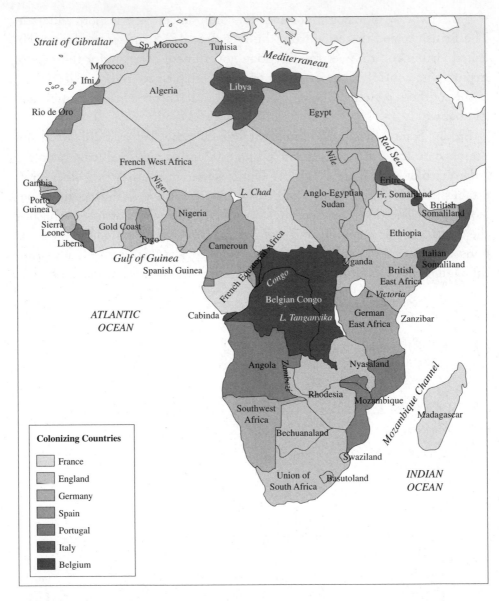

FIGURE 19.1   Europe's African Colonies in 1914

QUIZ

1. Peasants were of high social rank in Tokugawa Japan because _____.
   A. they were the best-educated people in the country
   B. they produced the rice on which Japanese survival depended
   C. they were the wealthiest class
   D. they had more respect for tradition than the other classes

2. The Manchu took advantage of _____ to seize power in China.
   A. economic depression
   B. military weakness
   C. widespread popularity
   D. political chaos

3. European religious organizations approved of their governments' efforts to colonize foreign countries primarily because _____.
   A. they believed in European racial superiority
   B. they wanted to recruit new converts
   C. they no longer felt welcome in Europe
   D. they hoped to make economic gains

4. Why were rural Africans less affected than urban ones by the occupying Europeans?
   A. They were less accessible.
   B. They were less educated.
   C. They were less wealthy.
   D. They were less intimidated.

5. The Dutch were able to demand high prices in Europe for Javanese sugar, coffee, and tea because _____.
   A. it cost them a lot of money to transport them to Europe
   B. Europeans did not often travel to Java
   C. the Suez Canal was not opened until 1869
   D. these crops could not be cultivated in the European climate

6. The Southeast Asian nation of _____ remained independent throughout the period of European colonization.
   A. Java
   B. Siam
   C. Vietnam
   D. Singapore

7. Tokugawa Ieyasu moved the capital from Heian to Edo because _____.
   A. Edo was Japan's largest city
   B. Edo was the location of the fortified family estate
   C. the emperor and the court were located in Edo
   D. Edo was the cultural and artistic center of Japan

8. _____ was the major cause of discontent in the merchant class under the Tokugawa shogunate.
   A. Their lack of social and political standing
   B. Their unfairly large share of the nation's tax burden
   C. Government controls of pricing
   D. The outlawing of Christianity

9. Why were the Dutch the only Western traders allowed to remain in Japan after its ports were closed?
   A. because their products were of the highest quality
   B. because they did not try to convert the Japanese to Christianity
   C. because they were not missionaries
   D. because they did not represent a great European power

10. The Suez Canal connected the Red Sea with the _____.
    A. Mediterranean Sea
    B. Indian Ocean
    C. Bay of Bengal
    D. Arabian Sea

Europe and the Ottoman Empire in the Nineteenth Century, 1815–1914

The nineteenth century in Europe is often described as a century of peace, with no major wars breaking out among the great powers between 1815 and 1914. In fact, however, all was not peaceful; this was the century of the popular uprising. Where most wars in the past had been fought *between* nations, this century saw a series of revolutions fought *within* nations, as the people rose up and demanded their independence. Examples of constitutional governments in Britain, France, and the United States led to loud calls for written constitutions in many European nations. One wave of European revolutions took place in 1830 and another in 1848. These revolutions can be understood as a struggle between the forces of liberalism and conservatism, the two mainstream political movements of the day. Liberalism, which supported representative forms of government, triumphed in the nineteenth century, although several conservative governments were still in power in 1914.

Nationalism also contributed to the decline and fall of the Ottoman Empire. Beginning in 1798, the Ottomans began steadily losing territory and influence until the empire was finally eliminated altogether after World War I. Other contributing factors included European aggression and the inability of the Ottomans to match European military and technological progress. The year 1923 saw the creation of Turkey, a secular Islamic republic; meanwhile, the Middle Eastern portions of the empire clung to their Islamic faith and culture.

CHAPTER OBJECTIVES

- Name and describe the major European political movements of the early to mid-nineteenth century.
- Discuss the changes in European society and government during the nineteenth century.
- Define the Romantic Movement in the arts and name its key figures.
- Describe the decline and fall of the Ottoman Empire.

Chapter 20 Time Line

1815	Congress of Vienna
	Formation of the Holy Alliance
1830	Charles X of France abdicates; Louis Philippe becomes king
1830–1831	Belgium becomes an independent nation
1832	Reform Act in Britain
1837	Queen Victoria is crowned
1848	*The Communist Manifesto* published
	Revolutions in France and other nations
1853–1856	Crimean War
1861	Emancipation of serfs in Russia
	Unification of Italy
1867	Creation of Austro-Hungarian Empire

- 1870–1871   Franco-Prussian War
- 1871   Unification of Germany
- 1882   Egypt becomes British protectorate
- 1905   Decembrist Revolution in Russia
- 1916   Arab Revolt
- 1923   Founding of Republic of Turkey under Mustafa Kemal
- 1924   Final dissolution of the Ottoman Empire

Europe: The Age of *-isms* in Politics

Conservatism and liberalism— words whose meanings have changed some-what in contemporary American politics—were the mainstream political philosophics of nineteenth-century Europe. Broadly speaking, conservatives distrusted the common people and thus believed in authoritarian rule by the upper classes; liberals trusted the common people and thus believed in rep-resentative government. Conservatives opposed freedom of the press because they believed the monarch was the best judge of what should and should not be published; liberals believed in the Enlightenment ideals of free speech and a free press. The conservative ideal was a benevolent, enlightened hereditary monarch who would use his or her powers for the good of society; the liberal ideal was a freely elected representative government of checks and balances in which the legislature should have the greatest power. Neither conservatives nor liberals believed that the lower classes should have a voice in the political system, on the grounds that working people did not own property and were largely uneducated. Instead, they believed that a good government would, as a matter of course, look after the working poor.

Nationalism

The revolutions of the nineteenth century encouraged nationalism—pride in one's native country—by defining national borders and making them perma-nent. By 1900, nationalism was deeply rooted all over Europe—at least among the educated classes. It was a unifying force in culturally homogenous nations such as France, but in a culturally and ethnically diverse empire such as Austria-Hungary, it could be explosive.

Socialism

Socialism is a form of government in which the good of the community is more important than the rights of the individual. A socialist government controls major institutions such as education and major industries such as the production of steel. In a capitalist economy, by contrast, businesses and industries are privately owned, and the laws of supply and demand set prices. By the end of the twentieth century, most European nations would have mixed capitalist-socialist economies.

Marxism

The Communist Manifesto (1848), written jointly by Prussians Karl Marx and Friedrich Engels, is the founding text of communism. Marx and Engels argued that human history was a power struggle between social classes. After centuries of oppression, it was time for the proletariat (working class) to take over society by means of a violent overthrow of the existing order. In *Das Kapital* (its three volumes were published from 1867 to 1894), Marx argued further that the worker who produced goods was a far more valuable member of society than the owner, who produced nothing. Thus Marx not only predicted, but encouraged, a sweeping reorganization of the European social order, thereby arousing opposition across the political spectrum. The wealthy and comfortable dismissed his arguments as the ravings of a madman. Conservatives decried him because he suggested overturning the social order in which they believed. Liberals opposed him because he was too democratic. Nationalists scorned him because he insisted that one's country of origin counted for nothing. Capitalists despised him because he insisted that workers, not owners or managers, should enjoy the profits and run the industries themselves.

The Great Powers and the Holy Alliance

In September 1815, just after the Congress of Vienna, the leaders of Austria, Prussia, and Russia formed what became known as the Holy Alliance. These three nations agreed to assist one another in maintaining what they saw as the peace and stability of the new European map of 1815. As conservatives, Holy Alliance leaders viewed popular rebellions and insurrections as serious threats to political stability. As it turned out, the three nations would frequently have to send troops to put down such rebellions. Their superior military strength led them to success in most cases, but ultimately the tide of history was against them.

Austria: From Kingdom to Empire

Empress Maria Theresa and her son Joseph, who ruled Austria jointly until 1780, were more enlightened monarchs than most European rulers of the day. For example, they abolished judicial use of torture in 1776. They also presided over a much simpler, less ostentatious court; when Joseph II assumed full powers in 1780, he often described himself as "first servant of the state." However, Joseph was still an autocrat. The difference between him and a monarch like Peter the Great (see Chapter 16) was that Joseph intended to be a benevolent despot. Just as a good nineteenth-century father considered himself the wisest and most mature individual in the home, thus deserving of total authority, Joseph II believed his royal birth made him the person best fitted to run his own kingdom.

The Hapsburgs were generous patrons of the arts; Vienna, the capital, was perhaps the most cosmopolitan city in Europe in the late 1700s. The Viennese Rococo style of architecture was light and fanciful, with elaborate decoration, spacious and airy interiors, delicate and graceful furniture, and light and pretty color schemes. Composers Christoph Willibald von Gluck, Franz Joseph Haydn, and Wolfgang Amadeus Mozart made Vienna the center of the musical world; Ludwig van Beethoven also spent much of his musical life in Vienna.

One of Joseph's first acts as emperor was to relax censorship, which led to an immediate rise in book publication. In 1781, he abolished serfdom throughout Austria. In addition, he reorganized the civil service into an efficiently functioning bureaucracy.

Unlike many previous Hapsburgs, Joseph understood the importance of religious tolerance in creating a stable realm. In 1781, he issued the Toleration Edicts, which expanded civil rights for non-Catholics throughout Austria (although social customs continued to pressure Jewish citizens to assimilate). In a true union of church and state, the Austrian Catholic clergy became civil servants, their salaries paid by the government. Joseph also instituted a mandatory level of education for priests.

Among his other social reforms, Joseph founded Austria's General Hospital—the first of its kind in Europe—and one of Europe's first free public school systems. He passed agricultural reforms that made conditions much easier for individual small farmers. It was no wonder that ordinary Austrians, particularly those of the poorer classes, came to regard Joseph as their defender and protector.

Given his liberal social policies, it is not surprising that Joseph aroused strong opposition from the Austrian nobility. The aristocrats did not welcome any measure of social equality; they preferred to keep their special privileges and status for themselves. The Catholic Church hierarchy also resented what they perceived as interference. In 1790, Joseph reluctantly bowed to pressure and revoked numerous reforms in the Hungarian region of the empire. He died later that year.

In 1804, the Kingdom of Austria under Francis II officially became the Austrian Empire. Francis assumed the imperial title largely as a symbolic gesture of rebuke to the upstart Napoleon, who had just assumed the title "Emperor of the French." The Napoleonic wars (see Chapter 18) reduced Austria practically to the status of a French satellite by 1810, only to have its former status restored by the Congress of Vienna in 1815. The new Austrian Empire created at that time included Hungary, Transylvania, Croatia, the Czech states of Bohemia and Moravia, and the Italian states of Lombardy and Venetia.

The forces of nationalism and self-determination created political and social instability in this culturally and ethnically diverse empire. Bohemia and Moravia were a mix of ethnic Germans and Czechs; the Germans were satisfied with Austrian rule, but the Czechs demanded greater independence. Additionally, the Italians and the Hungarians in the empire rose up in 1848. Although the Austrian army crushed both rebellions, it was clear that at least some measure of independence would soon become a fact. In 1867, Austria and Hungary formally declared a dual monarchy, the Austro-Hungarian Empire. Emperor Franz Joseph of Austria ruled both kingdoms, and joint ministries oversaw all foreign affairs and finances, but Hungary had a separate constitution and a separate legislature. Hungary now found itself a large nation with a discontented, diverse population in its turn, and it granted Croatia a measure of self-rule in 1878.

In 1878, Austria made the Balkan nation of Bosnia into a protectorate, then annexed it in 1908 in a move to protect Austrian control of certain trade routes. Bosnia's Serbian population immediately began agitating for Bosnian independence. This Serbian nationalism would contribute largely to the outbreak of World War I in 1914.

Britain

With its constitutional monarchy and strong parliament, Britain was much further along the road toward republicanism than any continental European nation. However, there were major causes of social and political discontent: overcrowding in prisons, working conditions in factories, and Irish nationalism.

The Annexation of Australia

Prison reform had been a concern in Britain since the late 1700s; the North American colony of Georgia, in fact, had been founded as a penal colony. In 1770, Captain James Cook voyaged to Australia. The interior of this small continent was largely barren plains, which was why the substantial Maori population of Australia lived near the coast. Cook's reports convinced the British government that here was an ideal penal colony; accordingly, the British began sending shiploads of convicts to what it named Botany Bay in 1778. As usual through history, Europeans found it relatively easy to subdue a tribal culture and take over its homeland.

With good ranching land for the taking, Australia appealed to many Europeans, and it did not remain solely a penal colony for long. In fact, it became a group of separate colonies, which united in 1901 as the Commonwealth of Australia.

Industrial Reform

The Reform Act of 1832, passed by a Whig majority, created labor laws that barred women and children from working in the extremely dangerous and unhealthy conditions in Britain's coal mines. The liberals hoped that this would enable children to attend school and women to take care of their families. The act also adjusted the number of representatives each borough could send to the House of Commons, giving the larger (urban) areas more votes; since there were more workers in urban areas, this would favor industrial reform. In 1867, the Conservative (formerly Tory) leadership in Parliament passed a Reform Bill that extended suffrage to most homeowners and renters. This gave many working-class men a political voice for the first time.

In 1849, Prime Minister Robert Peel repealed the Corn Laws, which had maintained high import duties on grain. In the late nineteenth century, Prime Minister Benjamin Disraeli saw a number of domestic reforms through Parliament. The Public Health Act and the Artisans' Dwelling Act (1875) respectively improved sanitation and provided public housing for those in need.

The Whigs and Radicals combined forces late in the nineteenth century to form the Liberal party. Its leader was William Gladstone, who became prime minister. Gladstone oversaw numerous important social reforms:

- Promotion in the military governed solely by merit, not social rank
- Reform of the civil service
- Introduction of compulsory free public education
- Introduction of the secret ballot
- Extension of the franchise to include farm workers
- Second redistribution of seats in Parliament to make representation proportional

Irish Nationalism

Although Ireland was represented in Parliament, Irish Catholics (that is, most Irishmen) were barred from office by an "Anglicans-only" law. During the 1820s, the Tory majority in Parliament passed two major bills repealing religious restrictions on eligibility for office.

France

Despite the creation of a new, strong legislative assembly, the nineteenth century was a chaotic era in French politics, with a variety of factions that could not agree on the kind of government they wanted. Republicans wanted the legislature to have control, radicals wanted the people to have control, and royalists wanted the monarch to have control.

In 1824, Charles X succeeded Louis XVIII. An old-fashioned monarchist and conservative, Charles was unable to accept the limited role the liberal legislature intended him to play. In 1830, he dismissed the legislature, established censorship of the press, and revoked voting rights for certain categories of citizens. This provoked a popular uprising, and Charles abdicated in the face of the violent demonstrations.

Louis Philippe ruled as a moderate liberal until 1848, but his reforms did not do enough for the working class. Parisian mobs took to the barricades again, and Louis Philippe abdicated in his turn. Again, liberals and radicals could not agree on what kind of new government they wanted. The radicals persuaded the liberals to support a system of worker-owned factories on an emergency basis; when the elections of 1848 brought in a moderate National Assembly, the new government disbanded the factory system. This led to another Paris uprising—the "June Days" of 1848. In the end, the National Assembly created a constitution for a new French republic, with a strong president, a unicameral legislature, and voting rights for all adult men. Louis Napoleon Bonaparte was elected first president of the Second Republic; he soon took advantage of widespread popular support to declare himself emperor, taking the name Napoleon III. Despite this title, his policies were moderate and liberal.

Napoleon III's reign ended abruptly when he failed to check the spread of Prussian power. In 1871, France lost the Franco-Prussian War (see "Prussia and the Unification of Germany" in this chapter) and the new National Assembly of the Third Republic negotiated the peace with Prussia, including the surrender of Alsace and Lorraine. This treaty was highly unpopular in France, especially in Paris; the Parisian radicals soon declared Paris independent from France and established a new government of their own, the Paris Commune. The Commune turned out to be no match for the national army and was obliterated at the cost of twenty thousand lives.

By 1875, the National Assembly accepted that it would be impossible to restore the monarchy in any form. The deputies devised a new legislative structure modeled after the United States Congress. The lower house was popularly elected, the upper house chosen by the political parties, and the president elected by members of both houses.

Prussia and the Unification of Germany

Prussia was largely conservative and antinationalist, but there were enough Prussian liberals to succeed in a rebellion against the government. In 1848, the liberals pressured Frederick William IV to summon a new legislative assembly, the National Parliament of the German Confederation, and to agree to a new constitution.

Internal disagreements quickly weakened and divided the liberals. The king soon disbanded the National Parliament and replaced the constitution with a more conservative version. In Prussia as elsewhere in Europe, the liberals and socialists, who should have been natural allies against the conservatives, could not agree on what they wanted. When the liberals formed a parliament in Frankfurt and asked the king to rule a united Germany as a constitutional monarch, he refused. With no executive, and with parties that were constantly at odds, the parliament broke up in 1849.

In 1862, Wilhelm I of Prussia appointed Otto von Bismarck prime minister. Bismarck's name has become closely identified with the term *Realpolitik*, or "the politics of realism." Like Richelieu of France and Cavour of Italy, Bismarck was a very able man, both pragmatic and focused. A political conservative, Bismarck was determined to have a united Germany with a strong monarch. Faced with a hostile liberal majority in the parliament, he directed the nation's attention to foreign affairs; this would allow him to maintain control of the domestic policy. History shows that civilian populations have always accepted special government controls and restrictions during wartime.

Prussia and Austria defeated Denmark to gain joint control of the duchies of Schleswig and Holstein; Bismarck then attacked Austria, which quickly ceded him full control. Prussia had now formed what would be the nucleus of a united Germany. In 1867, Bismarck oversaw the annexation of the free city of Frankfurt and three more German states, bringing all the German-speaking lands north of the Main River under Prussian control.

The opportunity for the final step in German unification arrived in 1870. Bismarck's goal was to unite all the German states with Prussia against a common enemy, France. He changed the wording of a press release to make it appear that the Prussian king was insulting the French emperor in print. On reading the statement, Napoleon III immediately declared war on Prussia.

The war can accurately be described as "Franco-German" rather than "Franco-Prussian" because, as Bismarck had foreseen, many German states besides Prussia took part. The superior strategy of the German military brought about a quick French surrender. The peace treaty gave Germany control of Alsace and Lorraine and forced France to pay Prussia five billion francs in compensation; although Prussia had provoked the war, France had technically been the aggressor and, at any rate, was on the losing side. This peace settlement created deep resentment in France, which would become an issue in the next century.

On January 18, 1871, Wilhelm I of Prussia was officially crowned emperor of Germany. In a final insult to the French, the Germans held the ceremony in the Hall of Mirrors at Versailles.

The legislative assembly of the new German Empire was bicameral, with a Federal Council (*Bundesrat*) of hereditary nobles and an Imperial Diet (*Reichstag*) of popularly elected representatives. All men age twenty-five and older had the right to vote for their representatives in the *Reichstag*; the princes in the *Bundesrat* inherited their seats, just as the British peers inherited their places in the House of Lords. Both the *Bundesrat* and the *Reichstag* had to pass any given bill in order for it to become German law. The King of Prussia became the emperor, or kaiser, of Germany; although Wilhelm I found such a pompous title silly and personally embarrassing, it was a source of pride among his subjects. The imperial title suggested a connection between the German Empire and the Holy Roman Empire—although, in fact, the Holy Roman emperors had ended up as the ruling family of Austria, not Prussia.

Nationalism was a major force in the creation of the German Empire. Both the nobles and the common people supported unification, and troops were strongly motivated by nationalism during the Franco-Prussian War. It was nationalism that motivated the leaders to press Bismarck to demand heavy reparations from France at the end of the war, despite the minister's belief (which would be justified by future events) that the demand was vengeful and unwise.

Prussia had worked toward control of a unified German state since 1640; unsurprisingly, it became the most powerful province in Germany. The Prussian king became the hereditary German emperor; Prussian generals were in charge of the German army; the efficient Prussian bureaucracy administered the civil service; and the Prussian capital, Berlin, became the capital of Germany.

The Russian Empire

The Russian government would remain autocratic throughout the nineteenth century, despite the passage of some degree of social reform. Liberalism was strong among Russian intellectuals, but they had little influence; power lay with the nobles, military officers, and high-ranking clergy, who were mainly conservative.

Alexander I ordered his aides to draw up a plan for abolishing serfdom (it had been achieved in the Baltic provinces in 1818), but he was forced to abandon this unpopular idea by 1820. However, the serfs did achieve some rights and privileges in the 1820s and 1830s: a measure of self-government, village schools, and health clinics. As was so often the case in Russia, all these reforms were chaotic in their administration, however neat they appeared on paper.

Nicholas I succeeded his brother Alexander in 1825; he soon proved to be an old-style autocrat, very different from his generally liberal predecessor. Nicholas believed in keeping the lower classes in what he regarded as their proper place. Under his rule, only the nobility could attend secondary schools and universities, and the civil rights of religious and ethnic minorities were curtailed. In foreign affairs, Nicholas supported any monarch facing a popular uprising.

Russia continued its policy of territorial expansion, reaching the Aral Sea in 1853 and the Afghanistan border in 1885. Russia also took over territory on the

Pacific coast, establishing the port city of Vladivostok; Russia could now begin overseas trade from the Pacific Ocean. The completion of the Trans-Siberian Railroad in 1904 made overland travel from Vladivostok to Moscow possible. These two developments were extremely important for trade.

In 1853, war broke out in the Crimea, a region controlled by the Ottoman Turks on the coast of the Black Sea. Nicholas I entered the war with two goals: first, to take over Turkish-controlled provinces along the Danube River, and second, to seize control of certain Christian shrines within the Ottoman Empire. The Russian invasion of the Crimea aroused the opposition of Britain and France, who had their own Mediterranean interests to protect. Historians agree that the Crimean War was disastrously mismanaged on all sides, particularly the British. Russia concluded a peace treaty with the Turks in 1856, but it did not last; Russia and Turkey were at war again by 1877.

Nicholas I died before the Crimean War was over. His politically moderate son Alexander II would rule until 1881. Alexander's major contribution to history was the emancipation of the serfs—a long and complex process that involved major changes to the judicial system and to local government, besides compensating landowners for their financial losses. Emancipation became official in 1861.

Despite this great step toward human rights, many liberals in Russian society felt that Alexander's social reforms did not go far enough. During the 1870s, violent demonstrations became common. This period of unrest ended abruptly in 1881 when Alexander was killed by an anarchist's bomb. Alexander III succeeded his father; no doubt blaming the liberals for his father's death, he suppressed all liberal tendencies in society. He strengthened the central bureaucracy, extended the powers of the police, and revoked freedom of the press.

The year 1905 was pivotal for Russia. The country lost the Russo-Japanese War, in which Japan halted Russian expansion into China (see Chapter 21). It was also the year of a major popular uprising known as the 1905 Revolution. This revolution had several contributing causes. First, Russian intellectuals and workers had enthusiastically espoused Marxist and socialist ideas. Second, the government had instituted widespread industrialization in Russia without understanding or providing for the consequences to either the peasants or the workers. Third, a severe famine in 1891 had taken its toll on the people.

Workers throughout Russia went on strike in 1905, establishing *soviets*—the word means "workers' councils"—everywhere. These bodies, intended to serve as local governments, were based on the Marxist ideal of turning society over to the rule of the workers. They did not last but would return in 1917. Peasants also rose up in fury over social conditions, especially the issue of land owner-ship. All of these issues would play into the Bolshevik Revolution and the end of the empire in 1917.

The Unification of Italy

Italy was a natural breeding ground for nationalism and unification. First, it already had a history as a unified empire, in the days of ancient Rome. Sec-ond, its people were still culturally, ethnically, and linguistically homogenous, despite the regional differences that occur in any sizeable geographical area.

In 1815, the Congress of Vienna parceled out the Italian provinces to several different rulers. Nationalist forces in Parma and Modena rebelled in 1831 and again in 1848 without success. Republican forces declared the Republic of Rome in 1848; French and Austrian troops, united in the desire to maintain a divided and weak Italy, put down the rebellions. French troops occupied Rome until 1870.

In 1852, Count Camillo di Cavour become prime minister of Sardinia, a kingdom that included both the island of Sardinia and the Piedmont region of northern Italy. Crafty, clever, and pragmatic, Cavour used national alliances to achieve his goal of uniting all of Italy. A Crimean War alliance with France led to an Italo-French attack on Austria; as a result, Austria lost Lombardy to Sardinia in 1859. Later that year, most of the rest of northern Italy joined the union of Italian states.

In 1860, the fiery republican Giuseppe Garibaldi and his followers, the Red Shirts, liberated Sicily and Naples. Although Cavour was a monarchist and Garibaldi a republican, they found common ground in their desire to unify their people. With Garibaldi's support, Cavour called for a vote in which the people of southern Italy would decide whether to join the union. The Papal States (the city of Rome and the surrounding area) held out, as Italian unifica-tion would rob the pope of his status as a head of state, but the rest of Italy favored unification, which officially took place in 1861. The king of Sardinia was crowned Victor Emmanuel II of Italy later that year; the new Italian parlia-ment, meeting in 1860, was officially referred to as "the eighth session of the Sardinian Parliament." The new government granted voting rights to literate, property-owning men over the age of twenty-four—about 8 percent of all Ital-ian men of that age.

The new nation had to contend with two divisive factors: regional division and the hostility of the pope. Southern Italy resented the dominance of the northern Piedmontese in the army, the provincial governments, and the civil service. At the same time, in retaliation for the loss of his authority, Pope Pius IX encouraged the foundation of Catholic political parties whose goal was to undermine the new Italian state.

When the French troops occupying Rome were pulled out to fight the Prussians in 1870, the Italian army marched in to complete the unification process. Rome, the center and apex of Classical civilization, was immediately named the new Italian capital. Hostility between the Church and the Italian state intensified; it would not be resolved until Prime Minister Benito Mussolini named the Vatican an independent city-state in 1929.

Poland

Polish rebellion against Russian Czar Nicholas I broke out in the Kingdom of Poland—a region centered around Warsaw—in 1830. The Poles won the first skirmishes and achieved a short-lived independence, which was crushed by the Russian troops in 1831. This was followed by a campaign of "Russification" under the czar, who revoked many Polish rights and privileges in an attempt to replace Polish language and customs with Russian ones.

Spain

Liberals and socialists had far less support in conservative Spain than elsewhere in Europe, but the Spanish middle class did urge reform to the best of its limited ability. In 1820, the army forced Ferdinand VII to agree to Spain's first written constitution. However, French troops came to the king's aid, suppressing the rebellion and murdering most of the rebels. In 1875, the Cortés (legislative assembly) gained acceptance of a liberal constitution. However, the Spanish idea of a constitutional monarchy was far more conservative than the ideas prevailing in Britain or France. The real power remained where it had always rested—in the hands of the great landowners, the Church, and the army.

The Romantic Movement

The nineteenth century saw the birth of a major movement in literature and the arts—Romanticism. Writers, musicians, and artists of the Romantic era celebrated their own individuality in their poetry, symphonies, songs, and paintings.

Romanticism was something of a revolt against the Classical or Neoclassical era that had begun in the late 1700s and lasted through about 1815. This had been an era of rigidly controlled artistic forms, such as the sonata in music.

Where the Classical era concentrated on form, the Romantic era concentrated on content. As an outgrowth of the Enlightenment, Classical music and art celebrated reason; as an outgrowth of nationalism, Romantic music and art celebrated emotion. It was a glorification of the artist as a creative individual—an era in which each artist cast aside fixed rules and consciously placed his or her individual stamp on his or her work.

In literature, Romanticism lasted from about 1830 to 1850. Johann Wolfgang von Goethe of Frankfurt and Jean-Jacques Rousseau of Geneva were early influences on the Romantic writers, who included E. T. A. Hoffmann (Prussia); Aleksandr Pushkin (Russia); Samuel Taylor Coleridge, Charlotte and Emily Brönte, and Mary Shelley (Britain); and Victor Hugo (France).

In music, the Romantic Movement lasted from about 1830 to about 1900. The great Romantic composers are often included under the misleading label "classical music"; in fact, the Classical era in music was very short, lasting only from about 1750 to 1820. Classical composers begin and end with Franz Joseph Haydn, Wolfgang Amadeus Mozart, and Ludwig van Beethoven; the last is considered a bridge to the Romantic era in music. Major Romantic composers include Franz Schubert of Austria; Robert Schumann, Felix Mendelssohn, and Richard Wagner of Germany; Frédéric Chopin of Poland; Pyotr Ilich Tchaikovsky of Russia; Hector Berlioz of France; and Giuseppe Verdi of Italy.

The Breakup of the Ottoman Empire

During the nineteenth century, the Ottoman Empire disintegrated. Between 1815 and 1912, the empire lost all its European, Mediterranean island, and North African territory (except for a tiny patch of Europe between the Aegean and Black seas). In 1924, its existence was formally ended.

There were multiple causes for the fall of the Ottoman Empire. First and probably most important, it had fallen far behind Europe in terms of military organization, weapons, technology, education, and literacy. This enabled its European enemies to outmaneuver it with relative ease. Second, the same nationalistic fervor that was playing a major role in European politics seized the imaginations of the diverse peoples of the empire. Third, the Ottoman leaders could not find a way to modernize and reform their institutions quickly enough to preserve the empire.

France delivered the first decisive blow to the Ottoman Empire when Napoleon invaded Egypt in 1798. The Ottomans were able to repel his advance only with the aid of the British. This incident made it clear to Ottoman leaders that Europe had outstripped the Near East in military matters and that major changes would be necessary to survive.

In 1808, Mahmud II became emperor. He instituted a program of enlightened reform, calling for unified legal and tax codes that would apply throughout the empire and for uniform requirements for citizenship that would apply to all subjects. Unfortunately for the future of the empire, these ideas alarmed some of the most powerful conservative interests among the leadership and the wealthy.

Realizing that to catch up with Western progress, his people would need to understand Western methods, Mahmud sent a number of military officers to the West for education and training. These men returned to the empire having studied and absorbed a mass of Western ideas, including nationalism. They brought with them a mood of enthusiasm for remaking Ottoman society and institutions along Western lines. Because such changes could not happen overnight, enthusiasm quickly led to frustration and discontent. Widespread social unrest followed, as some ordinary people pushed for change while others held back.

In 1876, Abdul Hamid II became the new sultan of the empire. An old-style autocrat, Abdul Hamid overturned the new Ottoman constitution and reinstated older policies. This attempt to turn back the clock on progress failed, primarily due to the efforts of the Committee of Union and Progress, better known to history as the Young Turks. This group, largely composed of Turkish military officers, hoped to create a European Turkish state; its members were less interested in the Middle Eastern portions of the empire. Dissatisfied with autocratic rule, the Young Turks deposed Abdul Hamid II in 1909, installing his brother on the throne in his place. They soon realized that their Turkish-centered goals would be all but impossible to achieve in a diverse empire with so many non-Turkish groups. The situation would not be resolved until the end of World War I.

Throughout the nineteenth century, the European powers pursued a policy of colonization in the Ottoman Empire. European economies had become dependent on international trade, and European logic decreed that protection of trade routes in the empire meant colonizing the lands through which those trade routes ran. Over a fifty-year period beginning in 1830, France colonized or annexed Algeria, Morocco, and Tunisia in North Africa. Meanwhile, the Russians took over Turkestan and, along with Britain, achieved supremacy over Iran and Afghanistan. In 1912, Italy annexed Libya. Due to military weakness and diplomatic impotence, the Ottoman leaders were unable to withstand the foreign takeovers.

By the outbreak of World War I, Greece and almost all the Balkan states had won their independence from the Ottoman Empire: Greece in 1827, Romania and Serbia in 1878, Thessaly in 1881, Bulgaria in 1908, and Albania and Macedonia in 1913. Bosnia-Herzegovina remained under Austrian control.

World War I brought about the formal demise of the Ottoman Empire. The Arab Revolt of 1916, in which a united force of Bedouin tribes rose up against the Turks, freed most of the Arabian Peninsula from Ottoman rule. In 1923, the world officially recognized the Republic of Turkey, a secular Islamic state under the leadership of Mustafa Kemal, known as Atatürk (Father of the Turks). The Ottoman sultanate was abolished in 1924. Despite achieving independence from a Muslim empire, the region did not undergo widespread religious conversion; it remained overwhelmingly Muslim.

Egypt

Muhammad Ali, an Albanian soldier in the Ottoman army, became governor of Egypt in 1805. He guided Egypt through the transition from traditional ways to modern ones. Under Muhammad Ali's administration, the military and the civil service were remodeled along Western lines, with new tax codes and other bureaucratic reforms. Egypt became a major exporter of cotton; it also acquired its first modern printing presses, which greatly eased the reorganization and improvement of the educational system.

Muhammad Ali led successful military campaigns against the Sudan, Arabia, Syria, and Anatolia, thus largely eliminating Ottoman power in Egypt. He might well have taken over the empire if the British and French had not united to prevent him. The Europeans were well aware that the Ottoman Empire was on the wane; they did not want a strong, capable leader taking it over and perhaps reshaping it into a formidable rival to European supremacy.

Egypt's resurgence slowed and then halted after Muhammad Ali's death in 1848. His successors proved to be men of much less than his ability. Economic crises came along with weak government. The market for Egyptian cotton collapsed in 1865, when the United States resumed its substantial European cotton trade, which had been interrupted by the American Civil War. With the loss of revenue from cotton exports, Egypt was unable to pay the debts it had accumulated as a result of the construction of the Suez Canal, a French-administered construction project that created a shipping link across the narrow neck of Egypt that separated the Mediterranean and Red seas. The British seized the canal in 1875 when Egypt was unable to repay its foreign debt; soon after, Britain made Egypt into a protectorate, largely for the sake of maintaining control of the canal.

QUIZ

1. Which group would most likely welcome rule by a constitutional monarchy working with a popularly elected legislature?
   A. conservatives
   B. socialists
   C. liberals
   D. Marxists

2. The main reason for the breakup of the Ottoman Empire was _____.
   A. it did not have a coherent foreign policy
   B. it was in a strategically unimportant region of the world
   C. it was religiously and culturally homogenous
   D. it had fallen behind the times both politically and militarily

3. _____ is an important historical figure because he first suggested that the heretofore lowly worker was the most valuable member of society.
   A. Benjamin Disraeli
   B. William Gladstone
   C. Karl Marx
   D. Otto von Bismarck

4. _____ is credited with overseeing Egypt's entry into the modern era.
   A. Mustafa Kemal (Atatürk)
   B. Muhammad Ali
   C. Abdul Hamid
   D. Mahmud I

5. The political trend in Britain in the nineteenth century is best described
   as _____.
   A. conservative
   B. repressive
   C. communist
   D. reformist

6. Which best describes the main reason for the political turmoil in France during
   this period?
   A. the lack of a written constitution
   B. a series of incompetent monarchs
   C. disagreement among the political factions
   D. defeat in the Franco-Prussian War

7. _____ rebelled unsuccessfully against the czar in 1830 and 1831.
   A. Austria
   B. Greece
   C. Poland
   D. Russia

8. Otto von Bismarck provoked the Franco-Prussian War with the goal
   of _____.
   A. achieving German independence from the Ottoman Empire
   B. achieving German independence from the Austrian Empire
   C. making Prussia the strongest of the German states
   D. uniting all the German states against a common enemy

9. _____ is historically significant for his role as the architect of Italian
   unification.
   A. Count Camillo di Cavour
   B. Giuseppe Garibaldi
   C. Otto von Bismarck
   D. Vittorio Emanuel

10. In which nation-state would nationalism be most likely to cause political and
    social instability?
    A. an empire with an ethnically diverse population
    B. a heavily industrialized nation with a large population of workers
    C. a nation-state whose people shared a common cultural and linguistic heritage
    D. a state that practiced religious toleration

chapter 21

The Americas and Asia in the Nineteenth Century, 1815–1914

Many changes took place in the United States during its first full century as an independent nation. An exceptionally bloody and brutal civil war fought over the issue of African slavery tore the nation apart between 1861 and 1865. Although the Africans gained their freedom in name, racism was so deeply ingrained into the culture that they would gain little measure of true equality for a further century. Other developments included the rise of big business, westward migration and expansion, and important social and political reforms. The United States began the century as a fledgling nation and ended it as a powerful empire.

In the early nineteenth century, Latin America exploded in a series of violent struggles for independence. In a period of less than twenty years, Mexico and the entire South American continent (except tiny Guiana) shook off Spanish control. At the same time, Brazil peacefully declared its independence from

Portugal. Because the revolutionaries had very little political experience, Latin America would be mired in political and economic difficulties for decades to come.

China and Japan also underwent great changes in the nineteenth century, with China's star falling and Japan's rising. Relations with the West were the key element in the destiny of both nations. China began the era in a position of power, exporting far more than it imported; however, neither its leaders nor its military were able to defeat a fiendish British scheme to reverse that situation. The result was economic and political disaster, culminating in a full-scale civil war (the Taiping Rebellion) and the fall of the Manchu dynasty. The situation was quite different in Japan; a timely overthrow of the Tokugawa shogunate paved the way for sweeping changes to the government, the economy, and society. Japan absorbed everything it could of Western methods and applied itself to taking its place among the world's great powers. The conquest of Korea made Japan's imperialist aims plain to the rest of the world.

CHAPTER OBJECTIVES

- Describe the key events and trends in the United States in the nineteenth century.

- Describe the achievement of independence in Latin American countries.

- Discuss and analyze the effect of foreign relations on the fall of the Manchu Qing dynasty in China.

- Discuss the modernization of Japan during the Meiji Restoration.

Chapter 21 Time Line

●	1817–1825	Venezuela, Chile, Colombia, and Peru declare independence from Spain
●	1822	Brazil declares independence from Portugal
●	1840–1842	First Opium War
●	1851–1864	Taiping Rebellion
●	1852	*Uncle Tom's Cabin* published
●	1854	Kansas-Nebraska Act

- 1856–1860   Second Opium War
- 1859   Raid on Harpers Ferry
- 1860   Abraham Lincoln elected president of the United States
- 1861–1865   American Civil War
- 1863   Emancipation Proclamation in the United States
- 1868   Meiji Restoration in Japan
- 1871   Iwakura Mission to the West
- 1900   Boxer Rebellion
- 1901   Theodore Roosevelt elected president of the United States
- 1905   Russo-Japanese War
- 1910   Japan annexes Korea

The United States in the Nineteenth Century

The United States began the nineteenth century as a brand-new republic. By the end of the century, it had become a massive empire stretching from the Atlantic to the Pacific and from Mexico to Canada. Major trends in nineteenth-century American progress included an attempt at resolving the issue of African slavery, westward migration and development, the rise of big business and industry, and an era of Progressivism (social reform). These developments made the United States a powerful and prosperous society by the eve of World War I.

The American Civil War

The issue of African chattel slavery had divided the nation since its beginnings; Northern delegates had been forced to concede to the South on this issue to pass the Declaration of Independence. During the early nineteenth century, two cultures and two economies developed in the United States. The Northern economy was based on industry, the rise of cities, European immigration, and mercantile trade. The Southern economy was based on agriculture and slavery.

Southern slaveholders justified slavery on two grounds: economics and racism. They argued that the Southern cotton crop was highly important to the national economy and that it would be much too expensive to work the plantations with a wage-earning labor force. They also convinced themselves—and continued to teach every generation of their children—that African Americans were an inferior race fit only for slavery. Southerners argued that black people were neither smart enough nor capable enough to take care of themselves; therefore, white slaveholders were actually playing a good and necessary role in taking care of them.

Abolitionists argued that such ideas were nonsense. They pointed out that slaveholders forced slaves to live in conditions of poverty and ignorance and then blamed them for being poor and ignorant—the slaveholders, not the slaves, were to blame. They could also accurately point out that a large number of slaves were at least half European, because free Southern white men fathered thousands of children by African women. It was absurd to argue that slaves were racially inferior to people of European descent, when so many slaves had a substantial proportion of European genes. For many abolitionists, the wrong of treating people as property overrode any other consideration.

In 1857, the Supreme Court declared that a slave was a slave no matter where he traveled, even into free territory. This overturned the long-standing custom that if a slave managed to escape to a free state, he or she automatically became free. Thousands of slaves had run away and gone north at enormous risk to their lives; if recaptured, runaway slaves faced severe punishments of branding, beating, mutilation, and even death. Working together, slaves, former slaves, and black and white abolitionists created the Underground Railroad—a secret organized system to help runaway slaves gain their freedom. It was not a literal railroad with trains, but rather a route along which African-American runaways could find help—friends who would provide clothing, food, temporary shelter, money, and emergency aid. In the decades before the Civil War, the Underground Railroad helped countless slaves escape.

Western states banned slavery; both California and Oregon insisted on entering the Union as free states. When Senator Stephen Douglas of Illinois proposed that the Kansas and Nebraska territories be allowed to decide for themselves whether they wanted to be slaveholding or free, he provoked outraged reactions on all sides. Northerners were furious because Douglas's proposed Kansas-Nebraska Act overturned the earlier Missouri Compromise, which had outlawed slavery in the territories. Southerners were angry because they thought Douglas should have fought to make Kansas a slave territory.

Americans took action on both sides of the issue. Missouri "Border Ruffians" stormed into Kansas Territory before an election and illegally voted a proslavery legislature into office. White abolitionist John Brown and his supporters tried unsuccessfully to start an armed slave uprising in Harpers Ferry, Virginia.

Former slave Frederick Douglass spoke out powerfully against slavery and published the narrative of his own experiences. Harriet Beecher Stowe published *Uncle Tom's Cabin*, a dramatic story that opened Northern eyes to the corrupting influence of slavery on everyone it touched. And in Illinois, a self-educated lawyer named Abraham Lincoln decided to run for national office.

Although Lincoln lost his campaign for a Senate seat, he won the presidency in 1860 as the candidate of the newly created Republican Party. As a result, seven Southern states seceded from the Union, declaring themselves the Confederate States of America; four more states would later join them. Tension was high because forts throughout the South were, of course, still staffed by U.S. troops. War officially began in April 1861 when the Confederates fired on U.S. troops occupying Fort Sumter in South Carolina.

The Southern motive for war was clear—Southerners were not willing to change their economic and social system, all the more so because they believed that Northerners had no right to interfere in a system they themselves did not participate in. The Union (Northern) motive for the war was more ambiguous. Lincoln's primary goal was to restore the United States of America; he personally opposed slavery, but freeing the slaves was only a secondary motive for war.

The Confederacy faced many disadvantages at the start of the war. It was much smaller than the Union and thus had a much smaller population of boys and young men who could serve in the military. The South had few factories, little heavy industry, and much less money than the North. On the other hand, it did have greatly superior generals. This fact alone made the Civil War last probably three years longer than it otherwise would have.

The war began with a string of important victories for the South. In 1862, Lincoln issued a preliminary to the Emancipation Proclamation. This executive order would free all slaves in the Confederacy as of January 1, 1863, and it invited African Americans to enlist in the U.S. Army. More than one hundred eighty thousand of them would eventually serve.

The Confederates scored major victories at Fredericksburg and Chancellorsville, Virginia, in early 1863. When they invaded the North and attacked at Gettysburg, however, they lost all hope of winning the war. They would never again penetrate into the Northern states. The Battle of Gettysburg was lost on the same day that Vicksburg fell in the South. War dragged on for another year and a half, but in April 1865, the Confederacy surrendered to the Union.

The cost to both sides was heavy. An entire generation died on the battlefield or from wounds, disease, or starvation—more than six hundred thousand boys and young men. There had been little armed combat in the North, but many

Southern towns and cities were largely or entirely in ruins. Railroad lines had to be rebuilt and mail service reestablished. Slaves freed by the Emancipation Proclamation suddenly found themselves unemployed and homeless. The defeated white South cherished a bitter hatred toward the Northerners—a destructive emotion that would flourish in the South for many decades to come and that found immediate expression in the tragic assassination of President Lincoln by John Wilkes Booth, an emotionally unstable Southern sympathizer, days after the war ended.

Reconstruction

A Republican Congress was eager to reform the old Confederacy along the lines of the North. However, two obstacles stood in the way of this planned Reconstruction of the Old South. The first was Lincoln's successor Andrew Johnson. The second was the old guard of the Confederacy.

Johnson had supported the Union during the war, but he despised African Americans and did his best to block congressional attempts to extend their rights. Congress had veto powers that allowed it to overcome Johnson's opposition; it passed a series of laws making it possible for African Americans to vote, to hold political office, and to enjoy other important civil rights. Between 1865 and 1870, the states ratified three constitutional amendments that made slavery illegal, provided equal protection of the laws to all citizens, and extended voting rights to former slaves. However, no Congress ever convened would be able to remove deep-seated prejudice, bitterness in defeat, and racism simply by passing laws.

Southern whites were determined to restore society to exactly what it had been before the war. While they were forced to accept the Thirteenth Amendment, which made slavery illegal, they passed many laws curtailing the rights and privileges of African-American citizens. Using terrorist tactics of violence and intimidation, the South managed to defeat Reconstruction reforms and push African Americans back down to the lowest rung on the social and economic ladder. Racial segregation and discrimination would continue to exist in the American South for another century.

Westward Migration

The mid-nineteenth century was a period of great change and development west of the Mississippi River. For the American Indians, these years brought disaster. For most other Americans, the West offered opportunity and freedom.

The United States continued to push the Indians farther and farther from their ancestral lands. A deep cultural divide existed between the two groups. Indian experience of dealing with other tribes had been limited and had not taught them that treaties were easily broken. The European Americans, on the other hand, were descended from nations that had warred with their neighbors throughout history, making treaties on the best terms possible and then breaking them as soon as necessary. To these Americans, broken promises were a natural part of foreign policy—and to the U.S. government, the Indians were a foreign population. To the American Indians, broken promises were baffling; this difference in viewpoint caused deep resentment and fury toward the U.S. government and its people. When negotiation failed, the Indians resisted with force of arms, but they lacked the strength and the numbers of the federal troops. By the end of the nineteenth century, they were settled on reservations and facing the end of their former dominance over the North American continent.

The U.S. government and big business between them worked hard to settle the West. Table 21.1 shows three of the most important laws the government passed.

Table 21.1 The Government Land Acts of 1862	
Homestead Act	Anyone who staked a claim to up to 160 acres of land could keep it if he or she farmed and lived on the land for five years.
Pacific Railway Act	Railroad companies could apply for land grants on which to develop and build a transcontinental railroad system.
Morrill Act	The government granted 17 million acres of federal land to the states, requiring that they sell this land and use the money to found agricultural and engineering colleges.

The government offered generous land grants to any companies willing to build railroads. Companies jumped at the offer and the railroads became the largest employers of the day, hiring millions of people to work on every aspect of developing and building the national transportation system. The railroad was largely built with immigrant labor. Chinese laid the track for the Central Pacific, which began on the west coast and led eastward. On the Union Pacific, which began in the east and headed west, the workers were overwhelmingly Irish, supplemented by young Civil War veterans and freedmen.

The California Gold Rush of 1849 ushered in an era of mining in the West, where major further discoveries of gold and silver deposits occurred. The Civil

War temporarily halted the westward flow of people, but it began again in 1865, specifically among three groups: immigrants, freedmen (and women), and middle-class whites. The American West provided every opportunity for prosperity—land for the taking, a variety of well-paid jobs, and relative freedom from the oppression and discrimination that prevailed against blacks in the Reconstruction South and against recent immigrants in northeastern port cities. (Discrimination against the Chinese was the exception to this rule; the U.S. government passed a Chinese Exclusion Act that denied them even the opportunity to become citizens.) The government made prairie land free for ranchers' cattle to range on, making ranching an attractive and profitable venture to many entrepreneurs, large and small.

American Capitalism and Big Business

In U.S. history, the postwar nineteenth century is sometimes called the Second Industrial Revolution. It was a period in which new inventions that would have seemed miraculous to a previous generation—instant long-distance written communication (telegraph), the ability to speak to someone in another city (telephone), a machine that could produce a perfectly printed letter (typewriter)—became everyday and commonplace.

These technological breakthroughs caused a boom in heavy industry. Since it was suddenly much easier and cheaper to convert iron ore to steel, there was a surplus of steel—which meant that it could be put to a variety of uses, such as skyscraper building and bridge construction. People at the head of large corporations made fortunes.

Until the Civil War, most American businesses had been small, usually owned and operated by one or two people and a small staff. Such an organizational plan was not practical on a large scale because costs were too high. Instead, an ambitious businessman (or woman) would acquire partners; together, they would set up a corporation, selling shares of stock to investors and paying them dividends based on company profits.

In the same way that individuals united to form a corporation, corporations united to form trusts. A board of trustees runs all its corporations as a single enterprise. When a trust gains control of all corporations within one industry, it becomes a monopoly. Owners prefer a monopoly because it eliminates competition and they can set prices as high as they please. Consumers oppose a monopoly because competition benefits them; each corporation has to try to attract their business by making the most attractive offers.

As public criticism of trusts grew, Congress reluctantly acted by passing the Sherman Antitrust Act. The act banned trusts and monopolies but failed to define exactly what a monopoly or a trust was. Without strong leadership in Washington that was determined to fight the abuses of big business, the act was impossible to enforce.

As big businesses grew, the United States underwent the change from an agricultural economy to a manufacturing and consumer economy. Middle-class and wealthy Americans enjoyed an era of unprecedented consumer choices on which to spend their money. New stores were opening on every city block, selling mass-produced goods of all kinds, both necessary and frivolous.

Fourteen million immigrants came to the United States between 1860 and 1900, principally from China and southern Europe. They formed a lively and colorful presence in cities, where they gathered in small replicas of their old neighborhoods at home. Many of them took factory jobs; big business and industry meant wage-earning opportunities for millions of workers. However, working conditions were horrible and wages were at starvation levels.

Business and industry can be seen as a system of checks and balances. In the nineteenth century, the owners had all the power. Society eventually devised two powerful checks on the owners. The first was government regulation. The second was the labor union—the organization of workers into a group with the power to negotiate. The first attempts to organize labor into unions began soon after the Civil War. One of the first unions to form was the Knights of Labor, a national union begun by Philadelphia garment workers under the leadership of Uriah Stephens. It began as a union for white male workers, but in the 1880s, it expanded to include women and African Americans (although it excluded Chinese workers). Membership was open to both skilled and unskilled workers of all types. Important leaders of the Knights of Labor included Terence V. Powderly and Mary Harris "Mother" Jones.

By 1886, the Knights of Labor had over seven hundred thousand members and was growing. The union fought for an eight-hour workday, equal pay for equal work (at that time, women were paid less than men, and black workers less than white), and the passage of laws against child labor.

The Progressives

The term *Progressive* refers to an American who supported social and political reform. In 1901, Theodore Roosevelt became the first of a series of Progressive presidents. He believed that a democratic republic like the United States should have no social classes; that all should prosper; and that the government must regulate big business, since business had demonstrated that it would not treat either its workers or its customers fairly on its own.

Under Roosevelt and his successor William Howard Taft, the federal government passed important legislation to regulate business and sued numerous trusts and monopolies. Roosevelt was concerned with reform on all levels—social, political, and economic. Meanwhile, Progressives across the nation pushed for local and state political reforms. They succeeded in making many changes in the electoral process, giving the people greater direct voice in their own government. For example, the Seventeenth Amendment called for direct popular election of U.S. senators.

Investigative journalists and novelists also concerned themselves with social ills of the day. Magazine articles exposed the shady and dishonest business dealings of men like John D. Rockefeller of Standard Oil. Full-length books informed readers about immigrant living and working conditions in city slums and big factories. When details about the filthy conditions in meat-packing and food-processing plants were published, comfortable, middle-class Americans were horrified and pushed for change.

When Woodrow Wilson became president in 1912, he continued to fight for reform. Wilson signed much important legislation that protected workers and regulated business practices. He reformed the national financial system, creating the powerful Federal Reserve. The ratification of the Nineteenth Amendment under Wilson marked the greatest triumph of the era of reform, granting women age twenty-one and over the right to vote.

Latin America

In 1800, almost the whole of Latin America was under Spanish domination. By 1831, the entire area (except Guiana) was a mass of independent republics. This was a strikingly short period of time for so much change across such a vast geographical area.

The Napoleonic wars had an important effect on Latin American independence. When Napoleon invaded Spain and installed his brother Joseph on the throne in 1808, the Latin Americans had to decide which of the two Spanish monarchs to obey—Joseph Bonaparte or the deposed hereditary monarch Ferdinand VII. This question created an atmosphere of confusion—the perfect conditions for successful rebellion. In 1823, the United States made its position clear in a statement known as the Monroe Doctrine. This document promised noninterference with existing European colonies; at the same time, it pledged aid to any Latin American country invaded by an outside power. In other words, the United States would not help the colonies to gain independence but would support them if they broke free successfully on their own.

Economic concerns also played a role in the struggle for independence. As the ruling colonial power, Spain had a monopoly on Latin American trade—just as Britain had controlled all trade in the Atlantic coast colonies that eventually became the United States of America. The Spanish colonists greatly resented this interference with their economy, as they knew their coffee and other exports would find profitable markets in Britain and the United States. Independence brought an end to the trade monopoly, and Latin America was soon trading internationally. With the advent of refrigeration in the late nineteenth century, beef became—and would remain—a major export from a continent whose lands were perfectly suited to ranching.

Between 1817 and 1825, three leaders were responsible for liberating Venezuela, Chile, Colombia, and Peru: Simón Bolívar, Bernardo O'Higgins, and José de San Martín. O'Higgins would become the first president of Chile. The inland nation of Bolivia was named for Bolívar, who is revered throughout the continent as a great hero. By 1831, Mexico and the entire South American continent (except for tiny Guiana, divided among Britain, the Netherlands, and France) was independent.

The Spanish colonies of South America did not correspond exactly with the nations on today's map; there were a few large colonies rather than many small ones. Incipient nationalism led various groups in the newly independent colonies to wish for self-determination—not only independence from Europe, but independence from one another. In the end, a number of smaller republics were created from a few larger colonies. Because the borders were artificial creations in many cases, their establishment led to a long period of squabbling among the various republics.

Spanish colonial society had two rival upper classes: the *peninsulares* and the *creoles*. The *peninsulares*, who had the upper hand, were born in Spain; the *creoles* were Latin American–born people of Spanish descent. Spain was among the most conservative nations of Europe, and it passed on its rigid notions of social hierarchy to the colonies. The *peninsulares* always received preference when high offices or positions of authority were available. This naturally aroused *creole* resentment; it also deprived the *creoles* of valuable practical experience in governing and administration. Independence had been largely driven by the *creoles*—but they did not know how to manage it once they had acquired it. In the end, most of the nations of South America became more or less military dictatorships.

As a Portuguese rather than a Spanish possession, Brazil achieved independence by a different means. In 1808, with the Napoleonic wars raging, the prince regent of Portugal decided to abandon Europe for the safety of the West. He established his court in Rio, which appealed to him so much that when the Peninsular War ended in Napoleon's defeat, he decided to become Brazil's new king. Brazil officially declared its independence from Portugal in 1822, without the violence and economic collapse that characterized the revolutions throughout the rest of the continent.

Latin American countries did away with slavery during the nineteenth century. Abolition did not require an all-out war like the American Civil War; it happened much more easily, both as a by-product of revolution and by the order of the new governments. Former slaves did not immediately and magically acquire comfort and social acceptance, but they were assimilated into society far more easily and with far less resistance than was the case for former slaves in the United States.

In 1794, Haiti had become the first of the Caribbean islands to declare independence. Napoleon sent French troops to subdue Haiti back into the fold, but in 1804, it regained and held its independence. Spain controlled the sizeable islands of Cuba and Puerto Rico; Britain, France, and the Netherlands dominated the smaller Caribbean islands.

China: The Fall of the Manchu Qing Dynasty

In 1800, the Qing dynasty was enjoying an era of power and prosperity. The Western desire for Chinese exports had increased so much that China was making enormous profits. Tea was in the greatest demand, as the favorite beverage in Britain; it was followed by sugar and silk.

The Trade Balance

China's superior position in trade had two causes. First, the Chinese were not interested in acquiring Western goods; therefore, they had the upper hand in bargaining. Lack of interest in bartering led directly to cash profits, because the Chinese insisted on silver in exchange for their tea. Second, Chinese leaders did not welcome the idea of cultural exchange with the Westerners. This unwelcoming attitude toward Westerners meant that only certain ports were open to traders, and the behavior of those who went ashore was strictly regulated. This system allowed China to keep Western "contamination" far from Beijing and also to collect the export duties far more easily. By the late eighteenth century, entry into China for trade was limited exclusively to the southern port city of Canton.

Westerners pressured China to relax these restrictive policies, but to no avail—until the British hit on the brilliant but morally bankrupt notion of offering opium in trade instead of silver. Opium could be cultivated in India, which was now a British possession, then exported to China. The nineteenth century was an era of abysmal medical ignorance, and both Western and Eastern doctors prescribed opium as a painkiller. However, society was well aware that opium was a hallucinogenic, used illegitimately (not illegally in all countries) as what is today called a "recreational" drug. The Chinese had used opium for medicinal purposes for centuries but banned its purchase or use without a doctor's prescription. However, China was not without its drug dealers and opium addicts. The sudden rise in the availability of opium allowed the Chinese underworld excellent opportunities for profit.

When the first cargo of opium docked in Canton, the trade balance between China and Britain shifted 180 degrees. Almost immediately, China was buying more than it was selling. The demand for opium was so outpacing the supply that China soon found itself paying in cash for opium shipments. This led swiftly to the loss of the silver reserves, the disappearance of revenue China had earned from its exports, and a massive economic depression.

The Opium Wars

When the Manchus banned the importation of opium, British warships fired on China, inaugurating the First Opium War in 1840. By 1842, the Chinese, unable to match the British military power, conceded defeat and accepted British demands to resume the importation of opium and to sign new treaties. Historians refer to these agreements as "unequal treaties" because they were all but signed at gunpoint, with one side dictating all the terms. The treaties specified that the Chinese would open several ports for trade, that China would provide equal access and privileges to all Western trading partners, and that foreigners accused of crimes in China would be tried by their own nations rather than in Chinese courts—a proceeding known as "extraterritoriality." The First Opium War effectively ended China's reign as a world power until after World War II.

Britain and France formed an alliance and won further concessions from the Manchus in the Second Opium War, fought from 1856 to 1860. At the same time, Russia took the opportunity to seize a large expanse of Siberian territory from China. After two more wars, one with France and one with Japan, China was cornered. The West forced the Qing government to adopt a free-trade policy; although the Qing emperor remained on the throne, he had little authority over events. Britain, France, Germany, Japan, and Russia established spheres of influence over most of China.

The Taiping Rebellion

The First Opium War gave rise to a wave of Chinese nationalism; the nationalists had never been happy under Qing rule, since the Qings were ethnically Manchurian rather than Chinese. Hung Hsiu-ch'üan, a minor civil servant and the founder of a fringe religious movement, had attracted a large number of followers by 1850. Hung called for the overthrow of the Manchus and the establishment of what he called a "Heavenly Kingdom." (The name *Taiping* comes from the Chinese for this phrase.) The Manchus took the movement seriously enough to pass a number of reforms the rebels called for; however, Hung and his followers clearly would not be satisfied with anything less than a complete change of government. When this became apparent, the Manchus sent out troops and the Taiping Rebellion soon became a full-scale civil war. Fighting lasted until 1864; in the end, the government had to call in Western troops to defeat the rebels.

The Taiping Rebellion had several immediate effects. First was a tremendous loss of life; historians estimate that at least 20 million Chinese died during the war. Second, the fertile area around the Yangtze River valley was devastated, bringing widespread famine that would kill millions more. Third, the Manchu dynasty remained technically in power but, in fact, had ceded almost all real authority to the provinces. Fourth, it was clear that the Manchu government was weak, disunited, and unable to act effectively in any national crisis.

The Fall of the Qing Dynasty

Nationalist resentment against the foreigners continued to simmer among the Chinese people. This resentment boiled over again in 1900 in an incident called the Boxer Rebellion. The Boxers (the rebels actually called themselves "Righteous Fists of Harmony") surrounded the foreign legation in Peking and laid siege to it. An international force put down the rebellion and executed many of the rebels. The common people had enthusiastically supported the Boxers; the brutal efficiency with which the Boxer Rebellion was put down did nothing to reconcile them to foreign influences in their country. However, China could not block out the ideas of the West. Many young Chinese had gone abroad for their education; they found much to their liking and were eager to help incorporate new ideas into traditional Chinese ways. When the government eliminated civil service examinations in 1905, the way was open for those who did not belong to the aristocracy to enter government service.

In 1911, another uprising finally brought down the Manchu government. Many of these rebels—a diverse group of angry young men, Taiping Rebellion veterans, civil servants, and peasants—were inspired by the radical Sun Yat-sen, who was less a revolutionary leader than an organizer. Educated in Hawaii and Hong Kong, Sun Yat-sen did not share the traditional Chinese disdain for Western ideas. He sought alliances with both Japan and France in his attempts to bring constitutional government to China.

When actual armed rebellion broke out in 1911, Sun Yat-sen was overseas; former Manchu general Yüan Shih-k'ai led the rebellion. The last Manchu emperor (a six-year-old child) abdicated, and the provinces proclaimed Sun Yat-sen as president. Sun-Yat-sen graciously withdrew his claim in favor of Yüan Shih-k'ai, who in 1912 became the president of the Republic of China.

The Modernization of Japan

In the mid-nineteenth century, Japan took two decisive steps that abruptly ended its serene medieval existence and would make it a major force in international affairs. First, the Tokugawa government ended the policy of isolation. Second, the shogunate gave way to imperial rule.

The Opening of Japan

The Tokugawa government was aware that isolation had created many social problems in Japan; however, reformers could not agree on how to solve them. In 1853, the United States forced Japan's hand, sending Commodore Matthew Perry and four ships to Tokyo Bay with official papers setting forth the American demands for trade privileges with Japan—masked, of course, in polite diplomatic language. The fact that the United States was demanding rather than requesting was clear from the military nature of the convoy—a naval officer in command of four warships armed with heavy guns.

The Japanese were in no position to spurn the Americans. They were well aware they were no match for the American military and preferred graceful concession to a humiliating military defeat such as China had experienced during the First Opium War. The agreement did not happen overnight, but in 1858, Japan signed a treaty with the United States. Treaties with other Western nations would follow, all "unequal treaties" like those China had been forced to sign after the First Opium War. The Japanese treaties contained similar provisions, including extraterritoriality.

The Meiji Restoration

Many Japanese reacted to the opening of their nation with hostility, resentment, and fear. Although the step had been inevitable, the people considered that their government had lost face—the ultimate sin in Japanese culture. The shogunate, which had already lost a great deal of its power to manage the country effectively, was now the target of all but open contempt. It was clear that a change of government was needed. This took place abruptly in January 1868, when the *daimyos* announced from the royal palace that the Tokugawa shogunate was over. The Meiji emperor would now be the ruler of Japan; his long reign would not end until 1912.

The Japanese emperor had always been, and would continue to be, a symbolic monarch rather than an active administrator or even a participant in the government. Even more than the British constitutional monarch, the Japanese emperor was a figurehead. However, his symbolic value had great importance as a unifying factor for Japan.

The Meiji Restoration was a time of immediate and drastic change to Japanese society. The leaders quickly concluded that if Japan were forced to join the modern, Western-dictated world, it would do whatever was necessary to be treated as an equal in that world. This meant westernization on a sweeping scale; the government, the military, the society, and the economy were all reorganized along Western lines.

The government decided that in order to be respected in the West, Japan should imitate Western methods of imperialism. Military might would enable Japan to pursue an aggressive foreign policy, thus protecting itself from possible invasion and takeover. The hereditary warrior class was eliminated and replaced with universal military service for all Japanese men. Japan proved as ruthless as any Western nation in pursuing imperialist ambitions. The Sino-Japanese War of 1894 to 1895 and the Russo-Japanese War of 1905 led to the annexation of Korea, which Japan would rule with an iron fist.

In 1869, the hereditary social hierarchy was abolished; all Japanese were now free to enter whatever occupation they wished, regardless of their birth.

Because of their role in the bureaucracy, the samurai were placed in the unique position of having to rid themselves of their own historic privileges. In 1871, the government organized an expedition to the West with the purpose of studying its legal, political, and economic systems. Named for the man who led it, the Iwakura Mission gave the Japanese much crucial information that would help to reshape their nation. The government rewrote criminal and civil law codes along Western lines, extended the railways, and instituted compulsory education.

The Meiji constitution took effect in 1890. It called for a bicameral legislative assembly and a prime minister. In a sign that Japan was still in some ways a traditional Asian nation, the government ruled that criticism of the new constitution was an act of treason. The Japanese economy underwent a rapid conversion from subsistence agriculture to manufacturing and heavy industry. In a sign that the West approved Japanese progress toward modernization, the burdensome treaties from the period when Japan first reopened its ports were overturned.

Korea

Korea had been an independent monarchy since the seventh century, although it was subordinate to China. The Korean king paid the Chinese emperor regular tributes, in exchange for which China made no attempt to take over Korea. Both sides profited from the trade relationship.

Korea enjoyed a remarkably stable and peaceful existence until 1876, when Japan imitated Western methods of diplomacy and forced trade and diplomatic relations on its Asian neighbor. This created conflict between China and Japan, since both wanted to dominate Korea; it ultimately led to the Sino-Japanese War of 1894.

In 1905, Korea fell victim to an agreement between Japan and the United States; the United States recognized Japanese authority over Korea in exchange for Japanese acknowledgement of U.S. authority over the Philippines. Korea became a Japanese protectorate; it was annexed outright in 1910 and would remain under Japanese control until 1945.

Koreans deeply resented the Japanese presence in their country, all the more so because Japan showed no respect for Korea as an independent cultural entity. The Japanese did stimulate modernization in Korea, but they also attempted to suppress the Korean language and culture in favor of their own.

QUIZ

1. **Which best describes the long-standing relationship between China and Korea?**
   A. Korea was a Chinese colony.
   B. Korea was an independent state that recognized Chinese supremacy.
   C. Korea was a Chinese province with some degree of self-rule.
   D. Korea and China were equal powers with a nonaggression agreement.

2. _____ **characterized the Progressive era in the United States.**
   A. Social and political reform
   B. Civil war
   C. Westward expansion
   D. Imperialism

3. _____ **was the only Latin American country to gain its independence without resorting to armed rebellion.**
   A. Argentina
   B. Brazil
   C. Chile
   D. Venezuela

4. **The Taiping Rebellion in China had all these effects except _____.**
   A. a tremendous loss of life
   B. widespread famine
   C. the overthrow of the Manchu government
   D. the devastation of the Yangtze Valley

5. **The Japanese agreed to open their ports to Western trade in the 1850s because _____.**
   A. they were eager to bolster the Japanese economy
   B. they had decided to westernize their society
   C. they felt this was the best alternative to a popular uprising
   D. they did not want to risk an almost certain military defeat

6. **The Northern states began the American Civil War with all these advantages over the South except _____.**
   A. command of America's heavy industry
   B. more money in its treasury
   C. superior military commanders
   D. a larger male population of fighting age

7. **What was the overall effect of the First Opium War?**
    A. China banned the import of opium.
    B. China ceased to be a respected world power.
    C. China established favorable treaties with its Western trading partners.
    D. China reorganized its government along republican lines.

8. **The Meiji emperor is best described as _____.**
    A. the chief administrator and executive of the government
    B. a constitutional monarch with limited power in foreign affairs
    C. an autocrat and military commander
    D. a symbol to unify the people

9. **The most important Chinese export during its era of supremacy in international trade was _____.**
    A. ceramics
    B. opium
    C. silk
    D. tea

10. **By midcentury, Britain was able to dictate terms to China for all these reasons except _____ .**
    A. Britain was allied with Japan
    B. the Chinese economy was failing
    C. the British military was superior to the Chinese
    D. Chinese nationalists were rebelling against the government

chapter **22**

The Era of World Wars, 1914–1945

The twentieth century began violently with the outbreak of the Great War in 1914. (The name *World War I* did not come into use until later, since, of course, no one knew in 1914 that there would be a World War II.) Nationalism on one side provoked an attempt on the other side to restore the balance of powers. In the end, all the nations of Europe, particularly Germany, were severely weakened; the United States, on the other hand, emerged from the war as the world's strongest nation.

The Russian Revolution—the violent overturning of the social order by the workers as predicted in *The Communist Manifesto*—was unique in European history to that point because its aims were much broader than a mere overthrow of the current government. Instead, it was the beginning of an attempt to replace the social and political order throughout Europe. Although it claimed to be a revolution of the people, in fact it was simply the replacement of one tyrant with another. The new head of state was an autocrat like the czars; he commanded the loyalty of the army and police just as the czar had; and he tolerated no opposition or dissent.

During the 1920s and 1930s, totalitarian governments arose in Italy, Germany, Spain, and Eastern Europe; by 1937, Japan was also under strict military rule and Communist forces were on the rise in China. A combination of social and political conditions of the period gave rise to these dictatorships. The first was the new trend that gave ordinary citizens a voice in their government. The second was dissension among the forces or parties of the political left and their helplessness to deal effectively with the worldwide Great Depression caused by the U.S. stock market crash of 1929. The third was the large class of combat veterans who made an enthusiastic audience for nationalist rhetoric.

In practice, as it turned out, fascism and communism amounted to the same thing—totalitarianism. Each dictatorship of the period was fiercely nationalist, espousing an extreme form of patriotism that, at least in Germany's case, developed into active, malevolent racism. Each established government controls over what had been a market economy. Each used the army as an instrument to control the people. Each employed a police force that reported only to the dictator and that was hated and feared by the citizens. None tolerated dissent in any form; none tolerated free speech, free expression in the arts, or a free press.

The Axis Powers of World War II (Germany and Italy) had the upper hand on the battlefield until late 1942. As the aggressors, they controlled the course of events. Their well-planned invasions of 1938 to 1941 took the Entente, or Allied Powers, (Britain, France, and the USSR—the United States would join the Allies later) more or less by surprise, and the German troops were extremely well-disciplined. Between them, Germany and Italy controlled almost all of Europe and a sizeable chunk of North Africa. However, numerical strength eventually turned the tide in favor of the Allied Powers. The United States and the Soviet Union had the largest armies, and, in 1943, Italy changed sides, leaving Germany alone. Additionally, the distant American factories were well out of danger of being bombed or captured, so the Allied source of tanks, munitions, and so forth never dried up.

Perhaps the major reason for the German defeat in the war lies in the personality of Adolf Hitler. As sole dictator of Germany, Hitler made all the crucial decisions in the early days of the war; many of these turned out to be serious strategic errors. As the war dragged on, Hitler seemed less and less aware of reality; historians are generally agreed that he was not entirely sane.

The war is accurately called a "world war" because of fighting outside of Europe. Japan's 1932 annexation of Manchuria led to full-scale war against China; growing diplomatic hostility with the Western powers led Japan to attack the United States in 1941. After more than three years of fighting in the Pacific, the United States resorted to atomic bombing to force Japan to concede defeat in 1945.

The costliest war in history, World War II ended the era of European domination. A power struggle between the United States and the Soviet Union would dominate world affairs for the next forty-five years.

CHAPTER OBJECTIVES

- Discuss the causes and effects of World War I.
- Discuss the causes and effects of the Russian Revolution.
- Explain the rise of totalitarian governments after World War I.
- Discuss the Great Depression and its effects on the international community.
- Analyze the causes, major events, and effects of World War II.

Chapter 22 Time Line

1914	Gavrilo Princip assassinates Franz Ferdinand and Sophie of Austria-Hungary
	Austria-Hungary declares war on Serbia
	Russian troops mobilize against Austria-Hungary
	Germany declares war on Russia and France
	Battle of the Marne
1915	Trench warfare begins
1917	United States declares war on Germany
	Russian Revolution
1918	Treaty of Brest-Litovsk
	Worldwide influenza epidemic
	German surrender; signing of armistice
1919	Peace conference and signing of Treaty of Versailles
1920	League of Nations is formed
1922	Soviet Union is formally founded
1924	Lenin dies; Stalin takes power
1922	Benito Mussolini becomes prime minister of Italy

- 1928 First Five-Year Plan in USSR
- 1929 U.S. stock market crashes, causing worldwide Great Depression
- 1930 Nazi Party rises to power in Germany
- 1932 Japan annexes Manchuria

   Franklin D. Roosevelt elected U.S. President
- 1933 Adolf Hitler becomes chancellor of Germany
- 1936–1939 Spanish Civil War
- 1937–1945 Sino-Japanese War
- 1938 Germany annexes Austria
- 1939 Germany annexes Czechoslovakia and western Poland

   Britain and France declare war on Germany
- 1941 Germany invades USSR; USSR joins Allied side

   Japan attacks United States; Germany declares war on United States
- 1943 Italy switches to Allied side
- 1944 D-Day; Allied forces land on Normandy beaches

   Battle of the Bulge

   Battle of Leyte Gulf
- 1945 Yalta Conference

   Battle of Iwo Jima

   Germany surrenders

   Potsdam Conference

   United States bombs Hiroshima and Nagasaki

   Japan surrenders

World War I

The Buildup to the War

In the decades since its unification in 1871, Germany had become Europe's strongest nation, surpassing Britain in industrial output and investing heavily in its army and navy. National prosperity and military might gave rise to an excess of boastful national pride—particularly as embodied in Kaiser Wilhelm II, crowned in 1888—that made Germany unpopular among its neighbors.

Between German unification and 1910, the European powers formed a series of alliances (see Table 22.1). These agreements established relationships that would pit the nations of central Europe against the nations on either side.

Table 22.1 European Alliances, 1881–1907	
1881: "Three Emperors' Alliance"—Germany, Russia, Austria	This alliance crumbled because Germany quickly came to view Russia as a threat rather than an ally.
1882: "Triple Alliance"—Germany, Austria, Italy	This alliance brought all of central Europe together. It divided the eastern and western nations, making it difficult for them to help one another; on the other hand, it meant that the Central Powers would have to defend themselves on two fronts if war broke out. The alliance with Italy did not last; Italy joined the Entente Powers in 1915.
1894: France and Russia	These nations were natural allies against the threat of the nations that lay geographically between them. Neither had enough natural resources or manpower to defeat the Central Powers on its own. France and Germany were traditional enemies; France especially resented the German reannexation of Alsace and Lorraine in 1871.
1904: France and Britain	France and Britain had been enemies ever since the Norman conquest. However, German industrialization and the massive buildup of the German navy alarmed Britain and contributed to British desire for a strong ally on the continent.
1907: Britain and Russia	This agreement cemented the "Triple Entente" among Britain, France, and Russia.

The alliances showed another new factor that had emerged in European politics—the direct involvement of Britain. Britain's geographical detachment from the continent had generally reflected its lack of central involvement in major power struggles among the other nations. This changed with the series of alliances made after 1900.

Ironically, three of the European monarchs were closely related family members: George V of Britain and Kaiser Wilhelm II of Germany were first cousins, and Czar Nicholas II of Russia was their first cousin by marriage. However, the family relationships among the monarchs did not prevent them from going to war against one another.

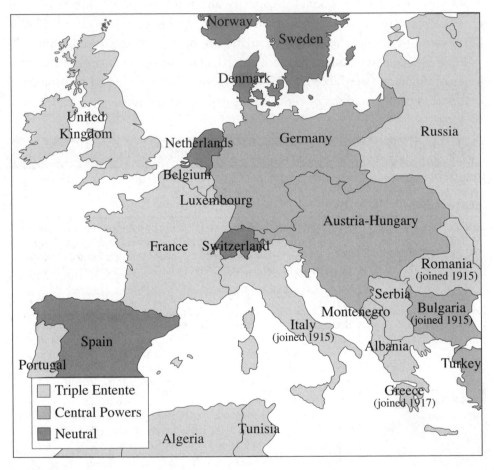

FIGURE 22.1   Europe in 1914

The Outbreak of War

The Balkan nation of Serbia had hoped for a political union with Bosnia so that the two states together could form one larger and stronger one. The Austrian annexation of Bosnia ended this hope and caused deep-seated Serbian resentment. In June 1914, the Serbian Gavrilo Princip shot and killed Austrian

Archduke Franz Ferdinand and Archduchess Sophie as they rode in an open car through the streets of Bosnia's capital, Sarajevo. Many historians believe that if Austria had immediately invaded Serbia in response, the war would have been between these two nations only and would have ended quickly. Instead, while Austria hesitated, Russia began to mobilize its army in preparation for the defense of Serbia, which it would support as a fellow Slav nation. Germany considered this mobilization a serious threat of war and promptly came to Austria's defense by declaring war on Serbia. (See Figure 22.1 for the European alliances as of 1914.)

The Western Front

The German military had long assumed that it would one day have to fight a war against France and Russia. The Schlieffen Plan, named after the officer who designed it, called for a decisive victory on Germany's Western Front before the Russians would have time to attack in the east. The German army would march into France via Belgium and capture Paris; then the entire German army would be free to face the Russians. This plan eliminated the need for dividing the German army on two fronts.

A departure from the Schlieffen Plan led to an unexpected French victory in the Battle of the Marne. The Western Front would now become a setting for trench warfare. By this time, Britain had declared war on Germany as well.

Both sides dug hundreds of miles of trenches; the two lines, separated by a zone of open, barren ground called "no-man's land," stretched from the North Sea to the border of Switzerland. The trenches served the infantry on both sides as both home and fort throughout four years of useless fighting—useless because, although millions of soldiers were slaughtered, neither side ever advanced its position more than a few miles into enemy territory. Both German and French leaders had apparently envisioned trench warfare as close-up, hand-to-hand combat in no-man's land. They failed to see that modern machine guns and hand grenades made this kind of battle obsolete. As long as the defenders stayed in the trenches, they could easily fire on the attackers advancing over the open ground and kill most of them without exposing themselves. This situation made the Western Front a stalemate.

The War at Sea

The British navy blockaded Germany, inspecting all ships entering the North Sea and intercepting any goods bound for Germany. The German U-boats were highly effective weapons because they could sail silently underwater, unheard and unseen, and then suddenly blow up ships on the surface. The Germans published advertisements warning the public that passenger ships were vulnerable to attack, but many people still took the risk of sailing. The German sinking of the British passenger liner HMS *Lusitania* killed more than a hundred Americans and proved a major catalyst in the U.S. decision to join the war in 1917.

The Eastern Front

The Germans won a major early victory against the Russians at Tannenberg on the Russian border. The Russians fought back decisively during 1915, but, over the next two years, the German army advanced some distance into Russia. Events took an unexpected turn when Russia's new revolutionary government abruptly withdrew from the war to settle its domestic affairs (see "The Russian Revolution" in this chapter). In the Treaty of Brest-Litovsk, Russia surrendered a good deal of territory in exchange for the German army's withdrawal. This freed the German army to turn all its attention to the Western Front.

The End of the War

In the fall of 1917, French troops began to mutiny, fed up with the nightmare of trench warfare. Fortunately for the Allied cause, American reinforcements arrived at this time, bringing fresh supplies and weapons as well as manpower. In the autumn of 1918, the Battle of the Argonne Forest led to the German surrender, with the abdication of Kaiser Wilhelm on November 9 and the signing of the armistice on November 11.

The Terms of the Peace

The peace conference convened at Versailles. It had been deliberately chosen to intimidate the German delegation and to stand as a symbol of French greatness.

For the first time in history, a non-European nation would play a major role in the peace settlements of a European war. The United States had played a decisive role in the victory, its industrial and economic might dwarfed all the European nations, and its losses had been minor compared to what the Europeans suffered. Fighting side by side with the British and French cemented good relations between the nations and gave the United States a level of power and influence over Europe that would persist through the coming century. The United States had achieved the status of a major world power.

The victors at Versailles were divided in their goals. U.S. president Woodrow Wilson wanted to establish a lasting peace in Europe. Premier Georges Clemenceau of France wanted to humiliate Germany. Prime Minister David Lloyd George of Britain wanted to achieve a balance of power between Germany and France on the continent. Italian Prime Minister Vittorio Orlando wanted to recover certain Italian territory from Austria.

Despite having fought on the winning side, Russia—soon to become the Soviet Union—took no part in the negotiations at Versailles. Far too much mutual distrust existed between Russia and the Western Europeans on both political and economic grounds. The Russians resented the lack of European support for their new government, while the Europeans considered that the Russians had sold them out by withdrawing from the war and making a separate peace with Germany. Economically, the forces of communism and capitalism were inherent enemies.

Provisions of the Treaty of Versailles

- Created new nations (Czechoslovakia and Yugoslavia)
- Restored the independence of Poland, Finland, Latvia, Lithuania, and Estonia
- Restored Alsace-Lorraine to France
- Gave France control of Saarland region until 1934
- Designated the Rhineland a demilitarized zone between Germany and France
- Created the League of Nations, an international peacekeeping force
- Drastically reduced the German military on a permanent basis
- Forced Germans to admit full responsibility for the war
- Charged Germany billions of dollars in reparations

Restoring the balance of powers and achieving peace involved three measures. The first was to redraw European borders along ethnic lines to achieve self-government by nationality. The leaders created new states, expanded others, and broke up the Austro-Hungarian Empire.

The second measure was to reduce Germany's strength and increase France's. Alsace and Lorraine were returned to French control. The Rhineland on Germany's western border would be maintained as a demilitarized zone. Additionally, the Germans were to admit full responsibility for the war, to pay enormous reparations, and to reduce their army and navy to small defensive forces. Although the United States argued against these punitive measures, France insisted on them. A storm of protest from the German delegates had no effect. The "war guilt clause," as it came to be known, would largely contribute to the German aggression of the 1930s and 1940s.

The third measure toward maintaining a balance was President Wilson's suggestion for an international peacekeeping force. Wilson had recently given a speech in which he laid out "Fourteen Points"—a list of measures that he believed would lead to a lasting peace throughout Europe and the world. The last point on his list proposed an international peacekeeping organization that would protect large and small nations on an equal basis. Members of this League of Nations could discuss conflicts over a conference table and resolve them peacefully, with war becoming a last resort. If one nation behaved aggressively, all other nations would unite against it, effectively putting a stop to attacks.

The League of Nations eventually came about in 1920. Ironically, the United States did not become a member of the league. The American system of government required that Congress approve international treaties; the opposition party refused to approve the League of Nations clause in the Treaty of Versailles on the grounds that it committed the United States to defend any European nation attacked by an outsider.

The War's Impact on Civilization

Mechanized warfare was a horror that no one had anticipated. Thirty-seven million people—an entire generation of Europeans of all nations—were either killed or severely wounded in the war. Millions more died of a severe flu epidemic that raged through the whole world. Many soldiers were left in a condition of mental illness called shellshock. (Today, doctors refer to these reactions to combat—chronic nightmares, hallucinations, severe depression, lethargy, and outbreaks of violent behavior—as post-traumatic stress disorder.) Additionally, with the presence of the United States at the conference table, the balance of international power had shifted from the Old World to the New. The United States was on its way to becoming a superpower.

The Russian Revolution

The Great War played a major role in bringing about the Russian Revolution. The advance of the German army into Russia brought mass slaughter, famine, and starvation; it smashed the Russian railway system in the west; and it diverted thousands of able-bodied men from their jobs to serve in the army. As it had elsewhere in Europe, war brought industrialization to a halt and wrecked the economy. It was easy for ordinary Russians to see that Czar Nicholas II, who had succeeded to the throne in 1894, was helpless to take control and improve matters. The concessions Nicholas had made toward republicanism in the wake of the 1905 uprising were too timid and slight to satisfy any but the most conservative. Resentment against the czar led to a popular uprising in 1917, as a result of which Nicholas abdicated.

There was no orderly transfer of power. In the wake of the czar's abdication, the socialists and moderates set up the Provisional Government, which shared its power with the Petrograd (formerly St. Petersburg) Soviet of Workers' and Soldiers' Deputies. The two organizations did not see eye to eye on priorities. The goal of the Provisional Government was to defeat the invading Germans, while the goal of the Petrograd Soviet was to set up a legislative assembly to address pressing domestic concerns—concerns about land ownership, grain prices, and food shortages.

Vladimir Ilyich Lenin, the leader of the Bolshevik (Russian for "majority") Party, soon became a prominent public figure with constant repetition of the slogan "Peace, Land, and Bread"—these were the three issues of greatest concern to the common people. In November, the Bolsheviks staged a successful coup d'état, orchestrated by Lenin's close associate Leon Trotsky; Lenin became leader of a one-party government.

Lenin had no interest in defeating Germany nor in maintaining alliances with Western capitalist nations. To begin solving Russia's enormous domestic problems, he had to end Russian participation in World War I. The quickest way was through diplomacy. In December 1917, Germany agreed to withdraw troops from Russia in exchange for a vast swath of territory (Latvia, Lithuania, Russian territory in Poland and Finland, and the Ukraine). The terms were made official in the Treaty of Brest-Litovsk, signed in March 1918.

Russia's European allies considered Brest-Litovsk a betrayal and an abandonment; the distrust it created between them and Russia would last for the rest of the century. Additionally, many ordinary Russians were alarmed at the loss of the valuable western territory; it was better developed, more densely populated, and more industrialized than central and eastern Russia. However, Lenin ignored all opposition to the treaty; he believed that as the head of a new government, he could not afford to show any weakness or hesitation. Had Russia sent a delegation to Versailles in 1919, it might have recovered some of the western territory it had ceded to Germany. With Russia absent from the conference table, the territory was made into independent nations.

The Russian Civil War

By 1918, a full-out civil war was raging in Russia between the Reds, who supported the Bolsheviks (now renamed Communists), and the Whites, who hoped to overthrow the new government. The Red Army's loyalty and support would make it one of the Communist Party's most effective tools in the following years. The Whites were a mix of royalists, moderates, anti-Communists and non-Russian Europeans, all of whom opposed the Bolsheviks but did not necessarily agree on who or what should replace them. The Reds prevailed after about three years of fighting. They outnumbered the Whites, they were better organized, they had a strong leader (Lenin) whose goals were clear, they controlled Moscow and the railroads, and they enjoyed tremendous popular support within Russia. Russian workers supported them because they were the workers' party, while peasants did not believe the Whites had their interests at heart. Political leaders considered the Whites to be foreign interlopers.

Russia and the Soviet Union Under Lenin

With no experience of governing, Lenin and his associates had to create a system by trial and error. Lenin insisted on an autocratic regime with himself as dictator; he believed that a parliamentary system was simply a rubber stamp for the capitalist forces that he intended to obliterate from Russian society.

Because most Europeans enjoyed voting rights (at least for adult men) and representation, European socialists were not sufficiently dissatisfied with conditions to overthrow their governments as the Russians had done. Lenin hoped to change this complacency; nothing less than the violent overthrow of the entire existing social order would satisfy Communist goals. The International Communist Party, or Comintern, was founded in 1919 to help bring this about. Moscow controlled the Comintern from the early 1920s.

War with Poland broke out in 1920, and a Russian-Polish border was established in March 1921. Poland had a long-standing history of resentment toward Russian oppression; it was capable of holding its own in a struggle with Russia; and the Poles were fiercely anti-Bolshevik, in part because Poland was largely a Catholic nation and the Bolsheviks were atheists.

The early 1920s in Russia can accurately be called "a Second Time of Troubles." Lenin's New Economic Policy of 1921 called for peasants to sell their surplus grain to the state at a fixed price in either money or kind (such as clothing or tools); the grain would be used to feed the urban industrial workers. Peasants reacted to the government orders in a way the Communists had not foreseen. With the promised payments rarely materializing, peasants hoarded their grain, fearful of not having enough to feed their families. With no grain coming in from the country, many urban workers fled to the country in search of food. Severe droughts at this time led to widespread famine; historians estimate that perhaps six million Russians died of starvation and disease during this period.

In 1922, Russia officially became the Union of Soviet Socialist Republics, called the Soviet Union or USSR for short. The individual republics—Georgia, Kazakhstan, Russia, and the others—were coequals, each with its own soviet and all under the central control of the dictator.

The Communists made it clear to the old guard that there was no place for them in the new workers' state. In the Soviet Union, there was no private property; the homes of the wealthy were turned into apartment houses for workers (with the original owners perhaps being allowed to rent one room as their own family apartment). At least two million Russian aristocrats fled to Western Europe; those who stayed had to learn hard manual labor like all other Soviet citizens.

Stalin Takes Power

After suffering a series of strokes, Lenin died in 1924 without naming a successor. Leon Trotsky and Joseph Stalin emerged as the most likely candidates. Both of them had been close to Lenin, but he believed that neither of them should rule. Born within two years of each other, both had risen to prominence among the Communists, and both had had serious disputes with Lenin. Both were known by aliases: Lev Bronstein took the name Trotsky when he escaped from political imprisonment, and Joseph Dzhugashvili began using Stalin as a pen name when he founded the worker's newspaper *Pravda* (*Truth*). Stalin won the power struggle and became dictator. He soon forced Trotsky to leave the country for good.

Stalin is considered by many to be history's most ruthless dictator, with the possible exception of Adolf Hitler. Under his rule, the Soviet Union could accurately be described as a police state. Stalin enforced his policies with no evidence of a conscience and no regard whatever for human life. Historians have estimated that about thirty million Russians died during his regime— some succumbed to starvation or disease, but most died as the result of either execution or the brutal conditions of the labor camps. The government concealed Stalin's brutality from the outside world; even many Russians were not aware of its full extent.

The Five-Year Plan

Some Soviet officials believed that since the grain harvests were needed to feed the industrial workers, the state should try to gain the peasants' support. Others believed that it was not necessary to conciliate the peasants, since the state could force them into obedience. Stalin was one of the latter group. His policy, called the Five-Year Plan, was implemented in 1929. It involved two goals, collectivization and industrialization. Collectivization forced small independent farmers (known in Russian as *kulaks*) and subsistence farmers to pool their land and work the new, giant farms together—with the state dictating prices. The *kulaks* were accustomed to independence; their lack of cooperation made Stalin, who considered them nothing more than a means for providing the urban workers with food, decide to get rid of them. Between 1930 and 1933, more than two million *kulaks* and "sympathizers" were deported, either to collective farms far from their own districts or to prison camps.

The second goal of the Five-Year Plan was to develop heavy industry. Before World War I, Russian industrialization had begun to catch up to the rest of Europe; as elsewhere, it was halted when the fighting broke out. By 1927, however, production had risen nearly back to its 1913 levels. The Five-Year Plan called for major public-works projects, including the Moscow Metro, railways, canals, and power plants; many of these were built with prison-camp labor. Employment doubled and industrial output more than doubled by 1932—but not without taking a toll on the workers. During this period, the Soviet Union experienced severe food shortages, peasant opposition to collectivization, mass migrations to the cities, a typhus epidemic, and, in 1933, a famine that probably killed more than four million people. The nation's economic gains during this period are especially impressive considering the harsh conditions in which the people were living.

Bold experimentation had occurred in the arts during Lenin's regime, but Stalin put a stop to this. He believed that art's only legitimate purpose was to serve the state. Books, films, popular songs, symphonies, paintings, plays—all were banned if they hinted at any criticism of the regime or suggested that social conditions in the USSR were anything short of ideal. Some artists left the country; those who stayed did their best to come to terms with the policies.

During the mid-1930s, a wave of executions and banishments known as the "Great Purges" did a great deal to establish Stalin's historical reputation. Interpretations of the Great Purges vary, but most historians agree that Stalin set about them as a means of preserving his autocratic powers. Between 1936 and 1939, at least seven hundred fifty thousand people were executed or banished to the labor camps. Anyone who opposed Stalin publicly, or was unfortunate enough to be caught denouncing him privately, was purged—military officers, high-ranking politicians or economists, artists and intellectuals, and political dissenters.

Communism Elsewhere in Europe

Lenin had originally expected the Communist Revolution to sweep through Europe. His expectations were only partially fulfilled. Short-lived socialist and Communist uprisings took place throughout Germany and Eastern Europe, but European socialists could generally find room for their ideas under a parliamentary government. Only in China in 1949 was a large Communist government established without Russian force being used.

Germany underwent a chaotic period of popular uprisings during the fall of 1918. In January 1919, the Weimar Republic replaced the monarchy; it was named for the city in which the legislative assembly met and wrote the new German constitution. The Weimar Republic lasted only until the rise of Adolf Hitler in 1933.

The Communists were closest to achieving success in Hungary, where a workers' republic was established in 1919 under Béla Kun. This Communist state lasted five months—a period of brutal oppression known in Hungary as the "Red Terror"—before it was replaced by something resembling a constitutional monarchy under former diplomat and naval commander Miklós Horthy. Communists in Bavaria and Slovakia also established workers' states, but each only lasted for a few weeks.

Totalitarian Governments Form in Europe and Asia

Italy

In 1919, the Italian economy was suffering from massive unemployment and high inflation. Towns in battle zones lay in ruins and would have to be rebuilt. Politically, the country was divided between the socialist and nationalist parties. The situation was ripe for the rise to power of Benito Mussolini, a well-read combat veteran and former journalist. He had once been a committed socialist, but his ideas changed during the war. In 1919, Mussolini held the first meeting of the group that would become the Fascist Party of Italy. (The Italian word *fascio* means "union" and comes from the Latin *fasces*, a sheaf of grain that had been a symbol of the authority of the Roman state in ancient times.)

As the leader of the Fascist movement, Mussolini explicitly encouraged violence against the socialists, thereby attracting those whose extreme nationalism found expression in gang-style violence. In April 1919, Mussolini's supporters stormed into the offices of the Milan newspaper *Avanti* (*Forward*) and destroyed the printing presses. This act of violence was typical of the terrorist tactics that would become the signature of the totalitarian regimes of the next two decades.

Mussolini had one serious rival in the person of Gabriele d'Annunzio, a playwright, poet, and World War I hero. In September 1919, D'Annunzio led his followers into the Yugoslavian city of Fiume, nearly 90 percent of whose citizens were ethnic Italians. Once in power in Fiume, D'Annunzio behaved like the Caesars, staging military parades and bombastic daily speeches to impress and intimidate the people. In exchange for Yugoslavia making Fiume independent, Italian Prime Minister Giovanni Giolitti forced D'Annunzio to step down. Guided by pragmatism rather than principle, Mussolini treated the chastened D'Annunzio generously, thus winning the loyalty and support of D'Annunzio's followers.

Between November 1920 and April 1921, the Fascists destroyed the offices of Labor Exchanges, dragged labor organizers into the street and beat them up, and smashed printing presses of any newspapers whose editors favored socialist politics. At the same time, the Fascists won support among the peasants by giving some of them land outright. This convinced many farmers to desert the socialists; they preferred private rather than state ownership of their own farms.

The Fascists stepped up their campaign of terror and intimidation, taking over entire towns and cities. With the help of local police, nationalist veterans, and their own organized military squads, called "Blackshirts" after the color of their uniforms, the Fascists occupied public buildings and forced local governments to do what they wanted, including instituting public-works programs that gave jobs to many of the unemployed. Naturally, this won them a great deal of support among the people.

By May of 1921, the Fascists had become so strong that Giolitti formed a coalition government with seats in Parliament for Mussolini and thirty-four other Fascists. In October 1922, Mussolini staged what became known as the

March on Rome. Hundreds of Blackshirts commandeered and boarded trains to Rome from three different starting points, taking over towns along the three routes. The new prime minister, Luigi Facta, resolutely prepared to stop them, assembling troops and asking the king to declare martial law in Rome. The king refused, however, fearing that a confrontation between the Fascists and the Italian army would lead immediately to civil war. Unwilling to risk this, he offered the office of prime minister to Mussolini. Four years later, Mussolini had become *Il Duce*—the absolute dictator of a one-party Italian government. (*Duce* is Italian for "leader.")

European economies collapsed in the crash of 1929 and the Great Depression (see "The Great Depression" in this chapter); Italy's economy was no exception. In 1935, Mussolini ordered the invasion of Ethiopia, for both political and economic reasons. Politically, the invasion was a sign of the typical fascist desire to subdue and control other lands. Economically, Mussolini intended Ethiopia to provide Italy with natural resources and a market for Italian goods.

Germany

The rise of an extreme nationalist party in Germany was all but inevitable after the Treaty of Versailles. Already bitter because they had lost the war, thousands of German veterans now found themselves out of a job. Blaming the Weimar government for abandoning them, they took revenge at the polling place. Between 1919 and 1933, coalition governments came and went with bewildering rapidity. Conservatives, monarchists, and democrats could not work together effectively. As Germany lost a series of arguments over Versailles Treaty provisions, Germans grew more nationalist and, at the same time, more contemptuous of their own government. When they learned of the agreement to pay France and Britain reparations of more than 130 billion marks, they were furious. They saw this demand as pure revenge on a defenseless nation. Moreover, the money simply was not there.

The French, deciding to take in fuel what Germany would not hand over in money, marched into the Ruhr—the coal-producing region of western Germany that had been made a demilitarized zone by the Treaty of Versailles. This brought economic ruin to Germany, with inflation soaring to unimaginable levels. In December 1921, a loaf of bread cost 4 marks; in December 1922 it cost 163 marks; by December 1923, the price had risen to a staggering 400 *billion* marks!

At this point, the tide turned. France and Britain compromised over the payment of reparations, and France withdrew its troops from the Ruhr. The United

States loaned money to Germany, and the German economy recovered. The Western nations even welcomed Germany into the League of Nations in 1926. In addition, the Weimar Republic became famous for bold, experimental works by such artists as composer Kurt Weill, writers Bertolt Brecht and Thomas Mann, painters George Grosz and Wassily Kandinsky, and film director Joseph von Sternberg.

The Great Depression halted Germany's economic resurgence. The German government, faced with strikes, demonstrations, and rising unemployment, collapsed. The Nazi Party (short for National Socialist German Workers' Party) now rose to power under its founder and leader, an obscure Austrian named Adolf Hitler.

Adolf Hitler Comes to Power

A failure at many jobs and a World War I veteran who had served with some distinction, Hitler felt great personal bitterness over Germany's defeat. He was neither an experienced leader nor a creator of logically thought-out social programs. Therefore, the established German political parties made the great mistake of underestimating him and his mass appeal—and mass appeal Hitler had. He used simple slogans and propaganda calculated to appeal to Germans' national pride, emotions, and prejudices. His rhetoric about the greatness of the German Empire—delivered in spellbinding style—hit a nerve with people who desperately needed decisive leadership.

In 1930, the Nazis won a large number of seats in the Reichstag, the elected arm of the legislature. Largely by means of intimidating key figures in political power, Hitler contrived his own appointment as chancellor in 1933. Soon the new chancellor was calling himself "Führer (Leader) of the Third Reich" and establishing one-party rule. The SS (a rogue militia like Mussolini's Blackshirts) and the Gestapo (a secret state police force) carried out the executions and other acts of brutal violence against German citizens that have cemented Hitler's reputation as the greatest villain in modern European history.

Where Hitler differed from other autocrats of the era was in his profound racism. He considered that Germans and northern Europeans were racially superior to Slavs and southern Europeans. His overall plan for Germany was to expand its borders, thus providing living space for the Aryans (his term for the racially superior) while at the same time subduing the *Untermenschen* (literally, subhumans). His persecution of the Jews was the most obvious manifestation of his prejudices; under Hitler's rule, German Jews were soon stripped of all civil rights, deprived of their professions, and forced into menial jobs—with worse to come. Historians estimate that perhaps one-fourth of all German Jews fled the country in the early 1930s. Many German intellectuals, artists, journalists, and teachers who found Hitler's policies appalling also packed up and left the country.

In 1933, Germany withdrew from the League of Nations and began to rearm despite the ban contained in the Versailles Treaty. Rearming increased considerably in 1936, as Hitler made it clear that he expected Germany to be ready to launch a war of aggression by 1940.

Spain and the Spanish Civil War

Spain spent the first half of the 1930s trying to settle what type of government it wanted: republican or nationalist. The dictatorship of Miguel Primo de Rivera ended in 1930; it was replaced by the republican administration of Prime Minister Manuel Azaña. For three years, Azaña carried out a program of egalitarian reforms, but in 1933, his opponents forced him out of office.

Over the next three years, the left-wing Popular Front (communists, anarchists, and socialists) and the right-wing National Front (conservatives, monarchists, and establishment Catholics) fought for supremacy. The Popular Front carried the 1936 elections, executing Primo de Rivera by firing squad and restoring Azaña to power.

General Francisco Franco had been waiting with the army in Morocco for news of the elections. When he learned that the National Front had been defeated, he led an invasion into Spain, where he laid siege to Madrid. The fascist Falange party supported Franco, as did Italy and Germany; the Germans were able to supply Franco through Portugal, whose ruler was a fascist sympathizer. The USSR supported the Popular Front for a time; when it withdrew its support, the National Front won the civil war and Spain became a military dictatorship under Franco.

Other European Nations

The small states of Eastern Europe were the perfect breeding ground for totalitarianism for three reasons. First, nationalism was a divisive factor in these ethnically diverse countries. Second, this area suffered economically as much as any other during the Great War. Third, several of these nations were newly created, and none had more than a few decades' experience in self-government.

All these factors combined to create unstable societies that were ripe for a seizure of power. Except for Czechoslovakia, which established and managed to maintain a democratic government, all the nations of Eastern Europe succumbed to dictatorship between 1919 and 1936.

Japan

From 1918 to 1931, Japan was a liberal society; by 1925, all Japanese men could vote, and Prime Minister Kato Komei supported important social programs. The Great Depression, however, undid much of this work as power shifted from freely elected representative government to forced rule by the military. In 1931, the Chinese nationalist movement challenged Japanese supremacy in Manchuria, a region in which Japan had considerable financial interest. While the government debated how to respond, the army staged an explosion and blamed it on the Chinese, thus manufacturing an excuse for a full-scale Japanese invasion. (Such an action was typical of imperialist behavior; in the same way, the United States had taken advantage of an accidental explosion on board the battleship *Maine* to invade Cuba in 1898.) In 1932, Japan made Manchuria a protectorate; when the League of Nations objected, Japan resigned its membership.

Prime Minister Inukai Tsuyoshi, who opposed the annexation of Manchuria, was assassinated; in the wake of a series of failed military coups, the government began cracking down on liberals to demonstrate its own nationalism. Widespread Japanese support for an invasion of China led to military dictatorship in all but name by 1937 and to all-out war with China.

China

The end of Manchu rule brought about an era of total chaos in China, with various warlords and factions ruling different small regions of the nation. In the early 1920s, Chinese leader Sun Yat-sen founded the Kuomintang, a Chinese nationalist party. Sun worked to bring the Chinese Communists into the fold of the Kuomintang but died in 1925 before this could be accomplished. Chiang Kai-shek stepped into Sun's leadership role; he unified the Kuomintang by 1930 and, after a series of military campaigns, forced Mao Zedong and his Communist supporters to march north in 1936. With the Japanese invasion, Chiang's fortunes fell. With the Japanese surrender in 1945, the Communists and the Kuomintang resumed their civil war; by the end of 1948, the Communists emerged victorious.

The United States: The Great Depression and the New Deal

The Great Depression

The U.S. stock market crashed in the fall of 1929. It had been soaring on an insubstantial foundation of margin buying and unpaid debts. When Americans began selling stocks to pay debts, people lost confidence in the market and it collapsed with stunning speed. When the market collapsed, the banks failed; when the banks failed, the businesses closed; when the businesses closed, the workers lost their jobs and could find no others. This economic failure is known to history as the Great Depression. It affected worldwide markets because international trade and commerce had become central to all their economies. Banks closed and prices dropped; no one could find a market for goods because no one had cash with which to buy them.

The New Deal

Ironically, given that the United States and the USSR were to become such deadly enemies in the Cold War era, the United States was one nation whose government shifted towards socialism rather than fascism in the wake of World War I and the Great Depression. Elected in 1932 at the height of the Great Depression, U.S. President Franklin D. Roosevelt (FDR) established the New Deal—a group of programs that offered immediate relief. Roosevelt referred to his New Deal as "a war against the emergency"; Congress granted him special powers to take action against the severe economic crisis. The New Deal marked a complete break with the Republican policies of the 1920s. It consisted of a set of fifteen programs designed to provide jobs for the unemployed, to help the economy recover, and to install safeguards so that no such major financial crisis could ever occur again. The New Deal did not end the depression, but it did create millions of jobs and restore the nation's banks to a sound financial footing. During Roosevelt's first term, unemployment dropped by about 8 percent. Unsurprisingly, he was reelected in 1936 in the greatest landslide in a hundred years.

In 1940, the U.S. economy was beginning to recover from the worst of the Great Depression, and America's possible entry into in the war in Europe became the major issue in the campaign. Both Roosevelt and his opponent Wendell Willkie pledged to keep the United States neutral—Willkie at all costs, FDR if possible. Roosevelt made it clear that the United States would not seek a battle with any nation but would immediately defend itself if it were attacked directly. Roosevelt won the election; historians agree that the uncertainty of the times made Americans prefer to stick with familiar leadership.

World War II

The Beginning of German Aggression

As German rearmament continued during the late 1930s, Hitler and his generals planned a European takeover. Their goal was to create a central European empire, ruled by Germany, with a number of Eastern European satellite states. The first step was to retake the Rhineland, which Nazi troops were occupying as early as 1936. In 1938, the German army invaded and annexed Austria (the Germans referred to this event as the *Anschluss*, or "union"), and in 1939, it invaded Czechoslovakia. These steps aroused concern among many European leaders, but there was no popular support anywhere for another war with Germany: the memories of World War I were too strong. Hitler therefore proceeded almost unchecked; when any leader did protest, Hitler's response was brutal and effective intimidation.

Having taken over Austria and Czechoslovakia, Hitler then met with Stalin. Secretly, they agreed to invade Poland from opposite sides and divide it between them, while promising not to attack one another. Stalin's motive was to recover Polish territory that had been under Russian control before the Great War. Hitler's motive was to recover a stretch of Polish territory known as the Danzig Corridor, which the Versailles Treaty had signed over to Poland. This corridor cut East Prussia off from the rest of Germany and also provided overland access to the Baltic; retaking it would reunite all of Germany into one land mass. The invasion of Poland would also allow the German army direct overland access to the Soviet Union—something the usually distrustful Stalin apparently had not considered.

Britain and France had formally guaranteed Poland's sovereignty. Hitler's closest associates had, therefore, tried to dissuade him from provoking a war against the Allies by invading Poland. Hitler refused to listen to them, considering the agreement a bluff. He promptly realized his mistake; Britain and France declared war on Germany immediately after the German invasion of Poland (see Figure 22.2).

1940: The Fall of France and the Battle of Britain

In April 1940, the German army invaded Denmark and Norway. In May, the army staged a successful two-pronged attack on France, with one division

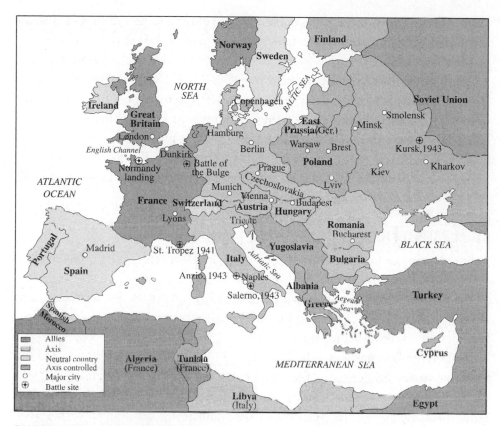

FIGURE 22.2   World War II, 1939–1945

invading though Belgium and the other through the Ardennes, south of Paris.
The advancing German divisions cut off the British troops, who were forced
to retreat across the Channel; on June 21, Marshal Philippe Pétain of France
asked for an armistice. Thus, Hitler won an easy victory over Germany's historic
enemy. The Germans would occupy Paris until late 1944; Hitler maintained
control over southern France, Morocco, and Algeria through the Vichy regime.
Named for the southern French city in which it was headquartered, the Vichy
regime was a puppet government. Pétain was its titular head, but in fact it was
a tool for the Nazis. The Vichy regime would remain in place until the Allies
liberated France in late 1944.

At this time, Winston Churchill was chosen prime minster of Britain. Having warned Parliament for years about German rearmament and its probable
consequences, Churchill may have been the only man in Europe whom Hitler
could not intimidate. His refusal even to consider the possibility of a British
defeat communicated itself to his people in his radio addresses. Churchill and

the royal family set an example of courage by refusing to leave London, despite the nightly bombing of the capital by the German air force.

This attack from the air is known as the Battle of Britain; it lasted until the summer of 1940. The bombardment began as a prelude to a planned German invasion of England that never took place. The Germans lost more than half their fighter planes in the attacks; they took revenge by bombing London and other heavily populated areas. The purpose of the Blitz, as this attack on the cities is called, was to intimidate the British into surrender; by 1941, the Germans acknowledged their failure. They would return to bomb London again in 1943, but, for the moment, the Battle of Britain was won.

The Eastern Front

When Germany invaded the Soviet Union in 1941, the Soviets were taken completely unawares. However, they soon rallied, proving fierce and stubborn in opposition. The German attack immediately brought the Soviet Union into the war on the Allied side. With its enormous army, the USSR would be a crucial factor in the ultimate Allied victory.

The German attack was a strategic error: Hitler seriously underestimated the vast size of the Soviet army, the production capacity of the Soviet munitions factories, and the discipline the Soviet people had acquired under Stalin's harsh rule. Ironically, given his peacetime skill at inspiring his people with terror, Stalin proved an important unifying force for the Soviets during World War II.

In September 1941, the Germans laid siege to Leningrad; the siege was not lifted until 1944, by which time more than a million Soviet civilians had died of starvation and related illnesses. (The Soviets would retaliate for this when they marched into Berlin in 1945.) In the summer of 1942, Stalingrad became a major battleground. The Germans nearly secured a victory, but the Soviets refused to give up, eventually winning the battle in January 1943. There were enormous casualties on both sides, but this hurt the Germans more than the Soviets, as the Soviets had a much larger population from which to draw reinforcements.

The United States Enters the War

In 1941, Japan bombed the U.S. naval base at Pearl Harbor in a surprise attack. This was an enormous shock to the Americans. Isolated on the east and west by oceans, with friendly Canada to the north and impoverished Mexico to the south, the United States had always considered itself invulnerable to invasion. Japan had signed an alliance with Italy and Germany in 1940; as a result,

Britain and the United States had broken off trade relations with Japan. After increasingly sharp exchanges between Japanese and American diplomats, Japan attacked Pearl Harbor with the intention of wiping out the U.S. navy and reducing the United States to the status of a second-rate power.

Roosevelt made good his threat to respond to any attack by declaring war on Japan immediately. As an ally of Japan, Hitler then declared war on the United States. He seriously underestimated the efficiency and promptness of the American response.

North Africa and the Italian Front

Under the command of American Dwight D. Eisenhower, the Allies invaded North Africa in November 1942; they soon blocked supply lines between Italy and Germany. In May 1943, the Allies forced the surrender of Axis troops in Tunisia, their last African stronghold. The combinations of victories on the eastern and northern African fronts turned the tide of war in the Allies' favor. In July, the Allies invaded Italy, which gave way promptly; many Italians had come to despise the Fascists. With Mussolini deposed and arrested, the new Italian government signed an armistice with the Allies; the Italians themselves took part in the liberation of Naples and Rome.

The Western Front

The Allies bombed Germany throughout 1943, seeking both to destroy strategic locations such as railroad lines and factories and to break the spirit of the German people. Allied bombs killed tens of thousands of German civilians and reduced virtually every large German city to rubble; the bombing of the ancient and beautiful city of Dresden later became a byword for vicious, strategically unnecessary destruction.

The United States and Britain agreed to launch a surprise offensive in Normandy. Working with Allied military staff, Eisenhower laid a trail of false clues that led the Germans to expect an invasion at Calais, some distance away. On D-Day, June 6, 1944, Allied troops landed on the beaches of France and began marching toward Paris. No German troops were there to stop them; Eisenhower's deception had fooled Hitler. On August 25, the Allies liberated Paris.

After the shock of losing the French capital, the Germans launched a fierce assault in the Ardennes, pushing Allied troops so far back that they nearly broke through the line of defense, thus giving the Battle of the Bulge its name. This was the last gasp of German strength; by January, it was clear that the Germans could not possibly overpower the Allies. In February 1945, Churchill,

Roosevelt, and Stalin met at Yalta to plan for the peace they knew the Allied armies would soon achieve. Stalin promised that after Germany surrendered, Soviet troops would help the United States defeat Japan. The three leaders then agreed to occupy Germany after the war and discussed plans for a new League of Nations.

The End of the War in Europe

The German troops had behaved with exceptional brutality in their invasion of the USSR; when the Soviets marched into Berlin in April 1945, they took full revenge on the civilians. Unable to contemplate the punishment and public humiliation he would undergo as the loser of the war, Hitler committed suicide on April 30. Germany surrendered a week later, ending the war in Europe.

As the British and American troops marched eastward, liberating Austria and Poland, they discovered the concentration camps where millions of Jews and other "non-Aryans" of Central and Eastern Europe, notably the migratory Sinti and Romany peoples, had been rounded up for slaughter in a deliberate massacre of innocents known to history as the Holocaust. Although there was at least some general knowledge of these camps and their purpose, and many courageous individuals had helped to hide and protect their Jewish friends and neighbors, no nation had made any official attempt to put a stop to what was happening, almost certainly because national leaders were fully occupied with the survival of Europe as a whole. The sight of the survivors, mere skeletons of flesh with numbers branded on their arms, horrified the troops and would shock the world when the news was made public.

Results of the War

After the war, the Allied leaders met in Potsdam for a peace conference. They had an enormous rebuilding task before them.

Many of the cities of Europe had been reduced to heaps of loose bricks and stones by the bombing. Transportation systems across the continent were wrecked. Everyday necessities such as fresh water, fuel, electricity, and food were unavailable. Governments were in disarray or had been removed from power.

The Nazi Party was disbanded and discredited; many of its key figures killed themselves or fled to South America. A number of the rest were tried as war criminals. Germany lost all the territory it had conquered since 1936. Soviet casualties totaled about 9 million soldiers and 19 million civilians; other European casualties totaled about 5 million soldiers and 7 million civilians, including the refugees who died of starvation, disease, or stray bullets. Approximately 6 million Jews, Sinti, and Romany were massacred in the concentration camps. Thousands more Europeans were lucky enough to emigrate overseas before or during the war; most would never return.

European domination of the globe was ended. For the next fifty years, only two nations dominated world affairs: the United States and the Soviet Union. War production had completely reinvigorated the American economy; U.S. casualties had been very low compared to European losses; and, of course, the United States was far from the combat zones, apart from the attack on Pearl Harbor. The Soviet Union had suffered tremendous losses but had taken advantage of the chaos to spread its sphere of influence across Eastern Europe.

Provisions of the Potsdam Conference

- Austria and Germany would each be divided into four zones of occupation: Soviet, British, United States, and French.
- The capital cities of Vienna and Berlin would be divided into four zones of occupation, as above.
- The Allies would help to rebuild German industry and reestablish local German governments.
- German refugees would be helped to return to their homes.
- Poland would retain German territory it had taken during the war.
- Germany would pay reparations to all Allied nations, with the Soviet Union taking the largest share as the greatest sufferer.

The leaders at Potsdam were outwardly civil but inwardly distrustful of one another. Stalin did not want the United States imposing a capitalist economy on Germany. In addition, he deeply resented the fact that the Allies had waited until 1944 to invade Normandy, while Soviet soldiers were fighting desperately in the east. On his side, U.S. President Harry Truman did not want the Soviets to gain too much control over Poland and Eastern Europe. These mutual suspicions grew as time went on. Before long, they led the world into the Cold War.

The United Nations

The League of Nations had failed to prevent World War II. National leaders agreed that they needed to design a new, stronger peacekeeping organization. Delegates from the United States, China, the Soviet Union, and Britain wrote a proposal for an organization to be called the United Nations. Delegates from fifty nations then met to discuss the proposal and write a U.N. charter. It established a General Assembly in which all member nations would have an equal voice and a fifteen-member Security Council. Ten of the fifteen seats on the Security Council would rotate among nations; the other five would be permanently held by Britain, China, France, the Soviet Union, and the United States.

The War in the Pacific

Japan bombed U.S. naval bases in the Philippines, Burma, Hong Kong, and other places. After the onslaught on the Philippines, General Douglas MacArthur led a U.S. retreat to Australia. The Japanese took thousands of American prisoners at Bataan and forced them on a death march through the jungle on the way to the prison camps. More than ten thousand of the prisoners died.

By 1942, Japan was planning to invade the Pacific coast of the United States. In three battles at the Coral Sea, Midway, and Guadalcanal, the U.S. fleet and the air force won victories, with some help from the British.

The United States planned to advance north in the South Pacific Islands, taking over each island on the way and using the islands as power bases to continue the advance toward Japan. In 1944, the Battle of Leyte Gulf became the turning point with a major U.S. victory. In February 1945, the Japanese finally gave way on Iwo Jima after six weeks of fighting, with thousands of dead on both sides.

With the European war ending in the spring of 1945, the United States could turn all its attention to the war in the Pacific. President Truman gave the order for the use of the world's deadliest weapon: the atomic bomb, developed in the Manhattan Project between 1942 and 1945. Although it was clear the bomb would wreak unimaginable destruction on its target, Truman believed it would end the war and thus save lives in the long run. The United States bombed the Japanese city of Hiroshima on August 6; it killed over seven hundred fifty thousand and laid every building flat. After a second bomb was dropped on Nagasaki three days later, the Japanese finally surrendered.

QUIZ

1. _____ was forced to assume total responsibility for World War I.
   A. Austria-Hungary
   B. France
   C. Germany
   D. Russia

2. Britain's main source of anxiety during the years before 1914 was _____.
   A. the buildup of the German navy
   B. the success of Russian industrialization
   C. the status of its colonies in the Middle East
   D. the Austrian annexation of Bosnia

3. Why did communism not take a stronger hold on Europe after the Great War?
   A. Socialists were contented with representative European governments.
   B. There was no international Communist party.
   C. Europeans were shocked by stories of Stalin's brutal policies.
   D. Nations were too busy rebuilding their economies.

4. _____ was the catalyst that brought the United States into World War II.
   A. The German and Soviet invasions of Poland
   B. The German bombing of Britain
   C. The Japanese attack on Pearl Harbor
   D. The forced march from Bataan

5. Trench warfare resulted in a stalemate primarily because _____.
   A. weather conditions made it too problematic
   B. modern weapons were not suited to that style of combat
   C. the German army had to divide its forces on two fronts
   D. the French trenches were badly and hastily dug

6. Truman ordered the bombing of Hiroshima and Nagasaki in order to _____.
   A. force an immediate Japanese surrender
   B. test the capacities of the atomic bomb
   C. persuade the Soviets to take part in the war against Japan
   D. avenge American losses in the Pacific theater of war

7. **Wilson's "Fourteen Points" is best described as** _____.

   A. a declaration of war

   B. a program for international peace

   C. an economic policy

   D. a redesign of the American military

8. **The king of Italy refused to put down the Blackshirts because** _____.

   A. he was personally afraid for his own life

   B. he did not command the loyalty of the Italian Army

   C. he wanted to avoid a full-scale civil war

   D. he had made a secret bargain with Mussolini

9. **Stalin is considered an especially brutal dictator because** _____.

   A. he led the nation into wars it could not win

   B. he was an absolute ruler who did not accept advice or counsel

   C. he ordered the exile, imprisonment, and/or execution of millions

   D. he used the army and police as tools of oppression

10. **A major "first" in World War I was** _____.

   A. the outbreak of battles in the empires outside of Europe

   B. the impressive military force demonstrated by Germany

   C. the alliance between France and Russia

   D. the decisive participation of a non-European nation

chapter 23

The End of the Twentieth Century, 1945–1991

The treaties signed at the end of World War II did not bring peace. Instead, a new era of conflict began—the so-called Cold War that would last for forty-five years. The era was known as a "cold" war because the major opponents—the United States and the Soviet Union—did not actually fire shots at one another. Instead, they maintained a hostile standoff—the capitalist nation against the Communist nation, the philosophy of representative government against the philosophy of autocratic one-party rule. Each side tried to contain the other's sphere of influence. Both sides stockpiled nuclear weapons, more for their own defense than because either had any serious intention of launching a nuclear war. All of Eastern Europe (those countries under the sphere of influence of the Soviet Union) got caught up in the Cold War. After dragging on for decades with no real progress toward peace, it ended abruptly between 1989 and 1991. A variety of reasons led to the fall of communism: foremost were the persistent underground resistance to communism behind the Iron Curtain and the USSR ruining its own economy trying to keep up with the pace of U.S. defense spending.

From the Asian point of view, the term *Cold War* is a misnomer. When civil wars erupted in Korea and Vietnam, the Soviets backed one side and the United States the other. Hundreds of thousands of civilians and soldiers died during the Korean and Vietnam wars, neither of which made much difference to the overall Cold War. The first ended in a stalemate, the second in a Communist victory.

Just as its own staggering World War II losses and its excessive defense spending made it economically impossible for the Soviet Union to maintain its influence in Eastern Europe by 1989, the smaller European powers had no resources to spare for their colonial empires; all their energies and resources were concentrated on rebuilding. The postwar era therefore saw a wave of independence throughout all of Africa. This was not gained easily, peacefully, or overnight, and, in some African nations, it led to an era of harsh military rule, corruption, and violent social and political unrest. India also finally broke free from British rule and was divided into two separate states; a Hindu India and an Islamic Pakistan. Millions of Indian Muslims immediately crossed the border into Pakistan, while Pakistani Hindus fled to India.

As one giant Communist nation declined, another rose. The Soviet Union was no longer so imposing after the death of Stalin, but China became stronger and more economically viable after the death of Mao Zedong. The Soviet Union collapsed in 1991, breaking up into individual republics; China, although it continues to suffer grave social problems, enjoyed a tremendous economic boom. Japan, which suffered perhaps more destruction than any other nation during World War II, rewrote its constitution, redesigned its government, and rebuilt its economy in a remarkably short space of time.

The post–World War II era became the era of international organizations. Created in the wake of World War II, the United Nations served as a peace-keeping force. Smaller groups of nations with common interests created other organizations to oversee mutual defense, free-trade agreements, mutual economic interests, and the administration of international justice.

CHAPTER OBJECTIVES

- Discuss the Cold War; identify nations on both sides of the conflict.
- Describe the armed wars fought in Korea and Vietnam during the Cold War era.

- Describe the breakup of the old European colonial empires, specifically the achievement of independence in India and throughout Africa.

- Discuss developments in the United States, China, and Japan in the post–World War II era.

- Identify the various international organizations and treaties and discuss their importance.

Chapter 23 Time Line

1946	Winston Churchill gives "Iron Curtain" speech
1947	Independence of India
	Creation of Pakistan (former northeast India)
1948	Marshall Plan goes into effect
	State of Israel founded
1949	North Atlantic Treaty Organization (NATO) founded
	People's Republic of China founded
1950	Korean War begins
1953	Death of Stalin
1955	Warsaw Pact signed
1956	Hungarian uprising
1956–1962	Most African nations declare independence
1957	Treaty of Rome establishes European Economic Community (EEC; later, the European Union)
1960	Vietnam War begins
	Creation of OPEC
1961	East Germans put up Berlin Wall
1962	Cuban Missile Crisis
1964	Civil Rights Act in the United States
1966	Great Proletarian Cultural Revolution in China
1968	Prague Spring

●	1976	Death of Mao Zedong
●	1980	Formation of Solidarity in Poland
●	1985	Mikhail Gorbachev becomes head of Soviet Union
●	1989	Velvet Revolution in Czechoslovakia
		Grósz lifts Iron Curtain in Hungary
		Berlin Wall falls
		Communist governments throughout Eastern Europe fall
●	1990	East and West Germany are reunited
		Civil war begins in Yugoslavia
●	1991	Soviet Union is dissolved
		Commonwealth of Independent States is established

Communism Spreads Through Eastern Europe

In 1946, Winston Churchill made an important speech on the state of world affairs. He spoke the following memorable sentences:

> From Stettin in the Baltic to Trieste in the Adriatic, an iron curtain has descended across the Continent. Behind that line lie all the capitals of the ancient states of Central and Eastern Europe. Warsaw, Berlin, Prague, Vienna, Budapest, Belgrade, Bucharest and Sofia, all these famous cities and the populations around them lie in what I must call the Soviet sphere, and all are subject in one form or another not only to Soviet influence but to a very high and, in many cases, increasing measure of control from Moscow.

Between about 1944 and 1947, Churchill's analysis was proved correct. Every Eastern European nation except Greece either established a Communist state (usually called a "people's republic") or was absorbed into the Soviet Union (see Figure 23.1). One-party rule by a dictator was the most common form of government in these small states; all of them answered to the absolute authority of the Soviet dictator, just as Churchill had described. Stalin claimed that the USSR needed these allies as a safety zone between itself and the West

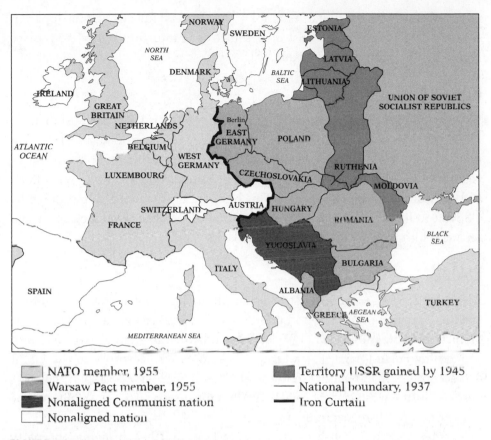

NATO member, 1955
Warsaw Pact member, 1955
Nonaligned Communist nation
Nonaligned nation

Territory USSR gained by 1945
—— National boundary, 1937
—— Iron Curtain

FIGURE 23.1 Europe During the Cold War

for its own security, to prevent any further repetitions of the devastating German invasions.

Czechoslovakia

After World War I, Edvard Beneš and Tomáš Masaryk had made Czechoslovakia a democratic republic. Subdued by the Nazi regime during World War II, the nation was reestablished in 1945 as an independent socialist state under President Beneš. In 1948, the Communist Party managed to shoulder Beneš aside, replacing him with Communist Klement Gottwald. Czechoslovakia struggled under an oppressive dictatorship until 1968, when the moderate Communist Alexander Dubček took power; in a brief burst of reform that became known as the Prague Spring, he abolished censorship and granted real legislative powers to the National Assembly. The Soviets, furious at this apparent defection from the Communist bloc, sent troops into the country to replace Dubček and restore the status quo.

Hungary

The Soviets drove the Nazis out of Hungary in 1944. In 1947, Stalinist dictator Mátyás Rákosi took power. Moderate Imre Nagy replaced Rákosi in 1953 but was forced out of office when he tried to introduce economic reform. Three years later, Nagy led a successful popular uprising, formed a new government, and instituted widespread reform. This brief era of freedom was put down by a Soviet military invasion in November 1956; the Soviets executed Nagy and replaced him with their own candidate, János Kádár.

Poland

After the 1939 German-Soviet invasion, the Polish leaders fled the country, eventually making their way to London. The Soviets installed a puppet regime of their own in Lublin in 1944. At Yalta, Stalin was granted two demands concerning Poland. First, Poland must give up eastern territory to the USSR and accept German territory in the west in exchange—in effect, both Poland's borders shifted westward. Second, the Allies must recognize the Lublin regime as the official Polish government.

The first postwar Polish elections were held in 1947, bringing one-party Communist rule to the nation. This marked the beginning of a long period of political and social unrest in Poland.

Yugoslavia

The state of Yugoslavia was highly unstable even before World War II broke out; it contained too many ethnic groups that would be satisfied only by self-determination. The Serbs were the dominant group and were thus the target of most of this resentment; the Croats hated the Serbs so much that they actually regarded the invading Nazis as liberators. Yugoslavs soon found themselves divided into two warring factions. The Chetniks were Serbian and royalist; the Partisans included Communists, anti-Nazis, and a variety of Yugoslavs who wanted to escape Serbian supremacy. In 1945, the Allies agreed to support Partisans leader Josip Broz, who had taken the alias Tito on his release from prison for political protest in 1933.

Although Marshall Tito ruled as a Communist dictator, he refused to recognize Soviet authority over Yugoslavia. When he expelled the occupying Russian military forces in 1948, the Comintern revoked his Party membership.

Germany

At Potsdam, the Allies agreed to occupy Germany. Their purposes were to purge Germany of Nazism and punish any surviving Nazis; to help the Germans set up a new, democratic government and a new bureaucracy, including a police force; and to reestablish society and the German economy.

The Soviets occupied the eastern half of Berlin; the western half was divided into American-, British-, and French-occupied zones The three Western powers united their zones into one for economic purposes; Stalin's refusal to include his zone in the plan effectively made Berlin into two cities.

Since Berlin was many miles behind the Iron Curtain, West Berlin was entirely isolated and geographically very vulnerable to threats from the Soviets. In 1948, the USSR blocked all ground access into West Berlin, claiming they had the right to do as they saw fit with East German roads, bridges, and railways. To counter this blatant attempt at a siege, the United States organized the Berlin Airlift, which brought in food, fuel, and other supplies by plane; on some days, a flight landed every few minutes. In 1949, the Soviets accepted defeat and ended the blockade. Soon after this, West Germany officially parted from East Germany. The Federal Republic of Germany (West) became a parliamentary democracy headed by Chancellor Konrad Adenauer, and the German Democratic Republic (East) became a one-party Communist state headed by Chancellor Walter Ulbricht.

During the 1950s, hundreds of thousands of East Germans emigrated by the simple means of walking or taking the metro to West Berlin, then relocating to West Germany or another Western nation. By 1961, nearly 20 percent of the East German population had defected. The East Germans and the Soviets knew that this westward flight was the worst possible publicity for their system, especially as so many of the emigrants were artists, professors, scientists, and other valuable and highly trained professionals. They therefore took drastic measures to halt the emigration. One August morning in 1961, Berliners woke up to discover that during the night, the army had begun construction of a physical barrier that entirely encircled West Berlin—a barbed-wire fence that would soon be replaced by a massive concrete wall, complete with armed guards and dogs.

From that time on, East Germans had to have special permits to cross the Berlin Wall and could only stay in the West for very limited periods of time. Travel from West to East Berlin was still unrestricted, but West Berliners had to carry identification proving their right to cross back over the border. West-bound Berlin metro trains now terminated on the eastern side of the barrier, and passengers on westbound international trains had to disembark in East Berlin if they were citizens of Iron Curtain nations.

Despite the armed guards, many people were still determined to escape the Communist society. Some hid in the trunks of cars; some clung to the under-carriage of trains; some openly made a run for it. Some escapes were successful; others ended in death. The Berlin Wall soon became the most recognizable symbol of the Cold War era. In June 1963, U.S. President John F. Kennedy gave a memorable speech on the western side of the wall, in which he summed up the basic flaw in the Communist system thus: "Freedom has many difficulties and democracy is not perfect, but we have never had to put a wall up to keep our people in—to prevent them from leaving us."

China After 1945

Having defeated the Kuomintang in the Chinese civil war, Mao Zedong estab-lished the People's Republic of China in 1949; China was now unified for the first time since the downfall of the Qing dynasty. Despite its name, the new nation was a one-party dictatorship. Voting rights meant nothing in a country where only one political party existed.

Foreign Relations

At first, China was hostile to the United States and friendly with the Soviet Union. By the 1970s, this situation had changed, partly because of border dis-putes between China and the USSR and partly due to Mao's resentment of Soviet attempts to interfere with him. In 1972, Richard Nixon became the first U.S. president to visit Communist China. Nixon and Chinese premier Zhou Enlai agreed to work together to maintain peace in the Pacific region and to develop trade relations. Nixon also agreed to withdraw U.S. troops from Taiwan if the Chinese would do the same in North Vietnam. Full diplomatic relations between China and the United States were established in 1979.

Domestic Policy

In 1958, Mao instituted a campaign known to history as the Great Leap Forward. Following the model created by Stalin, it called for the collectivization of Chinese farms. The program turned out to be badly named; the combination of collectivization with a series of natural disasters led to widespread crop failure and famine, with a death toll in the millions. Mao's attempts at boosting industrial production similarly failed.

By the mid-1960s, new men were beginning to challenge Mao's supremacy. To secure his position of power, Mao instituted the Great Proletarian Cultural Revolution in 1966. This called for the notorious policy known as "reeducation," in which anyone who appeared to have unorthodox ideas or who disagreed even slightly with Mao's own philosophy was ordered to work on a collective farm. In most cases, the victims were urban workers, often college graduates. The Cultural Revolution also saw censorship and bookburning and the rise of the Red Guards, student groups whose goal was to expose and denounce unorthodox activities and to promote and spread Mao's own teachings, which were spelled out in the famous *Little Red Book*.

Mao died in 1976; the more moderate rulers who succeeded him reversed many of his strictest policies. The Communist Party remains in power in China; examples of its insistence on control of the people include the 1989 massacre of public protestors at Tiananmen Square and the refusal to free political dissidents despite worldwide pressure. However, China has undergone a major economic recovery and, as it did in the days before the Opium Wars, enjoys an enormous international trade surplus.

International Organizations

Since the Communist and non-Communist members of the United Nations were mutually hostile and distrustful, many heads of state felt that they would do well to form smaller international unions for their mutual protection. Two such organizations were formed, the North Atlantic Treaty Organization (NATO) and the Warsaw Pact; members agreed that if any nation in their group were attacked, all the others would come to its defense (see Table 23.1).

Table 23.1 International Organizations			
Organization	**Date Formed**	**Members**	
North Atlantic Treaty Organization (NATO)	1947	Belgium	Luxembourg
		Britain	The Netherlands
		Canada	Norway
		Denmark	Portugal
		France	*Turkey
		*Greece	United States
		Iceland	*West Germany
Warsaw Pact	1955	Albania	Hungary
		Bulgaria	Poland
		Czechoslovakia	Romania
		East Germany	Soviet Union

* nation that joined NATO after 1947

Rebuilding Europe

When Communist forces took over Czechoslovakia in 1948, the U.S. Congress realized the seriousness of the Soviet threat to European democracy. They voted for full funding of the European Recovery Program, universally known as the Marshall Plan in honor of the U.S. secretary of state who created it. The United States offered an outright gift of enough money to repair Europe's cities, highways, and railways—the final total came to $13 billion. Stalin, who regarded the Marshall Plan as a blatant American attempt to subjugate Western Europe, would not allow any nation behind the Iron Curtain to accept American aid.

Thanks to its own superhuman efforts plus the boost provided by the Marshall Plan, Western Europe returned to normal much faster than anyone would have expected, given the destruction wrought by the war. Many difficulties, including food shortages and rationing, still existed for some time after the war, but a genuine spirit of cooperation grew up among Western nations, including the United States. With everyone working busily to rebuild and repair, employment was high and the atmosphere was one of courage and hope. Eastern nations also had to repair and rebuild, but without the freedom to choose their own employment, to form trade unions, or to install the latest technology, they felt less of a personal stake in the outcome. The atmosphere was one of stagnation and resignation.

Communist rule meant full employment, but jobs were assigned without regard to individual preference and wages were low. Housing was overcrowded—for example, an entire Russian family typically shared a one-room apartment without a private kitchen or bathroom. Necessities were always in short supply and luxury goods were a thing of the past. Long lines of customers would appear as if by magic when word got out that a market had just received a load of fresh eggs or potatoes, as it might be the last chance to buy potatoes or eggs for a month or more. People carried shopping bags called "perhaps-bags" everywhere they went, just in case—perhaps—there might be something to buy and carry home. Barter, rather than cash purchases, became common. The state owned and ran all businesses and industries, so no one had any personal pride or vested interest in doing a good job or seeing his or her business succeed.

Rebuilding Japan

After the Japanese surrender in 1945, the American military occupied Japan. The goal was similar to the occupation of Berlin: to help the Japanese rebuild their infrastructure and economy. American General Douglas MacArthur was in charge of this massive undertaking. It included the restoration of democratic government instead of the military rule that had characterized Japan during the 1930s. The new Japanese constitution included important social reforms such as freedom of the press and equal rights for women. The most notable provision of the constitution was an absolute ban on Japanese participation in, or declaration of, war. To this day, Japan maintains an army solely for the purposes of defense; only recently has it begun contributing troops to international peacekeeping missions.

The rebuilding of Japan was so successful in such short order that the U.S. occupying forces withdrew in 1952, after both sides signed a treaty that cemented friendly relations between these formerly bitter enemies. Japan also restored peaceful diplomatic relations with China, Korea, and the Soviet Union.

With no call to spend much on its small and purely defensive military, Japan was able to invest heavily in rebuilding its commerce and industry. Economic growth was astonishingly rapid. By 1960, Japan had become an economic superpower—the world's largest exporter of high-quality manufactured goods at reasonable prices.

The Creation of Israel

In the wake of the Holocaust, thousands of European Jews were left homeless and with a growing conviction that they required their own country and their own army so that they could defend themselves from future persecution. The United Nations decided in 1947 to divide Palestine, which had become a British mandate in 1920, into separate Jewish and Arab states. This provoked civil war between Jews and Arabs in Palestine; when the state of Israel was formally declared in 1948, the war turned into a conflict between Jewish Israelis on one side and the Arab states of Syria, Egypt, and Iraq on the other. The war ended in victory for Israel in 1949. Although Israel claims to be a parliamentary democracy, it is a two-tier society, with Jews enjoying greater privileges and opportunities and a higher standard of living than Arabs.

Armed violence continues to this day between Israel and its Arab neighbors. Control over Jerusalem is a major factor in the hostility. So is Israeli occupation of the West Bank and Gaza—land to which Israel has no rights, according to the beliefs of the Arabs and many others in the international community. The United States has played a leading role in a number of attempts to broker peace settlements between Israel and the Palestinians, but none has succeeded. Israel continues to claim that its belligerence is necessary for its own defense; the combination of open hostility between Jews and Arabs in the region plus Israel's nuclear capacity has raised international concern.

Cold-War Conflicts

Until 1949, only the United States had the technology to make nuclear weapons. When Soviet scientists built their own bomb in 1949, a nuclear arms race ensued. The possession of nuclear weapons made both superpowers very cautious. The bombing of Japan had proved exactly how destructive such weapons were; neither side in the Cold War wanted to cause a nuclear holocaust. However, they played key roles in two conventional wars and arrived at one dangerous standoff.

Korean War

When Japan surrendered in 1945, it lost control of Korea. After the war, the victorious Allied leaders agreed to divide Korea geographically. The Soviets occupied the industrial North, which was proclaimed the Korean Democratic People's Republic under chairman Kim Il Sung in 1948. The Americans occupied the agricultural South, withdrawing in 1949 after Syngman Rhee was elected president of the Republic of Korea. In 1950, North Korea invaded South Korea, intending to unite the divided nation under Communist rule. U.S. troops fought on the side of South Korea, while Communist China sent troops to aid the North Koreans. Fighting ended with a 1953 truce that left matters where they were in 1950—with two independent Koreas, one Communist, one democratic.

Cuban Missile Crisis

The closest the world came to nuclear war was an event known as the Cuban Missile Crisis. In 1959, rebel leader Fidel Castro seized power, turning Cuba into a Communist dictatorship. The presence of a Soviet ally ninety miles from the U.S. coast was a grave concern to the Americans. The Bay of Pigs invasion—a botched American attempt to remove Castro from power—increased Cold War hostility between the superpowers.

Soviet premier Nikita Khrushchev, Stalin's successor, first met U.S. President John F. Kennedy at a European summit and mistook Kennedy's youth and inexperience for weakness. Believing the United States would be easy to intimidate, Khrushchev began building up nuclear arms in Cuba. In response, the United States established a naval blockade of the island. Both sides prepared for battle, but, at the last moment, the Soviet ships turned back. Khrushchev offered Kennedy an exchange; if the United States would withdraw its nuclear missiles from its European bases, the USSR would do the same with the Cuban missiles. Nuclear war had been avoided. From that time forward, both sides worked slowly and cautiously toward achieving what later became known as *détente*, loosely translated "peaceful coexistence."

Vietnam War

France controlled what it called Indochina—Vietnam, Laos, and Cambodia—from 1883 to 1945. Japan occupied Indochina during World War II; when the Japanese withdrew, rebel leader Ho Chi Minh declared Vietnamese independence. The United States backed France's refusal to grant independence for two reasons: first, because Ho was a Communist, and second, because the United States was a longtime French ally. Communist China supported Ho and his followers, the Vietminh, who defeated the French at Dien Bien Phu in 1954.

France, Britain, the United States, the USSR, China, Vietnam, Cambodia, and Laos all met for a peace conference in Geneva. The conference ended in a stalemate, dividing Vietnam into a northern half ruled by Ho and the Vietminh and a southern half ruled by France. The representatives agreed that in 1956, the two Vietnams would hold general elections and reunite under one government.

With American backing, government official Ngo Dinh Diem became president of South Vietnam. Widely and deservedly unpopular, Diem refused to hold the agreed-on election because he was certain he would lose. Meanwhile, the Vietminh began sending weapons to their allies and supporters in the South—this rebel force would become known as the Vietcong.

Fighting dragged on from the early 1960s through 1975, with the Vietminh and Vietcong fighting a jungle guerrilla war in a method that the Westerners could never master. French troops abandoned the area in 1956; the Americans held out much longer, finally acknowledging in 1975 that they had reached an impasse. The war ended in a victory for the Communists, who were quick to unite the two halves of the nation under their rule.

The United States: The Civil Rights Movement

By the 1960s, the continuing oppression of African Americans was becoming an international embarrassment to the United States. Americans were horrified and repelled by Hitler's atrocities toward Jews and Romany in Europe; after the war ended, they realized that their own Jim Crow policies were equally indefensible. In 1948, President Truman issued executive orders integrating the armed forces and the federal bureaucracy. By the mid-1950s, federal legislation and important Supreme Court decisions had desegregated public schools and public transportation. In 1960, the Student Nonviolent Coordinating Committee (SNCC, pronounced "snick") began staging sit-ins at segregated restaurants throughout the South. The Southern Christian Leadership Conference, under the leadership of Martin Luther King, Jr., organized other nonviolent protests. The quiet, well-behaved protesters, exercising their First Amendment right to "peaceably assemble," provided a strong contrast to the brutal armed policemen and the jeering crowds of segregationists. The protesters won public opinion over to their side, and, by 1964, the Civil Rights Act had been signed into law, ending segregation in fact about one hundred years after the civil rights amendments to the Constitution had ended it in law. However, racism continues to be a problem throughout the United States to this day.

The End of the European Empires

One of the major consequences of World War II was the dismantling of what remained of the European colonial empires. The reasons were twofold. First, the former Great Powers of Western Europe were badly impoverished by the war; they had no resources to spare for colonial administration. Second, the forces of nationalism caused public uprisings and eventual independence throughout two vast areas of the world—Africa and India.

Africa: The Achievement of Self-Determination

Most of Europe's African colonies achieved their independence in the early 1960s. In the decades since the great wave of European colonization (see Chapter 19), African nationalism had become a powerful force. Apart from the nations along the continent's northern coast, Africa played no direct role in World War II.

As the European powers worked to rebuild after the war, they turned to their African colonies for raw materials. Because of the colonial relationship, the buyer, in this case the European nation, could set the prices; thus, the African colonies were exploited.

World War II deprived the African colonies of many of their European civil servants and bureaucrats. In their place, a new, educated African elite found that it was quite capable of administering its own people. With colonization no longer economically viable after World War II and feeling newly capable and strong, the African colonies began the drive toward independence. This was achieved peacefully in some colonies and violently in others. For example, Ghana's transition to independence in 1957, under Kwame Nkrumah, was relatively peaceful; after a period of autocracy and a military coup, Ghana eventually settled down as a constitutional republic. On the other hand, armed disruption and rioting characterized the Congo's declaration of independence from Belgium in 1960 under Prime Minister Patrice Lumumba, former head of the Congolese National Movement. The province of Katanga declared its independence from the Congo, adding further confusion to the chaos. Lumumba was kidnapped and murdered, apparently by U.S. and Belgian agreement. The

Congo has since undergone several rebellions, changes of government (many rife with corruption), economic crises, failed peacekeeping missions, and terrorist violence. It is unsettled to this day.

Figure 23.2 shows Africa in the postcolonial era. Compare this with the map in Chapter 19.

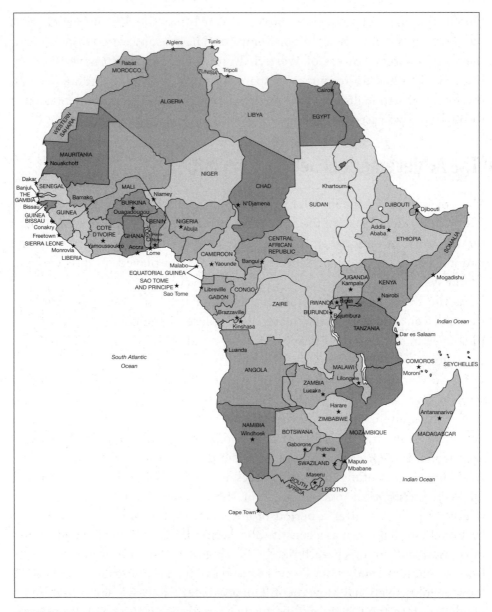

FIGURE 23.2 Independent Africa

The Partition of India

In the period following World War I, Indian nationalism grew. It was personified by Mohandas Gandhi, who called for nonviolent protest against British oppression. Gandhi's approach would strongly influence Martin Luther King, leader of the American Civil Rights Movement of the 1960s. Gandhi's followers, the Indian National Congress Party (NCP), reflected the Hindu majority; their main goal was independence from Britain. Meanwhile, the Muslim League, which had existed since 1906, hoped to create an independent Islamic state for India's sizeable Muslim population; League leadership had no faith in the possibility of Muslim equality in a Hindu-dominated India.

At first, Britain reacted with contempt to the Indian independence movement; the British genuinely believed that Indians were incapable of self-government. Their first response was repression; both Gandhi and Jawarhalal Nehru were political prisoners for a time. Britain made enough concessions in 1935 that Indians—particularly NCP members—achieved control of most of the provincial governments.

World War II was the decisive factor in Indian independence. Economically, Britain could no longer afford to govern India. In 1947, India became two independent nations: a Hindu India, led by Prime Minister Nehru, and a Muslim Pakistan, led by the Muslim League's President, Muhammad Ali Jinnah. The new state of Pakistan was actually two widely separated regions, West Pakistan in the extreme northwest and East Pakistan in the extreme northeast (East Pakistan would later become the independent state of Bangladesh). Anticipation of religious persecution caused massive migration of Hindus and Sikhs from Pakistan into India and of Muslims from India into East and West Pakistan. However, India remains more than 10 percent Muslim. Tensions between India and Pakistan, including conflict over the region of Kashmir, and Indian fear of Chinese aggression led both nations to develop nuclear capability.

The Rise of the Middle East

A massive demand for oil in the post–World War II era led to an enormous economic change in the Middle East. As the source of most of the world's oil, the region leapt into a position of international consequence and great prosperity almost overnight. In 1960, five of the Arab nations created OPEC—the Organization of Petroleum-Exporting Countries—with the purpose of regulating oil prices and controlling the supply of oil to the rest of the world. Today, OPEC has twelve member nations, including four in Africa and two in South America.

With the exception of democratic Turkey, the Middle Eastern states are either military dictatorships or monarchies. Both types of government exercise strict control over the press. Conservative Islamic leaders provide constant pressure to revoke ordinary rights and privileges from the people, particularly women. In the post–Cold War era, the area has been politically volatile. (See the Afterword.)

Soviet Leadership After Stalin

The Death of Stalin

The major turning point in the rise and fall of the Soviet Union took place in 1953 with the death of seventy-four-year-old Joseph Stalin. The Soviet heads of state who succeeded Stalin would never impress their personalities on the nation as he had done; they lacked both his brutality and his insistence on personal control over every aspect of Soviet life as well as Soviet government.

Stalin had deceived the United States and the world into believing that the USSR was much stronger militarily than was in fact the case. In truth, so many millions of Soviets had been killed during the wars and the western region of the country had been so badly damaged by the German invasions that the USSR would take a long time to recover. Stalin created an atmosphere of secrecy and mystery that was highly successful in maintaining the illusion of the Soviet state as a mighty superpower. The purpose of his bluff was mainly defensive; he wanted at all costs to prevent an American attack on the USSR. In fact, there was never any real danger of such an attack; the United States had no desire to engage in all-out war with the Soviet Union unless such a situation absolutely could not be avoided. Stalin, however, considered the capitalist United States his natural enemy and always believed in the danger of an American attack.

The Thaw

A gradual thaw in Soviet foreign and domestic policy followed Stalin's death. Beginning with a 1956 speech in which Khrushchev denounced Stalin's crimes against humanity, the cult of personality that Stalin had cultivated began to fade; he was no longer officially venerated in the USSR. This "de-Stalinization" process helped lead to the Hungarian revolution of 1956 (see "Hungary" earlier in this chapter).

Khrushchev also oversaw substantial domestic reforms. Although he could not have predicted the eventual breakup of the Soviet Union, he helped lay the groundwork for it by decentralizing the bureaucracy, shifting authority from Moscow to the fifteen individual republics. He also relaxed censorship in the arts, although he did not by any means eliminate it. New agricultural policies led to a short-term economic surge. In addition, Khrushchev presided over the space race, in which Soviet astronaut Yuri Gagarin became the first person to orbit the Earth.

In 1964, Communist leaders forced Khrushchev to resign; he lost support due to a downturn in the economy and long-standing discontent with some of his policies. His successor, Leonid Brezhnev, is most notable for signing the Strategic Arms Limitation Talks (SALT) Treaty with U.S. President Richard Nixon. This treaty limited the number of intercontinental nuclear missiles for both nations. In addition, the two leaders discussed relaxing trade restrictions between their countries.

The milder political climate under Stalin's successors gave the Soviet people the courage to begin giving open expression to their discontent with social and political conditions. A particularly sore point was the inequality in living conditions. The Party elite lived in comparative luxury, with expensive cars and nice apartments, while the workers were badly housed, poorly paid, and had little access to consumer goods or even much choice in basic items like groceries. Since the Communist ideal was equality for all citizens, this had long caused resentment among the people. For the first time, that resentment began to find public expression.

Soviet intellectuals, artists, and even ordinary workers were especially opposed to censorship in the arts; they considered it an international embarrassment, particularly in the nation that had produced Leo Tolstoy, Aleksandr Pushkin, and Anton Chekhov. Unfortunately, it would be some time before censorship was revoked. Boris Pasternak, an acclaimed poet and the author of the novel *Dr. Zhivago*, was ordered to refuse the 1958 Nobel Prize for literature, and Aleksandr Solzhenitsyn was deprived of his Soviet citizenship because he wrote honestly about the gulags (the notorious Soviet prison camps).

The Gorbachev Era

In 1985, Mikhail Gorbachev became the head of the Soviet Union. Although he was a Communist, Gorbachev knew that the old policies were failing. He instituted policies of *glasnost* (openness) and *perestroika* (a restructuring of the economy and society). *Glasnost* was intended to encourage open debate about the economic and social challenges facing the USSR; Gorbachev believed the problems were so vast that they demanded input from all segments of society, not just Party members. He relaxed censorship to demonstrate his seriousness about wishing writers and intellectuals to discuss and help improve conditions.

Perestroika called for increases in foreign trade and reductions on military spending. During a 1987 meeting with U.S. President Ronald Reagan, Gorbachev signed the Intermediate-Range Nuclear Forces Treaty, eliminating all medium-range nuclear missiles from Europe. This made Gorbachev very unpopular with the Soviet military, who were convinced he had made the USSR vulnerable to attack.

In 1988, Gorbachev thoroughly reorganized the Soviet government. He called for a Congress of People's Deputies whose members would then elect the Supreme Soviet (the federal legislative assembly). This transformed the Supreme Soviet from a rubber stamp for the Communist Party into a powerful lawmaking body. One-third of the deputies for the Congress represented the interests of the many nationalities within the USSR, one-third were freely elected on a geographical basis, and one-third were directly nominated by major institutions such as the Orthodox Church, the trade unions, and the Communist Party. The new Supreme Soviet was bicameral and would meet twice a year for three- or four-month sessions. The era of one-party rule in the Soviet Union was over; non-Communists were allowed to run for office at the national, republic, and local levels in 1989.

In July 1988, due to a severe economic slump and in acknowledgment of the changed atmosphere in Eastern Europe, Gorbachev announced that the Soviet Union would withdraw from any interference in the self-government of other nations. Eastern Europe would have to take care of itself from now on; the Soviet Union could no longer afford to control and monitor nations outside its own borders. By 1990, due to a combination of Soviet withdrawal and popular uprisings, all the Communist governments of Eastern Europe had fallen.

The Breakup of the Soviet Union

In 1991, Communist Party leaders attempted a coup against Gorbachev, who had been losing popularity due to a severe economic crisis and the Communist Party's dismay at the loss of Soviet influence in Europe. Additionally, the Baltic republics had been agitating for self-determination.

The actual coup attempt failed, but it gave the Baltic republics the opportunity to seize their independence. Gorbachev realized that he could no longer hold the Soviet Union together. In late 1991, all the Soviet republics became independent nation-states; all except Latvia, Lithuania, and Estonia formed an association known as the Commonwealth of Independent States (CIS). This association is a successor to the USSR, which was officially dissolved on December 31, 1991. CIS members are entirely independent, self-governing nations; the CIS unites them for purposes of security, economics, internal and external trade, and justice.

The End of the Cold War in Europe

The basic philosophy behind communism is that each person should contribute what he or she can to society and the economy and take as much as he or she needs. Most would agree that such an idea is compassionate, generous, and fair. Unfortunately, communism in practice did not reflect its philosophy. It meant censorship and oppression. When people are not permitted to say what they think, to write what they please, to travel where they wish, or to describe accurately the conditions in which they live, they are not free. Communism was intolerable to many precisely because it refused to allow such freedom. Throughout the Cold War, Eastern Europeans resisted it—some vocally, some silently, but all consistently. Without their courageous resistance, communism would not have fallen throughout Europe in the way that it did.

Poland

In 1978, international attention focused on Poland when Karol Cardinal Wojtyla became Pope John Paul II—the first non-Italian to hold the Catholic Church's highest office since the early 1500s. The Polish government's desire to shine in the spotlight played a significant role in bringing about political reform.

Beginning in 1980, soaring prices led Polish laborers to stage a series of strikes and to demand the right to form trade unions. Winning their point in September, the workers formed Solidarity, a national council to coordinate independent trade unions. Solidarity members wanted real reform, not just higher wages: a union's right to strike, the release of imprisoned dissenters, and the lifting of censorship. Dock worker Lech Walesa, who headed Solidarity, would later become the president of a democratic Poland.

The Polish government was naturally hostile to Solidarity, which had made itself a national political party rather than just a labor organization. Despite an outright 1981 ban on Solidarity, the political tide had turned in Poland. By 1989, the government was forced to legalize Solidarity once again; the party swept the elections held that year. These events, combined with Gorbachev's public withdrawal of Soviet influence in Iron Curtain nations, thrust aside the Communist Party in Poland for good.

Hungary

Although several years of Stalinist repression had followed the 1956 rebellion, Hungary had been gradually flexing its political muscles since the Soviet thaw of the early 1960s. In 1968, Hungary announced the New Economic Mechanism, which removed state controls on the market and allowed for free enterprise. Károly Grósz, who took office in 1987, supported Gorbachev's policies; with the 1989 withdrawal of Soviet interference in Hungarian affairs, Grósz ordered the opening of the border between Hungary and Austria. This was the first official lifting of any part of the Iron Curtain and caused an immediate flood of Eastern European immigrants into Hungary and thence across the border.

Czechoslovakia

In the wake of Communist crackdowns meant to prevent the workers from uniting in imitation of Solidarity, popular demonstrations occurred in the streets of Prague and other cities in the fall of 1989. In a series of events known as the Velvet Revolution, the Communist premier Gustav Husak resigned and was replaced within the month by the democratically elected Vaclav Havel. Alexander Dubček, the hero of the Prague Spring, became the head of the Czechoslovak Parliament. Long-standing ethnic hostility between Czechs and Slovaks caused the 1993 separation of Czechoslovakia into two nations—Slovakia (also called the Slovak Republic) and the Czech Republic.

East Germany

Perhaps the most emotional and dramatic moment of the entire Cold War came on November 9, 1989, when the Berlin Wall came tumbling down.

In the wake of Gorbachev's official visit to Berlin in October, German travel restrictions were relaxed in early November. On the evening of November 9, one ill-prepared official, flustered by a reporter's question, announced that the new rules would "immediately" take effect at the border. East Berliners flooded to the Berlin Wall checkpoints in such huge crowds that the guards could not hold them back. By midnight, young Germans were attacking the wall on both sides with sledgehammers and pickaxes, clambering to the top and pulling up their friends to dance and cheer alongside them. Berliners poured freely through the Brandenburg Gate in both directions for the first time since 1961. During the following weeks, border restrictions throughout Eastern Europe were removed, and Easterners could freely travel to the West once again. In 1990, East and West Germany were formally reunited under one government. After nearly fifty years, the Iron Curtain had come down.

Yugoslavia

Marshall Tito governed Yugoslavia from 1945 until his death in 1980, managing to keep the mutually hostile forces of ethnic nationalism under control. In the great revolutionary year of 1989, however, civil war broke out. Serbians wanted to dominate the power structure of the nation, while Croatians, Macedonians, Slovenians, and Bosnians agitated for independence and self-determination. Fierce and bloody fighting among the various ethnic groups continued through 1995. By 2008, Yugoslavia had broken up into independent states—Slovenia, Croatia, Bosnia-Herzegovina, Serbia, Montenegro, and Macedonia.

The European Union

The foundation of the European Union goes back to the 1957 Treaty of Rome. This treaty began as a Franco-German agreement to create an international organization that would administer the coal-rich region on their border so that all of Europe could benefit from the coal. In 1957, what was then called the European Economic Community (EEC) and the European Atomic Energy Commission had six members: France, West Germany, Belgium, the Netherlands, Luxembourg, and Italy. In addition to overseeing coal production, the nations lifted tariffs among themselves, thus encouraging internal trade, and agreed to establish common tariffs for imports from non-EEC nations. Membership expanded in 1973; in 1991, the present European Union (EU) was founded with fifteen member nations. Between 2004 and 2007, membership was extended to almost all the nations of Eastern Europe.

Member nations of the EU are entirely separate and self-governing, but they share a common foreign and security policy and cooperate on domestic affairs and affairs of international justice. Since 1999, the EU nations have also had a shared currency, the euro. Member states are required to have stable, freely elected governments; to guarantee basic rights and protections to their citizens; to manage their economies; and to abide by EU laws and treaties.

QUIZ

1. _____ issues provided the primary motivation for the creation of the European Economic Community/European Union.
   A. Cultural
   B. Philosophical
   C. Economic
   D. Political

2. The political concept of *glasnost* welcomes _____.
   A. free expression of political opinions
   B. universal suffrage for adults
   C. the lifting of restrictions on travel
   D. the establishment of a strong legislature

3. Which best describes the change in the Soviet government after the death of Stalin?
   A. It became substantially more harsh and repressive.
   B. It became somewhat less repressive.
   C. It became more centralized.
   D. It became radically more democratic.

4. Indians who supported the partition of their nation were determined to achieve _____.
   A. religious self-determination
   B. ethnic separatism
   C. popular democracy
   D. freedom from British domination

5. **The Marshall Plan offered aid to _____.**
   A. all the nations of Europe
   B. all nations behind the Iron Curtain
   C. all nations that had fought for the Allies during the war
   D. all nations west of the Iron Curtain

6. **The Berlin Wall was built in order to _____.**
   A. prevent Westerners from entering East Berlin
   B. prevent East Germans from entering West Berlin
   C. block Allied or Western access to West Berlin
   D. prevent violence from breaking out in Berlin

7. **At the end of the civil war in Vietnam, the North and South were united under _____ .**
   A. a constitutional monarchy
   B. a democratic republic
   C. a Communist dictatorship
   D. a hereditary monarchy

8. **_____ was one advantage of life under Communist rule.**
   A. Freedom of expression
   B. Comfortable housing
   C. High wages
   D. Full employment

9. **Which best describes the purpose of the Red Guards in China?**
   A. to take up arms in China's defense when called upon
   B. to expose behavior that appeared to criticize the government
   C. to provide the dictator with a loyal personal bodyguard
   D. to administer the collectivization of Chinese farms

10. **_____ is unique among the world's nations for its constitutional ban on participation in war.**
    A. India
    B. Japan
    C. The United States
    D. Germany

PART THREE EXAM

1. What was the main factor in the economic crisis that led to the French Revolution?
   A. reform of the French tax system
   B. major public-works projects in the cities
   C. excessive spending on the military
   D. the personal extravagance of the royal family

2. The Ottomans repeatedly attempted to capture the city of _____ in an attempt to gain a foothold in Europe.
   A. Constantinople
   B. Athens
   C. Rome
   D. Vienna

3. During the revolutionary period and the civil war in Russia, members of the old guard _____ by the thousands.
   A. joined the Red Army
   B. emigrated to the West
   C. committed suicide
   D. ran for political office

4. As a result of the Taiping Rebellion, the Manchu government _____.
   A. lost most of its effective control of China
   B. came to an abrupt end
   C. instituted sweeping reforms to modernize China
   D. revoked many human rights and freedoms

5. What effect did the first Five-Year Plan have on the Russian peasants?
   A. They gained the right to own their own land.
   B. They were forced to work on collective farms.
   C. They gained the right to vote.
   D. They lost the right to vote.

6. _____ was established after World War II as an international peacekeeping organization.
   A. The Quadruple Alliance
   B. The League of Nations
   C. The United Nations
   D. The Warsaw Pact

7. Spain and Portugal's Latin American colonies gained their independence in the wake of, and partly as a result of, which important European event?
   A. the French Revolution
   B. the Peninsular War
   C. the demise of the Holy Roman Empire
   D. the Crimean War

8. In the Arab Revolt of 1916, the Bedouin tribes drove _____ out of the Arabian Peninsula.
   A. the Israelis
   B. France
   C. Britain
   D. the Ottoman Turks

9. All these European nations were major participants in the African slave trade except _____
   A. Britain
   B. France
   C. Italy
   D. Portugal

10. One major reason the Latin American *creoles* desired independence from Spain was _____.
    A. they were born and raised in Spain
    B. they had more experience at politics and government than other social ranks
    C. they were socially and politically subordinate to the *peninsulares*
    D. they were eager to establish military dictatorships

11. Which person was considered the lowest in the social scale of Tokugawa Japan?
    A. an artisan
    B. a samurai
    C. a farmer
    D. a merchant

12. The language, culture, and artistic styles of _____ dominated the great Islamic empires of the 1600s.
    A. the Turks
    B. India
    C. Persia
    D. Egypt

13. Motives for European colonization in the sixteenth century included all of the following except the desire to _____.
    A. enlarge one's power base
    B. establish independent new nations
    C. convert "heathen" populations to Christianity
    D. discover viable sea routes to Asia

14. The Industrial Revolution began in Britain because of Britain's _____.
    A. year-round temperate climate
    B. northern European location
    C. stable government and society
    D. role in the Enlightenment

15. The only South American nation to achieve independence peacefully was _____.
    A. Brazil
    B. Guiana
    C. Venezuela
    D. Ecuador

16. Which two nations were allies in the Seven Years' War / French and Indian War?
    A. Austria and Britain
    B. Britain and Prussia
    C. Prussia and Austria
    D. Britain and France

17. The USSR installed nuclear missiles in Cuba in order to _____.
    A. expand its power base
    B. make an ally of Cuba
    C. intimidate the United States
    D. fulfill a United Nations requirement

18. As a result of an agreement with Mussolini, the Catholic Church _____ in 1929.
    A. ceded control of the public-school system
    B. officially recognized the state of Italy
    C. supported the underground anti-Fascist movement
    D. shut down its seminaries throughout Italy

19. All the following nations remained absolute monarchies throughout the nineteenth century except _____.
    A. Austria
    B. France
    C. Prussia
    D. Russia

20. The Ottoman Empire lost much of its North African territory to _____ during the nineteenth century.
    A. Egypt
    B. France
    C. Italy
    D. China

21. _____ was the first European power in the modern era to establish trade relations with India.
    A. Britain
    B. France
    C. The Netherlands
    D. Portugal

22. The Progressive era in American politics lasted from about _____.
    A. 1850 to 1860
    B. 1880 to 1900
    C. 1900 to 1920
    D. 1930 to 1940

23. American _____ was the fundamental motive for the American Revolution.
    A. bitterness over having lost the French and Indian War
    B. refusal to accept taxation without representation
    C. desire to rewrite the colonial charters
    D. hope to expand their borders westward

24. The _____ provided an important shortcut for ships trading between Europe and Asia.
   A. Mediterranean Sea
   B. Panama Canal
   C. Suez Canal
   D. Adriatic Sea

25. In the 1850s, _____ became the first nation to use "gunboat diplomacy" to force Japan to open its ports for international trade.
   A. Britain
   B. the Netherlands
   C. Russia
   D. the United States

26. _____ is notable for being the only Communist head of state in Eastern Europe to successfully defy the authority of the Soviet Union.
   A. Vaclav Havel
   B. Josip Broz (Tito)
   C. Walter Ulbricht
   D. Konrad Adenauer

27. Egypt was strategically important to the European economy because of the presence of _____.
   A. the Suez Canal
   B. the Orange Free State
   C. diamonds and gold
   D. mineral deposits

28. What was the purpose of the Iwakura Mission of 1871?
   A. to rewrite the Japanese constitution
   B. to share Japanese arts and culture with the Western world
   C. to study Western political, legal, and economic systems
   D. to convert Westerners to Buddhism

29. In 1870, the southern German states allied themselves with Prussia and the north German confederation against their common enemy _____.
   A. Austria
   B. Britain
   C. France
   D. Russia

30. Which two forms of government amount to exactly the same thing?
    A. communism and fascism
    B. communism and anarchism
    C. fascism and republicanism
    D. democracy and fascism

31. The term *Velvet Revolution* refers to a regime change in _____ in 1989.
    A. Czechoslovakia
    B. East Germany
    C. Poland
    D. Yugoslavia

32. Which best describes the goal of the Committee of Union and Progress, also known as the Young Turks?
    A. to expand the Ottoman Empire into central Europe
    B. to add Safavid Persia to the Ottoman Empire
    C. to modernize and westernize the Ottoman Empire
    D. to make Turkey a culturally European nation-state

33. Which nineteenth-century political philosophy was most likely to appeal to the poorer classes of society?
    A. conservatism
    B. liberalism
    C. Marxism
    D. nationalism

34. Politically, the National Front in 1930s Spain is best described as _____.
    A. Communist
    B. socialist
    C. conservative
    D. democratic

35. Control of Java in the nineteenth century was very valuable to the Dutch for _____ reasons.
    A. economic
    B. political
    C. imperialistic
    D. missionary

36. All of the following are major composers of the Romantic Movement in Europe except _____.
    A. Frédéric Chopin
    B. Franz Joseph Haydn
    C. Giuseppe Verdi
    D. Richard Wagner

37. The activities of Christian missionaries after about 1800 had all these positive practical effects on sub-Saharan Africa except _____.
    A. to provide much-needed medicines and medical care
    B. to open schools and thus spread literacy in both African and European languages
    C. to combat harmful primitive customs such as human sacrifice
    D. to put an end to intertribal warfare

38. _____ took over most of the Vietnamese peninsula, which became known as the Union of Indochina under its authority.
    A. China
    B. France
    C. Britain
    D. The Netherlands

39. What motivated most combat veterans of World War I to support Fascist leaders?
    A. extreme nationalism
    B. economic concerns
    C. income-tax issues
    D. the desire for peace

40. In the Sepoy Rebellion of 1857, India rose up against the occupying forces of _____.
    A. Britain
    B. China
    C. the Netherlands
    D. the Ottoman Turks

41. Trench warfare during World War I resulted in a stalemate primarily because of _____.
    A. the technological changes in weapons
    B. the imbalance in numbers of troops on the two sides
    C. the location of the trenches in central Europe
    D. the lack of sufficient weapons, rations, and other supplies

42. **Prime Minister Azaña of Spain was forced out of office due to the opposition of the _____.**
    A. reformers
    B. liberals
    C. workers
    D. establishment

43. **Korea was under the control of _____ from 1905 to 1945.**
    A. China
    B. Japan
    C. Russia/USSR
    D. the United States

44. **In Tokugawa Japan, the _____ became more prosperous as the *daimyos* became less so.**
    A. samurai
    B. emperor
    C. merchants
    D. shoguns

45. **Which best describes the shift in thinking between the Scientific Revolution of the seventeenth century and the Enlightenment of the eighteenth century?**
    A. a rebirth of interest in Classical values and ideas
    B. a falling-off of the belief in the omnipotence of God
    C. a new interest in discovering how the universe functioned
    D. a reawakening of conservative ideas and ways of thinking

46. **Traders from _____ were the only Westerners allowed any access to Japan once Tokugawa Ieyasu closed all the ports.**
    A. England
    B. the Netherlands
    C. France
    D. the United States

47. **Mughal emperor Akbar's greatest contribution to India was _____.**
    A. his introduction of Persian artistic styles
    B. his value as a unifying force in a land of diverse peoples
    C. his insistence on maintaining the old ways
    D. his personal supervision of every aspect of government

48. **The Meiji Restoration of nineteenth-century Japan is best known for the emperor's decision to _____.**
    A. close off the kingdom to all outsiders
    B. collectivize small independent farms throughout the islands
    C. modernize the entire social and political order
    D. allow young Japanese to go abroad to study

49. **All of the following individuals made significant contributions to the abolition of slavery in the United States except _____.**
    A. John Brown
    B. Frederick Douglass
    C. John Wilkes Booth
    D. Harriet Beecher Stowe

50. **The Great Powers redrew the European map at Versailles in 1915 in order to _____.**
    A. create new states on the basis of a population's ethnic identity
    B. take Russian territory away from the new Communist government
    C. create an alliance between Germany and France
    D. eliminate the need for European nations to maintain standing armies

Final Exam

1. The earliest human civilization was located _____.
   A. on the Pacific coast
   B. in the Near East
   C. on the Indian subcontinent
   D. on the steppes of Central Asia

2. Which was the first nation to establish settled colonies in North America?
   A. England
   B. France
   C. Germany
   D. Spain

3. Iron Curtain nations refused to accept Marshall Plan aid because _____.
   A. they blamed Germany for destroying the European economy
   B. there was too much distrust between the former Allied and Axis nations
   C. they knew they would never be able to repay the United States
   D. Stalin refused to allow any ties between his satellites and his only strong national rival

4. Which aspect of Chinese culture or tradition was most enthusiastically embraced in early Japan?
   A. Confucianism
   B. merit examinations for government posts
   C. literary and artistic styles
   D. occasional changes of the imperial dynasty

5. At the end of the Thirty Years' War, _____ emerged as the dominant European power.

    A. England
    B. France
    C. the Holy Roman Empire
    D. Sweden

6. The religious beliefs and social structure that characterize Hinduism are based on _____.

    A. individualism
    B. sacrifice
    C. logic
    D. freedom

7. The Peace of Augsburg of 1555 declared that each elector in the Holy Roman Empire _____.

    A. could choose the religion of his state
    B. could cast one vote for Holy Roman emperor
    C. must vote for a Protestant for the post of Holy Roman emperor
    D. must vote for a Catholic for the post of Holy Roman emperor

8. Under the Roman Republic, the plebeians had all these ways to balance the power of the patricians except _____.

    A. one of the Senate's two consuls was always a plebeian (after 366 BC)
    B. the plebeian tribunes had veto power over the patrician senators
    C. the plebeians did not have to serve in the army
    D. the plebeians had the right to protest publicly against the government

9. In nineteenth-century Europe, both conservatives and liberals believed that _____.

    A. there should be separation among the branches of the central government
    B. a written constitution was necessary for political stability
    C. a nation should be ruled by a benevolent, but absolute, hereditary monarch
    D. the working class should not have any voice in the government

10. Which of these ancient American civilizations was the least aggressive militarily?

    A. the Aztec
    B. the Moche
    C. the Inca
    D. the Maya

11. **What was the purpose of the Great Purges of the 1930s?**
    A. to eliminate political opposition in the Soviet Union
    B. to massacre specific ethnic groups within Europe
    C. to provide necessary labor for major construction projects
    D. to draft men into the armed forces in the Axis nations

12. **The first inhabitants of northern North America lacked all the typical elements of advanced civilizations except _____.**
    A. literacy
    B. cities
    C. bureaucracies
    D. artistic ability

13. **Britain and France went to war in North America over conflicting claims to _____.**
    A. the Ohio River valley area
    B. the city of New Orleans, Louisiana
    C. territory west of the Mississippi River
    D. the colonies along the Atlantic coast

14. **The Greek civilization contributed the concept of _____ to the future world.**
    A. rule by divine right
    B. government by the citizens
    C. imperialism
    D. monotheistic religion

15. **Which major figure of the Enlightenment first suggested a government of multiple branches with checks and balances?**
    A. Descartes
    B. Montesquieu
    C. Rousseau
    D. Voltaire

16. **At its greatest extent under Genghis Khan, the Mongol Empire included almost the entire continent of _____.**
    A. Africa
    B. Asia
    C. Europe
    D. South America

17. During the 1400s, _____ established a hereditary monarchy in Russia.
   A. Peter the Great
   B. Prince Dmitri
   C. Vasili II
   D. Ivan III

18. The Romans described the peoples of northern Europe as barbarians because _____.
   A. their ethnic origins were Central Asian
   B. their men wore full beards
   C. they did not have sophisticated, settled civilizations
   D. they were militarily weak

19. Michelangelo's Sistine Ceiling is an important reflection of its historical period because _____.
   A. it treats Christian and pagan elements equally
   B. it covers an enormous surface
   C. it is almost entirely the work of a single painter
   D. it was commissioned by the pope

20. After the Byzantine Empire collapsed, what rose in its place?
   A. the Ottoman Empire
   B. the Persian Empire
   C. the Republic of Turkey
   D. the Republic of Greece

21. One reason the Industrial Revolution was slow to come about on the European continent was the lack of political influence among the _____.
   A. aristocracy and nobility
   B. mercantile middle class
   C. working class and farmers
   D. students and intellectuals

22. In ancient times, the geographical features at the edge of the Indian subcontinent protected it from invasion from all directions except _____.
   A. the northeast
   B. the northwest
   C. the southeast
   D. the southwest

23. **What was the most important purpose of the Berlin Wall?**
    A. to prevent any possibility of a Berlin airlift during the blockade
    B. to prevent Iron Curtain nations from accepting Marshall Plan aid
    C. to prevent West Germans and other Western Europeans from defecting to East Germany
    D. to prevent citizens of East Germany and other Iron Curtain nations from defecting to the West

24. **After the fall of Constantinople, the emperor of _____ declared himself the last defender of the Eastern Orthodox faith.**
    A. Byzantium
    B. Poland
    C. Rome
    D. Russia

25. **The ancient Egyptians believed that the pharaoh _____.**
    A. ruled by divine right
    B. was literally descended from the gods
    C. could not be killed in battle
    D. must obey the same laws as the common people

26. **The Punic Wars pitted the Romans against _____.**
    A. the Athenians
    B. the Carthaginians
    C. the Etruscans
    D. the Persians

27. **Machiavelli's *The Prince* was revolutionary because it asserted _____.**
    A. that a ruler should do whatever was necessary to maintain power, including acting unethically or dishonestly
    B. that women were just as competent and qualified to rule kingdoms as men
    C. that rule over a nation-state should be decided by merit, not by birth
    D. that all human beings had certain natural rights

28. **All these things except _____ characterized the Ming dynasty in China.**
    A. a rise in food production
    B. economic prosperity
    C. brisk international trade
    D. a rapid rise in literacy

29. **Which nation changed sides during World War II?**
    A. Austria
    B. Italy
    C. Poland
    D. the Soviet Union

30. **The ancient Israelite code of the Ten Commandments was revolutionary because _____.**
    A. its origins were explained by means of legend
    B. it applied equally to all, regardless of rank or class in society
    C. it was religious rather than legal in nature
    D. it contained unresolved contradictions

31. **The Japanese word _____ means "military dictator."**
    A. *bushido*
    B. *daimyo*
    C. *samurai*
    D. *shogun*

32. **_____ brought an abrupt end to the European economic recovery of the late 1920s.**
    A. Hitler's rise to power
    B. Stalin's rise to power
    C. The Great Depression
    D. The Spanish Civil War

33. **Which European nation emerged from World War II as a great world power?**
    A. Britain
    B. France
    C. Poland
    D. the Soviet Union

34. **The Confucians of the Zhou dynasty argued that _____ would ensure peace and prosperity in China.**
    A. a legal code that would apply equally to all
    B. responsible behavior and respect for tradition
    C. daily reading and study of the *Tao Te Ching*
    D. the imposition of military discipline on society

35. The invention and development of the _____ allowed Galileo to make crucial observations about the planets and other heavenly bodies.
    A. pendulum clock
    B. printing press
    C. telescope
    D. microscope

36. Aesop, Aristotle, Herodotus, and Pindar are all key figures of the golden age of which ancient civilization?
    A. Persia
    B. Macedonia
    C. Greece
    D. Rome

37. The term *Indochina* refers to a group of Southeast Asian states collectively ruled by _____ at the end of the nineteenth century.
    A. Britain
    B. France
    C. Germany
    D. the Netherlands

38. _____ culture was the most influential in the Near East in the sixteenth century.
    A. Arabian
    B. Turkish
    C. Persian
    D. Greek

39. Ancient Rome is most remarkable for its achievements in the field of _____.
    A. engineering
    B. philosophy
    C. ceramics
    D. religion

40. During the Reformation, which nation adopted a Protestant religion by legislative act rather than popular rebellion?
    A. Germany
    B. France
    C. England
    D. Sweden

41. **Britain imposed its authority on Egypt in the late nineteenth century in order to maintain _____.**
    A. a trade monopoly on Egyptian cotton
    B. a friendly alliance with a large Arab nation
    C. control over the Suez Canal
    D. control of Egypt's foreign relations within Africa

42. **The Phoenicians are notable for their trading supremacy _____.**
    A. across the Indian Ocean
    B. across the Atlantic Ocean
    C. in the Mediterranean
    D. along the rivers of China

43. **Which nation was the aggressor in the Crimean War of the 1850s?**
    A. Britain
    B. France
    C. Russia
    D. Italy

44. **What was the result of Saladin's overthrow of the Fatimid dynasty in Egypt in 1171?**
    A. the founding of the Ottoman Empire
    B. the restoration of Sunni Islam authority
    C. the conversion of Egypt to Christianity
    D. the downfall of the Mamluk Turks

45. **Why did the Catholic nation of France not support the Catholic side in the Thirty Years' War?**
    A. because the king of France was married to an Austrian princess
    B. because the pope was a traditional enemy of the French kings
    C. because a Catholic defeat in the war would strengthen France's position
    D. because France's ministers were sympathetic to the Protestant side

46. **Britain drove _____ out of power in South Africa and the Orange Free State.**
    A. the Dutch
    B. the French
    C. the Portuguese
    D. the Germans

47. **The USSR and the United States nearly reached the point of nuclear war during _____.**
   A. the Cuban Missile Crisis
   B. the Strategic Arms Limitation Talks
   C. the partition of Germany into four zones of occupation
   D. the signing of the Warsaw Pact

48. **As a result of the 1438 Council of Florence, _____.**
   A. Martin Luther published his Ninety-Five Theses in Wittenberg
   B. a major cultural and intellectual exchange took place among scholars
   C. Pope Leo X commissioned Michelangelo to paint the Sistine Chapel ceiling
   D. the Italian city-states became a unified nation under one monarch

49. **Which group became the dominant culture in Eastern Europe during the "Dark Ages"?**
   A. the Franks
   B. the Slavs
   C. the Turks
   D. the Vikings

50. **The Assyrian Empire was most notable for its _____ achievements.**
   A. artistic
   B. agricultural
   C. literary
   D. military

51. **Which best describes the major overall goal that united all the eighteenth-century *philosophes*?**
   A. education
   B. freedom
   C. anarchy
   D. political unification

52. **In *The Communist Manifesto*, Marx and Engels stated that _____ was the most valuable member of society.**
   A. the constitutional monarch
   B. the soldier
   C. the worker
   D. the artist or intellectual

53. The ancient Greek city-state of Sparta is best described as a _____ culture.
    A. mercantile
    B. military
    C. monotheistic
    D. literary

54. Constantinople was named "the Second Rome" or "New Rome"; _____ later became known as "the Third Rome."
    A. Madrid
    B. Moscow
    C. Paris
    D. Vienna

55. The great bulk of the army that opposed the Western Europeans during the Crusades was _____.
    A. Arabian
    B. Persian
    C. North African
    D. Turkish

56. Which best explains why communism, as it was practiced, was not satisfactory to the peoples of Eastern Europe?
    A. It left them feeling constantly vulnerable to foreign invasion.
    B. It refused them basic freedoms they demanded as a human right.
    C. It was a corrupt system of government.
    D. It was a barrier to economic progress.

57. Ancient Ethiopia was the site of the _____ civilization.
    A. Axumite
    B. Egyptian
    C. Nubian
    D. Byzantine

58. The emperor Constantine is historically significant because he _____.
    A. divided the Roman Empire into two halves
    B. made Christianity the state religion of the empire
    C. was the first pope of the Roman Catholic Church
    D. reestablished the Roman Republic

59. **Which best describes the realm of France under the Merovingians?**
    A. a feudal system
    B. an absolute monarchy
    C. a vast empire
    D. a military dictatorship

60. _____ **is historically significant because he founded the Mughal Empire in India.**
    A. Babur
    B. Akbar
    C. Mahmud
    D. Saladin

61. _____ **was the first modern European nation to establish a constitutional monarchy.**
    A. Belgium
    B. England
    C. France
    D. Italy

62. **Zheng, the founder of the Qin dynasty, ruled China according to the Legalist belief in _____.**
    A. popular democracy
    B. a centrally controlled state
    C. a feudal system
    D. military dictatorship

63. **The American term _Progressive_ refers to someone who supports _____.**
    A. rampant capitalism
    B. social and political reform
    C. socialism
    D. a universal military draft

64. **All these factors contributed to the downfall of the Persian Empire in the fifth century BC except _____.**
    A. lack of great military commanders
    B. weak and/or incompetent emperors
    C. geographical overexpansion
    D. resentment and hostility among various peoples of the empire

65. The history of Russia as a nation-state began during the era when the Russians managed to expel _____ from their lands.
    A. the Chinese
    B. the Indians
    C. the Tatars
    D. the Arabs

66. The Shang dynasty of ancient China was characterized by all the following except _____.
    A. the manufacture of beautiful ceramics
    B. the development of a written language
    C. a feudal system of small city-states
    D. the military conquest of most of southern Asia

67. _____ was the major battleground during the Thirty Years' War.
    A. Austria
    B. France
    C. The Holy Roman Empire
    D. Poland

68. The original purpose of the Great Wall of China, completed in the late third century BC, was _____.
    A. to encourage international trade
    B. to protect China from invasion
    C. to serve as a permanent border between Korea and China
    D. to impress the world with China's engineering prowess

69. Why was Newton's discovery and explanation of the principle of gravity important?
    A. It proved that travel in space would be possible one day.
    B. It disputed the findings of previous scientists and astronomers.
    C. It showed that the workings of the universe were intelligible to ordinary people.
    D. It demonstrated that the Earth and other planets moved around the sun.

70. The Arabs' most significant contribution to world history is their _____.
    A. literature
    B. art
    C. religion
    D. culture

71. The Hittites of Asia Minor prospered economically for all these reasons except _____.
    A. the ability to work with iron
    B. control over important trade routes
    C. the invention of paper
    D. an abundance of natural resources

72. The Declaration of the Rights of Man and of the Citizen contains important ideas from _____.
    A. the Glorious Revolution
    B. the Renaissance
    C. the Enlightenment
    D. the Scientific Revolution

73. After the death of Alexander the Great, his empire _____.
    A. broke up into small independent kingdoms
    B. was handed down intact to his oldest son
    C. was immediately absorbed into the Roman Empire
    D. became the world's first example of a republic

74. All these ethnic groups played significant roles in early Russian history except _____.
    A. the Slavs
    B. the Vikings
    C. the Mongols
    D. the Romans

75. Why do historians believe the Indus Valley was a peaceful civilization?
    A. It lasted for a thousand years.
    B. Its written records have not yet been deciphered.
    C. Its cities were built according to the same street plan.
    D. It has not left behind any advanced weapons.

76. Which religion does not share the same basis as the other three?
    A. Buddhism
    B. Christianity
    C. Islam
    D. Judaism

77. _____ constituted the greatest military threat to ancient China.
   A. The Roman Empire
   B. The tribes of the Central Asian steppes
   C. India
   D. Korean and Japan

78. What kind of government did Japan establish in 1890?
   A. a hereditary monarchy
   B. a military dictatorship
   C. a parliamentary system
   D. a popular democracy

79. The original motive for sponsoring European voyages to other continents was _____.
   A. to establish foreign military bases
   B. to expand the empire by setting up permanent European colonies
   C. to convert native populations to Christianity
   D. to establish profitable trade relations

80. In the nineteenth century, both _____ were forced, more or less at gunpoint, to make favorable trade agreements with foreign nations.
   A. Italy and Egypt
   B. Egypt and China
   C. China and Japan
   D. Japan and Italy

81. According to Muslims, Muhammad was _____.
   A. the divinely begotten son of God
   B. God's last and greatest prophet
   C. God manifested on Earth in mortal form
   D. a god who would live eternally among men

82. The merit examination given to applicants for the Chinese civil service, from the Han dynasty until the early 1900s, had all these effects on Chinese society except _____.
   A. to prevent absolutely the possibility of a commoner serving in the bureaucracy
   B. to give all Chinese bureaucrats the same kind of background and training
   C. to ensure that China would always be a Confucian state
   D. to forge a strong link between government and scholarship

83. One important reason the French Revolution succeeded in abolishing the monarchy was that _____.
    A. France had no formal political parties and no legislative assembly
    B. the king was unable to escape from Versailles
    C. the hereditary aristocracy did not want to give up any of its privileges
    D. the armed National Guard sided with the common people

84. A key reason the Roman Empire lasted so long was _____.
    A. its manageable geographical size
    B. its tolerance of diverse cultural and religious elements
    C. its emperor's insistence on being regarded as a god
    D. its establishment of the Latin language as universal in the West

85. The Ming dynasty in China ended with all of the following except _____.
    A. an end to international trade
    B. an imperial suicide
    C. a foreign takeover
    D. a popular uprising

86. Conflict between King Charles I and the British Parliament erupted into open warfare over the issue of _____.
    A. the balance of power between the legislature and the throne
    B. religious disagreements between England and Ireland
    C. Parliament's dislike of being ruled by a Protestant monarch
    D. Charles's prospective marriage to a French Catholic princess

87. Before the great changes of the mid-nineteenth century, which factor was most important in determining a Japanese person's life?
    A. physical beauty and strength
    B. intellectual and artistic ability
    C. birth into a particular social rank
    D. religious beliefs

88. The Muslims conquered and held sway over most of _____ for several centuries.
    A. Italy
    B. Britain
    C. France
    D. Spain

89. After Tokugawa Ieyasu closed off Japan to Westerners, he agreed to allow the Dutch traders _____.
    A. to live in an enclosed area of Nagasaki
    B. to maintain a trading post on a tiny offshore island
    C. to leave Japan safely within a specified period of time
    D. to become Japanese citizens so that they could continue to trade

90. The Kingdom of _____ eventually became the core of a united German nation.
    A. Austria
    B. Bohemia
    C. Poland
    D. Prussia

91. As of the ninth century BC, all these civilizations flourished on the Italian peninsula except _____.
    A. Etruscan
    B. Greek
    C. Phoenician
    D. Roman

92. Most victims of the Black Plague died in urban areas because _____.
    A. urban areas suffered more from air pollution
    B. there were fewer doctors and clergymen in cities
    C. most Europeans at that time lived in cities
    D. urban conditions were crowded and unsanitary

93. Which ancient civilization had the least contact with the others?
    A. China
    B. Egypt
    C. India
    D. Rome

94. All of these are important early works of Indian thought and literature except _____.
    A. the *Mahabharata*
    B. the *Odyssey*
    C. the *Ramayana*
    D. the *Upanishads*

95. **Which nineteenth-century political philosophy is furthest to the political left?**
    A. conservatism
    B. communism
    C. liberalism
    D. socialism

96. **What was the most important reason for the Europeans' success in establishing dominance over the native populations in the Americas?**
    A. They had deadlier weapons.
    B. There were more of them.
    C. They were physically healthier and stronger.
    D. They were more familiar with the local geography.

97. **_____ was created at the end of the Napoleonic wars to maintain a peaceful balance of power in Europe.**
    A. The League of Nations
    B. The European Union
    C. The Quadruple Alliance
    D. The United Nations

98. **The peoples of the Central Asian steppes generally migrated in which two directions?**
    A. south and east
    B. east and north
    C. north and west
    D. west and south

99. **All of these except _____ were important in shaping the thinking of the delegates at the Constitutional Convention held in the United States in 1789.**
    A. the Magna Carta
    B. *The Spirit of Laws*
    C. the English Bill of Rights
    D. the code Napoleon

100. **What was the effect of Amenhotep IV's new law establishing monotheism in New Kingdom Egypt?**
    A. It stimulated a cultural and artistic renaissance.
    B. It caused a major civil war.
    C. It weakened the empire.
    D. It caused a change in dynasty.

Afterword
The World Since the Cold War

A typical world history survey course will end with the fall of communism in the USSR and Eastern Europe. The course is called *history*, not *current events*, because it deals with the past. However, it is a good idea to arm yourself with knowledge of developments that have taken place among the nations of the world since the early 1990s. This Afterword describes some of the trends and issues that world leaders are trying to come to terms with for the future.

Immigration

Since about 1990, Europe has had to absorb an enormous influx of immigrants, almost all of them from Africa and the Middle East. Immigration has had a tremendous impact on the economy, as many of these immigrants have entered Europe illegally and are working without proper documentation.

Immigration has also had a significant cultural impact. Many Europeans feel grave concern that their own cultures are disappearing as African and Arab populations rise and the native population falls. Unlike the United States, a nation populated entirely by immigrants and their descendants (even the "native" peoples of the Americas originally came from Asia), European countries have been, for the most part, culturally homogenous for centuries. Racial and ethnic prejudice against immigrants is definitely on the rise in Europe, and there are frequent outbreaks of race-based violence.

Immigration—mostly from Latin America—has also had a significant cultural and economic impact on the United States. It is an economic concern for two reasons. First, Americans are afraid of losing jobs to Latinos who will gladly work for lower wages. Second, many Latino immigrants have entered the country illegally and thus are probably not paying taxes. Culturally, unlike all previous immigrant groups, the current wave of Latin American immigrants is resisting assimilation into the American culture; instead, the culture is changing to meet the needs of the immigrants. For example, the government and most businesses provide information and customer assistance in both Spanish and English. A nativist backlash against this has developed among some segments of the U.S. population.

Foreign Relations

Immediately after Saudi terrorists attacked the United States in September 2001, U.S. foreign policy became aggressive—so much so that the initially sympathetic international community began to view it with alarm. The European Union would have preferred a more restrained response. A 2008 change of leadership in the White House has gone some way toward mending the transatlantic friendships; however, it is impossible to predict what the near future will bring.

The United States continues to fight wars of aggression in Afghanistan and Iraq, although it has pledged to pull its troops out of Iraq by the end of 2011. Islamic resentment toward the West in general and toward the United States in particular continues to be strong.

In addition, Europe and the United States no longer have a monopoly on nuclear weapons. China, India, Israel, North Korea, and Pakistan all possess strategic nuclear weapons—a fact that European heads of state must constantly keep in mind. With deep mutual hostility between India and Pakistan and between Israel and its Arab neighbors, all nations must use care in negotiations.

European Union Membership

The European Union currently includes twenty-seven members, all of which have agreed to abide by its requirements. These include the observance of basic human rights, the maintenance of a free-market economy, and the establishment of a popularly elected representative government.

Among states that have applied for membership but have not yet been accepted, the case of Turkey is the most controversial. Many European heads of state have grave concerns over admitting a nation that would be one of its largest members; the size of Turkey's population would guarantee it the largest number of seats in the European Parliament, significantly changing the current balance of power. Some member nations argue that Turkey should not be eligible on the grounds that almost all its landmass is in Asia with only a small corner in Europe. Others argue that with its Muslim population, Turkey is culturally non-European and does not belong in the EU. Still others point to Turkey's practice of censorship and its other controls over the lives of its people. Discussion over admitting Turkey to the EU has been going on since 1987 with little likelihood that it will soon be settled.

Apart from the Baltic republics, none of the former states of the USSR has been admitted to the EU. These nations have still not recovered economically or socially from the long era of Communist domination. Although the former Soviet republics have their own union, the Commonwealth of Independent States, their exclusion from the EU may become a significant issue in the future.

Within Europe, the people appear to have a mixed view of the EU. While many enjoy the advantages it brings, others express concerns. Principally, there is a fear that the member states will lose their unique individual cultural identities and that Europe will become a second United States—a federal republic whose states all share one central government and whose people consider themselves all one nationality. Only time will determine the influence the EU will have over its members and over the future of Europe as a whole.

The Rise of Democracy in the Middle East

The twenty-first century has ushered in a wave of popular revolt in the Middle East—revolt against censorship, against the denial of basic individual freedoms, against one-party rule, and against political and religious oppression. This began in Egypt in 2003, with the founding of *Kefaya*, also called Egyptian Movement for Change. In 2011, a series of large- and small-scale protests throughout the region have led journalists to begin using the phrase "Arab Spring."

Massive public demonstrations in Cairo forced Egyptian President Hosni Mubarak to resign and the Egyptian Parliament to disband. Egypt is to hold free elections in the fall of 2011. Full-scale civil war erupted in Libya; it continues as of this writing. A revolution took place in Tunisia, sending its longtime president into exile. It is far too early to predict the long-term results of any of this activity; however, the story of this book suggests that in the end, humanity has always progressed toward individual and political freedom.

Answer Key

CHAPTER 1 QUIZ

1. c   2. b   3. a   4. b   5. a   6. d   7. a   8. c   9. b   10. d

CHAPTER 2 QUIZ

1. b   2. a   3. c   4. b   5. a   6. a   7. c   8. d   9. c   10. c

CHAPTER 3 QUIZ

1. b   2. c   3. a   4. d   5. b   6. a   7. c   8. a   9. d   10. c

CHAPTER 4 QUIZ

1. c   2. d   3. b   4. c   5. d   6. b   7. c   8. c   9. a   10. a

CHAPTER 5 QUIZ

1. a   2. d   3. b   4. d   5. b   6. a   7. c   8. c   9. d   10. d

CHAPTER 6 QUIZ

1. d   2. b   3. c   4. a   5. a   6. c   7. d   8. b   9. a   10. d

CHAPTER 7 QUIZ

1. b   2. d   3. c   4. a   5. a   6. b   7. c   8. b   9. d   10. c

PART 1 EXAM

1. b   2. b   3. a   4. b   5. d   6. b   7. a   8. c   9. a   10. b   11. d   12. c
13. a   14. c   15. c   16. d   17. a   18. b   19. c   20. c   21. d   22. c   23. a
24. d   25. a   26. b   27. d   28. a   29. c   30. d   31. b   32. a   33. d   34. b
35. c   36. c   37. a   38. d   39. b   40. c   41. d   42. a   43. c   44. c   45. c
46. b   47. d   48. a   49. b   50. c

CHAPTER 8 QUIZ

1. b   2. d   3. a   4. b   5. b   6. c   7. b   8. a   9. c   10. d

CHAPTER 9 QUIZ

1. b   2. c   3. d   4. b   5. c   6. c   7. a   8. c   9. d   10. b

CHAPTER 10 QUIZ

1. c   2. b   3. c   4. c   5. a   6. b   7. c   8. d   9. d   10. c

CHAPTER 11 QUIZ

1. d   2. a   3. b   4. a   5. d   6. a   7. c   8. d   9. a   10. c

CHAPTER 12 QUIZ

1. d   2. d   3. a   4. b   5. a   6. c   7. d   8. b   9. d   10. b

CHAPTER 13 QUIZ

1. b   2. d   3. b   4. c   5. d   6. c   7. c   8. b   9. a   10. a

CHAPTER 14 QUIZ

1. c   2. c   3. b   4. b   5. d   6. b   7. b   8. a   9. c   10. a

PART 2 EXAM

1. a   2. b   3. c   4. c   5. d   6. b   7. c   8. b   9. a   10. a   11. d   12. c
13. d   14. c   15. c   16. a   17. d   18. b   19. a   20. d   21. b   22. b   23. b
24. c   25. d   26. b   27. c   28. b   29. a   30. b   31. c   32. c   33. b   34. a
35. d   36. b   37. a   38. c   39. d   40. b   41. a   42. b   43. c   44. c   45. d
46. c   47. a   48. b   49. b   50. b

CHAPTER 15 QUIZ

1. a   2. b   3. d   4. a   5. c   6. d   7. c   8. a   9. c   10. a

CHAPTER 16 QUIZ

1. d   2. a   3. a   4. c   5. b   6. d   7. c   8. a   9. b   10. a

CHAPTER 17 QUIZ

1. c   2. b   3. c   4. a   5. d   6. b   7. c   8. a   9. a   10. b

CHAPTER 18 QUIZ

1. d   2. c   3. c   4. d   5. c   6. c   7. a   8. b   9. b   10. c

CHAPTER 19 QUIZ

1. b   2. d   3. b   4. a   5. d   6. b   7. b   8. a   9. b   10. a

CHAPTER 20 QUIZ

1. c   2. d   3. c   4. b   5. d   6. c   7. c   8. d   9. a   10. a

CHAPTER 21 QUIZ

1. b   2. a   3. b   4. c   5. d   6. c   7. b   8. d   9. d   10. a

CHAPTER 22 QUIZ

1. c   2. a   3. a   4. c   5. b   6. a   7. b   8. c   9. c   10. d

CHAPTER 23 QUIZ

1. c   2. a   3. b   4. a   5. a   6. b   7. c   8. d   9. b   10. b

PART 3 EXAM

1. c   2. d   3. b   4. a   5. b   6. c   7. b   8. d   9. c   10. c   11. d   12. c
13. b   14. c   15. a   16. b   17. c   18. b   19. b   20. b   21. d   22. c   23. b
24. c   25. d   26. b   27. a   28. c   29. c   30. a   31. a   32. d   33. c   34. c
35. a   36. b   37. d   38. b   39. a   40. a   41. a   42. d   43. b   44. c   45. b
46. b   47. b   48. c   49. c   50. a

FINAL EXAM

1. b   2. d   3. d   4. c   5. b   6. b   7. a   8. c   9. d   10. d   11. a   12. d
13. a   14. b   15. b   16. b   17. c   18. c   19. a   20. a   21. b   22. b   23. d
24. d   25. b   26. b   27. a   28. d   29. b   30. b   31. d   32. c   33. d   34. b
35. c   36. c   37. b   38. c   39. a   40. c   41. c   42. c   43. c   44. b   45. c
46. a   47. a   48. b   49. b   50. d   51. b   52. c   53. b   54. b   55. d   56. b
57. a   58. b   59. a   60. a   61. b   62. b   63. b   64. a   65. c   66. d   67. c
68. b   69. c   70. c   71. c   72. c   73. a   74. d   75. d   76. a   77. b   78. c
79. d   80. c   81. b   82. a   83. d   84. b   85. a   86. a   87. c   88. d   89. b
90. d   91. c   92. d   93. a   94. b   95. b   96. a   97. c   98. d   99. d   100. c

Bibliography and Sources for Further Reading

Chapter 1: Early Civilizations

Bottéro, Jean. *Everyday Life in Ancient Mesopotamia*. Baltimore: Johns Hopkins University Press, 2001.

Freeman, Charles. *Egypt, Greece, and Rome: Civilizations of the Ancient Mediterranean*. 2nd ed. Oxford: Oxford University Press, 2004.

Kramer, Samuel N. *The Sumerians: Their History, Culture and Character*. Chicago: University of Chicago Press, 1971.

Chapter 2: The New Kingdom to the Fall of Babylon, 1550–550 BC

Ceram, C. W. *The Secret of the Hittites: The Discovery of an Ancient Empire*. New York: Phoenix Press, 2001.

Foster, Benjamin, and Karen P. Foster. *Civilizations of Ancient Iraq*. Princeton: Princeton University Press, 2009.

Leick, Gwendolyn. *The Babylonians: An Introduction*. New York: Routledge, 2002.

Chapter 3: The Ancient Middle East: Israel, Phoenicia, and Persia, 1800–323 BC

Allen, Lindsay. *The Persian Empire*. Chicago: University of Chicago Press, 2005.

Casson, Lionel. *The Ancient Mariners: Seafarers and Sea Fighters of the Mediterranean in Ancient Times*. 2nd ed. Princeton: Princeton University Press, 1991.

Holst, Sanford. *Phoenicians: Lebanon's Epic Heritage*. Cambridge: Cambridge & Boston Press, 2005.

Chapter 4: Ancient China and India

Auboyer, Jeannine. *Daily Life in Ancient India: From 200 BC to 700 AD*. New York: Phoenix Press, 2002.

Loewe, Michael, and E. L. Shaughnessy. *The Cambridge History of Ancient China: From the Origins of Civilization to 221 BC*. Cambridge: Cambridge University Press, 1999.

Chapter 5: The Greek Civilization and the Macedonian Empire, 2000–275 BC

Briant, Pierre. *Alexander the Great: Man of Spirit, Man of Action*. New York: Harry N. Abrams Inc., 1996.

Herodotus. *The Histories*. New York: Penguin Classics, 2003 (originally written circa 445 BC).

Kagan, Donald. *The Peloponnesian War*. New York: Penguin Books, 2004.

Martin, Thomas R. *Ancient Greece: From Prehistoric to Hellenistic Times*. Updated ed. New Haven, CT: Yale University Press, 2000.

Plutarch. *Lives*. 2 vols. New York: Modern Library Classics, 2001 (originally written circa AD 30).

Renault, Mary. *The Nature of Alexander*. New York: Pantheon Books, 1979.

Thucydides. *History of the Peloponnesian War*. New York: Penguin Classics, 1972 (originally written circa 430 BC).

Chapter 6: The Roman Empire and the Rise of Christianity, 900 BC–AD 476

Holland, Tom. *Rubicon: The Last Years of the Roman Republic*. New York: Anchor Books, 2005.

Mackay, Christopher S. *Ancient Rome: A Military and Political History*. Cambridge: Cambridge University Press, 2007.

Plutarch. *Lives*. 2 vols. New York: Modern Library Classics, 2001 (originally written circa AD 30).

Suetonius. *The Twelve Caesars*. New York: Penguin Classics, 2007 (originally written circa AD 100).

Chapter 7: Early Asian Empires, 400 BC–AD 600

Allchin, F. R. *The Archaeology of Early Historic South Asia: The Emergence of Cities and States*. Cambridge: Cambridge University Press, 1995.

Lewis, Mark Edward. *The Early Chinese Empires: Qin and Han*. Cambridge, MA: Belknap Press/Harvard University Press, 2007.

———. *China Between Empires: The Northern and Southern Dynasties.* Cambridge, MA: Belknap Press/Harvard University Press, 2009.

Liu, Xinru. *The Silk Road and World History.* Oxford: Oxford University Press, 2010.

Chapter 8: Europe and the Byzantine Empire to AD 1000

Geary, Patrick. *Before France and Germany: The Creation and Transformation of the Merovingian World.* Oxford: Oxford University Press, 1988.

McKitterick, Rosamond. *Charlemagne: The Formation of a European Identity.* Cambridge: Cambridge University Press, 2008.

Norwich, John Julius. *A Short History of Byzantium.* New York: Vintage Books, 1998.

Wickham, Chris. *Framing the Early Middle Ages: Europe and the Mediterranean, 400–800.* Oxford: Oxford University Press, 2007.

Chapter 9: The Rise of Islam, African Civilizations, and India to AD 1000

Armstrong, Karen. *Muhammad: A Biography of the Prophet.* New York: Harper, 1993.

Bennison, Amira K. *The Great Caliphs. The Golden Age of the Abbasid Empire.* New Haven, CT: Yale University Press, 2009.

Berkey, Jonathan P. *The Formation of Islam: Religion and Society in the Near East 600–1800.* Cambridge: Cambridge University Press, 2002.

Edwards, David N. *The Nubian Past: An Archaeology of the Sudan.* London: Routledge, 2005.

Parker, John, and Richard Rathbone. *African History: A Very Short Introduction.* Oxford: Oxford University Press, 2007.

Chapter 10: East Asian Civilizations to 1000; the Americas to 1500

Brown, Delmer M. *The Cambridge History of Japan.* Vol. 1, *Ancient Japan.* Cambridge: Cambridge University Press, 2003.

Coe, Michael D. *The Maya.* 7th ed. London: Thames & Hudson, 2005.

Coe, M. D., and R. Koontz. *Mexico: From the Olmecs to the Aztecs.* 6th ed. London: Thames & Hudson, 2008.

Kuhn, Dieter. *The Age of Confucian Rule: The Song Transformation of China.* Cambridge, MA: Belknap Press/Harvard University Press, 2009.

Lewis, Mark Edward. *China's Cosmopolitan Empire: The Tang Dynasty.* Cambridge, MA: Belknap Press/Harvard University Press, 2009.

MacQuarrie, Kim. *The Last Days of the Incas.* New York: Simon & Schuster, 2008.

Shively, Donald H., and William McCullough. *The Cambridge History of Japan.* Vol. 2, *Heian Japan.* Cambridge: Cambridge University Press, 1999.

Chapter 11: The Rise of the Turks, 1000–1500

Finkel, Caroline. *Osman's Dream: The History of the Ottoman Empire.* New York: Basic Books, 2007.

Maalouf, Amin. *The Crusades Through Arab Eyes.* New York: Schocken Books, 1989.

Madden, Thomas F. *The New Concise History of the Crusades*. Updated ed. Lanham, MD: Rowman & Littlefield Publishers Inc., 2005.

Chapter 12: Medieval Europe, 1000–1500

Clanchy, M. T. *England and Its Rulers 1066–1272*. 2nd ed. Oxford: Blackwell Publishing, 1998.
Hale, J. R., ed. *A Concise Encyclopedia of the Italian Renaissance*. New York: Oxford University Press, 1981.
Hicks, Michael. *The Wars of the Roses 1455–1485*. Oxford: Osprey Publishing, 2003.

Chapter 13: Medieval Asia, 1150–1600

Brook, Timothy. *The Troubled Empire: China in the Yuan and Ming Dynasties*. Cambridge, MA: Belknap Press/Harvard University Press, 2010.
Halperin, Charles J. *Russia and the Golden Horde: The Mongol Impact on Medieval Russian History*. Indianapolis: Indiana University Press, 1987.
Weatherford, Jack. *Genghis Khan and the Making of the Modern World*. New York: Three Rivers Press, 2004.

Chapter 14: European Reformation and the Age of Absolute Monarchy, 1500–1750

Goubert, Pierre. *Louis XIV and Twenty Million Frenchmen*. New York: Vintage Books, 1972.
Knecht, Robert. *The French Religious Wars 1562–1598*. Oxford: Osprey Publishing, 2002.
MacCulloch, Diarmaid. *The Reformation: A History*. New York: Penguin Books, 2004.
Reston, James, Jr. *Dogs of God: Columbus, the Inquisition, and the Defeat of the Moors*. New York: Anchor Books, 2006.
Wedgwood, C. V. *The Thirty Years' War*. New York: New York Review Books, 2005 (first published 1938).
Wheatcroft, Andrew. *The Habsburgs: Embodying Empire*. New York: Penguin Books, 1996.

Chapter 15: European Exploration and Colonization, 1500–1700

Clendinnen, Inga. *Ambivalent Conquests: Maya and Spaniard in Yucatan, 1517–1570*. 2nd ed. Cambridge: Cambridge University Press, 2003.
Dolin, Eric Jay. *Fur, Fortune, and Empire: The Epic History of the Fur Trade in America*. New York: W. W. Norton and Company, 2010.
Perdue, Theda, and Michael D. Green. *North American Indians: A Very Short Introduction*. Oxford: Oxford University Press, 2010.
Weber, David J. *The Spanish Frontier in North America*. New Haven, CT: Yale University Press, 1992.

Chapter 16: Russia and the Great Muslim Empires, 1500–1858

Axworthy, Michael. *The Sword of Persia: Nader Shah, from Tribal Warrior to Conquering Tyrant*. London: I. B. Tauris, 2009.

Bushkovitch, Paul. *Peter the Great*. Lanham, MD: Rowman & Littlefield Publishers, 2002.

Dale, Stephen F. *The Muslim Empires of the Ottomans, Safavids, and Mughals*. Cambridge: Cambridge University Press, 2010.

De Madariaga, Isabel. *Catherine the Great: A Short History*. 2nd ed. New Haven, CT: Yale University Press, 2002.

———. *Ivan the Terrible: A Short History*. 2nd ed. New Haven, CT: Yale University Press, 2006.

Figes, Orlando. *Natasha's Dance: A Cultural History of Russia*. New York: Picador, 2003.

Schimmel, Annemarie. *The Empire of the Great Mughals: History, Art and Culture*. London: Reaktion Books, 2006.

Chapter 17: Western Revolutions in Science, Industry, and Thought, 1550–1900

Fara, Patricia. *Pandora's Breeches: Women, Science & Power in the Enlightenment*. London: Random House, 2004.

Gay, Peter. *The Enlightenment: An Interpretation*. Vol. I, *The Rise of Modern Paganism*. New York: W. W. Norton and Company, 1966.

———. *The Enlightenment: An Interpretation*. Vol. II, *The Science of Freedom*. New York: Alfred A. Knopf, 1969.

Maury, Jean Pierre. *Newton: The Father of Modern Astronomy*. New York: Harry N. Abrams, 1992.

Starobinski, Jean. *Jean-Jacques Rousseau: Transparency and Obstruction*. Chicago: University of Chicago Press, 1988.

Weightman, Gavin. *The Industrial Revolutionaries*. New York: Grove Press, 2007.

Chapter 18: Political Revolutions in the West, 1688–1815

Borneman, Walter R. *The French and Indian War: Deciding the Fate of North America*. New York: Harper Perennial, 2007.

Fisher, Todd. *The Napoleonic Wars: The Empires Fight Back 1808–1812*. Oxford: Osprey Publishing, 2001.

———. *The Napoleonic Wars: The Rise of the Emperor 1805–1807*. Oxford: Osprey Publishing, 2001.

Furet, François. *The French Revolution: 1770–1814*. Oxford: Blackwell Publishers Limited, 1992.

Johnson, Paul. *Napoleon*. New York: Penguin Books, 2002.

Middlekauff, Robert. *The Glorious Cause: The American Revolution, 1763–1789*. New York: Oxford University Press, 2007.

Chapter 19: Asian Empires 1600–1815; Late European Colonization

Boahen, A. Adu. *African Perspectives on Colonialism*. Baltimore: Johns Hopkins University Press, 1989.

Rowe, William T. *China's Last Empire: The Great Qing*. Cambridge, MA: Belknap Press/Harvard University Press, 2009.

Totman, Conrad. *Early Modern Japan*. Berkeley: University of California Press, 1995.

Chapter 20: Europe and the Ottoman Empire in the Nineteenth Century, 1815–1914

Berlin, Isaiah. *Russian Thinkers*. 2nd ed. New York: Penguin Classics, 2008.

Ferber, Michael. *Romanticism: A Very Short Introduction*. Oxford: Oxford University Press, 2010.

Gay, Peter. *The Dilemma of Democratic Socialism*. New York: Collier Books, 1962.

Hopkirk, Peter. *The Great Game: The Struggle for Empire in Central Asia*. New York: Kodansha International, 1992.

Lincoln, W. Bruce. *Nicholas I: Emperor and Autocrat of All the Russias*. DeKalb, IL: Northern Illinois University Press, 1989.

Marx, Karl, and Friedrich Engels. *The Communist Manifesto*. Many editions.

Riall, Lucy. *The Italian Risorgimento: State, Society, and National Unification*. New York: Routledge, 1994.

Schorske, Carl E. *Fin-de-Siècle Vienna: Politics and Culture*. New York: Vintage Books, 1980.

Wawro, Geoffrey. *The Franco-Prussian War: The German Conquest of France in 1870–1871*. Cambridge: Cambridge University Press, 2005.

Chapter 21: The Americas and Asia in the Nineteenth Century, 1815–1914

Brands, H. W. *American Colossus: The Triumph of Capitalism, 1865–1900*. New York: Doubleday and Company, 2010.

Cohen, Paul A. *History in Three Keys: The Boxers as Event, Experience, and Myth*. New York: Columbia University Press, 1998.

Dubois, Laurent. *Avengers of the New World: The Story of the Haitian Revolution*. Cambridge, MA: Belknap Press/Harvard University Press, 2005.

Feifer, George. *Breaking Open Japan: Commodore Perry, Lord Abe, and American Imperialism in 1853*. Washington, DC: Smithsonian Museum, 2006.

Foner, Eric. *Reconstruction: America's Unfinished Revolution, 1863–1877*. New York: Harper & Row, 1988.

Hanes, W. Travis, and Frank Sanello. *The Opium Wars: The Addiction of One Empire and the Corruption of Another*. Naperville, IL: Sourcebooks Inc., 2004.

Howe, Daniel Walker. *What Hath God Wrought: The Transformation of America, 1815–1848*. New York: Oxford University Press, 2009.

Chapter 22: The Era of World Wars, 1914–1945

Audoin-Rouzeau, Stéphane, and Annette Becker. *14–18: Understanding the Great War*. New York: Hill and Wang, 2003.

Fest, Joachim C. *Hitler*. New York: Vintage Books, 1975.

Figes, Orlando. *A People's Tragedy: The Russian Revolution: 1891–1924*. New York: Penguin Books, 1998.

Fussell, Paul. *The Great War and Modern Memory*. Oxford: Oxford University Press, 1975.

Gilbert, Martin. *The Second World War: A Complete History*. Revised ed. New York: Holt, 2004.

Keegan, John. *The First World War*. New York: Vintage Books, 2000.

Kennedy, David. *Freedom from Fear: The American People in Depression and War 1929–1945*. New York: Oxford University Press, 2001.

Paxton, Robert O. *The Anatomy of Fascism*. New York: Vintage Books, 2004.

Rauchway, Eric. *The Great Depression and the New Deal: A Very Short Introduction*. Oxford: Oxford University Press, 2008.

Reed, John. *Ten Days That Shook the World*. New York: Penguin Books, 1977 (first published 1919).

Service, Robert. *Stalin: A Biography*. Cambridge, MA: Belknap Press/Harvard University Press, 2006.

Snyder, Timothy. *Bloodlands: Europe Between Hitler and Stalin*. New York: Basic Books, 2010.

Spector, Ronald. *Eagle Against the Sun: The American War with Japan*. New York: Vintage Books, 1985.

Chapter 23: The End of the Twentieth Century, 1945–1991

Dobbs, Michael. *One Minute to Midnight: Kennedy, Khrushchev, and Castro on the Brink of Nuclear War*. New York: Vintage Books, 2009.

Fitzgerald, Frances. *Fire in the Lake: The Vietnamese and the Americans in Vietnam*. Boston: Back Bay Books, 2002 (originally published 1973).

Freedman, Lawrence. *Kennedy's Wars: Berlin, Cuba, Laos, and Vietnam*. Oxford: Oxford University Press, 2000.

Furet, François. *The Passing of an Illusion: The Idea of Communism in the Twentieth Century*. Chicago: University of Chicago Press, 1999.

Goto-Jones, Christopher. *Modern Japan: A Very Short Introduction*. Oxford: Oxford University Press, 2009.

Hitchcock, William I. *The Struggle for Europe: The Turbulent History of a Divided Continent, 1945 to the Present*. New York: Anchor Books, 2003.

Karnow, Stanley. *Vietnam: A History*. New York: Penguin Books, 1997.

Kurlansky, Mark. *1968: The Year That Rocked the World*. New York: Random House, 2004.

Mitter, Rana. *Modern China: A Very Short Introduction*. Oxford: Oxford University Press, 2008.

Perlstein, Rick. *Nixonland: The Rise of a President and the Fracturing of America*. New York: Scribner, 2009.

Sebestyen, Victor. *Twelve Days: The Story of the 1956 Hungarian Revolution*. New York: Vintage, 2007.

Sheehan, Neil. *A Bright Shining Lie: John Paul Vann and America in Vietnam*. New York: Vintage Books, 1989.

Taylor, Frederick. *The Berlin Wall: A World Divided, 1961–1989*. New York: Harper Perennial, 2006.

Internet

The Internet can be a useful, even superb, tool for research—**when used with caution!** It is rich in texts of original primary source documents, some of which are difficult to find in print. However, the secondary source material online varies greatly in quality. Anyone can post anything he or she wishes on the Internet; it does not have the fact-checking, quality-control process that goes into the publication of nonfiction books. Therefore, the student is cautioned to use good judgment when consulting online secondary sources in the field of world history. Check for footnotes and citations of sources, and no matter how impressive an Internet site appears, it is always best to confirm the information in a print source.

Relevant Works of Literature

Presented here is a highly selective list of works of literature—novels, poetry, and plays—dealing with many of the major characters, issues, and events of world history. Of course, the student should not rely on fiction for exact accuracy of facts and dates. However, reading historical fiction and drama can enormously enrich a student's understanding of a period. Great historical fiction can bring an era to life and provide a vivid picture of a time and place.

The Trojan War: Homer, the *Iliad*

Ancient India: Herman Hesse, *Siddhartha*

The Peloponnesian War: Mary Renault, *The Last of the Wine*

The Macedonian Empire: Mary Renault, *Funeral Games*

The Roman Empire: Robert Graves, *I, Claudius*; Thornton Wilder, *The Ides of March*

The Heian Period in Japan: Murasaki Shikibu, *The Tale of Genji*

Medieval Europe: Geoffrey Chaucer, *The Canterbury Tales*; Giovanni Boccaccio, *The Decameron*; Miguel de Cervantes, *Don Quixote*

European Reformation: Robert Bolt, *A Man for All Seasons*

The Hundred Years' War: William Shakespeare, history plays

Scientific Revolution in Europe: Bertolt Brecht, *Galileo*

European Enlightenment: Voltaire, *Candide*

Napoleonic Wars: Leo Tolstoy, *War and Peace*

Industrial Revolution in Europe: Charles Dickens, *Hard Times*; Emile Zola, *Germinal*

Italy in the Nineteenth Century: Giuseppe de Lampedusa, *The Leopard*

France in the Nineteenth Century: Victor Hugo, *Les Misérables*

The Opening of Tokugawa Japan: Stephen Sondheim and Jerome Weidman, *Pacific Overtures*

American Slavery: Toni Morrison, *Beloved*; Harriet Beecher Stowe, *Uncle Tom's Cabin*

American Civil War: Russell Banks, *Cloudsplitter*; Stephen Crane, *The Red Badge of Courage*

Franco-Prussian War: Emile Zola, *The Debacle*

British Occupation of India: E. M. Forster, *A Passage to India*

The Rise of Big Business and Industry in the United States: Sinclair Lewis, *The Jungle*; Booth Tarkington, *The Magnificent Ambersons*

World War I: Erich Maria Remarque, *All Quiet on the Western Front*

Russian Revolution: Boris Pasternak, *Doctor Zhivago*

Weimar Republic: Christopher Isherwood, *Berlin Stories*

The Great Depression in the United States: John Steinbeck, *The Grapes of Wrath*

World War II in Europe: Joseph Heller, *Catch-22*; Erich Maria Remarque, *Arch of Triumph*

World War II in the Pacific: James A. Michener, *Tales of the South Pacific*

Soviet Union Under Stalin: Aleksandr Solzhenitsyn, *One Day in the Life of Ivan Denisovich*

Cold War: John le Carré, *The Spy Who Came in from the Cold*

Vietnam War: Graham Greene, *The Quiet American*; William Lederer and Eugene Burdick, *The Ugly American*

Index

Note: Page numbers followed by "f" refer to figures.